Stories of Democracy

Stories of Democracy

POLITICS AND SOCIETY IN CONTEMPORARY KUWAIT

Mary Ann Tétreault

Columbia University Press

NEW YORK

Columbia University Press

Publishers Since 1893

New York   Chichester, West Sussex

Copyright © 2000 Columbia University Press

All rights reserved

Library of Congress Cataloging-in-Publication Data

Tétreault, Mary Ann, 1942–

   Stories of democracy : politics and society in contemporary Kuwait / Mary Ann

   Tétreault.

      p.   cm.

   Includes bibliographical references and index.

   ISBN 0–231–11488–5 (cloth : alk. paper) — ISBN 0–231–11489–3 (pbk. : alk. paper)

   1. Kuwait — Politics and government. 2. Democratization — Kuwait. I. Title.

DS247.K88 T48 2000

320.95367 — dc21

99–047271

To Kuwait and its people

Contents

Acknowledgments

I have worked on this book for ten years, ever since I began writing what is now chapter 3 during my Fulbright semester in Kuwait. It is impossible to make an exhaustive list of everyone who took time from a busy life to help me with this project, so I will mention just a few whose contributions to this work were extraordinary and indispensable. Although errors surely remain, this manuscript has been both enriched and enlivened by the assistance of these generous people, along with the hundreds of others whose names are not mentioned here.

Intellectual interchange is crucial to scholarship, and I have been blessed by the willingness of Kuwaiti colleagues to engage with my ideas and interpretations of events. I would like especially to thank sociologist and sometime-collaborator Haya al-Mughni, with whom I have worked for five years on a number of articles on gender politics in Kuwait. Other intellectual companions include economists Eqbal al-Rahmani and Yousef al-Ibrahim; engineers 'Eisa bu Yabis, 'Khaled Buhamrah, and Sara Akbar; linguist Sa'd al-'Ajmi; sociologist Khaldoun al-Naqeeb; and political scientists Ghanim al-Najjar, Ma'suma al-Mubarak, Saif 'Abbas 'Abdulla, Shafeeq Ghabra, and Shamlan al-'Eisa. Philosopher Ahmad al-Rub'i straddles the categories of academic and political and therefore I put him here as a bridge between the two. Other "political" Kuwaitis whose generosity has been invaluable include 'Abdullah Nibari, Ahmad Baqr, Hamad al-Jou'an, Jasim al-Qatami, and Saleh al-Hashem.

Many other Kuwaitis also were very generous with their time, expertise, and their professional and associational networks. They include 'Abd al-Wahhab al-Wazzan, Adela al-Sayer, Ahmad al-Tamimi, 'Ali Murad,

Buthaina al-Muqahawe, 'Eisa al-Serraf, Fawzi Mossad al-Saleh, Jasim al-Sa'doun, Khaled 'Ali al-Attar, Khouloud al-Feeli, Lidia Qattan, Lubna Saif 'Abbas 'Abdulla, Nihaya al-Dashti, Mohammad al-Jasim, Muna al-Musa, Nader Sultan, Sa'ud al-'Eneizi, Suleiman al-Mutawa, and Waleed Hadeed.

Expatriates like me who were Kuwait residents during one or more of my visits also contributed in various ways to this volume. They include 'Ali Attiga, 'Usama Jamali, Jill Nanson, Hana, Shereen, and Ma'moun al-Rashy, Hilary Shadroui, Kristin Stilt, Ziad Taky, George Tomeh, John Watson, and 'Abd al-'Aziz al-Wattari.

This project taught me a lot about the international press and how it works—or doesn't. For the opportunity to get press credentials and access during the 1992 and 1996 elections, I thank Rifa' al-Sayer of the Kuwait Ministry of Information. Among the non-Kuwaiti journalists I consulted, three went out of their way to be especially helpful: Shaqib al-Otaki (Middle East Economic Digest), Michael Sullivan (National Public Radio), and Bob Hepburn (*Toronto Star*). I thank the *Middle East Economic Survey* proprietors and Gary Lakes for giving me access to the *MEES* Archives during the preparation of the final draft of this manuscript, and Middle East Institute librarians Betsy Folkins and Paul Yachnes, who also were instrumental in helping me with sources.

Diplomats are supposed to fade quietly into the background, but four of the many who assisted me were so outstanding that I feel compelled to thank them by name: Ryan Crocker, Alberto Fernandez, Sylviane Galland, and Nathanial Howell.

Many non-Kuwaiti colleagues also have provided sustained intellectual support and advice throughout this project. They include Paul Aarts, Nathan Brown, Jill Crystal, Eleanor Doumato, Mark Gasiorowski, Greg Gause, Kate Gillespie, Ellis Goldberg, Anh Nga Longva, Toni Mercandante, Gwenn Okhrulik, Mary Ottaway, Frank Randall, Susan Slyomovics, Robin Teske, Bob Vitalis, and the two anonymous reviewers for Columbia University Press. My students Karla Scheele and Leslie Pitt worked hard to help prepare the manuscript. I also want to give special thanks to my editor, Roy Thomas, who has been perfect in every way.

Funding for this project came from a Fulbright Fellowship and grants from the United States Institute of Peace, the president of Old Dominion University, and the Graduate College of Iowa State University. As always, my financier of last resort has been my family. I thank my husband Richard and my sons Paul and Charles for all they gave up so that I could do this work.

Families are important sources of many things in addition to love and money. The privilege of being able to enjoy the company of Kuwaitis being themselves in informal settings provided the foundation of my understanding of the public acts I recount in this volume. Many of the people I've listed here talked with me not only in offices and restaurants but also invited me to their homes for meals and long afternoons with their families and friends. Two of them were responsible for invitations from women in their families, each of whom accepted me as a guest in her home for stays varying from a few weeks to more than two months. Even more than diplomats, the women who preside over Kuwaiti households are supposed to be invisible to the outside world. Here I identify my two hostesses only by their personal names, Zaineb and Hussa, and I give them my deepest thanks. To harbor houseguests who are not members of one's family is rare in Kuwait. The openness of these two beautiful and accomplished women gave me an unparalleled view of the texture of everyday life in households at once comfortingly similar to and startlingly different from my own. There I could see a part of how culture in Kuwait is constructed and transmitted through the weaving of the bonds of love and obligation that connect human beings one to another across space and through time. Much of my affection for Kuwait and its people derives from my experiences as a temporary sojourner in these households. I always will be grateful for the generosity that made them possible.

Abbreviations

CB	Constitutional Bloc
CFK	Citizens for a Free Kuwait
FIS	Islamic Salvation Front
FKA	Free Kuwait Association
FKC	Free Kuwait Campaign
ICM	Islamic Constitutional Movement
INA	Islamic National Alliance
IOC	International Oil Company
IPA	Islamic Popular Alliance
KDF	Kuwait Democratic Forum
KIA	Kuwait Investment Authority
KIC	Kuwait Investment Company
KIO	Kuwait Investment Organization
KNPC	Kuwait National Petroleum Company
KOTC	Kuwait Oil Tanker Company
KPC	Kuwait Petroleum Corporation
KPI	Kuwait Petroleum International
KSHR	Kuwait Society for Human Rights
MP	Member of Parliament
OAPEC	Organization of Arab Petroleum Exporting Countries
OPEC	Organization of Petroleum Exporting Countries
PIC	Petrochemical Industries Company
POW	Prisoner of War
PPFC	Protection of Public Funds Committee
RFFG	Reserve Fund for Future Generations
WCSS	Women's Cultural and Social Society

A Note on the Transliteration of Names

Arabic words have been transliterated according to standard academic usage, but names appear here as they are transliterated by individuals themselves (from business cards and title pages, for example), as they are shown on street signs and spelled in local English-language newspapers, as they appear in specific sources used (such as the materials from British Foreign Office files) and, where none of these exists, by applying the standard rules. In cases of disparities among these various sources, the first two—occasions of local usage—are given priority. Thus, 'Abdullah Nibari and not "Naibari," because "Nibari" is how 'Abdullah spells his name on his card; and Hasan 'Ali al-Ebraheem, not al-Ibrahim, because the first is how Hasan's name is spelled in his publications. Fahahaheel and other place names are transliterated such that you'll know where to get off the motorway the next time you are in Kuwait. Even in names, however, I've indicated where the ayn and hamza occur to aid in pronunciation. Locals rarely do this.

Stories of Democracy

For more than two decades I have been deeply fasci-
nated by the politics and society of Kuwait. This interest began with my dissertation, which included an examination of Kuwait's role as a major oil-exporting
country and a founding member of OPEC and
OAPEC (the Organization of Petroleum Exporting
Countries and the Organization of Arab Petroleum
Exporting Countries, respectively). It grew as I learned
more about Kuwait's exemplary foreign aid program,
its eccentric brand of nonalignment during the Cold
War, and the development of KPC, the Kuwait Petroleum Corporation, its pathbreaking national oil company. As I explored these issues, I became curious
about what sort of people and what kind of political
system could devise and support so many "major
power" policies on such a tiny base.

In the spring of 1990 I spent five months in Kuwait
on a Fulbright fellowship to begin fieldwork for a book-
length study of the Kuwait Petroleum Corporation.
This was my second visit to Kuwait; it took place at an
interesting time. Kuwait's pro-democracy movement
was at the peak of its activities when I arrived in January, and clearly had been outmaneuvered by Kuwait's
amir, Jabir al-Ahmad, by the time I left at the end of
May. Ten days later, Kuwaitis elected members to an
extra-constitutional consultative body, the Majlis al-
Watani. This election marked a significant backward
step away from the real, though limited, popular representation provided for in Kuwait's constitution (which
had been suspended in July 1986), and in the lively parliament (also suspended that troubling summer) which
was its hallmark. Less than two months after the June
1990 election, however, Saddam Hussein invaded Kuwait and the political kaleidoscope shifted once again.

The political opportunities presented by Saddam's invasion arose as much from the skill of Kuwaiti citizens at exploiting the situation as from the deus ex machina himself. Kuwait's oil and its oil production policies were the ostensible causes of Saddam's invasion. However, as historians of the region know well, the causes of the "crisis in the Gulf" were far more complex. They involved Iran even more than Kuwait, and especially Iran's engagement with Iraq in competing versions of what Ghassan Salamé has described as the politics of "historic missions." This messianic style of politics has had devastating effects on the development of virtually every large state in the Middle East.[1]

Elsewhere I have called Kuwait's role in this recurrent clash a "sideshow,"[2] an assessment made from the perspective of the larger powers involved. For the Kuwaiti nation, it was the first (1980–1988) and second (1990–91) Gulf wars that were sideshows. Kuwait's "main event" throughout the twentieth century has been the repeated clashes between would-be citizens demanding civil and political rights and what has become over the period a deeply entrenched albeit variably autocratic "traditional" regime.[3] When a grant from the United States Institute of Peace enabled me to return to Kuwait in the fall of 1992 to witness the first parliamentary elections held there since 1985, it was to observe a political process that had been restored rather than derailed by invasion and occupation.

The shift in perspective that can move a single event of the magnitude of the second Gulf War from a central defining moment to a sideshow also characterizes much of my understanding of Kuwait's domestic politics. For example, by the end of the six years I spent studying and writing about KPC,[4] I had come to believe that the company should operate more openly and that Kuwaitis should take a more active interest in it and in its policies. Over the same period, and much to my surprise, I also came to believe that KPC should continue to pursue its generally successful strategy of multinational vertical integration as the best means to preserve Kuwaiti sovereignty and national autonomy. However, the implications of these two recommendations are not necessarily compatible. Few Kuwaitis approve of KPC's corporate strategy. Indeed, Kuwaiti preferences on economic issues are very similar to those of people living in the United States: they tend to be based on a poor understanding of the processes and consequences of globalization;[5] usually they are the product of private desires for personal gain rather than a strategic foreign policy vision or some definition of the public good. From this it might seem that greater transparency and popular involvement in oil company policies would be bound to undermine a corporate strategy heavily tilted toward furthering Kuwait's strategic interests. Looking at the problem a little differently, however, one also could envision transparency as the impetus for Kuwaitis to view KPC as a public asset underpinning their long-term security rather than as a wasting asset each had better grab a share of before someone else gets it first.

This question of perspective and its impact on evaluation becomes even more complicated when the topic is democratization rather than corporate strategy. In the Middle East, "democracy" is disparaged as a "Western" concept by those who benefit from the status quo and, as a result, both are problematic terms. Those of us who teach about the "Middle East" are fond of exploring the meaning of this label with our classes—middle of what? east of what? But we could as easily ask what or where is "the West"? Patricia Springborg finds the origin of our conception of the West as the positive pole representing civilized life in the city-states of ancient Greece, alongside the beginnings of what Edward Said calls "orientalism," the negative pole representing either primitivism or decadence, depending on the intention of the user.[6] Ironically, modern Greece, along with the Balkans which lie north and west of it on geographic maps, are well off the mental maps cherished by most of those who today think of themselves as Westerners.[7] In popular cultural representations such as the British play and later film *Shirley Valentine* (1989), Greece is an exotic locale where one finds authentic emotions among simple people living far from the demands of modern civilization. As the icon signifying the center of the rational world—if not of the entire universe—"the West" has moved far from its geographic origin at the time when Greeks invented it to describe themselves. Even so, its exact location on any kind of map can best be thought of as debatable.

Democracy is another concept that "moves" depending on one's assumptions. Like "the rational West," the concept of democracy developed from Greek roots. However, the tree that those roots nourish in the twentieth century is likely to shade parliaments of elected representatives in capital cities and vast, far-flung executive establishments—an imperial domain from the perspective of the citizens of ancient city-states. Democratic practices with which they were familiar relied on citizen assemblies and a face-to-face politics that is fundamentally local. In most of today's mass societies, such an intimate public sphere is difficult to realize except among elites or in subnational units such as towns and provinces, where the range of issues to be decided is relatively narrow.

Yet among the most notable aspects of Kuwaiti politics during the tense spring of 1990 was its close resemblance to the politics depicted in stories about classical Athens. During my long stay in Kuwait, I read Hannah Arendt's *The Human Condition* for the first time, and discussed with Kuwaiti philosopher Ahmad al-Rub'i parallels between the images of classical Athens that Arendt paints and the Kuwait we were observing in the present. Ahmad agreed that a surprising number of similarities between the two could be identified. Ghassan

Salamé also finds parallels between classical Athens and modern Kuwait, and exploring these parallels is part of the task I set myself here.[8]

The limits and the contradictions of that ancient democratic ideal also were evident in 1990 Kuwait. Modern classicists remind us that Athenian democracy was, despite Aristotle's prescriptions to the contrary, far from self-sufficient economically and also was enjoyed by very few persons—that is, absolutely, as a proportion of the city's inhabitants, and in terms of group representation. Classical Athens depended heavily on external financing and the domestic exploitation of slaves, noncitizen foreigners, and women called citizens who were, in reality, the subjects of their fathers and husbands.[9] To most Westerners, these aspects of the reality subsumed by the symbol "classical Athens" are suppressed or denied through "(re)traditionalization," the reinvention of the past to suit the needs of the present.[10] For me, however, the negative and the positive similarities linking 1990 Kuwait to many different representations of the ancient world encouraged me to examine Kuwaiti politics in a framework that incorporates references to its identity as a city-state.

Furthermore, I write from the perspective of one who believes that modernity is a global project. However much a nation is shaped by its history, it is equally and contingently shaped by myriad and various reactions by its people and their leaders to social forces, many disembedded from particular locations in time and space. Anthony Giddens calls this process of continuous interdependent adjustment "modern reflexivity."[11] Throughout, you will find explicit comparisons between "Kuwait" and various components of "the West" conceived as sharing a common functional experience of moving from "traditional" to "modern" status, albeit along very different historical trajectories. As I read and talked and thought about the history of my own "democratic" country as compared to Kuwait, it seemed that Kuwait encapsulates more of the classical understanding of day-to-day democratic practice than I or my own society do. But contradictions continued to present themselves because I also saw myself and my peers as enjoying freedoms and rights that all Kuwaiti citizens, especially women, could only dream about. Consequently, my conceptions of democracy and citizenship have changed to include aspects of an iconic past along with what I understand to be the practices of a number of contemporary polities. This process is reflected in the theoretical frameworks developed in the following two chapters.

Chapter 2 considers formal models of citizen-state relations and what is meant by public versus private life. As I argue, these meanings are shaped by history, culture, and the degree of penetration of society by the processes of modernization. These strong social forces produce patterns of interaction, some mediated by formal rules and institutions, that limit interplay between the political and social repertoires of key actors. The interpenetration of political, social, and economic structures and practices limits the rate and degree of change. At the same time, the rewiring of human social organization that we call "modernity" enlarges the repertoires of individual social and political actors along with their opportunities to shape their own lives. In chapter 3, I deal with these processes in the Kuwaiti context as sets of contending myths—about Kuwait and its history, its citizens, and its rulers. The interplay of these various stories defines the place of Kuwait and Kuwaitis in their country, their region, and the world.

The remainder of the volume focuses on the politics of democratization in Kuwait. In chapter 4, I trace the development of Kuwaiti notions of democracy from 1921, when Kuwaiti elites first tried to institutionalize formal curbs on the ruler, to the Iraqi invasion of 1990. Chapter 5 looks at how the invasion and occupation were assimilated to preinvasion ideas and practices and also were used as platforms by Kuwaiti democrats to push their political liberalization project forward. Chapter 6 concentrates on the election of 1992. This was not only the first postliberation election but, even more importantly, the first election held after the ruler had suspended for a second time the provisions of Kuwait's constitution that protect public political life. Its unfolding illustrates not only the political manipulation of structures and rules but also the spontaneous fragmentation characteristic of modern societies and the difficulties that stand in the way of managing reflexivity (see chapter 2), whether the manager is a democrat or an autocrat. Chapter 7 shows how even such a cataclysmic event as external invasion is limited in its capacity to effect lasting political change. It also looks at the common practices of normal political life and their role in producing or retarding political change and development. Chapter 8 looks at Kuwaiti domestic politics in the context of new social movements and the growing "internationalization" of citizen activism. In the final chapter, I draw some conclusions about Kuwait's democratic prospects and the forces I see shaping the country's political future.

The overall framework employed here for examining Kuwaiti political life is the concept of political space and how it conditions state-society relations. Democracy as an existential reality is centered on the experience of the individual as an autonomous public actor, but at the same time that totalitarian regimes were collapsing across Eastern Europe, Kuwaitis were chafing under a newly imposed return to autocratic rule. Encouraged by the spectacle of citizen activism as an agent driving the collapse of communism, the people of Kuwait flocked to their own pro-democracy movement.[12] Citizens from every social group petitioned their ruler, the amir Jabir al-Ahmad, asking him to restore their civil liberties and authorize new elections for the National Assembly. The pro-democracy campaign intensified in the winter of 1989–90, when a series of meetings at which prominent citizens challenged the legitimacy of the amir's actions were met with increasing levels of state repression. During the summer of 1990, the amir's extra-constitutional resolution of the immediate crisis was swept away by Iraq's invading army just a few weeks after it went into effect.

The invasion, occupation, and liberation of Kuwait were regarded by some analysts as having improved prospects for democratization, in Kuwait and possibly elsewhere in the Middle East.[13] But others were less sanguine. Doubters cited reasons ranging from culture to world-system pressures for concluding that the countries of the Middle East are unlikely to participate in an otherwise global convergence toward more open domestic political systems.[14] Some argued that Islam as a belief system and tribalism as a cultural pattern present formidable obstacles to democratization in the Middle East.[15] Others, dismissing arguments based on Islam and tribalism as little more than orientalism in modern dress, based their skepticism on structural conditions they see as impeding democratization in the Middle East and in other places where these same conditions hold true.[16]

Counterarguments based on religion and local culture challenge the first set of doubters. Islam, like Christianity, includes egalitarian ideals as well as traditions of debate and plural interpretations of doctrine.[17] This heritage is as available as the legacy of repression to serve as a basis for redefining tradition. Too, the local cultures of Arabs, Turks, and the Maghreb peoples, who are thought to be so resistant to democracy today, are the offspring of the same "Mediterranean" culture presumed to have invented democracy in the first place.[18] To attribute the origin of democratic practice to the urban civilizations of the Mediterranean encourages a reexamination of how democracy operates and a broader view of the conditions under which it can be realized. By looking at democratization as a complex process, we may be able to understand and devise multiple ways to check the power of elites, protect human rights, and expand individual freedom. As a result, "democracy" becomes not an end in itself, but rather a means for realizing what citizens together define as a good society.

Before the modern period, the Western political order was heteronomous and interpenetrated, with political units that were relatively undeveloped as compared, for example, to China, with its highly organized and closely controlled bureaucracy and judicial system.[19] Individual freedom in the West— what philosopher Isaiah Berlin calls "negative liberty"—was virtually nonexistent, limited by powerful religious, social, and economic institutions that sometimes supported and other times competed with political institutions for the labor and loyalty of populations. In the modern period, a combination of ideology, technology, and mass mobilization has created enormously powerful and destructive states all over the world.[20] At the same time, individual liberty and human rights are endangered by nonstate actors and institutions and by political entrepreneurs acting alone, in groups, and in formal as well as informal organizations, a phenomenon visible in developed democracies as well as in developing areas.[21] States, regimes, and governments themselves are vulnerable to predators and, as a result, may look to their populations to protect them in exchange for an expansion of citizens' rights.[22] Consequently, we should view the state not merely as a set of potentially repressive institutions but also as a potential supporter of liberty and human rights.

In this conception, the state is autonomous rather than a control apparatus run by dominant social, religious, or economic interests. This does not mean that state interests are independent of the interests of other holders of power. However, it does mean that state interests coincide only partially with those of other institutions or groups. It is the divergence of these various sets of interests that creates "political space," geographic and metaphoric locations within which it is possible for people to invent new identities, relationships, and institutions, including those that expand human freedom and the political capacity of citizens.[23] I have chosen to analyze the contemporary politics of Kuwait in terms of political space in order to emphasize the agency of individuals in the process of political change.

Political space as a concept owes much to Hannah Arendt's description of the "space of appearance," and her conviction that "the political realm rises directly out of acting together."

> Action and speech create a space between the participants which can find its proper location almost any time and anywhere. It is the space of appearance in the widest sense of the word, namely, the space where I appear to others as others appear to me, where men exist not merely like other living or inanimate things but make their appearance explicitly.[24]

Spaces of appearance are defined by four characteristics. The first is plurality, the fact that every individual is different from every other individual. Second is agency, the capacity of human beings to act, to speak, convince, and mobilize one another to do something together. Third is natality, the creation of something new—a new idea, a new way of looking at things one has seen before, actions whose conclusions cannot be foreseen or foreordained. Fourth is the existence of a place or places where individuals can show themselves—can appear—to others through their actions and words. A space of appearance also has strategic qualities: like the concept of energy in physics—the capacity to do work, possible only where there are differences in the energy levels of various components of a system—political power is the result of human beings of differing capacities operating in the same political space. It is realized when this plurality of individuals acts—moves—in concert.

Arendt contrasts power with strength. "Strength is the natural [material] quality of an individual seen in isolation, [but] power springs up between men when they act together and vanishes the moment they disperse." However, superior strength is not sufficient to guarantee that an actor will prevail. Arendt uses the concept of passive resistance to illustrate this point.

> Popular revolt against materially strong rulers . . . may engender an almost irresistible power even if it foregoes the use of violence in the face of materially vastly superior forces. To call this "passive resistance" is certainly an ironic idea; it is one of the most active and efficient ways of action ever devised, because it cannot be countered by fighting, where there may be defeat or victory, but only by mass slaughter in which even the victor is defeated, cheated of his prize, since nobody can rule over dead men.[25]

Plurality and agency are characteristics of human beings. Natality is an outcome of these qualities. Spaces of appearance as geographic and metaphoric sites also are outgrowths of human characteristics but as these spaces are expressed structurally rather than psychologically. Because I am interested in democratic politics, the spaces of appearance I concentrate on here are public spaces, that is, spaces to which any member of a community can claim access, although an individual's capacity for action in any particular public space may be constrained or enhanced by her or his status and/or resources. Spaces of appearance can be actual in the sense of assemblies of persons occupying a particular physical space at the same time. They also can be virtual, mediated by communication networks such as a free press where effective simultaneity is approximated by readers being more or less in the same place at more or less the same time, although cognitively rather than physically.[26] Spaces of appearance, therefore, depend on the existence of actual or virtual public arenas where individuals can listen and speak to one another, all of them spaces that are vulnerable to closure. Forbidding public gatherings such as parliaments, law courts, and club meetings, and censorship of books, films, and news media are examples of how despotic rulers erase political space. The continuation of politics under tyranny requires the existence of protected spaces to which access by repressive institutions can be limited effectively.

In the context of Kuwaiti politics, I have written about two protected spaces, the home and the mosque.[27] Both are protected from state encroachment by a culture whose social norms are strong enough to mobilize popular and elite resistance to the same effect as the passive resistance described above by Arendt. However, neither the home nor the mosque is a satisfactory democratic alternative to political space, public space to which every citizen has ready access for the purpose of political action. The home is private, and access is limited to idiosyncratically selected members of the community. It is too small physically and too limited socially to allow the full range of citizens' viewpoints on issues to emerge. The mosque, though it is public and offers a large physical space where people can gather, imposes religious controls on expression and action that deprive particular groups, such as women and non-Muslims, or particular points of view, such as secularism, from access to the forum it provides. Despite their limitations, however, both of these protected spaces support the partial mobilization of political resources and have proven themselves capable of maintaining the capacity of some Kuwaiti citizens to act in the name of the community even during periods of severe political repression.

Action also is limited by contingent factors—the particularities of one's situation. These include the finite nature of personal and group resources, the outcomes of previous actions, and the inability to control events even though one might have some power to influence them. Thus, action is limited by what can be brought to bear on a situation whose parameters have been shaped by history and whose outcome will be influenced by factors beyond the understanding and control of those initiating it. The power of the past to cast its shadow on the future is profound even when the action taken is directed explicitly at smashing its physical, social, and ideological authority.[28] Yet, although one may be tempted to be fatalistic in the face of contingency, such a position denies plurality, agency, and natality. If individuals do indeed differ from one another, and if each has some capacity to act, then the creation of new ideas, new forms, new relationships, and new institutions is a constant possibility. If it were not so, the variety we see in human society would not exist and political change would be impossible.

Action also is limited by basic human needs—"necessity." Necessity is an equalizer: everyone must eat, drink, find shelter, and protect the integrity of the social unit that maintains the physical survival of the individual and the group. With respect to political life, necessity involves more than physical sustenance. It includes as well emotional security and personal autonomy.[29] Plurality can be realized only after the demands of necessity are satisfied. Thus politics in the sense of free choice and action is impossible where basic human needs, physical and emotional, remain unmet.[30] Any institution that controls the means of satisfaction of basic human needs can eliminate freedom and thereby eliminate politics. This point is made frequently as an argument against state control of the economy, a primary source of the means to satisfy basic needs.[31] Institutions and actors other than the state also have the potential to deny freedom by depriving persons of life or the means of subsistence. Indeed, it is the fact of deprivation rather than the identity of its agent that must be the focal point of assessments of freedom and human rights in any society.

Any discussion of Kuwait's internal potential for democratization also must consider its external environment and the supports for and constraints on liberty that come from this source. Kuwaiti historian Hasan 'Ali al-Ebraheem is fond of saying that Kuwait is a small state living in a bad neighborhood, an observation that contains a great deal of truth. Kuwait was deeply affected by the Iraqi invasion and occupation. Even so, liberation did not reveal a "new Kuwait." The preinvasion struggle between Kuwaitis and their government over whether, how much, and in what direction to revise the social contract governing state-society relations simply resumed, but with an additional vocabulary and a new set of contending myths for each side to bring to bear on the other. Thus, despite the power of the external environment to alter conditions inside Kuwait and possibly to eliminate Kuwait entirely, it is the internal environment composed of Kuwaitis positioning themselves in the various spaces within which they define one another and act in concert that determines the parameters of Kuwaiti politics.

In some ways, Kuwait was more democratic under Iraqi occupation than it was before or has been since. Part of the reason is because the internal boundaries dividing Kuwaitis into groups were erased by the common experience of occupation. "When Saddam Hussein came, he treated us equally. He did not kill Sunna or Shi'a: he killed Kuwaitis."[32] Family, sect, and class lines faded into insignificance; Kuwaitis under occupation saw themselves as a unified national community, one very like what they imagined Kuwait had been in a past none of them had experienced directly.[33] The political meaning of this odd and unexpected experience of democratic life has not been lost in postliberation Kuwait. It enlarged the repertoire of strategies that democrats and antidemocrats have adapted and used throughout this century in the Gramscian war of position that characterizes modern Kuwaiti politics.

What I hope is reflected throughout this volume is a strong sense of the unique quality of life in Kuwait—what it might be like to be a Kuwaiti and what that identity means politically. I would like to think that the Kuwaitis depicted here are representative and therefore that the impressions of Kuwait they convey also are representative, but this is only partly true. In spite of the remarkable accessibility of Kuwaitis to foreigners, my direct knowledge of the Kuwaiti people remains limited. Most of the people I have interviewed formally are well-educated and hold responsible positions. Even so, I've met many others in less formal settings: in markets, at meetings and public gatherings, in households and businesses that I visited, or as friends and acquaintances of persons I already knew. Through queries, direct observation, and shameless eavesdropping at every opportunity, I continue to construct a collage of not entirely compatible images that signify "Kuwait" in my mind. In this volume I have tried to convey some of the diversity and complexity of my imperfect knowledge and understanding of "Kuwait." I have taken pains to do this using the words of Kuwaitis and other observers along with my own so that readers can understand how I came to see Kuwait as I do and yet be able to disagree with my interpretations and conclusions.

Another goal of this work is to present a textured view of Kuwaiti politics as it is experienced and conducted by various individuals in their personal and public lives. My training as a political economist predisposes me to look for structural explanations for social phenomena, and some of that predisposition is reflected here. However, I have concentrated in this work on writing about personal experiences in actual situations and how participants recall and understand them. I hope this will allow the reader to see the agency of individuals as well as to understand the structural constraints that limit their choices and shape the outcomes of those choices. One purpose of this approach is to show how different people have seen their opportunities and their obligations and have chosen how to act on them. Another is to show what happened to them as a result and, as well as I can, to explain why.

Given this practical goal, it may seem odd that I cast many of the stories I recount here as myths. The word *myth* is popularly understood as a fairy tale or fable, a story that isn't "really" true. But I mean something quite different by this word. Here, a myth is a paradigmatic story, one intended to convey concern for "issues transcending immediate data," such as stories of communal origin and depictions of individual and cultural values.[34] In this sense, a myth is more than true; it is "super true." The myths about Kuwait that I recount in chapter 3 are intended by their various tellers to delineate some essential aspect of "Kuwait" in much the same spirit as the Homeric tales convey essential aspects of what it means to be Greek and Old Testament stories essential aspects of what it means to be Jewish. Similarly, the models of democracy and citizenship I present in the next chapter are stories of origins and values through which "the West" imagines and understands itself and projects this identity to others. In this sense, all the stories and models recounted here are idealizations of a representative self and the group to which that self belongs.

As I make clear in chapter 3, myths are not monolithic and often develop as clusters of contending images. In the first three chapters of Genesis, for example, there are two myths of creation. The first is a story of women and men created as equals in the image of God. The second tells of woman as "Adam's rib," a story of divinely ordained female subordination and inferiority to men. Harold Bloom argues that the misogyny reflected in the second Genesis creation myth is due as much to inadvertent traditionalization through the choice of idioms by translators as to intentional interference by redactors—that is, that at least some normative aspects of myths are unintentionally created in the process of transmission.[35] However, Elaine Pagels insists that it is the instrumental goals of those who create and re-create myths that shape the choice of words, emphases, and understandings.[36] The Pagels perspective comes closer to what I see in the creation and transmission of political myths. From my position as an outsider, it appears to me that the founding myths of Kuwaiti nationhood and the stories Kuwaitis tell about the Iraqi occupation reflect not only the memories of experiences but also the feelings and the contending values, interests, and goals of those who recount them.

Making and interpreting myths is a basic task of political leadership.[37] Defining the content of myths is an objective in itself as well as a means to create instruments for achieving other objectives. Connections between myths and politics also are explored in this book. The thesis guiding this exploration is that the inability to harmonize or suppress contending mythic interpretations of national life mirrors a fundamental disagreement over the nature of power and its appropriate distribution and management by a people and its government. In contrast, "normal politics" marks a successful synthesis of contradictory theses or, perhaps even more, such a politics, when successful, keeps a regime and a society within the bounds of an Aristotelian mean, a broad middle path between contending sides whose full simultaneous expression would produce civil war rather than civil society. This point may be clarified by considering what Jean Leca has identified as the two basic ingredients of democracy in the context of modern Arab politics: populism, that is, the access of the masses to politics; and constitutionalism, the rule of law that protects specific spheres of life against arbitrary power.[38] The potential for conflict between these two ideals is well known when they are formulated as the opposition between majority rule and minority rights. Any Aristotelian mean between them is the product of a "political pact" or agreement establishing limits to the expression of each and rules for managing the conflicts that arise when these limits are exceeded.

The idea that there is such a thing as a social contract is another myth, one that justifies the establishment of a political regime; the story that describes any particular social contract rationalizes the unique distribution of power in that system. In Kuwait, the social contract has been a subject of open dispute since the time of Mubarak (r. 1896–1915). This dispute is conducted in forums ranging from *diwaniyyas* to marketplaces to legislative assemblies, and it fuels the struggle to control interpretations of other myths describing Kuwaiti history. It is complicated by a parallel struggle to dominate myths about democracy, many of which include various reasons why democracy is or is not suitable for Kuwait and Kuwaitis. In effect, pro-democracy forces tell stories integrating Kuwait and Kuwaitis into a larger world defined by universal values; antidemocrats speak of a world where Kuwaiti (or Muslim or Arab) society occupies a niche carved out by particularistic qualities like tradition, religion, and culture. The world defined by universal values is pluralistic—one world composed of many different parts that are morally equal in terms of responsibility for ideas and actions; the world defined by particularistic values is monadic, defined by a single hegemonic vision. This dispute is articulated most clearly in clashes between secularists and Islamists, but it also shapes other conflicts over the "true" nature of Kuwait and Kuwaitis.[39]

My story about Kuwait also is a myth. Like other stories that concentrate on individuals and actions, mine is intended not only to recount events but also to tell a story about democratization, to imagine what it is, whether it is possible, and whether it is worth the struggle to achieve it. I see conflicts among Kuwaitis over who is a citizen and whether to democratize or to suppress democracy as part and product of a frightening and often repressive process of global restructuring whose effects have evoked myriad countervailing social movements worldwide. Myths about Kuwait should be viewed in the context of this global process and the contest to control these myths and their meanings as part of the larger reconsideration of democratic values occurring worldwide, including in societies conventionally viewed as having achieved democracy once and for all.

Even from this point of view, of course, a story about Kuwaiti politics is a story about Kuwaiti politics. However, it also is a story about how we understand social contracts in political systems from North America to Southeast Asia. This story about Kuwait is itself a collection of myths: about Kuwait, about political change in the Arab or Muslim world, and about citizenship and democracy anywhere and at any time.

Political traditions are complex bundles of beliefs and practices that connect a community's collective past to the future. The importance of the past to these traditions is reflected in such terms as "national character" and "political culture," concepts implying that a community holds particular beliefs and behaves in particular ways because of its common history. We also talk of "revolution" as signifying a break with history, a new beginning that is sought even if its particular results may not have been chosen. Yet as Alexis de Tocqueville observed in France, little about the essential nature of French politics changed as the result of the revolution of 1789.[1] This is not to say that France has not changed during its history, but that new regimes and new styles of community, in France and elsewhere, are constrained by the past. "Development" marks a fundamental discontinuity between traditional society and modernity;[2] even so, the structures of modernity are shaped both by the pattern of the culture it replaces and the manner of its disintegration.[3] Consequently, what we call "revolution" is less an event inaugurating major political and social change[4] than a particularly violent episode in an ongoing series of adjustments to changing realities.

Modernity hastens change by expanding the number of points at which adjustment occurs and the speed at which it is demanded but, even so, political change remains highly constrained. How a people understands power, authority, and community is embedded in culture, geography, institutions, and personal relationships at so many points that the results of even a sudden violent change in regime may be less momentous than contemporaries believe. How power and authority are negotiated by members of political communities is the subject of this chapter. The intersection of culture and modernity is particularly important as the locus of change and how it is shaped.

Political Participation

Human beings tell many stories to explain how civil life developed, and this practice and its meanings have not changed much since we have begun to call these stories "models" and "theories." One describes civil society everywhere as evolving along a track from communal, kin-based relationships to contractual, interest-based associations.[5] This story is contradicted by Patricia Springborg, who argues that patterns of civil life are culturally shaped, regionally based, and continuous over time.[6] Her analysis of two "ideal types" of political community parallels distinctions made between two paradigms of political liberty, each of which underlies a radically different understanding of democracy and citizenship.[7]

Springborg believes that democratic traditions arise from particular historical experiences and that the two stories of democracy she finds in the Western tradition are rooted in separate *problematiques*.[8] The set of myths associated with each is intended to justify a particular hierarchy of values and enjoin a particular set of practices that its adherents claim are the heart of democracy in any culture. One set tells of the evolution of the highly autonomous cultures of Mediterranean city-states; the other describes a different historical trajectory traced by political cultures whose roots are in northern Europe. Springborg distinguishes them as

> properly political society—small-scale, urban, highly participatory and entrepreneurial . . . and northern European society, whose ancestry is feudal, rural, and decentralized. In these latter systems (excluding northern Italian city-states and the free cities of the Hansa League) participation in free and equal institutions is only a recent part of history, and absolutism, where the only public person was the king, was once the dominant mode.[9]

Mediterranean city-states, home of "properly political society," were the birthplaces of *public* life—that is, human existence embedded in face-to-face political communities and in *private* relationships centered on domestic life.[10] Describing the multiplicity of community life in such societies, Springborg notes that their citizens enjoyed many opportunities not only to define themselves as persons and express themselves as individuals but also to participate as members of multiple associations extending beyond the family group, relationships undertaken in part to increase security. In the absence of a powerful governing authority, individual and family security depended on such networks of mutual reliance.[11]

Otto Hintze finds a similar association between city-states and participatory politics. However, he emphasizes scale rather than diversity as the defining characteristic of a political community.

> What is common to ancient and modern constitutions of city-states is based, it seems to me, on the peculiar character of this political organization. Even where the foundation of a city-state was the work of a monarchical rulership, after it had come into existence it soon emancipated itself from monarchical authority; for close union simply in terms of space and intense communication among the inhabitants produced a vigorous, unified, collective political consciousness. . . .
>
> This communal spirit is responsible for the inclination toward a republican form of government common to all city-states.[12]

Hintze and Springborg, each proceeding from different national and temporal contexts, tell the story of the city-state as a unique sociopolitical form, one that carries with it an open and participatory style of political and social life. In support of this thesis, Ghassan Salamé offers a third argument, one whose *problematique* is located specifically in the modern Middle East.[13] Like Springborg and Hintze, Salamé believes that small communities invite political participation. However, he is less concerned with the micropolitics of face-to-face relationships than with the effects of scale on the terms of the social contract.

Salamé argues that the small state in the Middle East is one that is unable to suppress the inherent plurality of its population by asserting its authority in the context of a "historic mission." Unlike Egypt or Iraq, countries the size of Kuwait are simply too small for their rulers to argue credibly that they can lead an international crusade in the name of a cause such as Arab nationalism or anti-imperialism. Unable to create a sense of urgency strong enough to produce unity, regimes like Kuwait's are exposed directly to the plurality of citizens and their multiple demands; at the same time, they share a history that has made legitimacy crises endemic to the region. To rulers in this situation, democracy may look like an attractive political strategy: "It is the only system in a position to organize peaceful power sharing in a society where a hegemonic group [cannot] establish an exclusivist or, at least, an openly dominant position."[14] Because these small states are forced to recognize and deal with "their ethno-cultural pluralism" rather than being able to deny or suppress it, they are prompted to work out "pacts" or mutual guarantees that permit limited participation and also act as checks on state authoritarianism.[15]

The picture of political participation in city-state arenas is complex, with overlapping rather than sharply demarcated institutions, activities, and groups. The conceptual separation of populism and pacts as different types of politics is a legacy of a different path of political development. Empires, ancient and modern, along with modern authoritarian states, are enemies of the plurality, flexibility, and participation characteristic of the politics of city-states. Ancient city-states themselves found their politics profoundly altered by the spreading imperial power of Rome. By the second century C.E., the Stoic philosopher Epictetus could describe politics as "not in our power," a judgment that Michael Walzer feels

> represented a turning away from political interests and activity, a radical severance of private needs and aspirations from the public world of cities and empires. . . . Epictetus wrote in an age when citizenship had lost its meaning and all men had become, in one way or another, subjects, whose political existence had but one essential characteristic: that they obeyed impersonal, more or less legal commands.[16]

In such a political universe, there is no politics. Where there is only one "person"—the ruler—who monopolizes the public sphere, there can be no plurality and, consequently, no political speech or action.

The division of the life of the citizen of the ancient world into public and private spheres was transformed for the subject into a division between "communal elements" viewed as common or public, and private elements that included persons with special rights—"those with immunities and privileges." Without such immunities and privileges, the former citizen, now a subject, had neither a public existence nor private rights. Under the feudal order, what was "private" in the sense of particular or exempted from subjection became the core of the regime, though it also was referred to as "public" in the sense of *publicare* to claim for the lord or the ruler.[17]

> Sociologically, that is to say by reference to institutional criteria, a public sphere in the sense of a separate realm distinguished from the private sphere cannot be shown to have existed in the feudal society of the High Middle Ages. Nevertheless it was no accident that the attributes of lordship . . . were called "public"; not by accident did the English king enjoy "publicness"—for lordship was something publicly represented. This *publicness of representation* was not constituted as a social realm, that is, as a public sphere; rather it was something like a status attribute . . . its incumbent represented it pub-

licly. He displayed himself, presented himself as an embodiment of some sort of "higher" power.[18]

The European feudal order still left many sites of relatively autonomous political life. Some were the practical result of the inability of kings and princes to rule effectively throughout the territories they claimed; others resulted from overlapping claims and from a broad range of exemptions. These included the personal immunities and privileges noted above, along with the charters of cities and towns which conferred on such communities some of the social and political ambience of the ancient city-states. These sites of autonomy shrank during the early modern period, as royal absolutists, with the economic assistance of wealthy clients, acquired the military and bureaucratic capacity to control large territories and multicultural populations more effectively. The resulting restrictions and loss of "borderlands" where social control used to be multiply vested and/or highly diluted, evoked countermovements against the absolutist state.

> The Parliament, the Cortes, and Estates did ordinarily incorporate the principal segments of the population which had acquired or maintained liberties, privileges sanctioned by law, in the face of the sovereign. . . . Building strong royal power meant co-opting, subordinating or destroying these institutions; that program absorbed a large part of the energy of seventeenth-century kings. . . . The result of [their effort to concentrate power in the crown] was an enormous amount of conflict and resistance.[19]

John Keane identifies the equation of the early modern state with despotism as a product of eighteenth-century liberalism.[20] However, this comparison was made even earlier and by critics whose solution to tyranny was the antithesis of an expansion of privacy and personal freedom.[21] That critique was part of a social movement that produced the first modern revolution in seventeenth-century England, a movement that Walzer calls "the revolution of the saints." Unlike liberal challenges to state power, social experiments such as Calvin's Geneva and the movements that fueled the Puritan revolution in England were neither individualist nor hedonic. Rather than calling for negative liberty and the right to pursue happiness,

> Puritan zeal was . . . a highly collective emotion and it imposed upon the saints a new and impersonal discipline. . . . Puritan ministers campaigned against . . . personal extravagance . . . and deplored the role of "private inter-

ests" in politics. . . . The new spirit of the Puritans can be defined as a kind of military and political work-ethic.[22]

The Puritan critique may be difficult to recall as an attack against the absolutist state because it also was an attack against so many other things—the remnants of feudalism, the established church(es),[23] and the privacy rights increasingly claimed by bourgeois interests. Even so, the revolution of the saints was both an engine of modernity and a reaction against modernization. In contrast to Puritan efforts to eradicate private interests from public life, the liberal critique of absolutism which flowered in the eighteenth century advocated the expansion of private life and the protection of private interests through a grant of liberty that is essentially negative: freedom *from*—the king, the state, and even from society, described by the nineteenth-century libertarian John Stuart Mill as a "despotism . . . surpassing anything contemplated in the political ideal of the most rigid disciplinarian among the ancient philosophers."[24] Yet the ideology advocating human freedom from state and society had its philosophical roots in Greece and the Levant, where early Christians had claimed the right to choose a life path independent of the one marked out in advance by family, society, and state.[25] As Elaine Pagels argues, this movement was co-opted first by Rome and then from within by authoritarian church fathers. During its first two centuries, however, individuals and small communities of Christians asserted "God-given rights" to freedom from all but their consciences.

The Puritan critique of the absolutist state was a renewal of the early Christian conception of individual freedom in the context of the right of the believer to interpret scripture for her or himself rather than to depend on an often corrupted clergy. It also was a descendent of what Mill criticized as the "rigid disciplinarianism" of ancient philosophers, their understanding of liberty as an affirmative quality. In Isaiah Berlin's terms, such liberty is "positive." It is freedom *to*—to be "one's own master . . . to be a subject, not an object . . . to be . . . [responsible] for my choices and able to explain them by references to my own ideas and purposes . . . to be somebody, not nobody."[26] In the fifth-century *polis* of classical Athens, negative liberty would have been meaningless because

> man's existence is irreducibly social, and . . . no conception of morality or capacity to live by it attaches to men as individuals. . . . Protagoras' version of a naturalistic account of political society differs from the modern one in that the characteristic form of social life required for human survival is regarded as constitutive of a fully human life. That is, political society is not merely in-

strumental but rather essential to human well-being, and it secures not man's mere persistence as a sentient creature, but his development as a creature capable of genuine autonomy and freedom.[27]

To the seventeenth-century Puritan, increasingly hemmed in by royal absolutism and the dislocating effects of national economic integration, assertions of the right to live according to one's religion were embedded in communities of "voluntary, highly motivated and self-policing believers."[28] Like the voluntary associations formed by citizens of ancient city-states, these communities were designed to ensure the security of their members. However, they were intended to ensure security not just in this world but also, and more importantly, in the next. Puritan believers put themselves in opposition to powerful states, not by demanding negative freedoms that would enlarge the private sphere within which they as individuals or as congregations could do as they chose, but by demanding access to the public sphere of politics and the right to engage with others in defining a moral order that would be authoritatively enforced by the state.

The political passion of the Puritans was overtaken by the passion for individual privacy—perhaps the result of a tug-of-war between ideals and interests, but one whose exact genesis is not clear.[29] Privacy is only partially institutionalized in societies whose development was influenced strongly by Puritan ideology. As Nazih Ayubi points out, privacy is not a socially accepted norm in the Middle East where the public sphere comes closer to Habermas's description of the publicness of representation than to civil society concepts embedded in the political development of England and North America.

> In Muslim as in some Mediterranean societies, life is often "lived in public," and all things in life acquire a certain cruel publicity. Matters of personal conduct, sex and the family are often regarded as public morals that should be enforced collectively. The family has not (yet?) developed into an island of privacy and intense intimacy in the way it has on the whole done in North European and North American societies. The "public" realm is a realm of sociability mediated by conventions that allow social distance to be maintained despite physical proximity. . . . The "public space" here is a space of symbolic display, of interaction rituals and personal ties, of physical proximity coexisting with social distance. It is not conventionally a space for collective political action and is only rarely a space of a discourse that addresses common concerns. This latter type of space I prefer to describe as *civic*; it is the realm of public debate and conscious collective action or, in a word, of citizenship.[30]

While I agree with much of Ayubi's conclusion here, I see perhaps a larger scope both for individual privacy and for civic life in the Kuwaiti case than he finds in his survey of the many societies of the Middle East as a whole. The lacunae that supported political autonomy in premodern Europe also supported political autonomy in premodern Kuwait. Indeed, the rapidity of modernization in Kuwait preserved these small spaces of appearance and, even more important, the expectation among city-dwellers that political life was an entitlement of Kuwaiti citizens. As I discuss at greater length in chapter 7, Islamist movements are, at least in part, movements similar to Puritanism in their grounding in popular appropriations of religious authority to curb the powers of states whose capacity for coercion of their domestic populations expanded rapidly in the twentieth century. In Kuwait the political opposition is jointly composed of merchants seeking to ensure the rights—including privacy rights—of civil society, and mass movements reacting against the immorality of an unchecked authoritarian regime. This split in ideologies and strategies for democratization is reflected in divergences in the understanding of the meaning of citizenship among Kuwaitis today.

Citizenship

In two influential lectures, T. H. Marshall deals with the multiple character of citizenship as a status enjoyed by members of a political community. He describes the citizen's acquisition of rights as an evolutionary process. Taking the history of England as his *problematique*, Marshall asserts that, "in early times," the elements of citizenship were blended together. Civil rights (freedom-from elements), political rights (freedom-to elements), and social rights ("a different order from the others, because it is the right to defend and assert all one's rights on terms of equality with others and by due process of law") were "wound into a single thread," mostly because states were too small and rudimentary to support highly articulated institutions.[31]

Even though citizens' rights were conceptually undifferentiated, they were differently realized. Entitlement to rights and the capacity to exercise them depended on geographic location and social status. As early modern kings reduced the impact of locality by nationalizing politics and the economy, state institutions became increasingly differentiated. Separate institutions began to specialize in particular functions, though not all functions formerly performed by medieval communities—individual and collective welfare provision being chief among them—continued to be performed or performed as well because of "economic change."[32] Rights associated with highly developed institutions were more fully realized than others, but access to all institutions required new "machinery" because nationalization had changed not only their character and location but also the nature of their relationship to the citizen.

Marshall defines citizenship as a relation of political equality arising from the acquisition of civil rights by an entire population. Civil status—citizenship—was "democratic, or universal . . . [and] arose naturally from the fact that it was essentially the status of freedom, and in seventeenth-century England all men were free."[33] Civil rights such as habeas corpus, press freedom, property rights, and religious liberty were acquired one by one as elaborations of civil status—that is, they were acquired by every man when they were acquired by any man. In England, political rights, by which Marshall means essentially voting rights, depended for a long time on economic status. Their spread to the formerly disenfranchised took place in two ways. First, an individual could acquire property to meet current minimum standards; then, beginning in 1832, the property qualification itself was altered, initiating a trend of selective enfranchisement of whole sets of men formerly disqualified from voting. As Karl Polanyi also emphasizes in his discussion of the extension of the franchise in England, political rights were not seen from the outset as citizen entitlements but rather as the outcome of a struggle between citizen demands and client pressures to preserve first, the status of landlords and, subsequently, the security of capital.[34] However, despite the extension of the franchise to all adult men and all adult women (accomplished via separate acts passed in 1918), remnants of class bias in political rights remained in effect in England until 1948, when plural voting was abolished.

Social rights, according to Marshall, first took the form of universal education, itself something of a civil right in that citizens would not be able to understand or exercise other rights fully without it. More interesting than that, however, is Marshall's analysis of social rights as "class-abatement," that is, as an amelioration of the social effects of economic inequality.[35] Marshall notes that premodern efforts to alleviate the effects of poverty actually erased civil and political rights. Thus, the destitute lost civil rights by having to live in workhouses, poorhouses, or prisons, and political rights because they were disenfranchised. In the twentieth century, however, and increasingly so under the Labour government which assumed power after World War II, Marshall was satisfied that expanded social rights actually accomplished some degree of equalization. Means-tested benefits added directly to the income of the poor, although they also imposed a status disability that diluted their egalitarian effects. Universal flat-rate cash benefits marked a major improvement. Gains to individual citizens were inversely proportional to income, and the status disability of means-tested benefits was removed. Service benefits such as national health were even more equalizing because they were identical for all, transforming the "skyscraper" of class inequality into an egalitarian "bungalow."[36] Class-abatement allows all citizens to think of themselves as equal participants in a common culture even though capitalism ensures the practical persistence of class differences and substantial economic inequality.

Marshall's notions of citizenship remain highly influential despite the fact that they have been criticized on a number of counts. For example, their applicability in other settings, particularly to countries outside Europe and its colonies, has been questioned.[37] More problematic is Marshall's conclusion that the equality implied by citizenship can coexist comfortably with the inequalities inherent in capitalism as long as they are ameliorated by social rights. Bryan Turner argues that even though civil and political rights are necessary for capitalism to flourish, they challenge neither social nor economic hierarchies. In contrast, social rights, which imply redistribution and are highly vulnerable to rollback, do challenge existing hierarchies and require a very different kind of politics. Turner also takes issue with the assumption of evolution embedded in Marshall's story of citizenship rights, noting that the medieval Catholic Church supported a broader universalism than contemporary citizenship, and that an examination of the very different pattern of acquisition of rights by women who, even in England, had some social rights before they acquired any political rights or full civil rights, challenges the notion that civil rights are the bedrock of citizenship.[38] Barry Hindess's criticisms of Marshall concentrate on his tendency to equate formal equality with practical equality, particularly where social rights are poorly developed: "In the absence of social rights, then, the impact of a formal equality of civil and political rights will be somewhat restricted."[39] Hindess also criticizes Marshall's tendency to equate principles and formal statements with reality—whether the resulting gap is normatively positive or negative, it is likely to be filled with an array of different interpretations and an even larger variety of practices.[40] As I discuss below, both points have bearing on the Kuwaiti case.

Despite these criticisms, however, Marshall's conception that the elements of citizenship are independent allows them to be viewed as ideal types for the purpose of analysis, thereby supporting a range of narratives about how they arose and were combined in actual cases. Further, Marshall's connection of rights with institutional development indicates how one might develop alternative narratives of priority to the one he outlined. Finally, Marshall's observation that the provision of social rights is a strategy for reducing class conflict has a much wider applicability than to the particular case he examined. While much of what Marshall's critics say has merit, much of what Marshall says also is meritorious and worthy of consideration. This is especially so if we take a closer look at social and political development with respect to the continuity of traditional patterns into modern times.

Citizenship and the Nation-State

Anthony Giddens differs from both Springborg and Marshall, arguing that human institutions and patterns of behavior in modernity are only marginally connected to traditional forms. Giddens defines modernity as the

> institutions and modes of behavior established first of all in post-feudal Europe, but which in the twentieth century increasingly have become world-historical in their impact. "Modernity" can be understood as roughly equivalent to "the industrialized world." . . . A second dimension is capitalism. . . . Each of these can be distinguished analytically from the institutions of surveillance, the basis of the massive increase in organisational power associated with the emergence of modern social life. . . . This dimension can in turn be separated from control of the means of violence. . . . Modernity produces certain distinct social forms, of which the most prominent is the nation-state.[41]

Giddens sees all individual and institutional behavior as the outcome of "reflexivity," a continuous pattern of internal and external reality checks that modify self-understanding, behavior, and social structures. The speed and scope of reflexivity increase with the level of modernity but, as a process, reflexivity is the same mechanism that has produced social cohesion and cultural continuity throughout the history of human communities.

> All human beings routinely "keep in touch" with the grounds of what they do as an integral element of doing it. . . . This "reflexive monitoring of action" . . . [is] chronic . . . a consistent . . . monitoring of behavior and its contexts. . . . The reflexivity of modern social life consists in the fact that social practices are constantly examined and reformed in the light of incoming information about those very practices, thus constitutively altering their character.[42]

Giddens, like Polanyi, ties the processes associated with modernity to the rise of the nation-state and also to the penetration of traditional cultures by dominant states; both make modernity a global phenomenon.[43] These processes are highly visible in Kuwait where great wealth provides the means for Kuwaitis to initiate connections to individuals and institutions outside their immediate environment almost at will. Through reflexivity, cultural understandings and patterns of behavior are transmitted from one society to another. In the process, they are constantly modified by adjustments to local realities and, in turn, become the grounds of subsequent transmissions and modifications. Yet although this process appears to be globally homogenizing, in reality it is highly fragmenting, nationally and globally, as individuals form communities of choice independent of kinship, locality, and other premodern bases of identity-formation.

Another source of national fragmentation arises from the coexistence of modernity with premodern ideas and structures, including with respect to those statuses and identities associated directly with citizenship. Within most and across all states, the status of members of domestic communities differs widely.[44] We can think of these statuses as ranged between two ideal types of state-inhabitant relations. One creates "citizens," free persons, autonomous and equal partners in civil and political life. Each citizen is unique; this Arendtian plurality enables all of them together to construct their state as a corporate expression of their collective values, interests, and desires. The other ideal type creates "subjects," persons "subjected" to someone else's will. As Epictetus observed, subjects are neither autonomous nor partners in civil life but rather belong to the landscape of a ruler's estate. Perhaps no state today can boast of citizens who are entirely free, equal, and fully incorporated into political life; nearly every state harbors subjects of various sorts, among them persons who are nominally citizens.

According to Benedict Anderson, subjects belong to "the dynastic realm," a political order associated with a hierarchical and heteronomous premodern past.

Kingship organizes everything around a high centre. Its legitimacy derives from divinity, not from populations, who, after all, are subjects, not citizens. . . . In the older imagining, where states were defined by centres, borders were porous and indistinct, and sovereignties faded imperceptibly into one another.[45]

Also in the dynastic realm, time is experienced differently; "now" is eternal and distinctions between past and future are seldom made. Dynastic cycles that claim legitimacy from the transmission of authority from a heavenly source to a just ruler, and life cycles during which parents produce children to take their places in a cosmically regulated pattern of recapitulation without change—without "progress"—are divinely ordained pathways of life.[46]

Different understandings of the meaning of human life operate in the dynastic realm and in modernity. In Anderson's conception of the "older imagining," the world is monadic as well as timeless. Although each person—every thing—in it is singular, each also is iconic and essential, one self-contained facet of an eternity that embraces all of them at the same time. Destiny, one's location in eternity, determines each life. As in Verdi's 1861 opera *La Forza del Destino*, destiny may be interpreted by clerical intermediaries. However, it cannot be altered. This image of the world is captured in a Christian prayer, the Gloria: "As it was in the beginning, is now and ever shall be, world without end." Muslims say, "It was written," to convey a similar sense of a cosmic order over which human will has no power to prevail.

In contrast, the modern world is pluralistic. It exists in "homogeneous empty time . . . measured by clock and calendar."[47] In this world, persons and things exist during a limited lifespan, each in its particularity. Cosmology is separate from history. History is materially rather than spiritually manifested and also is subject to human agency. In the modern world we speak of "individuals," but this refers to interchangeability rather than singularity.[48] Individuals are units of society, atoms in the contingent construction of social aggregates. Unlike the "soul," individuals are neither unique nor immortal: to paraphrase Andy Warhol, anyone can be famous, but only for fifteen minutes.

Ernest Gellner offers another hierarchical and heteronomous image of premodern social orders which he calls "agro-literate" societies. Unlike Anderson, who sees the modern citizen almost as a spontaneous product of the spread of literacy and "print capitalism" (that is, a profit-seeking, market-driven publishing industry), or Giddens, who ties the creation of self-actualizing persons to the spontaneously organized processes of global modernization, Gellner depicts the modern state as a purposeful creator of equal and functionally interchangeable citizens. He tells us that citizens are produced by "exo-socialization, education proper," mass education provided by a national system as compared to the individualized training of agro-literate persons by parent, priest, and tutor.[49] In this view, the modern citizen is a commodity manufactured by the modern state. At the same time, modern citizens create the modern state by generating and then consuming the economic and political resources that maintain the state's legitimacy and sovereignty.

Some citizens of modern states are autonomous and interchangeable, but others are not. Gellner calls such citizens "entropy-resistant," marked in some obvious and unerasable way that allows their fellow citizens to reject and discriminate against them.[50] Inferior citizenship also can result from state action. For example, some citizens may be defined legally as having different entitlements to the resources of exo-socialization or access as adults to participation in the political, economic, and social life of the community. Women are persons most often so marked or legally set apart, but other groups such as members of ethnic and religious minorities also may suffer civil disabilities as a result of their entropy resistance.

Entropy resistance also can be exploited or created by political dissidents as a mark of resistance to a social and political order of which they disapprove. Anh Nga Longva emphasizes the importance of costume in defining "Kuwaitiness," especially among Kuwaiti men who nearly all wear the traditional *dishdasha* when they are in Kuwait.[51] This is especially true of Kuwaitis playing public roles. For example, when Shi'i cleric Husain 'Ali al-Qallaf was running for parliament in 1992 and 1996, among the arguments used against him was that he did not wear a Kuwaitily correct costume. His enemies often referred to him as "the turban" to emphasize his entropy resistance. In return, he challenged repeatedly their definition of Kuwaitiness as conforming to a specific mode of dress and thus of religious affiliation, insisting throughout the campaign that, if elected, he would indeed wear his turban in the parliament. A few other Kuwaitis choose secular costumes to mark their resistance. I never saw Ahmad al-Khatib, perhaps the most consistently independent dissident in Kuwait, wearing a *dishdasha*. Even in the parliament, he always wore a suit. Significantly, following the attempt on his life in June 1996, 'Abdullah Nibari, whom I had always seen in traditional dress in Kuwait before that time, returned to public life in Kuwait wearing a suit. With the spread of Islamism in Kuwait, other manipulations of costume and visage—such as the short *dishdashas* and untrimmed beards favored by the Salafin, and the demands for various types of veiling by female students at Kuwait University—mark sites of resistance where political activists use their own bodies to announce their disagreement with their opponents. Such concrete illustrations of both rejection and resistance confirm Marshall's observation that the elements of citizenship are separable.

As I show in subsequent chapters, inequalities of class, status, gender, and religion run through Kuwaiti political life and constitute dynastic elements in that nation. Despite the use of these inequalities as platforms for political action and criticism of the regime, the persistence of dynastic elements reinforces differences that are invidious to the consideration of citizenship as a status founded on the model of fraternal equality.[52] At its worst, such persistence introduces "intimate enemies" into the political community, persons who claim part or all of the entitlements of citizens but are treated as morally unfit for citizenship because of personal attributes—gender, religious affiliation, ethnic background—which mark them as suspect persons whose loyalty never can be entirely assured.[53] Such persons often are accused of having antisocial attitudes: clannishness, an unwillingness to put the community first when its demands conflict with their personal or family welfare, and even a propensity to treachery. Intimate enemies easily become scapegoats when communities or their leaders are under pressure.

In contrast to these dynastic elements, the collectivities we call "nations" define themselves in reaction to other nations.[54] National identity is a group identity focused on a historic territory, common myths and historical memories, and a common mass culture, all of which separate "the nation" from "aliens." National identity incorporates variously composed bundles of citizenship rights such as the ones identified by Marshall which were outlined above.[55] The cultural elements of national identity often are infused with familial imagery and notions of common descent, and some of the most passionate nationalisms are reactions to perceived wrongs against the national "family" and its "home" territory. Palestinian nationalism is an interesting example. It did not exist before the twentieth century, and began to take shape only after two decades of organized movement of large numbers of European Jews into a particular territory inhabited primarily by Arabs. After the formation of the State of Israel in 1948, and nourished by recurrent Arab-Israeli wars, Palestinian nationalism flowered as a complex psychological and social phenomenon based in a political project to achieve an independent Palestinian state. As I describe in the next chapter, a distinctly Kuwaiti national identity first began to coalesce around the defeat and expulsion of an invading army. Although it is complicated by sociocultural divisions in the understanding and experience of a territorial patrimony, Kuwaiti nationalism nevertheless is the repository of stories depicting the community as a social organism, and constitutes the distinctive ground for the Kuwaiti citizen's identity as one of its members.

Democracy and the Modern State

Citizenship and its practices are realized in a political community, itself the product of formal rules and informal understandings defining a membership, its rights and obligations, and the regime that enforces them. The modern nation-state, which claims a monopoly over legitimate violence, is the primary authority enforcing these rules, either directly or as a guarantor of non-state-sponsored institutions and arrangements. Such institutions and arrangements are elements of complex material and social systems within and transcending the nation-state, and all of them together constitute the integuments of modernity.[56] One example in which Kuwait is deeply implicated is the international energy regime. Unlike the systems that characterize traditional life, modern systems are guided by technical specialists—experts. Other participants trust the specialists to know their jobs. They trust the existence of interlocking systems of regulation designed to ensure that the proper specialists occupy places where they are needed, and they trust that the entire complex edifice will be managed in a predictable way.[57] Kuwaitis rely on experts to produce, refine, and market their oil so that their state and society will have the income needed to maintain their way of life. When results fail to live up to expectations, trust is diminished, not only in experts but also in the political leaders who employ and direct them. Consumers of Kuwait's oil also depend on those expert systems and on the continued willingness and capacity of Kuwait to provide the raw material and processing facilities that keep this particular set of systems going. Conflicts between consumer and producer interests often are masked by the aura of expertise, making interest definition and pursuit difficult. This adds to the loss of legitimacy by the state for its perceived failure to recognize and articulate national interests.

The nation-state, as a fundamental attribute of modernity, is both a collection of expert systems and a guarantor of other systems. Like its population, the state is far from a unitary actor.[58] Because state institutions are fragmented, they may work together or at cross-purposes, with or without domestic and/or foreign nonstate partners, and against or for what a disinterested observer might judge to be state or national interests. The complexity of the state and its activities, along with its propensity to act in ways that appear to be illogical, immoral, and/or inefficient, leads observers of various ideological persuasions to believe that the state is not an autonomous actor but merely an apparatus used by dominant classes to exploit subordinate classes. Such critics include socialists like Karl Marx and Friedrich Engels, along with many liberals.[59]

Charles Tilly and Barbara Geddes, among others, see the state as autonomous but far from independent. Domestic clients, enemies, and political entrepreneurs, both internal and external, constrain the state and limit its ability to act at will. Tilly points to the close connection between war-making and state-making, linking the interdependence of domestic capitalists seeking services from the state to the needs of the state to raise the funds necessary to defend itself against military threats.[60] The authority of the bourgeoisie comes from its wealth and the dependence of the nation-state on domestic investment and fiscal resources, much of which originate from this class. Insofar as their wealth is independent of landholding, members of the domestic bourgeoisie can counter the authority of the state by exiting—individuals and groups can take their moveable wealth and go elsewhere if the state imposes unacceptable demands and conditions on their activities. However, "where exit either is not possible or is difficult, costly, and traumatic . . . [voice], the attempt at repairing and perhaps improving [a] relationship through an effort at communicating one's complaints, grievances, and proposals for improvement," though nearly always more dangerous to the individual, is the preferred strategy.[61] Recognition that both sides have something to gain from accommodation, rulers and powerful domestic interests devise pacts to delineate their respective spheres and rights, establishing systems of trust enabling them to engage in conflict with a low risk of violence.[62] As I describe in subsequent chapters, the repeated failure of Kuwait's twentieth-century rulers to honor their pacts with domestic social groups keeps exit among the explicitly considered defensive strategies in the political repertoires of some Kuwaitis.

Pacts between rulers and powerful segments of domestic society can be as formal as constitutions and as informal as "gentlemen's agreements." As elements of constitutions, pacts are devices intended to minimize risk. Examples include guarantees of basic civil rights such as the right to own property, conduct private business within a legal framework, and enjoy free speech and press—crucial components of the transparency necessary for markets to operate effectively and, not incidentally, for coordinating criticism of and resistance to oppressive state behavior.[63] In this sense, transparency contributes to building the trust without which complex modern systems cannot operate effectively.[64] Constitutional pacts may restrict or enlarge the scope of political rights. Franchise restrictions, along with strict limits on naturalization, can support the status quo politically by limiting the range of interests as well as the number and status of persons permitted legitimate access to the public sphere. By establishing representative institutions and devising mechanisms such as elections for transmitting voice, positive liberty in the form of political rights to persons and groups who otherwise would not have them is extended. Gentlemen's agreements—monopolies, contracts, and other quid-pro-quo deals—are private pacts that involve few if any direct benefits for the population as a whole although they may bolster the trust of elites in the government and thus their confidence in the political system and their willingness to consent to its constraints.

Geddes concentrates on interests within the state itself, and the conflicts of interests that impinge on individuals in key positions within the state. She explains some of the inefficiency and immorality of state actions as the logical outcome of the inability of a political entrepreneur—an ambitious individual occupying a particular office—to do good and do well simultaneously. Consequently, while the national interest, the preferences of a large segment of the population (Geddes calls these "latent interests"), or some other ideal conception of "the good" may be what a political entrepreneur actually wants to achieve, the particular interests of well-organized and politically influential groups, coupled with a strong desire to remain in office, can force the political entrepreneur to support a contrary course of action. As I describe in subsequent chapters, such dilemmas are the constant companions of Kuwaiti parliamentarians and cabinet ministers. Geddes argues that the structure of interests and their relative political capacities by themselves do not explain this strange logic. Just as important are "institutional factors such as electoral rules and party procedures [which] have as much influence on politicians' decisions about whether to supply particular public goods as do latent interests."[65] This point too is very well illustrated by the Kuwaiti case.

Tilly and Geddes are directly concerned with persons, structures, and practices that occupy the gap between formal statements and substantive practices that was identified by Hindess as a flaw in those analyses of citizenship which assume them to be the same thing. To explain differences in democratic norms and practices depends on whether democracy is conceived primarily from the perspective of populism ("the access of the masses—temporarily or, more frequently, permanently—to politics"),[66] or of constitutionalism ("the 'rule of law' protecting specific spheres of life against arbitrary power").[67] As Polanyi notes with respect to England and Dean Burnham and Ellen Meiksins Wood with respect to the United States, constitutionalism can be a tool for undermining the effectiveness of the masses of the population as political actors at the same time that it appears to be expanding their access to political life.[68] However, persons excluded either by social practice or the rule of law from effective participation in politics are not confined to groups ordinarily associated with "the masses," as the experience of Kuwaiti merchants attests. In addition, formal or practical exclusion from political decisions that they think are important does not imply that affected individuals and groups surrender their positive liberties without a fight. The oscillation between democratic oligarchy[69] and autocracy that has characterized Kuwaiti political life for one hundred years displays some of these qualities.

Local political traditions are important influences on the principles and practices of citizenship, but traditions are far from static. They are constantly renewed and reconstructed, enabling a wide variety of political entrepreneurs to argue with some plausibility that their particular vision of tradition is the only "authentic" one.[70] The fluidity of tradition and its instrumental use by political entrepreneurs in the Middle East is most commonly addressed with respect to Islamist movements. As many scholars have argued,[71] Islamism is only partly related to traditional beliefs and customary behaviors of Muslims. Even in the high-profile realm of "Islamic dress," such as veiling for women, Islamism calls for practices that diverge substantially from what was acceptable in the past. Yet Islamism has reconstructed tradition successfully in the minds of millions of believers, a result of reflexivity mediated by the tape recorders and TV sets of modernity.[72]

Whether they are religious or secular, political entrepreneurs in the Middle East have access to a vast repertoire of ideological and structural tools for propelling themselves to positions of power and keeping themselves there once they arrive. At the same time, modernity also equips their constituents with handy tool kits full of useful implements along with directions for their use. Many of these tools can be used to make demands on the state for rights and entitlements. In a country like Kuwait, where small size and city-state ambience encourage the exercise of voice, clashes over political rights frequently center on the nature of citizenship itself. In the next chapter, I discuss myths describing Kuwaiti political traditions, and the citizen who is both their maker and their product. Competing versions of these myths provide many of the scripts for the play of politics in contemporary Kuwait.

Clashes among contending myths of citizenship and the state have characterized Kuwaiti domestic politics for nearly a hundred years. Although Kuwaiti status has come to be associated with material privilege, Kuwaiti national identity has a strong cultural foundation in stories, practices, and artifacts that predate the oil era. The passion with which Kuwaitis today argue over who is a real Kuwaiti and what is the real Kuwait is intensified by internal and external pressures to resolve the status of noncitizen populations and, among Kuwaiti citizens, adult women. Despite theoretical and practical shortcomings, Kuwait and "Kuwaitiness" are real concepts, and Kuwaitis of all kinds continue to be absorbed in the struggle to control their meanings.

Founding Myths

The dynamics of state-society relations in Kuwait are reflected in stories describing the community's social and political origins. One example comes from economist Robert Mabro.[1] As he tells it, in the early eighteenth century, three important families headed a group of nomads forced from the Arabian interior by a prolonged drought. Finding water at an oasis near the shores of the Gulf, they decided to settle there permanently. Then they were faced with a second decision: who would rule their group—who would be responsible for keeping the peace, settling disputes, dealing with foreigners, and doing the other jobs necessary if the rest were to live and work in comfort and security. The tribal elders met to talk about this. The head of the most important family was the first one asked to take the job, but he declined because running the government would interfere with his business. The head of the second-ranking family declined for the same reason. The Sabah were the poorest of the important families. When they were asked to provide a ruler for the city they agreed, both for the honor of it and because the opportunity costs for them were very low.

The rhythms of this story are familiar. They remind us of fairy tales in which the youngest sibling, despite the inequities of primogeniture, rises on merit to triumph in the end. A similar transformation has been worked on the Sabah. Although their precise position in the economic and social hierarchy of pre-oil Kuwait is a matter of some dispute, their present dominance over the economy and the state is not. This transformation has accompanied, indeed, been part of, a general shift in the old social order, unmoored by the flood of oil wealth that has altered the balance of power inside and outside Kuwait over the past fifty years. During the unsettled period immediately prior to the Iraqi invasion, the identity of Kuwait and hopes for its future were mirrored in the conflicting stories citizens and observers told about its political origins.

In their stories, Kuwaiti historians tend to emphasize the participatory nature of the politics surrounding the founding of the city and the choice of its ruler. For example, Hasan 'Ali al-Ebraheem says that the selection of the first amir, Sabah I, was made by his peers, that is, through consensus reached by an oligarchy.[2] This assessment is echoed in contemporary reports written by European travelers until nearly the end of the nineteenth century. For example, a French observer, E. Reclus, writing in 1884, remarked that "the people of this republic (Kuwait) is one of the freest peoples in the world."[3] Perhaps the most tenacious contemporary historian of Kuwait's ruling family is British author Alan Rush. His writings on the ruling family reflect the fragmentary nature of what we know, indicating merely that "[the Sabah] are said to have acquired the right to rule through a voluntary division of responsibilities between themselves and the other leaders of the community."[4]

Other outsiders tell stories built around images of domination by a leadership with an unassailable right to rule absolutely. Robert Stevens says that the Sabah founded a "dynasty [which] has continued to this day," a royalist perspective echoed by some other British writers.[5] A story H. R. P. Dickson reports as having been told by the amir 'Abdullah al-Salim (r. 1950–1965) has the tribal council selecting Sabah as their emissary to the Turks shortly after the migrating families had settled in Kuwait. They did this to avoid an attack from Constantinople in retaliation for appearing to be infringing on the imperial rights of the Porte.[6] But Dickson also tells another story, one he seems to like better. In this one, the Sabah establish their status as tribal leaders through fealty sworn by their retainers prior to a battle to defend the honor of the family from an importunate outsider wanting to marry the shaikh's daughter Mariam.[7]

The origin of the name "Kuwait" also is differently accounted for. Most agree that it comes from the Arabic word *kut* or "fort." Peter Mansfield says that such a fort on the site of modern Kuwait had been used by the then-dominant Bani Khaled tribe before the ancestors of the Kuwaitis arrived.[8] Dickson says that the word refers to the "stronghold" constructed in the center of their tent city by the settlers themselves.[9] Ahmad Mustafa Abu-Hakima says that the name Kuwait and the old name of the city, Grane, are both diminutives, one meaning a small fort and the other a small hill; both signify that the place was unimportant.[10] Hasan al-Ebraheem agrees, saying that Kuwait is the word for a little mud house, indicating the "insignificant origin of the town which later became the capital of the present state of Kuwait."[11] Local versions of the naming myth often project this defensive insignificance. The founding myth told by Kuwaiti merchant 'Abd al-'Aziz al-Saqr takes this self-deprecation even further. Some cowardly bedouins were chased out of their territory. They roamed for years and years through the desert until they came to Kuwait. It was very hot. It was dusty. There was no fresh water. "Let's stay," they said. "No one will bother us here."

Myths of Money and Power

Another history of Kuwait is told from the perspective of its wealth and who controlled it. These stories are not only about money but also about power, both political and social: who had it, what they did with it, and to whom. Particularly in a patriarchal society, this kind of myth is a "family romance," a story in which relationships among individuals in various familial roles echo the shape of the struggle for power in society as a whole.[12] In many of these myths, Kuwait's rulers are pictured as protectors of the common people against a rapacious oligarchy, while the merchants are portrayed as exploiters who put their private—their selfish—interests above those of the community as a whole.

Stories about Kuwaiti wealth vary, not only with respect to heroes and villains but also according to the period of time that the teller has in mind. Nearly everyone agrees that Kuwait became poor in the first half of the twentieth century.[13] Pearling, the main industry, declined throughout the region following the introduction of Japanese cultured pearls in the 1920s. Jacqueline Ismael blames Kuwait's poverty on a turn-of-the-century alliance between the British and merchants from some of Kuwait's founding families that led to Britain taking over Kuwait's local dominance of long-distance shipping. Ismael argues that the basis of this unholy alliance was the merchants' desire to freeze Ottoman competition out of Kuwait, and the British desire to freeze all their competitors out of long-distance trade.[14] However, in the Ottoman archives, Frederick Anscombe finds evidence that Kuwaiti merchants and the Ottomans were similarly injured by rising taxes on trade imposed by the Kuwaiti amir Mubarak (r. 1896–1915). Anscombe's research indicates that it was Mubarak's secret alliance with the British that hastened the substitution of British for Ottoman influence.[15]

Kuwait's entrepôt economy was further weakened by the disruption of local trade that occurred because of World War I. Afterward, it was ravaged by bedouin raiding, masterminded by a former Kuwaiti dependent, 'Abd al-'Aziz Ibn Sa'ud. Then it was hit by the Great Depression. The population of Kuwait grew during the Depression because of immigration from areas that were even worse off,[16] but the resulting surplus of labor further depressed per capita income, already devastated by declines in pearling and trade. World War II imposed additional hardships in the form of new disruptions in normal trade patterns and also reduced food supplies, especially the imported rice that is a staple of the Kuwaiti diet.

This dismal picture changes when the nineteenth century is the focus of consideration. The extent and diversity of Kuwait's trade then made it very lucrative, especially during the second half of the nineteenth century, although the prosperity was confined to a small elite.[17] Sailors and pearlers worked under a system of debt peonage. They borrowed money, often from their ship's owner or its captain, worked for an entire season—about ten months—to pay their debts and, if they were lucky, earned enough to have some left over. Few were so lucky. The average sailor earned fifty dollars per season.[18] Smuggling was the main source of income for sailor and ship's captain alike, and gold smuggling was one of the primary avenues for capital accumulation by Kuwaiti merchants.[19] W. G. Palgrave, a British observer, was impressed by Kuwait's mid-nineteenth-century prosperity. He attributed it to the high quality of its mariners, its low tariffs, and the "good administration and prudent policy" of the ruling family.[20] Palgrave does not mention inequalities in income distribution or any conflict between the ruler and the merchant elite over control of the surplus produced by the local economy.

The chief source of the surplus in the nineteenth century was the merchants' profits from long-distance trade.[21] As in Europe, merchants in Kuwait relied on the state for policing,[22] that is, for the provision of administrative infrastructure to support the community and its way of life—including enforcement of the labor contracts that allowed the merchants to accumulate significant wealth. This wealth also gave them economic leverage to use on the rulers, but its accumulation depended on the rulers keeping the system together.

When the rulers' requirements for financing from the merchants disappeared, this unequal but still effective interdependence also vanished, giving the rulers the upper hand.

Jabir I (r. 1812–1859) and Sabah II (r. 1859–1866) acquired the date gardens in Iraq that formed the basis of the family's independent wealth.[23] However, neither altered the relative superiority of the merchants in the domestic balance of power. Jabir I was preoccupied with foreign policy, and whatever attention he had left for domestic concerns was centered on the poor. He spent his disposable income to maintain "a sort of public table (of food) of a plentiful but coarse description to which every one appears to be welcome."[24] Sabah II did challenge the merchants, instituting customs taxes on imports during a period of booming trade. But when he tried to impose export taxes, the merchants "insisted that if he needed money he could ask for it but not receive it routinely as a right."[25] They also threatened to leave Kuwait if the amir's tax collector were not removed from office. Sabah II yielded on both points. He, like his father, is remembered for having used his money and prestige to help the poor of Kuwait, many of whom were exploited by the same merchants who opposed extending the ruler's authority.

Power Myths: Dragons and Dragon-Slayers

Stories about the development of autocratic state power in Kuwait are told in whispers—literally—by Kuwaitis. Not only students but their parents and teachers as well discuss the accession of the amir Mubarak (r. 1896–1915) in lowered voices.[26] Some Kuwaitis say that the ruling family tries to suppress any mention in textbooks of the manner of Mubarak's takeover to avoid being tainted by his actions. The family is assisted in its desire to legitimize the position of the present rulers by histories that put Mubarak's 1896 coup in a favorable light. These stories are centered on external threats from the Ottomans and the complicity of Kuwaiti merchants opposed to Turkish interests in the coup that established the current method of selecting Kuwaiti rulers. Frederick Anscombe's *The Ottoman Gulf*, which draws on extensive research in Ottoman archives, challenges many of these stories, painting Mubarak as a skillful political opportunist motivated primarily by greed. When Mubarak's strategy for adding to his wealth and political autonomy proved to be successful, Anscombe shows how it was emulated by other Arabian Peninsula princes who, like Mubarak, also aspired to be state-builders. This state-building activity contributed to the erosion of Ottoman power and prestige in the region prior to World War I.[27]

The older stories depict the successor of Sabah II, 'Abdullah II (r. 1866–1892), as forced by circumstances to align himself with the Ottomans. Prior to 'Abdullah's reign, Kuwait was said to have paid only "nominal recognition to Ottoman authority . . . [while] it pursued an independent policy" that included a refusal to deny asylum to political refugees from Ottoman Baghdad.[28] A dynastic struggle in neighboring Najd is said to have forced 'Abdullah into an alliance with the Ottomans in a war on the Arabian Peninsula, an involvement Anscombe reports as having been undertaken in self-defense.[29] Afterward, 'Abdullah accepted the Ottoman title of Quaimmaqam (subgovernor), which signified that Kuwait was a *qaza* or dependency of the *wilayet* (province) of Basra.[30]

Anscombe's account of this period is part of the story of Midhat Pasha, the visionary Ottoman governor of Basra, who "revived, altered, and pushed vigorously the idea of establishing Kuwait as Ottoman territory."[31] As part of Midhat's strategy to counteract growing British influence in the Gulf, he cut off the revenues from the Sabah date gardens, forcing the family to acquiesce in the extension of Ottoman suzerainty over Kuwait. Constantinople regarded this as resurrecting an old relationship rather than forging a new one, but still agreed to Midhat's accommodation of Kuwaiti requests that no revenues be collected from Kuwait and no Ottoman officials be stationed there.[32] There were occasional impulses to go back on these promises, but the Porte decided in 1893 to reinforce Kuwaiti loyalty with a carrot rather than a stick, giving 'Abdullah's brother and successor, Mohammad (r. 1892–1896), a generous annual stipend.

Some accounts depict Mohammad, who ruled almost in partnership with another brother, Jarrah, as orienting himself and his policies so closely toward Ottoman interests that Kuwaiti merchants became fearful of the potential "Iraqization" of Kuwait.[33] The merchants are said to have looked for an ally in a fourth brother, Mubarak, to assist them in their struggles, but that Mubarak exceeded their expectations when he and his sons assassinated Mohammad and Jarrah, after which Mubarak declared himself ruler of Kuwait. In contrast to this almost collegial depiction of Mubarak's coup, Jill Crystal tells the assassination story as Mubarak's response to his effective exile from the city, sent by his brothers on military campaigns to Hasa and among the tribes in Kuwait's hinterland, but with no funds.[34] Anscombe also recounts mixed motives, but concludes that "money more than politics caused the quarrel that resulted in the murder of Muhammad and Jarrah."[35]

Whatever the role of the merchants in encouraging Mubarak, the new ruler dissociated his interests from theirs and devoted considerable effort to curbing their power. The merchants—Kuwait's incipient bourgeoisie—were not without resources in their various struggles against Mubarak. Despite income from his date gardens and the payments Mubarak received from Constantinople and London,[36] the merchants remained the primary source of state revenues until the 1930s, and the country's chief employers until the 1950s.[37] Merchant power was social as well as economic: employers in a status-based society exacted "a loyalty that was almost absolute" from their employees.[38] As in the past, the merchants' greatest weapon against the government was to threaten to leave, and this remained their strategy in the face of Mubarak's incessant fiscal demands. The British political agent at the time observed that Mubarak liked to live well and that he was an expansionist who warred with local tribes to enlarge the scope of his control in the hinterland. But when he proceeded to raise taxes, camels, and conscripts for another desert campaign in 1910, some of the pearl merchants packed up and moved to Bahrain in protest. Mubarak was forced to send a delegation to woo them back and, in the end, nearly all of them did return. However, neither the merchants nor most other Kuwaitis ever liked Mubarak, who surrounded himself with armed guards for protection from "his own subjects, more and more of whom condemned his luxurious way of life."[39]

British protection enlarged Mubarak's powers tremendously, though British records and histories, along with Kuwaiti memories, tend to understate Britain's role in Mubarak's reign. The British gave Mubarak substantial political and economic independence from the Ottoman Empire, to which Kuwait remained nominally attached until World War I, as the result of a series of mostly secret agreements beginning in 1899.[40] Mubarak received large sums of money under the table every time he signed a new treaty ceding another portion of Kuwait's foreign policy autonomy to Britain.[41] Gradually, British authority spread over Kuwait's port, some of its commerce, and its as-yet-undiscovered oil and gas deposits. In return, Britain contributed to Mubarak's financial independence from his Kuwaiti constituents. British officials also guaranteed that, after he died, his sons rather than his remaining brothers or any of his nephews would succeed him.[42]

Mubarak's direct descendants aspired to rule as he did, but Kuwaiti merchants were unwilling to concede so much power to the ruler without a fight. Following the short reigns of Mubarak's two sons, Jabir (r. 1915–1917) and Salim (r. 1917–1921), they demanded that a system of consultation be established between the ruler and Kuwait's leading citizens. The merchants' first attempt at institutionalizing such a check on the ruler's power was to propose a consultative body that seems to have been a cross between a legislature and a cabinet. The merchants insisted that they would only accept as ruler someone who would assent to such a council, which was established under the leadership of Hamad ibn 'Abdullah al-Saqr, a member of an important merchant family. Of the three "candidates" for the job, the one who is said to have agreed to the council was Ahmad al-Jabir, who was duly appointed by his family and then approved by the British. But as Dickson says, the council met infrequently and, in any event, was ignored by the ruler, who preferred the older system.[43] Even so, the council represented the first formal "attempt at democratic rule in Kuwait and, for that matter, in the Persian Gulf and the Arabian Peninsula."[44] The precedent it set allowed subsequent attempts to establish representative government in Kuwait to be construed as reform rather than revolution,[45] and may explain some of the reason why, even though violence has been a part of this process, it has played a relatively minor role.

Myths of Representative Government

Parliamentary bodies periodically were formed and dissolved in Kuwait following the institution of that first council. This pattern held both before and after a Kuwaiti national constitution was adopted in 1962. The evolution of representative government in Kuwait also was conditioned by oil revenues, which tilted the social balance of power in two ways. First, oil revenues allow the ruler to be fiscally independent of the population, including the merchants who formerly were the primary financiers of the state and thus the primary checks on ruler autocracy. Any merchants who move to Bahrain today cannot hope to influence the government by reducing its disposable income—even if they were paying taxes at the old rates, these payments would be minuscule in comparison to oil revenues.

At the same time, the magnitude of Kuwait's oil revenues allowed the ruler to create and maintain a welfare state, shifting the allegiance of the population from the merchants to the regime. Kuwaiti social rights can be seen as manifestations of a complex system of Marshallian "class-abatement." Among them is the right to state employment. The importance of the merchant elite as employers of Kuwaiti workers has declined dramatically since pre-oil days. Social rights, in the form of extensive economic benefits dispensed by the government, thus both reduced the social status of the merchants and undermined their control over Kuwaiti society.

Following the decline and fall of oil prices in the mid-1980s, merchants and their allies engaged in persistent public complaints about the bloated public sector of Kuwait's economy, something they had been complaining about privately for some time.[46] The state pays the salaries of "about half of all working citizens in Kuwait,"[47] and provides a high level of social benefits such as free health care and child allowances (which go only to male state employees and those few female state employees whose husbands work in the private sector).

Government salary and benefit scales constitute a "minimum wage" floor for Kuwaitis, and their magnitude and downward rigidity have long encouraged Kuwaiti merchants to staff their enterprises with lower-wage foreigners. (Also see chapter 7.)

Oil revenues are mediated by markets which are indifferent both to the principles and to much of the behavior of owners of profitable investments. As a result, the replacement of British support by oil revenues also removed the important, if intermittent, external check on the regime's growing autocracy that Britain previously had exercised. British political agents had oscillated between supporting the ruler and pressing him to allow greater citizen participation in domestic politics.[48] However, as Kuwaiti rulers became less dependent on British economic and strategic resources, they also became less responsive to British political advice.

Ever since the initiation of Kuwait's oil industry, revenues have been appropriated directly by Kuwaiti rulers, who regard them as part of the autocratic domain that their state became thanks to the internal independence from checks on their power that their relationship with Britain had fostered.[49] After Kuwait's first democratic government was installed following elections in January 1963, the disposition of oil revenues was undertaken with the advice of cabinet officers, some of whom came from families other than the ruler's.[50] Even so, virtually all cabinet members are considered to be "yes-men" whose positions depend on their willingness to agree to whatever the ruler wants.[51] Few have the power to act effectively as checks on the ruler, especially those who also are elected members of the Kuwaiti parliament (see chapter 7). Within the cabinet and outside of it, those with the greatest power to check the ruler's behavior come from within the ruling family itself, which is one reason why I sometimes refer to the leaders of Kuwait's regime as "rulers" rather than "the ruler." The plurality of the rulers is itself a check on extreme behavior, a product of the family's collective interest in preserving the regime that gives them so much power.

The most important institutional check on the ruling family today is the elected National Assembly (Majlis al-'Umma) provided for in the 1962 constitution. In spite of its many institutional shortcomings and constant efforts by the regime and its allies to place it in an unfavorable light, the National Assembly is viewed by Kuwaitis from every social class as a check on executive power, though some contend that interference in elections produces a less-than-representative result.[52] What is so curious about the Kuwaiti parliament is that its authority persisted during the two extended periods when the amir dismissed it and suspended the constitution. During those times, the parliament's power was exercised through nonviolent resistance movements which successfully undermined the legitimacy of the regime in spite of its having halted the parliament's formal role as a legislative body.[53] Both times, when the parliament was restored it was in conjunction with other changes intended to check its power.[54]

Clearly, contests for political power and authority in Kuwait have broadened far beyond the conflicts between merchants and rulers which defined the fault-lines in Kuwaiti politics through most of the nation's history.[55] New groups, many from the "middle class" created and supported by oil-financed education and employment, demand greater participation in state and society. The resulting shifts in Kuwait's political universe both embrace a greater diversity of persons and generate conditions for the appearance of mass publics. Government payments fuel a politics of private desires that appeals to Kuwaitis of all income levels. The working masses of Kuwaiti citizens, that is, citizens who live on their wages—a group that is not a working class in the Marxian sense according to most observers[56]—have reoriented their allegiances as a result of how the state's oil income is translated into wages and social benefits. Before the development of mass-level civil or political rights, social and economic benefits such as jobs, education, housing, health care, and free utilities constituted the most valuable citizenship rights of Kuwaitis. The regime's mediation of the transfer of oil wealth in such highly visible ways bolstered popular support for the ruling family and allowed it to shift the status loyalty of the masses from the merchant elite to itself. These benefits also create an acute economic dependency between large numbers of citizens who otherwise are incapable of supporting themselves in today's Kuwait and a state that gives them jobs and services for very little effort.[57]

Elites also are seduced by gifts of private wealth. Crystal identifies a number of ways that Kuwaiti rulers use oil money to buy off traditional challengers to their authority.[58] One of the first programs to distribute Kuwait's oil wealth directly to elites was begun in 1946 and involved government purchases of land at highly inflated prices.[59] The Land Acquisition Policy has been criticized by Kuwaitis and foreigners for handing far more money to the already-rich, including many members of the ruling family, than to the working and *badu* "masses."[60] Between 1946 and 1971, about a quarter of Kuwait's total revenues from oil were distributed directly to individuals through this program, a sum that exceeded investments in foreign assets and almost equaled the total spent on economic development.[61]

Both old merchants and the new rich benefit from laws requiring every business to be majority-owned by Kuwaitis and every foreign worker to have a local sponsor.[62] These laws produced a growing group of "agents" and "sponsors" who take a substantial cut of the profits and wages earned by foreigners.[63]

Local monopolies are another example of the myriad gentlemen's agreements marking little pacts between the ruler and one or another of the influential merchant families, each of which is something of an interest group all by itself.

Citizenship Myths

During the second Gulf War, it became a commonplace to hear that there is no such thing as "Kuwait," that what we call Kuwait is an artificial construct with a very short history,[64] an "accidental state" consisting of little more than a rich family sitting on top of a large oil well.[65] This commonplace arises from envy as well as from ignorance—Saddam Hussein is an enthusiastic retailer of such anti-Kuwait myths. Kuwaiti nationalism is, in fact, far more fully formed and realized than Iraqi nationalism.[66] It is shaped by the city-state experience and, like other nationalisms worldwide, it was fired in the crucible of external attacks. Two twentieth-century invasions threatened Kuwait's independent existence. The more recent is Iraq's 1990–91 invasion and occupation of Kuwait. The other, an invasion by the Saudi-allied Wahhabi Ikhwan, was equally defining in terms of its impact on Kuwaiti nationalism and political culture.

The cultural legacy of the war with the Ikhwan rests on two collective experiences. Both occurred in 1920: the construction of the wall around Kuwait town and the battle of Jahra.' Like the Iraqi occupation, the building of the wall and the battle of Jahra' simultaneously united and divided the Kuwaiti people. The events themselves solidified perceptions by Kuwait's urban residents of their engagement in a common political enterprise, but they also initiated a system of differential status and rights that continues to work against the social cohesion of the Kuwaiti population as a whole.

Anthropologist Anh Nga Longva believes that notions such as nationality and citizenship are relatively new to the peoples of the Arabian Peninsula.[67] Formally launched as nation-states only in the twentieth century, these communities continue to reflect earlier conceptions of group identity that are primarily tribal, based on the principle of jus sanguinis, or entitlement to membership of a community by virtue of "the right of blood." In 1948 two decrees on citizenship were promulgated that added the principle of jus soli, entitlement to membership of a community by virtue of residence, to the rules establishing who could be a Kuwaiti citizen. These decrees defined persons as "originally Kuwaiti [asil]" who were "members of the ruling family, those permanently residing in Kuwait since 1899, children of Kuwaiti men and children of Arab or Muslim fathers also born in Kuwait."[68] The decrees also outlined procedures for naturalization.

Kuwait's 1959 nationality law, since amended but still the basis for deter-
mining citizenship today, reversed the 1948 inclusion as Kuwaitis of those entitled by jus soli. It made naturalization more difficult and exceedingly rare—
limited to fifty persons per year—and also changed the interpretation of the jus
sanguinis principle as it applies in Kuwait. Thus, the citizenship category "children of Arab or Muslim fathers also born in Kuwait" was dropped, while the
citizenship category "originally Kuwaiti" was enlarged to include the descendants of those who had resided in Kuwait in 1920.

> Until independence in 1961, the term "Kuwaitis" was used to refer exclusive-
> ly to the inhabitants of the town of Kuwait. Beyond it, the bedouin nomads
> were known by the names of their tribes and their sub-divisions. . . . Kuwaiti
> society, [like] most societies in the Arabian peninsula, consisted of two
> sharply contrasted communities, the sedentary town-dwellers (hadhar) and
> the nomads (badu).[69]

The hadhar, merchants, sailors, and others lived in the town and earned their
living, directly or indirectly, from the sea. The badu were herders of sheep and
camels who saw the town primarily as a market where they could exchange
meat, milk, and wool for salt and manufactured items like knives and guns.[70]
The badu could break camp and scatter if they were under attack, but the hadhar, as a community with a fixed abode, had to depend on mutual aid to defend themselves and their homes.

The year chosen as the demarcation was not arbitrary. The antagonism that
had simmered for some years between Ibn Sa'ud and the amir of Kuwait, Salim
al-Mubarak, came to a boil in 1920.[71] A small force of Kuwaitis sent by Salim to
camp at Manifa Mountain near Kuwait's southern border was almost entirely
massacred by invading Wahhabi Ikhwan forces in April. The massacre indicated to Salim that Ibn Sa'ud would not honor the boundaries of Kuwait set under
the unratified Anglo-Ottoman treaty of 1913, but the British resisted the idea
that Ibn Sa'ud was behind the Wahhabi attack. This, along with the harrowing
tales told by the few survivors, convinced Salim that he would have to defend
Kuwait on his own.[72]

Salim mobilized Kuwait town to construct defenses. For four months the
entire male population worked day and night to build a wall around the
town.[73] After the wall was built, Salim learned that the Ikhwan, led by Faisal al-
Duwaish, were on the verge of reaching the oasis of Subahiyya on their way to
Jahra', an agricultural community west of Kuwait town. Salim took a force of
armed men from the town to Jahra',

a village of Arab cultivators, tending date-groves and carefully irrigated gardens of lucerne [alfalfa]. They were settled inhabitants who shared neither the worldly sharpness of the Kuwait businessman, nor the maritime interests of the Kuwait sailor. . . . Most of them had come from Najd, and had made of this village a scene more typical of the oases of central Arabia than of the coastal settlements.[74]

Ideally, Salim would be able not only to prevent Faisal from taking Jahra', which occupied a strategic location on the road between Kuwait town and Basra, but also to inflict enough of a defeat on the Ikhwan to forestall an attack on the town altogether.[75]

Abu-Hakima calls the battle of Jahra' "one of . . . the most important events in the modern history of the shaikhdom of Kuwait."[76] The Kuwaiti forces, augmented by *badu* clients of the amir Salim, met a well-planned attack launched by Ikhwan fighters on the morning of October 10. The Kuwaitis were "considerably outnumbered."[77] After some three hours of fighting, they lost control of the village and had to withdraw to the Red Fort, located on the outskirts of the palm groves. That afternoon, a messenger from Faisal al-Duwaish offered safe conduct to the Kuwaitis to leave Jahra'. However, retreat would not have removed the Wahhabi threat to the town. Salim refused Faisal's terms and continued to fight, repulsing three assaults against the fort and inflicting heavy casualties on the Ikhwan forces. Meanwhile, Salim's nephew, Ahmad al-Jabir, who had been left in charge of the town's defense, heard the gunfire from Jahra' and mobilized a relief expedition which left the following morning. When these reinforcements arrived in Jahra', they found eight hundred dead among the Ikhwan and about a quarter of that number among Salim's forces. Faisal already had retreated back toward Subahiyya with his surviving fighters, taking along the camels and other goods they had looted from the people of Jahra'.[78] However, the backbone of the Ikhwan as a military threat to Kuwait had been broken.

The town wall, a symbol of the collective effort that had gone to build it, was transformed into "the symbol of Kuwaiti unity against external threats."[79] Longva says that "the battle of Jahra' . . . created a special bond between the town-dwellers who had taken part in the events and their descendants. These [persons] qualify today as full-fledged 'first category' Kuwaitis whose loyalty to Kuwait has never been questioned."[80] Yet the town-dwellers were not the only residents of Kuwait who had fought with Salim against the Ikhwan. "Badu" are recorded as having been part of Salim's forces, a designation that lumps together not only nomadic tribesmen but also settled Jahra' villagers. Zahra

Freeth recounts a story about the aftermath of the battle that she heard as a young woman from "badu" witnesses. The fighting had taken place in mid-autumn, a time of year when the weather in Kuwait is still very hot. The number of casualties, small by the standards of European wars, was huge in comparison to the size of the Jahra' settlement. Faisal had abandoned so many dead and wounded Ikhwan that it took days for the Kuwaitis to sort them out, and the fingernails fell off some of the corpses before they could be buried. "For a period after the battle whenever the wind rose human fingernails were blown like husks around Jahra', eddying and drifting among houses and tents, creating a weird rattling sound which was vividly described by those who had heard it."[81]

To the town-dwellers, mercifully far from the eerie noises made by these macabre relics of slain Ikhwan, the construction of the town wall (which was never assailed) and the battle at the Red Fort, which they had experienced as the sound of far-off gunfire, were remembered and recounted as singularly *hadhari* accomplishments. Today, Kuwaiti *hadhar* speak with pride about the defense of Kuwait town by their ancestors but are unashamed to say that they've never been to Jahra', a large urban area less than twenty miles from Kuwait City. Meanwhile, as carefully selected cohorts of *badu* were awarded full Kuwaiti citizenship, with its plenitude of social rights, to boost support for the regime,[82] indiscriminate prejudice against tribal Kuwaitis by *hadhar* Kuwaitis intensified. Tribal Kuwaitis whose ancestors had been settled inhabitants of Jahra' since before the Ikhwan wars are especially resentful at the inclusion of recently settled *badu* among first-category citizens when so many of their own number have been denied that status. The Iraqi invasion brought some of these antagonisms to the surface in charges by *hadhar* that "the badu" had fled before the Iraqis rather than standing to defend Kuwait.

Legal and cultural understandings of citizenship continue to divide the Kuwaiti people. The institutional translation of Kuwaiti identity into legal citizenship required heads of families to register with the government during limited open enrollment periods designated by nationality laws and their amendments. This process introduced discrimination against some groups among the settled residents of Jahra' and the nomadic population. Whether because of ignorance of the requirements or suspicion of the procedure, many family heads among the tribes failed to record themselves or their sons as Kuwaitis, either at the most advantageous of these designated times or ever. Those registering late received "second-category" citizenship, analogous to the status of naturalized persons. Second-category Kuwaiti men are deprived of political rights even though they are entitled to the same social and civil rights as first-category Kuwaitis. Nonregistrants are among the *bidun*, short for *bidun jinsiyya* or persons "without [documented proof of] nationality." The status of all Kuwaiti *bidun* was tainted by the incursion of large numbers of refugees during the Iran-Iraq war. Even those *bidun* who have worked their entire adult lives as soldiers or policemen in Kuwait continue to exist in a stateless limbo.[83]

Longva offers an interesting cultural hypothesis about citizenship to explain the depth and persistence of the division between town and tribe. The English word *citizen* is derived from a Latin root, *civis*, "city," coming through the French *citoyen*, the egalitarian term of address used among "fraternal" French revolutionaries. This linguistic legacy reflects the history of citizenship as a concept embedded in the experiences of urban life. In the Kuwaiti urban experience as well, national identity is bound up with the connection between the citizen and the town. As a result, despite a very different linguistic tradition, urban Kuwaitis share a cultural understanding of citizenship very similar to that of Europeans.

> Urban Kuwaitis . . . understand citizenship as *jinsiyya*, from the root verb *jns*, to make alike, to assimilate, to naturalise. . . . There is here an idea of similarity and horizontal solidarity. . . . Jinsiyya . . . does not posit *a priori* an idea of hierarchy or supreme authority. In this sense, it is . . . [close] to the Western concept of citizenship. Although jinsiyya [carries] no connotation . . . [of] the city, the urban Kuwaitis relate this notion with a territorialised community . . . previously the town, today the nation-state, rather than with a particular leadership. . . .
>
> [In contrast,] the tribes in Kuwait understand nationality and citizenship in the sense of *tabiʿiyya*, which can be translated as "following" or "allegiance" to a leader, in this case Kuwait's ruling family. The root verb of tabiʿiyya means, among other things, to walk behind someone, to be subordinate to, to be under someone's command. The concept is clearly built on an idea of hierarchy and vertical allegiance.[84]

While Kuwaiti *hadhar* experience citizenship in the context of modernity with its emphasis on equality and autonomy, significant numbers of tribally oriented Kuwaitis remain part of the old imagining. They are subjects of a ruler, personally tied to him by two-way vertical bonds of status and obligation.

The *badu* tradition, with its absence of attachment to a particular territory, is based on such leader-follower bonds, free of competition from crosscutting loyalties rooted in geography. Even among the *badu*, however, the leader-follower bond cannot be taken for granted. It also proceeds from a social contract, one that requires a leader not merely to reward his followers materially but also to reaffirm his competence and worthiness to retain their allegiance.[85] Salamé argues that a contemporary state organized along these lines follows a recipe first set down by Arab philosopher Ibn Khaldun.

Leadership (*ri'asa*) exists only through superiority (*ghulb*) and superiority only through group feeling ('*asibiyya*). Leadership over people, therefore, must, of necessity, derive from a group feeling that is superior to each individual group feeling. . . . [The] two ingredients of the state's strength . . . are, on the one hand, the actual capabilities of the state and, on the other, the recognition by others of these capabilities. Their recognition of this strength will make them accept it, obey it and shift their political loyalty to its possessors. The central concept of *iltiham* [the coalescence of subordinates around a superior leader] . . . . is then the ultimate form of hegemony in its insistence on social integration by and around the ideology professed by the ruling 'asibiyya.[86]

The *tabi'iyya* conception of citizenship, with its focus on actual or fictive blood relationships arranged in a hierarchy topped by a "superior leader," is the basis of the citizenship myth favored by Kuwaiti rulers. It is precisely this cultural manifestation of citizen-as-subject that Hisham Sharabi calls "neopatriarchy," a complex of nested hierarchical institutions modeled on the patriarchal family.[87] Habermas's concept of representation in premodern political formations as a process that "pretended to make something invisible visible through the public presence of the lord,"[88] is mirrored in the official myth of the Kuwaiti nation, which portrays the amir as the father of his people and citizenship as a family romance.

This version of Kuwaiti national identity is based on the concept of *al-'usra al-waheda*, the "one" or united family. In an effort to promote national cohesion, a campaign to associate this slogan with communal solidarity was undertaken by the government in the early 1970s. *Al-'usra al-waheda* resonates with individual family histories as well as with idealized images of the old-style tribal families of the Arabian Peninsula, idylls of a bygone age when everyone lived securely under the protective wing of the family patriarch.[89] This Kuwaiti national myth incorporates nomadic tribal values such as the subordination of women and young men, and emphasizes those such as that one's primary loyalty is to the '*asibiyya* and its leader.[90] Consequently, the national myth clashes with the entrepreneurial values of the town, not only because of the relatively more horizontal orientation of *hadhar* values but even more because of the town's connection to a particular place.[91] This divergence is bridged structurally by the legitimation of a pyramid of quasi-amirs, "princes" whose castle domains are the households and clans in which they claim entitlement to the absolute loyalty and obedience of their dependents. Consequently, the Kuwaiti national myth is heavily dependent on the acceptance of (neo)patriarchy as the paradigm of social organization and therefore on the continued subjection of women[92] and the acquiescence of young men in their own subordination to family heads. To support their positions, Kuwaiti rulers have given tacit and sometimes open support to those whom they hope are "safe" Islamists, neo-fundamentalists whose advocacy of this vision of "family values" adds religious legitimacy to the al-'usra al-waheda story.[93]

The cultural constraints that produce compliant women and obedient sons are beginning to dissolve as modernity reorganizes Kuwaiti family life. Modernity provides both alternative models for reflexive adjustment and structural support for personal autonomy.[94] Over fewer than fifty years, public education, including female education, has transformed a mostly illiterate population into one where large majorities of female and male adults can read. Increasing numbers of Kuwaiti women work outside the home[95] and marry later than their mothers and grandmothers; some do not marry at all. These changes already have begun to reflect different sets of family values from the ones Islamists promote, and even Islamist values regarding women are far from uniform. In fact, Islamist views of women "as people, and no longer as mere instruments of pleasure or reproduction," are among the strongest indicators of the modernity of Islamist political movements.[96] Modern Kuwait is the home of mixed-gender social organizations such as the Kuwait Graduates Society and the Kuwait Human Rights Organization, while gender itself has become an analytical category that activists use to sharpen arguments for a broadening of civil and human rights in other areas—for example, with regard to the rights of bidun.[97] Although citizenship rights for Kuwaiti women remain at this writing inferior to men's rights in every one of Marshall's canonical categories,[98] reflexivity mediates both the development of gender-equal models of citizenship and political mobilization to promote their wider acceptance and implementation.

At the same time that modernity is eroding traditional conceptions of citizen-as-subject among Kuwaitis themselves, the dependence of the country on immigrant labor embeds a huge population of subjects in the daily lives and consciousnesses of the Kuwaiti people. Longva's study of labor migration and its impact on Kuwaiti society in the 1980s demonstrates the confusion in identity that results from the overlay of large numbers of persons from different—and hierarchically ordered—national groups. One example of this confusion is how the concept of "masculinity" is experienced as a quality of persons. Longva argues that gender roles in Kuwait are unstable except for two groups, Kuwaiti men and Asian women. Kuwaiti men always behave as the masculine (i.e., dominant) partners in relations with members of all other groups: Kuwaiti women, Arab men, Arab women, Asian men, and Asian women; just as Asian women are always the feminine partners, that is, subordinate, without power, in their relations with members of every other group.[99] Consequently,

Kuwaiti women have "masculine" roles in some situations and "feminine" roles in others, contributing to the fluidity of their identities as they are experienced by themselves and perceived and reacted to by others. The dependence of Kuwaitis on a migrant population that outnumbers them by about three-to-one also tends to promote "traditional" values—examples include the contribution to high Kuwaiti birthrates from conscious and unconscious pressures arising from the minority status of Kuwaiti citizens, and the tendency to place responsibility for the size of the immigrant population on "lazy" Kuwaiti women. These multiple roles and identities add to psychological fragmentation and weaken the hegemonic authority of neopatriarchy.

Myths of the Rentier State

Shortly after the Organization of Petroleum Exporting Countries took control of member oil production and pricing away from the international oil companies, articles and books began to appear in the West comparing OPEC nations to sixteenth-century Spain. Awash in bullion from the New World, the Spanish government was said to have been too primitive and incompetent to deploy these vast financial resources in the long-run interests of the state. Some said that Spain's loss was Holland's and England's gain, and that the loot from America financed the capital accumulation that set the stage for Europe's industrial revolution.[100] After 1973 the Spanish theme was exchanged for a contemporary focus, first on the "problem" of petrodollar recycling and then on a formal theory of the *rentier* state.

> A rentier is . . . more of a social function than an economic category. . . . The distinguishing feature of the rentier . . . resides in the lack or absence of a productive outlook in his behavior. [With respect to the rentier state,] there is no such thing as a pure rentier economy. . . . Second . . . a rentier economy is an economy which relies on substantial *external rent*. . . . Third, in a rentier *state*—as a special case of a rentier economy—only a few are engaged in the generation of this rent (wealth), the majority being only involved in the distribution or utilisation of it. . . . Fourth, a corollary of the role of the few, in a rentier state the *government* is the principal recipient of the external rent.[101]

Early versions of the rentier state myth warn about the impact on the world economy of flawed economic and financial policies pursued by rentier states; later ones, many told by Arab nationalists and other advocates of regional redistribution of oil revenues, emphasize the moral shortcomings of rentier status.[102] Both offer structural explanations describing how rentier status disconnects the state apparatus from domestic checks on autocratic behavior. Some contrast oil rentiers with the former British colonies that became the United States. The American Revolution was fought on the principle that there should be no taxation without representation; in wealthy oil-exporting countries, these stories say, there is no representation because there is no taxation.[103] Most of these accounts are consistent with Charles Tilly's description of the evolution of the nation-state in modern Europe.[104]

Another way to look at the myths of the rentier state is to see them as parables contesting different patterns of differential accumulation. A concept developed by economist Jonathan Nitzan, differential accumulation reflects an understanding of capital as a crystallization of power, and its accumulation as the outcome of a struggle for dominance among competitors.

> Accumulation is usually associated with rapid mechanization and productivity gains, but these are technological processes; as such, they are not unique to capitalism and therefore cannot be equated with accumulation. . . . The value of capital represents discounted future earnings. Some of these earnings could be associated with the productivity (or exploitation) of the owned industrial apparatus, but this is only part of the story. As capitalism grows in complexity, the earnings of any given business concern come to depend less on its own industrial undertakings and more on the *community's overall productivity*. In this sense, the value of capital represents a *distributional* claim. This claim is manifested partly through ownership, but more broadly through the *whole spectrum of social power*. Moreover, power is not only a means of accumulation, but also its most fundamental end. . . . The ultimate goal of business is not hedonic pleasure, but *differential* gain.[105]

Nitzan's reintegration of capital with other manifestations of power explains the ferocity of the competition to acquire not simply "enough" for oneself but more than anyone else. By "beating the average," the successful competitor bests his rivals and also impairs their capacity to challenge his dominance. This reintegration explains some of the moral opprobrium heaped on the rentier state, whose military inferiority is seen as disqualifying it from the traditional source of entitlement to dominate other states. A comparison to the Soviet Union is instructive here. The Soviet Union enjoyed substantial rentier income from the oil, gas, and gold sales which produced the lion's share of its foreign exchange earnings. However, its dominance in the markets for these commodities—including its capacity to disrupt them—was not analyzed as an example of rentier state behavior, even though the connection between strategic economic power and strategic military power frequently was made in analyses of Soviet state behavior.[106] That the Soviet Union conformed structurally and politically to conventional conceptions of what it means to be a powerful state may explain some of this disparity.

In the context of differential accumulation, we can see myths of the rentier state as romances revolving around three stock characters: the undeserving rentier, the rent-seeking client, and the poor-but-worthy victim. The rentier state achieves its dominance by cashing in on unearned advantages, in this case, large deposits of natural resources. It is portrayed as the recipient of income to whose generation it contributes nothing because it lacks a "productive outlook." Income originates "outside" the state, a fiction it is possible to maintain if one forgets that the resources originate "inside."[107] Only a small segment of the domestic workforce is devoted to producing rentier income, which accrues to the government by virtue of its control of the state apparatus. As a result, the rentier state goes unchallenged domestically or internationally; it fritters its income away on hedonic consumption and rent-seeking clients who offer political support in exchange for differential access to a protected share of rentier spoils. Everyone else is a victim: those who do not share directly in the spoils and those from whom the spoils are wrested and accumulated.

The myth of the rentier state is the subtext of Saddam Hussein's criticisms of and justifications for invading Kuwait.[108] More broadly, it is the subtext of a whole set of criticisms of OPEC members and other developing-country mineral exporters who, during the 1970s, claimed authority over the production and pricing of their natural resources and used their positions as sellers in tight markets to demand a New International Economic Order.[109] Syrian diplomat and scholar George Tomeh points out how critics from developed countries used the concept of "interdependence" to challenge this authority, though they never cited interdependence as a reason why they themselves should exercise restraint with respect to the economies of developing nations.[110] It seems clear that the issue is less that some countries have the power to drain and/or destabilize the economies of others, but that the *wrong* countries have this power.

Rentier state mythology also underlies criticism by Kuwaitis of how the state allocates oil wealth internally. In this context, these myths are part of the competition among rent-seekers, those who want to be the most-favored recipients of whatever trickles down from the rulers' coffers. Rentier state mythology is the subtext of stories about "service candidates," payoffs, and gentlemen's agreements that are the subjects of one of the main genres of the rich oral literature of rumor and gossip that make up the Kuwaiti equivalent of urban legends.[111] Payoff legends explain how the deserving are cheated and the unworthy favored by an overly powerful yet seriously flawed state. Sometimes the state's flaws are moral: payoffs are quids pro quo for sycophancy and political support. Here the recipient is morally defective too. He sells his integrity for status when he agrees to become a candidate for an office he knows he cannot win; he sells his citizenship when he trades a vote for the money to buy a satellite dish or a fancier car; he sells his principles when he abandons the interests of his constituents to hold onto a plum job.

Other stories show the state to be "mentally" defective—it pays off the wrong people. The lazy and shiftless get government jobs and the economy staggers under their dead weight. Wealthy merchants get monopolies and dealerships, and in return they send their profits out of the country. *Badu* who neither care nor work for the community get citizenship and its many welfare benefits at the expense of "real" Kuwaitis. Islamists waiting for an opportunity to turn Kuwait into "another Egypt"—or worse, "another Algeria"—get payoffs of all kinds, despite the fact that they turn on the government if it makes even a small attempt to control them. In these myths, the "welfare recipients" are cleverer than the state because they succeed in maneuvering it into giving them something for which they have no intention of returning anything of equivalent value. These domestic urban legends resemble the foreign-generated rentier state myths. Both sets of stories are fables about injustice with moral points to make,[112] and both omit details and perspectives that might show the actions they criticize in a more favorable light.

Rentier state myths usually are recounted in a spirit of envy. It is not that the teller wishes for a more egalitarian state or a more even-handed system of distribution. Rather, he is arguing that someone else (perhaps himself?) would be a worthier recipient of the state's largesse or a more responsible holder of the ticket to rentiership than the subject of the story. The same perspective is evident in assessments by external critics from Saddam on down who see Kuwaitis in general as less worthy of Kuwait's oil wealth than they themselves would be. Analyzing myths of the rentier state as weapons in the war for differential accumulation encourages scrutiny of the position and likely agenda of the teller as well as a more comprehensive consideration of the position of the object of such stories.

Myths of Diplomatic Prowess

Kuwait is a very small country that is highly vulnerable to external threats. As in the past, the internal security of modern Kuwait depends on the ability of the state to keep foreign demands at an acceptable minimum. Even before the Iraqi invasion, doubts about the regime's ability to fulfill this obligation contributed to social unrest and widespread calls for domestic political change. At that time, Kuwait's political independence as a regional and global actor was frequently interpreted by Kuwaitis as the outcome of intentional and highly successful manipulations by Kuwaiti rulers of power balances among larger states and empires.[113]

In its various dealings with the international system, Kuwait has had two high cards to play: its strategic location and, for more than fifty years, its oil. Both also attract the envy of other states. Kuwait's small population and tiny territory make an independent military defense strategy against most external threats impossible.[114] Its existence as a more or less independent entity requires not just good luck but also diplomatic skill and the intelligence to play its cards so as to achieve consistently a "least unattractive" outcome. Since the Iraqi invasion, Kuwaitis' faith that the rulers can manage this on their own has declined dramatically.

In the late nineteenth century, Kuwait was the first choice to become the terminus of the controversial Berlin-to-Baghdad railway. This enterprise had grown out of a commercial alliance between the Ottoman Empire and Germany, whose leaders wanted to open a land route of access into regions where raw materials and markets were monopolized by maritime powers, chiefly Britain. The railroad also promised new economic opportunities for a state like Kuwait, whose wealth was almost entirely dependent on long-distance trade. However, it also threatened to insinuate Ottoman political control over and perhaps clear the way for Ottoman economic penetration of Kuwait, prospects far less attractive to Kuwaitis and their ruler. The railway also challenged British interests in the Gulf, India, and in Europe. It seemed potentially able to enhance the power and economic reach of Germany and to constitute an overland route culminating in a platform for the penetration of a "British sea" by other European powers, chiefly Russia. An understanding with Kuwait's rulers thus seemed desirable from the British point of view.[115]

The Kuwaiti-British arrangement is conventionally seen as one of several examples of Kuwait's standard strategy of embracing the least unattractive choice, but it also reflects the personal qualities of Mubarak as rent-seeker and political entrepreneur. The January 1899 bond with Britain imposed significant constraints on Kuwait's autonomy. Mubarak agreed for himself and his successors

> not to receive the Agent or Representative of any Power or Government at Koweit . . . without the previous sanction of the British Government . . . and to bind himself not to cede, sell, lease, mortgage, or give for occupation or for any other purpose any portion of his territory to the Government or

Subjects of any other Power without the previous consent of Her Majesty's Government.[116]

These provisions mandate a relinquishment of initiative in foreign investment and foreign policy, requirements that both Mubarak and his successors were able not merely to maneuver around but to flout. Their application to the development of Kuwait's oil was explicitly confirmed in a separate agreement signed in 1913. After a geological survey indicated a strong likelihood of finding oil in Kuwait, Mubarak exchanged letters with the British political representative, Percy Cox, promising that Kuwait would not grant an oil concession "to anyone except a person appointed from the British Government."[117] However, Kuwaiti rulers found themselves able to exercise significant autonomy in spite of the formal constraints imposed by their treaty obligations.

As I noted earlier, a key feature of the agreements between Kuwait and Britain is that they were secret.[118] The British insisted on secrecy because they did not want to provoke any Ottoman challenge to their relationship with Kuwait's rulers that might require them to devote serious resources to their Kuwait policy. The secrecy also protected Mubarak. It enabled him to continue to profess his allegiance to the Ottomans, and thus to collect honors and subventions from them, and also to keep both Constantinople and London off-balance by telling each what it wanted to hear while, as much as he could, doing whatever he liked.[119] Mubarak's status at home depended in part on his reputation as an astute diplomat, a reputation he might lose if it were known that he was a British dependent. Also, the secrecy hid the payments Mubarak received from Britain in return for his various concessions of sovereignty. The British political agent in Kuwait, Maj. Stuart George Knox, worried about how "Mubarak's subjects" would view the British role if they were to learn about it: "It will be an unpleasant moment for us when they arrive at a juster view of the situation and realize that it is our support chiefly that has enabled and will enable Shaikh Mubarak's despotism to flourish."[120]

Mubarak's deals with the British enhanced his power and that of his family, but they protected Kuwait as well. Abu-Hakima reports that Mubarak refused to sign the first agreement without written assurances that Britain would intervene in the event that Kuwait was attacked by a foreign power, a guarantee that Britain had not given to those Arab states with which it had regular protection treaties.[121] One could argue also that the Kuwaiti-British relationship kept Kuwait on the winning side in the conflicts that resulted in the defeat and dismemberment of the Ottoman Empire, and guaranteed its survival through the postwar period of mostly British-mediated state-creation in the region. Yet the British were willing to use Kuwait as a pawn when it suited them, such as in the Anglo-Turkish agreement of 1913 which named Kuwait an Ottoman province and acknowledged Ottoman authority over it, a status that no Kuwaiti ruler ever had conceded.[122] Despite the fact that the treaty was not ratified, it was used by Saddam to justify Iraq's 1990 invasion and annexation of Kuwait as well as earlier assertions by Iraqi rulers of their sovereignty over Kuwait's territory.[123]

This arrangement also elicited British support for an independent Kuwait during the postwar exercises in boundary construction which David Fromkin notes that, even by contemporaries, was seen as a "peace to end all peace."[124] Yet another apparent exception was the 1922 agreement establishing the boundaries separating Saudi Arabia, Kuwait, and Iraq. Despite the infatuation of Sir Percy Cox, then British High Commissioner for Iraq, for Ibn Sa'ud, Kuwait's long relationship with Britain limited the scope of "adjustments" to Kuwait's borders to benefit Saudi Arabia that Cox reasonably could justify.[125] David Finnie argues convincingly that the British protected Kuwait from territorial encroachments by Iraq for more than thirty years,[126] though it is possible that British failure to attend to the demarcation of the boundary between Kuwait and Iraq was a cause of the recurring border conflicts between the two countries in the first place. Finally, as I noted with respect to the exploitation of Kuwait's oil, the relationship between Kuwait and Britain did not foreclose maneuvering by a Kuwaiti ruler that resulted in a partnership between a British and an American company to exploit Kuwait's oil reserves, actions that attenuated the cliency relationship that Mubarak had initiated.[127] On balance, therefore, even though the arrangement had serious flaws it was not without its political benefits to Kuwaitis and their rulers.

British military protection was another benefit for Kuwait even after Mubarak's demise. Despite having had to defend themselves without British assistance from the Ikhwan invasion of 1920, Kuwaitis were protected by British forces on other occasions during the tribal warfare of the 1920s and 1930s.[128] After independence in 1961, Kuwait's first foreign policy crisis was precipitated by Iraq's threats to take it over, eliciting immediate direct military assistance from the British and only afterward from members of the Arab League.[129] Twenty years later, the Iran-Iraq war created a whole new set of threats to Kuwait. The government's ingenious defense against Iranian shelling of Kuwaiti oil tankers was a proposition to operate some of its ships under the flags of other countries, and it persuaded the United States and other major powers, including the Soviet Union and Britain, to intervene to protect its fleet.[130] Resolution was sought not in direct confrontation but in diplomatic efforts to convince powerful states that Kuwait's strategic interests coincided with their own.[131] The apotheosis of this strategy was achieved during the Iraqi occupation, when the Kuwaiti government orchestrated a campaign in coalition countries to persuade their leaders to mount a military offensive to retake Kuwait.[132]

Diplomatic skills achieved Kuwait's ends indirectly, often through the initiation of cliency relationships with extra-regional powers designed to defend the country against local threats to its survival. Oil money allowed the government to pursue state interests directly and to build constituencies out of nations on whose political resources Kuwait could draw. Such a strategy enlarged the range of foreign policy options available to Kuwaiti rulers. Two important components of Kuwait's oil diplomacy are its oil-financed portfolio holdings and direct foreign investment in developed and developing countries, and an aggressive preinvasion foreign aid program that targeted potential allies and neighbors, particularly those that threatened Kuwait.[133] The Iraqi invasion and occupation demonstrated shortcomings in Kuwait's foreign aid policy as a guarantee of its external security. However, Kuwait's direct foreign investment, especially in Europe, created strong mutual interests between the Kuwaiti government and the governments and societies of countries in the UN coalition supporting Kuwait's restoration as an independent state.[134]

Mythology and Politics

The prevalence of contending myths in Kuwaiti political discourse has many causes, among them a continuing disagreement among Kuwaitis about various provisions of their social contract, and a lack of adequate mechanisms for resolving domestic disputes in a way that can be seen as fair by concurrent majorities of multiple social groups. Kuwaitis are split politically across many dimensions. Some divisions draw class, sectarian, and gender lines; others draw cultural lines such as those dividing citizens from subjects, *hadhar* from *badu*, and secularists from religionists. Like citizens everywhere, Kuwaitis also are divided along myriad lines that separate reasonable people who disagree on various issues of policy. As elsewhere, these divisions frequently are crosscutting, limiting conflict by allowing people to find themselves on the same side on one issue when they are on opposite sides on another. In consequence of this reflexive experience, many Kuwaitis have come to see conflict as a function of external circumstances subject to change rather than as the result of a fundamental difference between the essential natures of a set of opponents.

Domestic divisions in Kuwait are greatly aggravated by political manipulation, not only by rulers who pit groups against one another to discourage the formation or persistence of an effective opposition, but also by political entrepreneurs with their own policy and interest agendas. In the next chapter, I trace

the development of some of the domestic political patterns of conflict and reconciliation that have characterized Kuwaiti politics throughout this century.
Political life in Kuwait oscillates between traditional monarchy and oligarchic
democracy. Each political cycle constitutes a set of reflexive processes; as such,
it is shaped by contingently altered grounds which, in turn, shape the next ensemble of institutions, expectations, and practices that compose the contemporary political universe. The repeated recurrence of broadly similar situations
and strategies indicates the inability of Kuwaiti rulers to "go back" to a stable
autocracy just as it reveals the inability of pro-democracy forces to "move forward" to a stable rule of law. How to get off the horns of this dilemma is the
fundamental issue to be resolved in Kuwaiti politics today.

In this chapter, I examine the patterns of struggle between Kuwaiti rulers and merchants beginning with
the rule of Ahmad al-Jabir (r. 1921–1950), a grandson of
Mubarak. As I noted in the previous chapter, Ahmad
had agreed to govern in consultation with a council,
but he never called it into session. After some years, the
merchants took matters into their own hands, electing
two "parliaments" that challenged Ahmad's right to
govern without their consent. Successfully crushing the
parliamentary movement allowed Ahmad to continue
to rule in the style of Mubarak, but his successor, 'Abdullah al-Salim (r. 1950–1965), chose a different path,
accommodating himself not only to some of the demands coming from the traditional merchant class, but
also to those from political classes that did not even
exist prior to the time of his rule. He created these new
classes through extensive programs to redistribute oil
wealth, and empowered them politically when he inaugurated constitutional government in Kuwait. Subsequent Kuwaiti rulers have tried to reverse his actions,
preferring the style of rule followed by Ahmad al-Jabir.
Thus, despite the adoption of a democratic constitution, Kuwaiti politics continued to operate in the shadow of autocracy throughout most of the period covered in this chapter.

Kuwaiti Political Space

Kuwait's constitution and parliament define the parameters of the formal public space of politics in Kuwait. Other public spaces that host limited political
activities include the marketplace, voluntary associations, the mosque, and kin-based associations such as

the *diwaniyya*, the traditional men's meeting usually held in individual homes. These informal spaces for political action are prepolitical spaces of appearance, but they are far from ideal because they limit the representation of both individuals and points of view. Even so, such spaces are crucial to political participation in Kuwait because, despite the superior capacity and transparency of public political spaces and their nominal protection by constitutional guarantees, such spaces in Kuwait have proven unexpectedly vulnerable to closure.

The Kuwaiti regime's interest in suppressing political activity intensifies when opposition rises. Twice in recent Kuwaiti history, in 1976 and 1986, challenges to the regime were perceived as so threatening that public political spaces were shut down completely. This action took the form of suspensions of constitutionally guaranteed civil liberties and the dismissal of the parliament. Although the Kuwaiti constitution does permit the amir to dismiss the parliament for cause, it also requires elections for a new parliament to be held within two months of any such suspension (article 107). This did not occur in either case.

The closure of parliament and the suspension of civil liberties such as press freedom and the right to hold public meetings push politics into protected spaces. As antigovernment pressure coming from these spaces builds up, the government encroaches there as well. However, the legitimacy of government intervention in protected spaces is minimal. Even the government's capacity to violate the boundaries of protected spaces in pursuit of its critics is tenuous, vulnerable as it is to a broadly based withdrawal of support from the regime. During both periods of constitutional suspension, the Kuwaiti regime continued by a variety of means to influence politics on its own behalf. However, it eventually found that its long-term survival required the restoration of constitutional rights and parliamentary rule. At the same time, the tacit threat of suspension exercises parallel restraints on the political opposition, even when constitutional guarantees are formally in effect. This tension between government and opposition helps to maintain a balance of power between an autocratic executive and a hypercritical legislature, but the long-term survival of constitutional government in Kuwait remains highly dependent on the persistence of protected spaces from which people can conduct politics by other means when necessary.

The line between state and society in Kuwait remains blurred despite more than a half century of state-building that institutionalized the separation of the ruling family from the rest of society. Separation enlarged the power of the ruling family to provide political leadership and also to control citizens' access to social and economic status and resources.[1] The historic pattern of relations among Kuwaiti notables that had held the Sabah to a status of primus inter pares for more than 150 years was vastly altered by the institution of the special relationship with Britain in 1899. Change accelerated after the advent of oil revenues because of the direct power oil income conferred on the ruling family, allowing it to reduce its economic and strategic dependence on the local population. As a result, citizens' threats to exit became virtually meaningless, while their claims to a voice in state decisions were profoundly weakened even though they were never successfully eliminated.

Oil income created and deepened already-existing channels through which the ruling family penetrates civil society. Oil wealth allows Kuwaiti rulers to manipulate elections by buying candidates and votes, and constrains the actions of voluntary associations by requiring them to obtain licenses and then funding their activities. It also enables ruling family members and their retainers to compete in the marketplace from a position of advantage. But civil society in Kuwait is so interwoven with the state that penetration works both ways. Some state employees elevate what they see as constitutional and functional responsibilities *to Kuwait* above loyalty to the ruling family, thereby bringing political opposition directly into the state. An official I interviewed in the fall of 1992 ended his discussion of the accomplishments of his agency by remarking that these achievements worked against the interests of "the government." Then he paused. "I say that even though some people might say that I am part of the government."

This attitude reflects more than a suspicion that the interests of the government and the interests of the nation might diverge. It demonstrates a readiness to behave politically under a wide variety of circumstances, a readiness that has been conditioned by repeated state suppression of public political activity. During such periods, political activity increases in spaces that enjoy a significant degree of normative, legal, and institutional protection from state intervention. This notion of "protected spaces" is an expansion of the ancient Greek distinction between the "private space" of the household and the "public space" of politics and markets.[2] According to this concept, although a man's[3] public actions are subject to external review and sanctions by peers and superiors, what he does in private is his own business.

Modern definitions of privacy differ substantially from this ancient distinction between public and private,[4] but the residence of the family, physically as well as metaphorically, is protected by the public-private dichotomy as it is delineated in Kuwait. The English maxim, "A man's home is his castle," describes the vernacular understanding of Kuwait's legal and constitutional provisions that explicitly protect the home from arbitrary intrusion. By definition, the home is the epitome of private space. Some public spaces also enjoy relative protection. Like the home, these are "protected spaces," privileged refuges from the full force of state power. The interplay between the state and social actors mobilized in protected spaces defines the limits of legitimate state intervention in society.

In Kuwait there are two social spaces that are substantially protected, by tradition and law, from state intrusion. As I have noted, the first is the home and, by extension, the family and kin-based institutions and associations such as the tribe, the family business, and the diwaniyya. The home is protected explicitly under articles 38 and 44 of the 1962 constitution and is the only secular space that enjoys such a high degree of formal protection. Ironically—but logically— this quality enhances its attraction to political organizers whenever public meetings are restricted or banned. Even during the worst of these times, such as the period of the 1989–90 pro-democracy movement, the privacy of the Kuwaiti home was rarely violated. When it was, the strength of citizen outrage forced the regime to moderate its behavior.

The mosque[5] is the other social space in Kuwait that enjoys extensive protection from state intrusion. The mosque occupies public space and is one of the few legal social structures anywhere in the Middle East available for mass political mobilization. The mosque's protection comes from a higher authority than the constitution; the space that it occupies is not only public but also sacred. This confers legitimate authority on religious leaders and groups independent of the authority of the state. During the Iraqi occupation of Kuwait, the authority of the mosque was strong enough to protect members of the Kuwaiti Resistance from molestation by Iraqi troops, and the secular as well as the religious relied on it to shield their political activities.[6]

Islamic principles often are interpreted as insisting that the state and the religious community are one and the same. However, in practice, Muslim societies accept a distinction between politics and religion similar to the distinction between church and state in Christian societies and analogous to the separation between politics and markets in capitalist societies.[7] Thus, these political, religious, and/or economic institutions are interdependent rather than either independent or identical, and their relations are marked both by cooperation and by interinstitutional struggles for power.

The 1938 Paradigm

The 1962 constitution was not the first document of its kind in Kuwait. Its antecedent was a charter written in 1938 by a small group of merchants who had more-or-less elected themselves to be the first Kuwaiti parliament. These merchants seized the initiative against the then-ruler, Ahmad al-Jabir, whose pro-

found self-centeredness at the height of the Great Depression threatened to di-
vert the entire income from Kuwait's newly discovered oil to his personal use.[8]
The merchants cited their grievances against the ruler to establish claims to a
share in the wealth generated by Kuwait's natural resources and to regain some
of the political authority lost after British intervention had altered the balance
of power between state and society in Kuwait.

By the late 1930s, Kuwaiti merchants and other dissatisfied citizens had accumulated a long list of political and economic grievances against the ruler.
They criticized his lack of attention to affairs of state and the administration of
justice; his rigging of local elections; his religious regulations that interfered
with the normal conduct of business; and his sequestration of state income,
which resulted in a lack of money for education, health care, and exploration
for domestic sources of water.[9] Popular discontent was fanned by a propaganda campaign masterminded by Iraq's King Ghazi, who hoped to annex Kuwait
to Iraq.[10] It "crystallized in . . . the flogging, etcetera, of one [Muhammad] al
Barrak, guilty of anonymous wall writings, ante-autocratic (*sic*) propaganda
and intrigues, by the Sheikh's town lieutenant."[11]

Muhammad al-Barrak was a taxi driver whose business had been hurt by
new regulations forbidding women to go outside the town walls after sun-
down. His leadership of a taxi strike against the regulations had resulted in a
public beating followed by imprisonment in 1937.[12] This probably explains his
antigovernment activities the following year. Popular reaction to the 1938 flogging was so intense that the British political agent, Capt. Gerald de Gaury, worried about its effects on "the smoothness of the relations of the Kuwait Oil
Company with the Kuwait Ruler." De Gaury also recommended that the British
appoint a minister of finance to deal with the fiscal issues.[13]

Before the British government could decide what to do, Kuwaitis took the
initiative themselves. A coalition of citizens that included merchants, proto-
Arab nationalist proponents of a political union with Iraq, and the amir's
cousin, 'Abdullah al-Salim, made formal proposals for reform organized
around the institution of a legislative council.[14] Their position was backed by
de Gaury, who believed that Ahmad al-Jabir's abuses of power had reached a
height justifying British support of curbs on the ruler.[15] De Gaury formally
protested the treatment of Muhammad al-Barrak to the ruler and at the same
time suggested that "any new democratic movement should be drawn by him
into useful channels," an idea de Gaury regarded as "beyond [Ahmad al-
Jabir's] comprehension."[16]

But Ahmad al-Jabir did understand and agreed to accept a legislative council that had already been elected by "140 persons consisting of the entire accepted heads of important families, communities, Sects, Localities (Firjis), etc.

in Kuwait, without consideration to their being poor or rich, Sunnis or Shi'as, Arabs or Persians."[17] The council convened that summer and wrote Kuwait's first constitution. It passed legislation abolishing monopolies; forbidding the ruling family to command forced labor or goods; and canceling taxes such as export duties, some import duties, and the pearl fishing tax. It also dismissed several corrupt public officials.[18] The council took positive steps as well, instituting a regular police force, trade and public health regulations, and a public works program.[19] As long as the council concentrated on domestic affairs, the British supported it. But when it intervened in the army and foreign policy, both the British and the ruler balked, the British because the council was transgressing on territory their several treaties with Kuwait had allocated to them, and the ruler because the council also had requested that he turn over his December check from the oil company.[20]

> When [Ahmad al-Jabir] first requested British intervention to deal with "troubles in the town" in August 1938, the British political agent responded evenhandedly, requesting the council to moderate its demands and pressing the amir to sit with the council instead of plotting against it. But later, as the council expanded its purview to include the army, British support for it cooled. When Ahmad al-Jabir dissolved the council in December, the British supported him.[21]

After he had dissolved the first council, Ahmad al-Jabir agreed to the election of a new one. This election was monitored by three groups. One represented the council and one represented the ruler, and each of these ran candidates. A third group served as official arbitrators. The second council pleased Ahmad al-Jabir no more than its predecessor. The two councils had many members in common even though the second was larger, had been elected by nearly three times the number of persons (four hundred), and "thus must be considered really representative of Kuwait."[22] The second council's chief sin was its opposition to the ruler's proposed new constitution, a charter that changed the council from a legislative to a consultative body and restricted its power to appoint officials and regulate the ruler's finances.[23] The council refused to accept Ahmad al-Jabir's constitution. On March 7, 1939, the ruler dissolved the council and immediately set to work to appoint—not elect—a new one.[24] He also asked the outgoing council to hand over its papers, including its handwritten copy of the first constitution. The council replied that it had sent the papers away for safekeeping and asked for time to retrieve them. Meanwhile, members continued in session as a sort of rump body that soon became a magnet for persisting Iraqi propaganda. On March 9 a Kuwaiti resident of

Basra, Ahmad bin Munais, addressed the rump council in its temporary chamber. He charged that the Sabah were unfit to rule Kuwait and advised council members to resist them until the Iraqi army should arrive. The council sent word to the ruler that night that it would turn over its papers the following evening, but the police came the next morning anyway, to arrest Ahmad bin Munais. On the way to the jail they were met by a small group of Kuwaitis protesting the arrest. During the resulting altercation, three Kuwaitis were shot. Yusuf al-Marzook was wounded; a police official who sided with the council, Muhammad al-Qatami, was killed after he fired at another policeman; and a shopkeeper was hit in the crossfire. Ahmad bin Munais was taken on to the jail where he was tried and convicted in a matter of minutes, shot, and then hanged in the main square until evening. Ahmad al-Jabir was himself a witness to some of these proceedings. He was reported as having been "slightly injured" in the fracas outside the jail, though not sufficiently to prevent him from doing a war dance in the main square at the end of the day to celebrate his conviction that "any hope of an elected council peacefully aiding him in the administration, [was] gone for a long time, if not for good."[25]

The tumultuous events of those few days in March 1939 marked the effective end of parliamentary democracy in Kuwait for a generation. Many council members and their supporters fled the country; those unwise enough to remain were arrested and imprisoned until 1944, when an amnesty freed them and also permitted the exiles to return home. Meanwhile, put off by the violence, Kuwaitis showed little enthusiasm for the ruler's opponents once the excitement had died down. Ahmad al-Jabir was further assisted in his efforts to restore the political status quo ante by the convenient death of King Ghazi on April 4. The ruler dealt with demands that he govern with the assistance of a council by choosing as his advisers a group of men in which members of his family were heavily represented. He had begun to incorporate family members into the government the previous year at the urging of de Gaury.[26]

Alongside this apparent restoration of the traditional order, a new Kuwaiti myth took root. It recast Kuwait's national history in terms not only of ruler-merchant equality but also in terms of a "tradition" of democratic opposition.[27] When the British departed in 1961 and a democratic constitution was written and then approved by the amir in 1962, Kuwaitis embraced democratic ideology and practices as homegrown elements from their national past rather than rejecting them as alien grafts from the imperial West. This myth has endured in spite of vigorous propaganda campaigns by religious and secular leaders in Kuwait and throughout the Middle East that insist on the foreignness of democracy and its unsuitability to local traditions and values.[28]

The events of the "year of the parliament" had other effects on Kuwaiti political institutions, ideologies, and practices. The ruling family became embedded in government as members of an elite state class with a large stake in the preservation of the regime and the position of the family as the supplier of its rulers.[29] At the same time, the British role in the crisis alienated many Kuwaitis, especially the merchants, from Britain and the West. The crisis thereby strengthened an already evident and distinctive Kuwaiti nationalism, as well as a larger Arab nationalism that linked domestic politics to events and movements taking place elsewhere in the region.[30]

Recursive Patterns

The style of the two elections in the year of the parliament confirmed already-prominent tribalist patterns in Kuwaiti politics.[31] For example, the ad hoc committee nominated as electors persons whose status was conferred by their positions as heads of families, sects, and associations. Unfortunately, they then failed to elect members from each of these groups to serve as direct representatives in the council, denying the losers both political status and assurances of security. The Shi'a were the most prominent among the groups omitted from direct representation. Terrified at the possible implications of their exclusion, thousands applied for British nationality.[32] Excluded groups also sought the ruler's protection. Shi'a, along with members of the tribes that functioned as military retainers of the ruling family, were among the ruler's main allies in the suppression of the assembly. Their rallying around the ruler no doubt confirmed the utility of balance-of-power politics in the domestic as well as the international arena.

Some of the patterns laid down during this crisis were repeated in subsequent clashes between Kuwaiti amirs and parliaments. Confrontations between the amir and the National Assembly in 1976 and 1986 resulted in the dissolution of the parliament and suspension of the constitution for long periods. During these suspensions the amir tried to change the electoral base of the parliament and otherwise limit its range of powers before calling it back. In 1981 he redistricted the country, changing the number of constituencies from ten to twenty-five and reducing the number representing each district from five to two. This diminished the electoral chances of the liberal/left opposition which, despite its minority status, had dominated the 1963 and 1967 assemblies. It also reduced the size of other voting blocs such as the Shi'a and the larger tribes, though not of the tribes per se.[33] In 1990, in what was advertised as an interim arrangement, the ruler persuaded a majority of Kuwaiti voters to accept a consultative council in place of a body with legislative powers.[34] The Iraqi invasion saved the contemporary generation of Kuwaitis from having either to accept the end of representative government as their grandfathers had in 1939 or, alternatively, to take to the streets to fight for it. But the same issues returned after liberation, even though the invasion and occupation had interrupted the post-1938 pattern.

The strategies of legislative assemblies and councils also carried over into the constitutional period. The decision of the second council to continue meeting, even after its official dissolution, was repeated by a large remnant from the 1985 National Assembly.[35] The membership of this rump parliament grew over time from twenty-six to thirty-two legislators and went on to organize a mass movement after repeated attempts to petition the amir to restore the parliament and the constitution were rebuffed (see below).[36] The concern of the 1938 council to take control of state finances also was mirrored by subsequent parliaments. Kuwaiti parliaments hastened the process of oil nationalization in the 1970s over the government's objections. They scrutinized and criticized government expenditures and investigated corruption and malfeasance so vigorously that their investigations are widely believed to have precipitated the 1976 and 1986 suspensions. In the 1990s, the 1992 and 1996 parliaments mounted investigations culminating in the legislation of oversight controls on government investment policies and defense expenditures. Both parliaments faced recurrent threats of dissolution. In May 1999 the 1996 National Assembly was dismissed under circumstances similar to those preceding previous parliamentary closures—with one notable exception. This time, the dismissal announcement was accompanied by a call for new elections within two months. This conforms to constitutional requirements for a legal dissolution (article 107). Despite this difference, however, the substantial persistence of these patterns of behavior reflects the persistence of divisions over the same key issues throughout the modern history of Kuwait. It also reflects a divergence in assumptions about the relative positions of citizens and governments and poorly developed repertoires of strategies to alter them. The consequence is the persistence of a family romance whose grip on political actors constrains their choices more than they might realize.

Democratization and Political Crisis

The pro-democracy movement of 1989–90 evoked a large number of contemporary comparisons to the democratization crisis of 1938–39. The driving forces behind the pro-democracy movement were similar to those that had produced the 1938 parliament. Both movements were rooted in widespread popular convictions that the government was corrupt, inept, and unresponsive to domestic needs, and both were led by elites who were personally threatened by government encroachments on their political autonomy, status, and liberty.

Beginning in July 1989, a broadly based popular movement seeking to liberalize the Kuwaiti regime organized in an attempt to force the amir to reinstate the constitution, much of which had been suspended in July 1986. Pro-democracy proponents, many from the political opposition, were invigorated by news of the progress of democratization in Eastern Europe.[37] The immediate goals of the movement, led by members of the 1985 parliament,[38] included restoration of the suspended portions of the constitution and elections to a reinstated National Assembly.[39] The regime defended its 1986 actions as responses to the "abuse of democratic life, exploiting the constitution for personal gains, spreading dissention and obstructing cooperation between the legislative and executive powers."[40] The opposition saw the amir's reasons differently. Parliamentary investigations into allegations of corruption and malfeasance in the Central Bank and four important ministries, including the Ministry of Oil and the Ministry of Finance, were widely credited with having triggered the suspensions.[41]

Allegations of government corruption and ineptitude persisted into 1990 and they arose from several sources. One was the continuing domestic economic crisis that had originated with the collapse of Kuwait's illegal stock market, the Suq al-Manakh, in September 1982. The crash swallowed financial assets held by individuals and firms at every level of Kuwaiti society, triggering a sharp contraction of the local economy.[42] Some of the biggest speculators in the Manakh transferred large sums of money out of the country to avoid its seizure for debt repayment.[43] Meanwhile, the prices of real estate and other assets fell as smaller investors liquidated to settle their debts. All but one commercial bank went into the equivalent of government receivership, and a number of local firms holding shares of the speculative Gulf company stocks traded on the Manakh went bankrupt. The government intervened by buying up depressed shares to support stock prices. In 1986 recession moved the government to purchase thirty-three of the "closed" companies, but both stock and bond markets remained depressed and the unresolved remainder of the Manakh debt continued to hang over the economy.[44] The largest debts, some rumored to be owed by members of the ruling family, including Crown Prince Sa'd al-'Abdullah, remained unresolved in March 1990 when the government agreed to adopt a new debt resolution plan proposed by the Kuwait Chamber of Commerce.

A second element feeding popular dissatisfaction centered on the state's controversial oil investments. Particularly aggravating to critics of the government was the 1981 purchase of Santa Fe International by Kuwait's national oil company.[45] The Santa Fe purchase was castigated as more than a money-loser. In 1983 the then-U.S. secretary of the interior, James Watt, cited Santa Fe's Kuwaiti ownership as his reason for curtailing the company's activities on land it had leased from the U.S. government. Although Kuwait sued and won its case, Kuwaitis were appalled at the foolhardiness of a government that would risk retaliation by the United States over an investment most of them thought was unwise to begin with. Santa Fe's poor economic performance following its purchase by Kuwait increased condemnation of the investment, especially by prominent private economists like Jasim al-Sa'doun, the head of the Al-Shall Economic Group. It also fueled parliamentary criticism of the oil minister, Shaikh 'Ali al-Khalifa. A member of the ruling family and protégé of the amir, Shaikh 'Ali's activities were under investigation when the National Assembly was closed in 1986.

A third factor contributing to perceptions of government corruption and incompetence was the persistent economic recession. The Kuwaiti economy began to stagnate in the backwash from the crash of the Suq al-Manakh, but the slowdown was aggravated by other local factors[46] such as the Iran-Iraq war, which disrupted oil exports and also diverted Kuwaiti reexport trade to the Saudi ports of Dammam and Jubail. But the most critical contributor to Kuwait's economic difficulties in 1990 was the sharp drop in world oil prices which had begun in the fall of 1985.[47] The consequent drop in government income led to reductions in non-oil-related government expenditures, especially for construction projects, further aggravating the domestic recession.[48] The persistence of the recession, along with its continual deepening, added greatly to the sense of insecurity inside Kuwait. It also amplified what Kuwaiti political scientist Abdul-Reda al-Assiri calls Kuwaitis' "siege mentality."[49]

Popular uneasiness mounted following the 1986 suspensions. In a manner similar to the continuation of meetings by the 1938 parliament, twenty-six members of the 1985 parliament, led by assembly speaker Ahmad al-Sa'doun, continued to meet regularly, often in the speaker's home. In July 1989 this group (which by then numbered thirty-two) broadened its base by recruiting thirteen nonparliamentarians who were selected to represent various social groups in Kuwait, including women, who are not allowed to vote or run for office under the state's electoral laws. The Forty-five petitioned the amir to restore the constitution and parliament. This petition was signed not only by the Twenty-six, the only ones to sign two similarly worded petitions submitted earlier, but also by thousands of other Kuwaiti citizens, most of them voters. Like its two predecessors, this petition too was rejected. The representatives taking it to the Amiri Diwan (the amir's executive office) also were refused an audience with the amir. Unsure of their next move, the Forty-five began a series of regular weekly meetings at preselected diwaniyyas. There they reported on events and sought the advice and assistance of their fellow citizens.[50]

Following the rule of thumb that politicians should go where the voters are, National Assembly candidates had been campaigning at diwaniyyas since the Kuwaiti constitution was adopted and the first elections under its aegis were held in 1963.[51] During the two constitutional suspensions, diwaniyyas became the primary sites for political activity because public political meetings were banned and censorship of the usually lively and informative Kuwaiti press made it impossible to carry on a critical dialogue about government actions in the media. This history made the earmarking of particular diwaniyya meetings for mass mobilization the next logical step. These special diwaniyyas were held on successive Monday nights, each time in a different location and nearly all at the homes of opposition leaders. The first was held on December 4, 1989, at the home of Jasim al-Qatami. Jasim is a brother of the policeman who was killed in the confrontation with the 1938 parliament and also was a member of the Group of Twenty-six. According to Ahmad al-Sa'doun, the primary purpose of the first Monday diwaniyya was to tell those attending "what was going on."

The government reacted to this new tactic in an inconsistent and hysterical fashion, sending riot police and police dogs to block access to the second Monday diwaniyya, held on December 11 at the home of Mishairy al-'Anjari. The interruption of a gathering in a private home was offensive to most Kuwaitis, and the use of dogs, animals that are ritually unclean in Islam, was particularly offensive. Many Kuwaitis sent telegrams to the amir to protest the police action. Seven members of the Group of Forty-five, including Ahmad al-Sa'doun, were invited to meet with the foreign minister, Shaikh Salim al-Sabah. According to the assembly speaker, Shaikh Salim "apologized for closing the diwaniyya and promised that it would not happen in the future." On the following Monday, the group's meeting at the Fatima Mosque in 'Abdullah al-Salim neighborhood attracted no police. Two weeks later (there was no special diwaniyya on Christmas day, which fell on the Monday of the intervening week), at Mohammad al-Marshad's diwaniyya in Khaldiya, there also was no sign of police.

On January 8, the Monday diwaniyya was held outside of Kuwait City, in Jahra.' The host was Ahmad al-Shriyan, a member of the Group of Twenty-six. Kuwaitis arriving for this meeting found their host sealed in his diwaniyya and troops surrounding the house. The troops refused to let anyone pass without showing their civil identification cards. As groups of guests coalesced around the sealed area, the troops attempted to dislodge them. "So we had a little scrimmage there," one guest told me. A number of persons were beaten, including an elderly former member of parliament, Mohammad Rushaid, and Mohammad al-Qadiri, a former ambassador. Several guests were arrested and detained overnight. Opposition leaders were permitted to use police loudspeakers to ask the crowd to disperse. They did so and also let everyone present know that there would be another diwaniyya the following week.

Two days after the disastrous encounter in Jahra', police arrested Ahmad al-Shriyan, charging him with attempting to hold an illegal gathering. They permitted him to make one telephone call, and he did, to Ahmad al-Sa'doun, who was presiding over a meeting of the Group of Forty-five that day. Ahmad al-Shriyan was taken to Kuwait City, another lucky break for the opposition because this was a more convenient as well as a more public location for demonstrations. Soon the jail was surrounded by protesters and, in a short time, the commotion ended in the release of Ahmad al-Shriyan. According to a friend, he was accompanied home by a "motorcade. We walked from the checkpoint to his house and then we had the speeches. So our diwaniyya was [just] delayed for two days."

Ahmad al-Sa'doun and the Group of Forty-five sent another strongly worded telegram to the amir to protest the police action in Jahra.' This time there was no change in policy. At the January 15 diwaniyya, hosted by Faisal al-Sana', the police used barbed wire for the first time, completely wrapping Faisal's house. As Ahmad al-Sa'doun recalls, "The diwaniyya was completely isolated. No one could reach it. Faisal al-Sana' was almost under house arrest. We could see him, but he could not come out and join us."

On January 22, 1990, the series of special diwaniyyas ended in what for Kuwait at that time was a shocking display of force. Two days before this meeting, the amir had made a televised speech calling for a dialogue with the opposition. Ahmad al-Sa'doun insists that he had responded in the same spirit of conciliation, sending a press release to the newspapers about the January 22 meeting scheduled for Farwaniya. He said that the press release announced that the meeting would not include speeches by the opposition, but that the organizers planned to present information about the amir's address and report how the Group of Forty-five had responded to it. However, government censors refused to allow the newspapers to publish the press release. When crowds of citizens and opposition leaders came to Farwaniya on the evening of January 22, they faced regular police, the Kuwait National Guard, riot police, and tanks shooting chemical foam. "For the first time, [the foam] was used. Stun grenades were also used, and tear gas. Even when the people went into the mosque, they put foam and tear gas inside the mosque." Six Kuwaitis were detained incommunicado for three days, and held an additional four days after that. The correspondents for Reuters and *Le Monde* also were detained by the police, and the Reuters correspondent was asked to leave the country following his release.

The level of violence, the desecration of a mosque, and the targeting of notables and members of the foreign press led the Forty-five to suspend the special Monday diwaniyyas. Widespread disquiet and tension continued, prompting Crown Prince Saʿd al-ʿAbdullah to hold a series of meetings with citizens' groups and members of the opposition in February and March 1990. During Ramadan, which began in mid-March, pro-democracy leaders made the rounds at various diwaniyyas to mobilize supporters. The government did not send police to interdict or interrupt these gatherings during Ramadan. Instead, government representatives also went to diwaniyyas to speak against the opposition, accusing it of being provocative and irresponsible. The opposition responded by criticizing the government, defending its strategy of mobilizing large numbers of citizens to make public demands on the amir as the only way to reinstate the constitution and the parliament. As in 1939, many Kuwaitis were reluctant to push the regime too far for fear of what might happen next. Yet even though the parliament had plenty of critics, its political legitimacy remained high, increasing pressure on the amir to act. As Ramadan drew to a close, the whole country waited for an announcement from the amir. Virtually everyone expected that he would either denounce the opposition, signaling renewed confrontation, or—what most hoped for—that he would call for new parliamentary elections and agree to the full restoration of constitutional freedoms and institutions.

On the first day of the ʿEid holiday following Ramadan, the amir made a brilliant speech. In it, he called for the election of a National Council, a Majlis al-Watani. The Majlis al-Watani was to be composed of fifty elected representatives, to which the amir would add an additional twenty-five appointed members. The speech and the subsequent Amiri decree outlining the purpose of the council and its manner of election noted that it was "designed for a transitional period during which it will have a special assignment of evaluating the country's previous parliamentary experience and proposing 'controls' for the future parliamentary process so as to avert 'a third crisis.' "[52] The council was portrayed as an interim body whose term would end with the election of a new parliament, though no prospective date for such an election was mentioned. While it sat, the Majlis al-Watani would not amend the constitution, but it would define relations between the parliament and the government. The cleverness of the proposal lay in its form and even more in its unexpectedness. Although the Majlis al-Watani was to have only advisory powers, the trappings of election and the promise of a forum in which elected representatives could air their grievances swayed many moderates to support the amir.

This unanticipated "third" alternative, which resembled Ahmad al-Jabir's proposal for a consultative council to replace the 1939 parliament, left the regime's opponents all but speechless. After some initial fumbling, most opposition leaders united against the Majlis al-Watani, root and branch. They made the rounds of diwaniyyas yet again, this time urging their fellow citizens neither to run for the Majlis al-Watani nor to vote in the June election. The police came back too, but with a different strategy this time. Rather than spraying homes with tear gas or wrapping them in barbed wire, the police simply plucked from them the primary sources of irritation to the regime. Several of the opposition's most prominent members, among them Arab nationalists Ahmad al-Khatib, 'Abdullah Nibari, Jasim al-Qatami, and Ahmad al-Rub'i, were arrested and detained, one by one from diwaniyyas where they were speaking. The arrests and detentions turned elite opinion against the amir. On May 20, 'Abd al-'Aziz al-Saqr, president of the Kuwait Chamber of Commerce, presented the amir with a declaration opposing the Majlis al-Watani that had been signed by two hundred merchants, professionals, and former members of parliament.

The amir retreated, but only a little. The charges were dropped against those arrested, and all were released within a few weeks.[53] However, the local press remained under strict censorship. Meanwhile, the government made strong efforts to recruit candidates to run for the Majlis al-Watani, and the elections were held, as scheduled, on June 10. Official turnout figures indicate that 62 percent of the eligible voters participated in the election,[54] far more than opposition leaders had predicted. Several individuals working for government agencies told me that they and their peers had been pressured heavily to vote. There is no reason to think that these reports are not true, but the relatively high turnout level also leads one to believe that many ordinary Kuwaitis continued to support the regime.

However, the opposition was successful in deterring all but a few politically prominent Kuwaitis from running for seats in the Majlis al-Watani. In the words of Ahmad al-Rub'i, candidate slates were dominated by "taxi drivers," that is, nonelite Kuwaitis from tribal backgrounds. Most of the winners, among both the few former parliamentarians and the many political newcomers, were "service candidates," men content to act as intermediaries between their constituents and the regime. In the brief time between its election and the Iraqi invasion on August 2, and during the period following liberation in 1991 when it reconvened, the Majlis al-Watani functioned primarily as a body dedicated to providing tangible benefits to voters and their families.

Democratization on the Eve of Invasion

The capacity of the Majlis al-Watani to defuse pressures for democratization in Kuwait remained untried. Tens of thousands of Kuwaitis left the country shortly after the June 1990 election to spend the hottest months of the summer abroad. Many were disgusted at the turn of events, but few had ideas about how to regain the initiative that had characterized the pro-democracy movement prior to the amir's shrewd riposte. Meanwhile, the government continued efforts to alleviate the economic problems fueling much of the discontent that the Forty-five had mobilized so skillfully. Chief among these was a policy it had pursued since mid-1989, when the pro-democracy movement leadership had reached beyond its base in the dismissed 1985 parliament to recruit active participants among various groups in the Kuwaiti population. This was to increase state income by selling additional crude.

The continuation of oil production above Kuwait's OPEC quota was neither a unique nor a novel tactic. It was something that virtually every other OPEC member with excess oil production capacity also was doing, and for much the same reason: to compensate for the fall in per-barrel revenues resulting from depressed oil prices. In fact, several were producing far more excess oil than Kuwait. The United Arab Emirates, for example, was producing up to a million barrels per day (bpd) over quota. In comparison, Kuwaiti overproduction reportedly averaged only a quarter of a million bpd.[55] At whatever level, the flaws in adopting overproduction as a strategy are obvious. Persistently applied, overproduction depresses prices even further. More serious for the future of Kuwait, however, was that its rate of oil production had triggered the rage of Saddam Hussein, the Iraqi president whose money problems were even more serious than those of the Kuwaiti amir.[56]

The relationship between domestic pressure on the regime and a desire to produce class-abatement—in this case, an abatement of the antagonism of Kuwaitis generally against the state class—is likely to have contributed to the government's decision to assume the risks of overproduction. The pro-democracy movement may have had another, more direct, impact on Saddam's decision to invade Kuwait. To the leader of a country where political opposition is forbidden,[57] evidence that citizens can oppose their government openly and survive is likely to be interpreted as a sign of serious weakness in the regime. Also, the prominence of Arab nationalists among the leadership of the Kuwaiti opposition may have convinced Saddam that his invasion not only would be welcomed but also would find a pool of potential quislings ready to lead the postinvasion government as his surrogates.

Instead, the Iraqi invasion demonstrated both the loyalty of Kuwaitis to their leaders and the loyalty of the leaders to the population, or at least to their own positions within Kuwaiti society as it had existed prior to the invasion. At the same time, the invasion deepened most Kuwaitis' democratic values and taught them new techniques for expressing these values in their daily lives. During the occupation, Kuwaitis inside Kuwait mobilized in protected spaces to maintain their society as best they could, aided by resources from outside smuggled to them by their fellow citizens. Kuwaitis inside and outside turned the occupation itself into a protected political space, one from which they continued, publicly and privately, to press their leaders for the restoration of the constitution after liberation. Thus, the Kuwaiti pro-democracy movement continued to work effectively during the occupation of the country by a foreign power, despite the upsurge in extranational influences on the domestic politics of Kuwait that the occupation and its rollback introduced.

chapter 5

Iraqi Occupation and
Kuwaiti Democracy

The takeover of a country by a foreign power is hardly recommended as a recipe for expanding freedom
and human rights. Yet one outcome of the Iraqi invasion and occupation of Kuwait was to increase the political capital of Kuwaiti opponents of domestic autocracy. The invasion also enlarged the arena where
the struggle for democratic reform in Kuwait was
fought. Individuals and groups formerly on the side-
lines mobilized to support reform domestically, while
foreign constituencies favoring liberalization also expanded. These changes helped to shift the balance between the regime and its opponents in favor of pro-
democracy elements.

In this chapter, I examine three primary reasons
why the Iraqi invasion effected a shift in the balance of
power between pro- and antidemocratization forces in
Kuwait. First, the invasion destroyed the myth of
diplomatic prowess that had been an important element in the regime's claim to popular support: a broad
spectrum of Kuwaitis agreed that the invasion marked
a failure of the system itself, not simply of the persons
occupying positions of responsibility at the time. It
also demonstrated the risks of censorship and of rely-
ing on a closed group to make life-and-death decisions
for the nation. Both pointed up the practical utility of
democratic rights and procedures.

A second element in this shift centers on the politics
of Kuwaiti exiles. During the occupation, the unity of
Kuwaitis outside the country was an important ingre-
dient in the campaign to mobilize support for the liberation of Kuwait by coalition forces. The regime's opponents used this leverage to pry concessions from the
ruling family regarding how Kuwait would be governed
after liberation. Although the government abused the

spirit and the letter of many of its promises, it was forced to keep the main one: following liberation, elections would be held for a new parliament. These elections took place in October 1992 and erased most of the amir's political gains from his 1990 Majlis al-Watani coup.

Third, the invasion altered the psychology of those Kuwaitis who embraced the experience of the occupation, at home or in exile, rather than hiding from, denying, or escaping it. These persons are a minority among Kuwaitis; postliberation Kuwait also is home to many people who seem virtually unchanged by their experiences, and to some whom the invasion and occupation left with psychological problems—especially terrified children and victims of Iraqi torture and abuse. Even so, the invasion produced a broad spectrum of Kuwaitis who are more confident and have clearer visions of what democracy means in daily life than they did before August 1990. These persons are a force for progressive reform and a reservoir of practical experience on how to achieve it. As long as they live and remain in Kuwait, they constitute as well a reservoir of information that contradicts the regime's revisionist campaigns about the invasion, and they embody some of its most valuable lessons about freedom and agency.

Regime Failure

Virtually every observer of the events of July and August 1990 was surprised by the Iraqi takeover of Kuwait.[1] From the perspective of most Kuwaitis, the actions of their government were primarily responsible, both for the invasion itself and for the complete unreadiness of the population and most of its putative defenders to protect themselves against it. Such criticism of the Kuwaiti government centers on two charges. The first is provocation—did Kuwait's oil production policy and then its diplomatic errors goad Iraq into invading? The second is the control of information and the means of defense—if Kuwaitis, including those in military and police forces, had realized the danger they were in, would they have been better able to protect themselves? And were Kuwait's defenses properly organized and supplied to do the job they were expected to do?

Even before the Iraqi invasion, many Kuwaitis expressed their uneasiness at Saddam's threatening reaction to Kuwait's persistent overproduction of crude oil.[2] The same critics also blamed government corruption and ineptitude for Kuwait's general economic malaise. Nearly all of them dismissed the importance of the global recession and the low world price of oil as factors explaining Kuwait's domestic economic situation. Some even said that Kuwait's overproduction was responsible for keeping world oil prices low—a judgment that vastly overstates Kuwait's market power, but one that coincided nicely with the views of Saddam Hussein.

The fervor of the opposition explains why the government was willing to risk foreign policy credibility in OPEC and other international bodies by ratcheting up oil production beginning in the summer of 1989. As more and more people and groups rallied to the pro-democracy movement, government leaders may well have believed that they had no choice but to resort to the only source of income they could influence directly—the oil market—for the resources needed to buy back popular support. And however unreasonable the opposition's condemnation of the government's economic strategy was construed to be by outsiders, these criticisms were based on observations and analyses that were widely shared among Kuwaitis.[3]

Oil policy is a contested issue in Kuwait. Since the 1970s, the government has gradually increased its control of the domestic oil industry and decisions on how to exploit it.[4] Citizens, however influential, had little hope of affecting Kuwait's oil policy except through parliamentary debate and action. Only when constitutional rights and protections were in effect could the parliament force the government to explain and perhaps to modify its decisions. For example, in 1974 the Kuwaiti government wanted to follow Saudi Arabia's lead and limit the percentage of foreign oil holdings to be nationalized. Debates in parliament publicized the issue and pushed the government to agree to nationalize completely before the end of the decade.[5] That same parliament also passed legislation limiting oil production, first to three million barrels per day (mbd) and then to two mbd. Members of the government feared that this would tie their hands in OPEC, but parliamentarians saw their position as protecting both Kuwaiti hydrocarbon reservoirs and OPEC's price structure.[6] The sharp difference in perspective on Kuwaiti oil and gas policy between the government and the parliament explains why many government initiatives in this regard, such as the 1980 creation of the Kuwait Petroleum Corporation, were launched during periods of parliamentary suspension.

Similarly, the composition of the nation's investment portfolio has been treated as a state secret. The parliament tried repeatedly to get accurate and complete information about Kuwait's financial position, but it was consistently checked by government intransigence and the threat of dissolution should it come too close to learning enough to challenge the legitimacy of the regime's control of the country's wealth. Several members of the 1985 parliament, along with independent economist Jasim al-Sa'doun, agree with parliamentarian and oil policy specialist 'Abdullah Nibari in attributing the 1986 suspension of parliament, at least in part, to its ongoing investigation of the government's fiscal activities, including those managed by the oil minister.[7] The 1992 and the 1996 parliaments contested the government's assertion that a minister cannot be tried in the regular criminal court for fiscal malfeasance connected to his position. The official in question is that same, now-former oil minister, Shaikh 'Ali al-Khalifa (also see subsequent chapters).

The personality as well as the policies of 'Ali al-Khalifa have always goaded the regime's critics. 'Ali al-Khalifa held positions in the finance ministry before, during, and after his tenure as oil minister, a job he assumed in 1978.[8] From all these positions, he influenced the nature and direction of Kuwaiti investments for many years, a time during which 'Ali al-Khalifa's activities attracted almost as much blame as praise from individuals and groups inside Kuwait.[9] 'Ali al-Khalifa had opposed the parliament's move to nationalize foreign oil holdings, perhaps most notably on a television program where 'Abdullah Nibari also was a participant. Jasim al-Sa'doun believes that 'Ali al-Khalifa did this to get attention and curry favor with government insiders. "By opposing the parliament, he got himself in good with the government. He came into the government after that. He is smart. He says things the rest do not understand. They accepted him as a permanent member—and he is a Sabah, after all."[10] However, the encounter between 'Ali al-Khalifa and 'Abdullah Nibari impressed the opposition far less than it impressed the government. A decade later, the parliament had no qualms about challenging his decisions as oil minister.

'Ali al-Khalifa seems always to have had nothing but disdain for the parliament as an institution and for its members as individuals, and remains convinced that few people in Kuwait understand the complexities of international finance.[11] Throughout his tenure as a government minister, he treated parliamentary demands for information and explanations of his policies as malevolent and pestilential attacks rather than as a normal part of political life. These attitudes help to explain why, as soon as parliament was suspended in 1985, 'Ali al-Khalifa halted oil ministry reporting of even the most basic industry data, such as oil production levels, to other government ministries. As a result, it became impossible for Kuwaitis to obtain official information on the domestic oil industry or the minister's activities. If they wanted to know what was going on in their own oil industry, an official in another ministry told me in the spring of 1990, "We have to read it in *MEES*."[12]

Already suspicious of the circumstances surrounding his decision to purchase Santa Fe International in 1981, 'Ali al-Khalifa's critics felt their fears as well as their hackles rising in response to his 1987 attempt to take a controlling interest in British Petroleum. The most knowledgeable among them said openly that 'Ali al-Khalifa was running amok. They viewed his preinvasion oil production policy as merely the most recent in a long line of bad decisions that endangered Kuwaiti national security. The provocation to Iraq arising from Kuwait's rate of oil production was interpreted by the opposition as a direct consequence of the lack of openness in government. Under 'Ali al-Khalifa, decisions were made after little consultation, and the minister was noted for his unwillingness to treat alternative proposals, however tactfully offered or technically well supported, as worthy of consideration.

A similar lack of openness and unwillingness to listen were cited as reasons for the refusal of Kuwaiti leaders to take Iraq's threats seriously or to negotiate with its representatives in good faith. The Iraqi version of the talks between Crown Prince Sa'd al-'Abdullah and the Iraqi representatives who met in Saudi Arabia on July 31, 1990, was widely publicized and dominated most contemporary interpretations of events.[13] In this version, the Kuwaitis were said to have behaved arrogantly, "like small-time grocery store owners."[14] The collapse of the talks was blamed on the Kuwaitis rather than on the Iraqis even though neither side seems to have made any concessions to the other.[15]

Kuwaiti leaders had difficulty believing that Iraq's threats were anything more than bluffing.[16] Few insiders took the threats seriously, despite reports from low-ranking Kuwaiti military officers stationed in Baghdad that they were sure that Saddam's military preparations meant he really intended to invade Kuwait.[17] Leaders of the Kuwaiti military also seemed unaware of the potential danger, and no attempt was made to recall any of the large number of senior officers out of the country on vacation.[18] In fact, Kuwait's troop alert level was "quietly" downgraded a short time before the invasion.[19] This action was taken in response to a call by Egypt's president Hosni Mubarak that each side work toward a reduction in tensions.[20]

The Iraqis continued with their war preparations. During the second week in July, Iraq's petroleum minister requested from his Kuwaiti counterpart permission for Iraq to send five technicians for training on the liquified petroleum gas facility at the Kuwait National Petroleum Corporation (KNPC), the KPC subsidiary in charge of domestic refining.

> Coming through the oil minister it was a bit fishy. But we brought five men to the South Pier for training. By the third of August they were in their uniforms. They were the officers for the troops that had come in. . . . [They understood] that the LPG was dangerous. . . . They were trained in Iraq and then here to lead the troops and handle the facility safely.[21]

Troops began massing on the border a week before the invasion. Shortly after, a meeting between Iraqi representatives and the Kuwaiti crown prince held in Jidda on July 31, ended in a stalemate.

Meanwhile, although the presence of masses of Iraqi troops on the Kuwaiti border was visible in U.S. satellite photographs made available to the Kuwaiti government, most Kuwaiti citizens were completely ignorant of the extent of the danger. "All except those who regularly monitored foreign radio knew little about the crisis, because censorship had banned any mention of it in local newspapers and broadcasts."[22] Even after the invasion was under way, the information ban continued.

> At that time there was nothing on the news whatsoever. Kuwait Radio is just giving slogans. I am not a radio listener. I looked for stations I had heard about, like VOA and BBC, but they are not clear except at night. The only station was from Saudi Arabia and they didn't mention anything. At 9:30 [A.M. on August 2] I got another call from my brother [in the Kuwaiti air force]. He said Iraqi tanks completely surrounded the airport and I knew that if they had gotten there it was all over.[23]

I have heard scores of stories from Kuwaitis about how their first inkling of danger came as they were awakened on the morning of August 2 by the sound of gunfire, or by telephone calls from friends and relations outside the country relating news they had learned on radio or television about Kuwait having been invaded.

The response of Kuwaiti military leaders to the invasion was just like the response of the Kuwaiti government. With a few notable exceptions, like brigade commander Salim al-Masaʿud, who commanded an armored unit that held the Iraqis off the Jahraʾ Ridge for several hours before the Kuwaitis ran out of ammunition and had to retreat,[24] they got out as quickly as possible. Military personnel below a certain level were not permitted to have live ammunition and thus could not even defend themselves in the absence of the officers authorized to distribute it. Desertion by their officers left troops without leadership as well.

> I instructed the people working for me, after they had secured their wells, to go home. The emergency room was open and we gave instructions. . . . After evening prayer [on August 2] we sat with the neighbors and tried to think what we should do. But we had no information. We passed the Ahmadi governorate and all the soldiers were sitting on their cars. They did not know what to do.[25]

A Kuwait Drilling Company supervisor described how his next-door neighbor, a general in the Kuwaiti army, had handed over the keys to his house the night after the invasion with instructions to "keep an eye on things." Then he got in his car and drove away.[26]

Such stories made the rounds quickly among Kuwaitis and confirmed their worst suspicions about the government's incompetence. However, the fact that the amir and crown prince had fled was viewed with mixed feelings. Every Kuwaiti I have discussed this with emphasized the importance of the amir as the symbol of Kuwaiti unity. Using terms that would be familiar to students of the relationship of the emperor to Japanese national identity, they stressed the centrality of the amir in efforts to mobilize Kuwaitis and non-Kuwaitis to liberate the country. High-level government employees who left Kuwait, some with reluctance, during the first weeks after the invasion, also underscored the necessity that persons with institutional authority avoid capture in case their physical custody could be used by the Iraqis to take control of Kuwait's overseas assets or provide a shield for an occupation government.

> The Iraqi plan [after Jidda] was to continue the talks in Baghdad and then capture the Kuwaiti prime minister and force him to denounce the amir. . . . In this case, the invasion would appear fairly legitimate; it would look like a ruling family quarrel with the Iraqis being generous to support the good ones in the family.[27]

According to Ghanim al-Najjar, the Iraqi press announced the continuation of talks in Baghdad but, the attempt to capture the crown prince having failed, had to search for another Kuwaiti notable to front for them. They attempted to get Faisal al-Sanaʻ, a Baʻathist and a member of the 1985 parliament, to form a government. He refused twice and, after the second attempt, was urged by his friends to leave the country. "But he rejected the idea. He was thinking he may be able to save some lives." Shortly afterward, Faisal was arrested, along with most of his family and, in 1999, remains a prisoner in Iraq.[28]

Politics in Exile

During the hot Kuwaiti summers, many residents take their vacations abroad. On August 2, 1990, about a third of the Kuwaiti population was out of the country. They soon were joined by a flood of refugees who managed to escape in the early days and weeks of the occupation, followed by a trickle of individuals and groups who continued to make their way out of the country throughout the occupation.[29] The refugees, most of whom were foreigners, made up another third of the population.[30]

Some exiles adjusted rapidly to their situation. They began to work within a short time of receiving news of the invasion, providing assistance to refugees, arguing on radio and television for international intervention to roll back the invasion, and planning for postwar reconstruction.[31] Their own outsider status made it difficult (though not impossible) for them to criticize their leaders for fleeing the country while other Kuwaitis suffered at the hands of Iraqi occupiers. Most of the exiles I interviewed recounted with pride the story of the one senior member of the ruling family, Shaikh Fahad al-Ahmad, who had died fighting Iraqis in the vicinity of the Seif Palace. This is the mythic ideal describing how Kuwait's leaders and defenders ought to have acted; but the story is told quite differently by some of the Kuwaitis who remained in Kuwait and since then have moved on from Kuwait's preinvasion family romance to a more autonomous vision of what it means to be a Kuwaiti citizen.[32]

Exiled Kuwaitis represented a broad spectrum of political views. Even though they were scattered geographically, activists continued to press these views on members of the government-in-exile in Saudi Arabia. Indeed, both because members of the opposition were overrepresented in the politically active exile community,[33] and because much of the non-Kuwaiti constituency that would have to be mobilized behind an allied invasion to retake Kuwait from the Iraqis saw little difference between the amir and Saddam Hussein,[34] the government was heavily pressured from several sides to show itself as the more democratic alternative.

During the first weeks of the occupation, the government—with the notable exception of the-then finance minister, 'Ali al-Khalifa—seemed to be paralyzed.[35] The cabinet was new, having been formed shortly after the June 10 election. Still, most cabinet members had had prior experience in the government. It was their bizarre situation that was so immobilizing. The amir had installed the government in the Saudi resort town of Taif. Life in luxury hotels in the sight of mountains was a surreal contrast to CNN's coverage of life in occupied Kuwait. The new routine for the government-in-exile was less like work than a vacation of indefinite length, with no one among them knowing when—or whether—they would be able to return to anything approaching the Kuwait they had known before.

The torpor of the Kuwaiti government was disturbed by a rising chorus of citizen complaints. These came from opposition leaders, who had begun meeting regularly in London shortly after the invasion, and from other Kuwaitis in various locations and from all walks of life. They asked pointed questions about the causes of the invasion and the responses of their government. They wanted to know why the army had withdrawn without a fight;

why there had been no attempt to negotiate a voluntary withdrawal during the early hours of the invasion; and who would manage, control, and reap the benefits from Kuwait's overseas resources, its blue-chip securities, and the oil industry assets owned by the Kuwait Petroleum Corporation (KPC) while the Iraqis held Kuwait.[36] Unlike most of their government, these Kuwaitis were not idle. The Kuwaiti capacity for self-government is attested by the spontaneous formation of numberless groups, inside Kuwait as well as among the exiles, set up to sustain the Kuwaiti nation. Some exiles established organizations to publicize the plight of occupied Kuwait.[37] The government-in-exile took over the financing of at least two of these groups, the Washington-based Citizens for a Free Kuwait (CFK) and the London-based Free Kuwait Association (FKA). The Washington group was taken over even further when most of its activities were centralized under the leadership of a "high-powered [American] public relations firm, Hill & Knowlton," hired by representatives of the government-in-exile.[38] The Free Kuwait Association seems to have remained somewhat more open, although the formation of another London-based group, the all-volunteer Free Kuwait Campaign (FKC), attests both to the lack of opportunity for grassroots activism in the FKA and the strong desire of Kuwaiti exiles to participate directly in efforts to liberate their country.

Other exiles organized themselves to prepare for the problems they expected to find after liberation. Many of these groups included persons working for KPC. Their company affiliation, together with their common concerns, facilitated communication and coordination. A group in Houston gathered information about oil well fire-fighting, spurred by reports from occupied Kuwait describing the Iraqi mining of oil wells which had begun during the second week of the occupation.[39] Later, an office was set up for this group to interview fire-fighting companies. The Houston group was an offshoot of a Washington-based committee working under nominal government leadership to coordinate planning for the postliberation period. The Washington planners were headed by Kuwait's World Bank representative, Fawzi Sultan, and included non-Kuwaiti employees of KPC affiliates, officials from the U.S. Department of Defense and the Central Intelligence Agency, and other representatives of the World Bank.

Meanwhile, the London offices of Kuwait Petroleum International (KPI), the holding company coordinating the operations of most of KPC's overseas operations, became the main operating base for Kuwait's oil-industry-in-exile. As soon as they heard about the invasion, KPC personnel, many on vacation in various parts of the world, headed for London. Their immediate attention allowed the company to salvage cargoes of Kuwait crude already on the water, as well as three ships that were in port in Kuwait at the time of the invasion. During the occupation, executives and managers crammed into KPI's London headquarters to run Kuwait's overseas oil operations. Whoever was in KPI's Bond Street offices on Friday afternoons met, sometimes for several hours, to exchange information and decide what do next.[40]

A group composed of seven operations managers also worked in the KPI offices—one participant who had been contacted in Kuwait in September was asked to come to London to join his peers—to develop comprehensive plans for oil industry reconstruction following liberation.[41] The several groups coordinated their activities so that each one's plans would support rather than compete with the rest. Every one of the exile groups that Kuwaitis formed on their own initiative, to do everything from locating the whereabouts of their fellow citizens to working for the liberation and eventual reconstruction of their country, confirms Hannah Arendt's conviction that individuals in their plurality have an enormous capacity for autonomous action.

In the face of the widespread criticism of the government and rapidly mounting evidence that Kuwaitis could manage their affairs very nicely without the direct participation of their rulers, the amir agreed to call a meeting of exiles in October 1990 to "make a show of national solidarity."[42] Before this meeting, attended by between 1,200 and 1,300 Kuwaitis, the crown prince cut a deal with two prominent opposition leaders, Ahmad al-Sa'doun, speaker of the 1985 parliament, and 'Abd al-'Aziz al-Saqr, president of the Kuwait Chamber of Commerce. The crown prince and 'Abd al-'Aziz al-Saqr made conciliatory speeches at the meeting, which was held in Jidda, Saudi Arabia, in mid-October. A communiqué was issued at the end of the meeting in which the opposition pledged to support the continuation of the Sabah as the ruling family of Kuwait and the ruling family pledged to restore the Kuwaiti constitution after liberation. At the Jidda meeting, the crown prince also agreed to set up a consultative committee that would include members of the opposition "in the critical decision making process undertaken by the government in exile."[43]

However, from the rulers' point of view, there was already entirely too much participation by the self-appointed in affairs they saw as rightfully theirs to dominate. According to Ahmad al-Sa'doun, there was no post-Jidda inclusion of representatives of the opposition in any of the committees planning for the postliberation period.[44] Instead, and in the name of broadening participation in the process, the self-organized committees planning for reentry were superseded by a regime-imposed gatekeeper who canceled most of the arrangements they had so painstakingly worked out.

The gatekeeper was former housing minister Ibrahim Shahin, who is connected to the Kuwaiti Islamist movement. He replaced Fawzi Sultan as the head of the Washington group, and was charged with approving all the contracts for supplies and services needed to put liberated Kuwait back together again. Industry personnel I spoke to agreed without exception that Ibrahim Shahin was unqualified to understand, much less to alter or overrule, their intricate plans for oil well fire-fighting and postwar industry reconstruction. But Ibrahim Shahin had not been appointed for his expertise. His ignorance and inexperience, helped along by the judicious planting of stories accusing participants on the independent committees of corruption, ended up by discrediting much of the work of those committees.[45] Meanwhile, committee members were encouraged by the rumor mill to believe that the appointment of Ibrahim Shahin had been masterminded by Kuwaiti merchants—including prominent leaders of the opposition—greedy for reconstruction contracts.[46] By this one appointment, the government was able to drive a wedge between the political opposition and committee technocrats which prevented them from developing common interests that could have united them after liberation.

The October Jidda meeting was a political gamble for the government, but it paid off. The apparent harmony between the government and the opposition pacified leaders of coalition governments, especially the United States, initially worried about the strength and depth of the regime's commitment to postwar democratization.[47] At the same time, the success of the even riskier strategy of appearing to broaden the base of the planning committees while scuttling most of their arrangements and discrediting their members enabled the rulers to increase their authority over the exile community. It also gave the government greater control of preparations for reentry, which initially were monopolized by the technocrats.

Kuwaiti leaders felt sufficiently secure to call a second meeting in Jidda in January 1991, shortly before the commencement of hostilities. At Jidda II, government spokesmen "harp[ed] on" the threat to national security from presumed Iraqi moles planted among the Kuwaiti population and, for the first time in public, singled out the Palestinians as the official scapegoats of the invasion.[48] Expressions of concern about possible subversives indicated that the rulers already were looking for ways to delay the elections promised at Jidda I, and foreshadowed the announcement made two weeks after the war began on January 15, which was that the government would impose martial law as soon as Kuwait was liberated.

Opposition leaders were openly angry about the way the government had violated the promises made at Jidda I. They demanded the resignation of the cabinet and the formation of a "government of national salvation" that would include secular nationalists along with Islamists. They referred by name to members of the ruling family in their criticisms. "Even the crown prince and

prime minister . . . who has generally maintained a much higher level of popularity than the amir . . . has been called a liar by such respected opposition figures as Dr Ahmad al-Khatib."[49] Yet despite their concerns, and the ugliness that
marked the reimposition of Al Sabah hegemony over Kuwaiti domestic politics
during the first months following liberation, Kuwaiti democrats did make
gains as the result of their activities during exile.

The democrats were assisted by the continuing interest of the foreign press
and the governments that had played leading roles in the coalition. The
promises of Jidda I to restore the constitution and hold elections were widely
reported and had been favorably reviewed. Opposition protests at the government's disregard of these promises also were reported, though less widely.
Other news reports told about government attempts to repress the opposition
following liberation. These included accounts of the closure by police forces of
public meetings in liberated Kuwait and attacks by death squads on two prominent opponents of the regime. Hamad al-Jou'an, a member of the 1985 parliament, was the only survivor of these attacks. His wife was a featured speaker at
a Washington conference in April 1991 sponsored by the National Republican
Institute for International Affairs. In town with her husband, who had come to
get medical treatment for complications arising from his wounds, she described the assassination attempt in detail and was an eloquent witness to the
climate of fear and violence that persisted in Kuwait despite the ouster of the
Iraqi occupiers.[50]

The perception among Kuwaitis that "the world is watching Kuwait," assisted by the pro-democracy efforts of Kuwaiti exiles and their foreign supporters,
improved prospects for postwar democratization. Before the invasion, the
main foreign interest in Kuwaiti domestic politics had come from Kuwait's immediate neighbors, chiefly Saudi Arabia, who dislike democracy on principle
and consistently have urged Kuwaiti rulers to crack down on their opponents.
Following liberation, a new external audience sought a postwar Kuwait worthy
of the massive effort that had been required to end the occupation. This meant
a Kuwait that was more than just an improvement over Iraq; postliberation
Kuwait was expected to show an improvement over its own preinvasion record.

The Transformation of Consciousness by Occupation

Abandonment by their leaders and defenders forced Kuwaitis remaining inside
Kuwait to fend for themselves against an occupying army busily engaged in
looting the country and abusing its residents. Within days, groups of Kuwaitis
had coalesced into pockets of organized resistance. Women and men, Shiʻa and

Sunna, the not-so-rich and the well-to-do, demonstrated, plotted, and engaged in commando operations until murderous reprisals forced a halt to their more provocative activities toward the end of October 1990.[51] Kuwaiti insiders also employed passive resistance against the Iraqis, with most refusing to go to work or assist the occupiers in any way. Of those who reported to their jobs, most did so in order to certify their employees for salary payments and to sequester data and equipment. A handful of engineers continued to operate utilities so that residents would have electricity and water, using their privileged positions as guarantors of the occupiers' comforts to gather information which they trans-mitted overseas by ham radio, satellite telephones, and fax machines.[52]

Other Kuwaitis, including lower-level military officers, members of promi-nent merchant families such as the Sultans and al-Wazzans, and at least three members of the Sabah,[53] worked in the Resistance. Merchants gave away food and consumer goods from their business inventories and distributed money to the Kuwaiti population so that people could continue to purchase what they needed from whatever source was available.[54] Among the most important sources and distributors of food during the occupation were the neighborhood cooperatives. In 1990 Kuwait's forty-two cooperative societies had more than 170,000 members. Their main activity is to purchase and sell retail meat, gro-ceries, fruits, vegetables, and household supplies, and at that time they con-trolled more than four-fifths of the market in these goods.[55] Their location throughout the country made the cooperatives useful for the Iraqis as well as for Kuwaitis. While Iraqis looted most other Kuwaiti businesses, the coopera-tives, like utility companies, were allowed to continue operating because they provided essential products and services to the Kuwaiti population, including the occupiers. Consequently, cooperatives continued to sell food and they also distributed goods to needy families. Their presence in every neighborhood, along with their pivotal role in the local cash economy, made them critical el-ements in Kuwaiti Resistance activities.

The physical presence of the premises of cooperative societies in every res-idential neighborhood, [made] the cooperatives . . . a focal point for com-munication. . . . The inter-connectedness of the cooperative societies meant that cooperative administrators could travel freely from district to district without attracting the suspicions of the Iraqi authorities . . . an invaluable channel of communication during the occupation. . . . Cooperatives [also] were able to enter into agreements with suppliers to obtain supplies on credit thus augmenting the funds available to them. An important use of the surplus funds was to pay bribes to the Iraqi authorities to secure the re-lease of detainees.[56]

Functioning businesses such as the cooperatives and privately owned merchant operations provided protected spaces from which Kuwaiti Resistance activists and those merchants who had stayed behind could learn about the weaknesses of the Iraqi occupation and decide how to exploit them for the benefit of Kuwaitis. Iraqi merchants paid Iraqi generals to let them enter Kuwait to sell goods.

> The Iraqi merchant gives a very small amount of Iraqi dinars [to be allowed to enter Kuwait and then be introduced to local merchants. I asked the general], how much did they give you. He said three hundred Iraqi dinars. I said, I will do better than that—thirteen thousand dinars. He couldn't believe it. He started working hard [to get more merchants to bring goods into Kuwait]. We gave them watches, perfume for their wives. These are big generals. They start to be different. Instead of trying to get things by force, let's be friends, to get what we want and to protect what we have.[57]

However, their activities were risky and some paid a heavy price for them. "Look at Khaled Sultan. He stayed and was captured and even tortured. Even some officers were captured. They kept changing houses even if they knew they would be killed if they were caught."[58] Defying the occupation always carried high risks and some Kuwaitis paid with their lives.

> Mubarak al-Nout was the director of the al-Ardhiah cooperative society and a friend of mine. We used to call him the poet of the constitutional movement. [During the occupation] he was active in distributing our underground newsletter, the "Popular Steadfastness." [After he was arrested by the Iraqis] he was brought to the parking lot of the cooperative and was shot in the head in front of everybody. I saw him only two days before he was executed. I was with a friend trying to get the cooperative to help handicapped people whose homes are near the society. I saw him keep Iraqi soldiers from entering the society without a permit.[59]

The social and economic poverty of the Iraqi military, which extended to the highest ranks, provided more than the opportunity to bribe soldiers and officers to get things Kuwaitis needed. It also disposed many among the occupation forces to see themselves and their positions in a different light.

> Small radios were distributed to soldiers to let them listen to outside. They are not allowed to do that. It puts fear in them. We gave them tapes. The Kuwaitis inside have done a lot to destabilize those people. Some young people come and sit with them and talk to them and help them, bring them food, tea. Be-

cause what they are receiving isn't much. Dry bread like a rock. Some of the generals, when they sit with me, they close the doors and start to talk about unhappiness. . . . They said they do not want to go back to Iraq. . . . So they turned their machine guns [over] to Kuwaitis.[60]

The unhappiness of well-placed Iraqi occupiers marks a strange contrast to stories from Kuwaiti activists that highlight their own satisfaction at all they managed to do under these difficult conditions. Here we should remember that, on the whole, the borders were relatively porous throughout most of the occupation, particularly for Kuwaiti nationals. I listened every morning to Deborah Amos's daily reports from Saudi Arabia on NPR. Periodically she would broadcast interviews with Kuwaitis—a number of whom I knew personally—who had just crossed the border. Some Kuwaitis traveled in and out several times, bringing money and supplies to those inside and carrying news in both directions. As counterintuitive as it seems, it is hard to escape the conclusion that many Kuwaitis who stayed inside throughout the occupation remained by choice.

We did not leave. We didn't want to sit or beg. I would rather die here, in front of my house, with my family, than go outside and beg. . . . This is our place and we can't be anywhere else. We want to cooperate with our ruling family but they don't trust us. Kuwaitis have to wake every morning [and face who they are]. No Kuwaiti cooperated with the occupier. [Kuwaitis] asked the ruling family to come [back to Kuwait].[61]

On the second day of the invasion, I went with two of my friends down near the Saudi border. I stopped cars going to escape. "Why are you leaving?" I asked them. I stopped a man with a wife and a small child. They had a Mercedes and were driving through the desert. "Do you know the way?" I asked him. "No," he said. "You have a very heavy car," I said. "What if you get stuck in the desert and you don't know where you are? You could die. Wouldn't you rather die in your own country?"[62]

How can you have a country where people desert? . . . These type of people, I can't depend on them. I moved back to Kuwait City to stay with my folks. In our neighborhood [in the city] we had twenty-one houses. Only one house was empty. The father and mother were out but the kids stayed [in Kuwait] and they came [regularly] to check the house. In Subahiya almost all fled. . . . Why did some stay in the country and others go out?[63]

The occupation gave Kuwaiti insiders the opportunity to see themselves in a different light.

I took another occupation. I became the imam in the mosque. It was very risky, especially for Friday prayers. You have to give a speech and you have to be careful. I didn't know how but I did it. I had to act brave and it taught me something. Even in the last days, when people were rounded up in the streets, I kept going.[64]

During the occupation, I did a lot of "nice" things. I was responsible for collecting all the rubbish in my area and also I secured some food for the people and some money also. I had some friends who forged some documents. But mostly I was in charge of rubbish. I protected my old mother and my sister. . . . During the invasion we experienced equality and the true spirit of the liberation. After the liberation we are going back more and more to the way it was before . . . and we are not the same Kuwaiti people as during the invasion.[65]

I was outside and came in for two months and then went back outside. I smuggled [myself] through the border on the ninth or eighth of August and stayed until October. During my presence I participated in the cooperative. I was responsible for my house block. I opened a small supermarket. I and my friends operated this supermarket. Also with my friends I was responsible for the British Airways crew, to hide them, feed them, and take care of them. The main reason for me to leave Kuwait was my sister who was late in her pregnancy. The only way to save her life was to [get her out of the country]. . . . Then I went to the army. I trained at Fort Dix. Then I . . . deployed to the eighth evacuation hospital.[66]

A few Kuwaitis returned once they discovered that it was possible to manage under Iraqi occupation. Some actually were recruited by insiders. Ghanim al-Najjar was part of a group of Kuwaiti insiders who started a weekly bus service between Kuwait and Iraq so that Kuwaitis could visit members of their families who had been arrested and taken out of the country.

After the invasion we had an organization that from November [1990] until January [1991] organized trips for the prisoners' families, taking them by bus from Kuwait to prisons all over Iraq. . . . We found out where various people were being held because some Kuwaitis knew high-ranking Iraqis. [Then] letters started to arrive—when you are under siege you hear all sorts of things and we had heard about the prisoners but nothing [certain]. Then we had a letter from my sister's husband [one of those who had been taken prisoner] and I took her [to Iraq] with some other women with sons and husbands in that prison. I rented a bus and we were able to see them. . . . [The Iraqis had cut all the telephone lines connecting Kuwait to the outside, but] we could phone people outside from Baghdad. We called people to tell them what the conditions were in Kuwait. They were very surprised—they wanted to know if it was possible to survive. We said yes and urged them to come back. They flew into Baghdad from Cairo, from the Emirates—I would bring an empty bus for them. My sister was in Saudi Arabia. I called her—"How are things?" she asked me. I said, "OK." She came back. I picked her up in Basra and took her home on the bus.[67]

Ghanim's wife and children were outside Kuwait when the invasion occurred and they too came back. Ghanim met them at the airport in Baghdad. "It was an emotional moment. I did not know whether I would ever see my wife and children again."[68]

Despite these examples, however, insiders are the first to say that not all those who remained behind or returned to occupied Kuwait were heroes.

Not all the people inside the town were courageous. Some stayed because they were afraid to leave their houses. You must have heard all the stories about Kuwaitis who spent the occupation in their basements. I know one. . . . Everyone convinced him to go out one day. He went for a walk into another block and the Iraqis surrounded it. He went to a friend and stayed there and the next day he went home and never came out again.[69]

In fact, many inside found the occupation stressful, not because it was particularly dangerous but because it was so boring.[70] Foreigners had to stay hidden, so they were shut in except when they were moving to another house. Kuwait University economist Eqbal al-Rahmani says that female residents, especially those who, like her, had an ill family member to comfort and care for, were confined almost as closely as the foreigners.

Throughout the occupation, thanks to the Resistance distribution networks, Kuwaitis were able to get food. With little else to do, many cooked—and ate—elaborate meals. But mostly they talked, read, and watched television. What they saw was not particularly reassuring.

We heard many reports about rapes, but I don't believe they were accurate. If six thousand women were raped you would have to know one of them. My friend in Doha works in a hospital and did not see any. . . . The news about war crimes was exaggerated in Europe and the United States. This propaganda scared Kuwaitis.[71]

The story of the occupation has been an object of struggle between insiders and exiles that began well before liberation. Reports of atrocities are part of this story. Even after liberation, exiles told many more stories about atrocities than insiders. During the occupation, atrocity stories were used to mobilize populations in coalition countries to support armed intervention to reverse the invasion. Documenting atrocities after the war was necessary to support war crimes claims and to bolster Kuwaiti efforts to retain United Nations sanctions on Iraq until all UN demands had been met by Saddam Hussein and his government.

But atrocity stories served other purposes as well, purposes that became clearer after liberation. Occupation stories told by insiders are tales of daring and triumph about how they coped and got the better of the occupiers while the exiles ran away. The traffic over the borders, and the relative ease with which Kuwaitis came into and occasionally even left the area through Baghdad, illustrate the agency of Kuwaiti insiders and their capacity to mobilize people and resources to meet their own needs. In contrast to the insiders' stories about their experiences, atrocity stories reverse the polarity between those who fled and those who stayed. They transform insiders into passive victims and exiles into heroic rescuers.[72] New atrocity stories continued to be produced after liberation. During the fall of 1992, atrocity vignettes featuring graphic scenes of violence and terror and ending with the rescue of occupied Kuwait were shown as fillers between programs on government-controlled Kuwait TV.

Dr. Buthaina al-Muqahawe, a Kuwaiti psychologist who remained inside throughout the occupation, reports that many exiles continue to live with severe guilt as the result of having been outside and safe while their country was under attack.[73] Such persons have a strong need to deny or assuage these feelings. A European diplomat stationed in Kuwait in 1992 told me that he thought the TV vignettes were intended to do precisely that.[74] The fact that former exiles outnumber insiders and occupy the majority of positions of power in Kuwaiti politics and society may explain why the feelings of insiders were and are so freely sacrificed for the psychological comfort of exiles. Additionally, atrocity vignettes rehabilitate the image of Kuwaiti leaders, quintessential outsiders with more than psychological needs to attend to.

Rape stories are almost a category by themselves in the rhetorical conflict between insiders and exiles. Sexual violation is viewed with greater horror than murder by many Kuwaitis because of the cultural importance of female chastity as the primary marker of family honor.[75] The "six thousand rapes" bolstered postliberation efforts to discredit those who had remained in Kuwait during the invasion. As one insider put it, "After the liberation, the people who returned said there were no women with honor [in families that had stayed behind] in Kuwait."

Like the campaigns against actual and potential opponents of the government among exiled activists, campaigns to minimize the work of the Resistance were subtle and designed to reestablish the regime's hegemony over Kuwaiti society. With notable exceptions, most Resistance survivors were ignored and some became targets of whispering campaigns like those directed against exiled technocrats and members of the political opposition. Rape stories dishonored Resistance members and implied that they were incompetent. Indeed, the Resistance figures most frequently honored during the first few years after liberation were "martyrs." For those who are dead, a street has been renamed and public ceremonies are held. A Martyr's Office was established in the Amiri Diwan, but its officials are reluctant even to publish a definitive list of martyrs because there is disagreement over who should be on it. Some Kuwaitis have declared their preferences by putting up their own street signs to honor individuals killed by the Iraqis. The government does not encourage this, not only because deciding who is a martyr is such a problem but because, no matter what criteria are chosen, there are too many names on the list.

The government devalued the Resistance by refusing to use its networks to distribute food and other supplies following liberation. The government had no alternative systems or personnel in place, and the population suffered hardships as a result of what were mostly avoidable shortages. This decision also prevented returning outsiders, who had had no firsthand experience of the effectiveness of Resistance organizations, from appreciating their capacity and competence. Consequently, they were unable to add to the pressure on the government to take advantage of these networks during the emergency, and had no opportunity to form an opinion of Resistance structures based on firsthand knowledge. Kuwaiti military forces trained abroad also were used to discredit the Resistance. They had no role in distributing supplies on the grounds that their job was to enforce martial law so they could disarm Resistance members said to be planning an insurrection against the government. Few Kuwaitis I spoke to gave any credence to the stories that Resistance activists were planning a coup, noting that no positive evidence had been offered in support of that contention.

Whispering campaigns—manufactured "urban legends"—were directed against prominent insiders, a number of whom are associated with the political opposition. Many are businessmen who were widely praised by insiders for their work distributing food, supplies, and currency, and for protecting foreigners wanted by the Iraqis to use as hostages. The whispering campaigns charged these men with having stayed in Kuwait during the occupation only to make money. They are accused of remaining to protect their property when the property of exiles was left undefended, dealing with the enemy for their own profit, and making money directly on their Resistance activities. The last charge was leveled at several involved in the distribution of currency, some of which came from inside and the rest from outside Kuwait. Dinars from abroad were said to have been tucked away or exchanged by the receivers into Iraqi dinars at highly favorable rates.[76] For several years, these negative stories cycled over and over; testimony by insiders to the selfless behavior of surviving Resistance activists seemed to evaporate as soon as it was uttered or printed.[77]

The only Resistance activists who appear to have escaped being tainted by such stories and rumors are Islamists. Following the changes in the electoral system in the early 1980s, Islamists used board memberships in cooperative societies to mobilize neighborhood bases of support for future parliamentary candidacies.[78] Working from the protected spaces of cooperatives and mosques, Islamists, along with secular members of the Resistance, distributed food and medical supplies.[79] Mosques also were primary venues of information dissemination—the reason why those Friday speeches, referred to above by 'Eisa bu Yabis, were such risky affairs—and they were dispensers of spiritual comfort. Many mosques relied on the services of "Friday preachers," individuals who saw a need for leadership in their communities and, like 'Eisa, stepped forward to provide it. Islamist candidates running for parliament in 1992 generally attracted high levels of early support, especially from young voters.[80] At least nineteen men elected to the 1992 parliament "had built their careers as members of cooperative society boards, or had some substantial involvement in the movement."[81] According to Kuwaitis living in districts with prominent Islamist candidates, Islamists were believed to have been the backbone of the Resistance. Khaled al-'Adwa, a young religious scholar running from a tribal district, was able to parlay his identity as an Islamist into a position in parliament even though he had spent the occupation in exile.

The anti-insider stories are matched, in feeling if not in the quality of their plot and action, by the stories insiders tell about exiles. Whether told by insiders or outsiders, these stories owe as much to imagination as to systematic fact-gathering.

The ones inside did the job. From outside, you are far from the fire, the front, living in a five-star hotel, breakfast in bed, receiving salaries—some three thousand pounds per month. And it was fascinating to be living outside.[82]

For a number of years I have been doing a survey of my classes about their attitudes toward political rights for women. In the last four semesters [at the time of the interview, the number since liberation], the first was very strong. The second, less. The third attacked women. They said women did nothing during the occupation. They were mostly bedouin in that class and the bedouin were the first to run away.[83]

Foreign nationals who remained in Kuwait are as scornful of the exiles as Kuwaiti insiders.

> There is a great division between them and us, those who stayed and those who were out. . . . The people who left could afford to leave. Some left because they had to. Some stayed because they were poor. Others stayed because they wouldn't leave their country. Look how many Kuwaitis didn't bring their families back. Sixty-five percent of school places are still vacant. For example, there are very few Mutawas back in the country. They are very wealthy with lots of property and business in the UK.[84]

Despite the conflicts between insiders and exiles to control the story of the occupation, however, Kuwaitis from both groups had many opportunities to test themselves against conditions of adversity and to realize their capacity to behave honorably and effectively. Insofar as this opportunity was seized rather than avoided, Kuwaitis shared a defining experience regardless of where they were during the occupation.

> I kept asking to join the army and eventually they called me and said we only want a few women and we think you would be good. Training was exciting. It was hard. But we earned the guys' respect and it is very hard to earn Arab men's respect. In the end they bragged that they were in the platoon with the girls.[85]

Many look back on the occupation as a time of personal dedication, long hours and days of work, and intense feelings of community with other Kuwaitis.

> It was very nice during the occupation. . . . Yes, people were rushing for available resources, but for one time we became the real genuine Kuwaiti society once again. We came to the people we know. Everyone knew how was the neighbor, did he need anything. We became the old fisherman society like the old days.[86]

> The FKC [Free Kuwait Campaign] was . . . the focus of action of the European press. We established very good relations with French TV and radio, Scandinavian TV and radio. . . . People manned the office until midnight— even through the night when things were going on. It's the people who matter. The FKC had dedicated volunteers who were willing to go all over the country. It was a grassroots effort. . . . Most of us came to it totally unpoliticized. We were doing it merely to achieve the goal of Kuwaiti liberation. We had everybody—the Kuwaiti student union is Islamic [sic] Brotherhood—

we would come in in jeans and they—they operate under codes. I don't know the percent of women involved, but everyone will admit that, throughout, the women have shone. This is a testament that we as Kuwaiti women never had to fight for the right to do the work—we just did it.[87]

We set up a KPC management group, but working as Kuwaitis, not as officials. We had . . . seven people. . . . We started planning with Bechtel, from November 15 until we reentered Kuwait. The planning, the material bought and stored in the Emirates, the scenarios—what if we came by sea and there are no port facilities—we planned for temporary port facilities down to the last crane. Bechtel had maybe two days for Christmas, but we all worked day and night.[88]

We enjoyed talking to the Iraqis. This was part of our challenge. We laughed from inside. We knew that they are coming to steal rather than to occupy. . . . They were afraid.[89]

The population stood really tall when the Iraqis came.[90]

Lessons

The occupation provided lessons in practical democracy to Kuwaitis, inside and outside, who devoted themselves to the assistance of their fellow citizens and the restoration of their country. The various groups set up to meet the needs identified by their organizers were run, for the most part, democratically. This was so for organizations that were normally more hierarchical than horizontal, such as the oil industry management group working at KPI headquarters, as well as for ad hoc Resistance groups and the all-volunteer Free Kuwait Campaign. Where the government intervened in these groups, hierarchical organization was (re)established and the quality of what was accomplished compared unfavorably with preintervention efforts and with the efforts of those who continued to work democratically, those substantially free from government control. Two examples show this well.

The first was discussed above, that is, the government's imposition of Ibrahim Shahin on the groups working on reentry and reconstruction. Although it is not possible to know how well the unobstructed arrangements would have worked, we do know that the intricate plans for reentry described above were seriously disrupted and that a procedure was imposed whose only clear-cut result was the introduction of systematic inefficiencies. Even firefighters were adversely affected by the Ibrahim Shahin "system," and it took the intervention of the U.S. embassy in Kuwait to exempt fire-fighting supplies and equipment from its constraints.[91] We know also that Ibrahim Shahin's appointment caused technocrats on the committees and members of the political opposition each to see the other as instrumental in corrupting if not sabotaging reentry and reconstruction activities. These attitudes continued to poison relations between the two groups during and after the 1992 election campaign.

The second example is the infamous atrocity story told by a young woman to a U.S. congressional committee, that she had seen Iraqi soldiers dumping premature infants from incubators in Kuwaiti hospitals. Her testimony was presented in November 1990, after Hill & Knowlton had been hired to orchestrate public relations activities formerly coordinated by Citizens for a Free Kuwait. It was contradicted by hospital personnel in Kuwait at the time, and by human rights workers investigating war crimes charges following liberation. The witness was completely discredited when it was discovered both that she was a member of the ruling family—the daughter of Kuwait's ambassador to the United States, Shaikh Saʿud al-Nasir al-Sabah—and that she is unlikely to have been present where the atrocities she alleged were said to have occurred.[92] Her exposure damaged the Kuwaiti cause, angering people who felt they had been duped by her testimony and casting doubt on the veracity of genuine witnesses to actual war crimes committed by Iraqis against residents of Kuwait. In contrast, the all-volunteer Free Kuwait Campaign, whose primary task was working with news media across Europe, remained untainted by accusations about manipulation throughout the occupation.

The occupation was a source of other lessons. For the insiders, these lessons at first mostly were positive. Insiders learned that it was possible to defy an autocratic regime and survive. Those who engaged actively in life under occupation learned how much they were capable of enduring and overcoming. Even though armed resistance was effectively halted after three months, other resistance activities continued until liberation. Strategies changed to meet changing circumstances. People took new "jobs" if they were prevented from continuing with their old ones. They did unglamorous work that they never did before or hadn't done for years, even dirty work like garbage collection and personal care of the ill and infirm. Families organized transnationally to protect those living inside, bringing in things that they needed and sometimes taking out individuals, such as the pregnant sister of Mohammad al-Muhanna (see note 60), whom they feared would not survive in occupied Kuwait. Neighbor looked out for neighbor. One result of these experiences is that most insiders are less intimidated by their government than they were in the past. As so many of them put it, "We aren't afraid of the Sabah. We survived Saddam Hussein."

As time passed, however, the insiders' feelings underwent a dramatic shift. Their exhilaration at having survived a horrible ordeal gave way to feelings of despair at the social and political chaos that continues to characterize postwar Kuwait. Insider pride at having coped so well has been undermined by the political dominance of the exiles and their myths of rescue. The exiles are seen by insiders as financially better off, having been supported while abroad and financially compensated after their return. Exile children are less likely to suffer the nightmares and behavior problems that are regular experiences in some insider households. Exiles were able to go on with their lives, to continue their educations, to work at "real jobs," and to be the focus of media attention—all the things that 'Abd al-Wahhab al-Wazzan meant when he said that it was "fascinating" to be outside. Compared to exiles, insiders were exhausted—emotionally, professionally, and physically. They found it harder to reassemble lives which had fallen apart in consequence of the invasion. Although it is true that most insiders aren't afraid of their government, few of them are as confident as outsiders that political life in Kuwait will change for the better in their lifetimes.

The exiles who reacted energetically to the occupation are more varied as a group. Their experiences differed more widely as compared to Kuwaitis who remained inside, depending on where they were and what they chose to do. After liberation, activist exiles were less inclined than insiders to interpret the occupation as proof that normal people can resist a dictator. Even so, they look back with pride at the occupation as a time when they rose above their private desires to devote their lives to regaining their country. Such activists probably always were competent and confident, endowed with the social, intellectual, and financial resources to succeed. The occupation gave them the added assurance of having been tried and found worthy.

A few exile activists became relatively detached from Kuwait, not only as compared to insiders but also as compared to their preinvasion selves. Disgusted by the rapid return of "business as usual" following liberation—martial law, death squads, the devaluation of the Resistance and the consequent aggravation of the suffering of the population—they expressed an alienation as profound as the despair of some insiders. Exiles once, they are not afraid to contemplate leaving a second time. As it was for the pearl merchants who took their boats to Bahrain when Mubarak's taxes became too onerous, the possibility of exit remains an item in their strategic repertoires. In 1990 many Kuwaitis remarked to me that it was impossible to be a Kuwaiti outside Kuwait. After liberation, several alienated exiles turned that statement around: it is impossible to have Kuwait without Kuwaitis. A number already have left the country. In contrast, despairing insiders rarely talk about life outside Kuwait.

By far the vast majority of Kuwaitis don't fit any of these general descriptions. These persons include most who were children, dependent women, and infirm elderly during that time. They also include the men who sat out the occupation, whether in basements in Kuwait or in five-star hotels in London and Cairo. For the most part, these people never were prominent in the networks of relationships that compose the public spaces of Kuwaiti society, politics, and the economy. Their lives continue to be lived primarily in the private spaces of home and family and in the sheltered spaces of government sinecures. During the war in Vietnam, Vietnamese counterparts of these Kuwaitis were called *attentistes*, those who watched to see which way the wind was blowing before they committed themselves to one side or the other. Kuwaiti politicians describe Kuwaiti *attentistes* using a term from the Nixon presidency, calling them Kuwait's "silent majority." The assumption carried by either name is that these Kuwaitis are fundamentally risk-averse and support the status quo.

As the Iraqi invasion recedes further into the past, its contributions to Kuwaiti national myths are assimilated to impressions left by the Ikhwan invasion of 1920. In both cases, activists who escaped the horrors of the battlefield seem to have come away with the most empowering sense of their Kuwaiti identity. The town-dwellers could sleep without hearing the rattle of blowing fingernails; exiles sleep without hearing the screams of the tortured or seeing the mutilated bodies of friends and relations. The exiles also appear to have won the battle of interpreting the occupation. Armed with their self-confidence and political prominence, exiles have dominated postwar struggles to define the politics and economics of liberated Kuwait.

The election of a new National Assembly was held a
little more than a year and a half after Kuwait was liberated from Iraqi occupation. A flood of reporters
came from all over the world to observe the last days
of the campaign, the balloting, and the counting of the
votes. The sheer mass of foreign observers lent credence to a conviction constantly repeated by Kuwaitis
throughout the campaign and election: "the whole
world is watching us." Although most of these "democracy tourists" departed well before a new government
was named and the new parliament convened, the impact of what their presence confirmed persisted. The
audience observing the rituals of domestic politics in
Kuwait included television viewers in Paris and readers of large-circulation newspapers and magazines in
Europe, east Asia, and North America. Far more critical of these political performances than the foreign audiences, Kuwaitis also expected great results following
the 1992 elections.

Launching and Covering the Campaign

The amir announced in June 1991 that parliamentary
elections would take place in October 1992, though an
election date was not set until more than a year later.
Most Kuwaitis were confident that the election would
be held by year's end, but the lack of a definite date
inhibited some potential candidates from formalizing
their plans, particularly among those who had not
run for office before.[1] Experienced politicians tested
the political waters in the winter of 1991–92, going to
diwaniyyas and meeting informally with potential
constituents.[2] In the spring, aspiring candidates

began to declare their intentions publicly. So-called "tribal primaries" were held in heavily bedouin districts. These clan meetings select one or two family members from among those who wish to run. Losers agree in advance not to contest the race, allowing the clan to concentrate its vote and improving the odds that a member of the group will win a seat.[3] By late August 1992, when the election date was officially proclaimed, early-identified candidates had been campaigning for several months.[4] Following the announcement, others rushed to join them, and the campaign soon dominated Kuwaiti public life.

The lack of a definite date for the election was not the only inhibiting factor in the campaign's slow start. The persistence of press censorship and the law against public assembly, both imposed in the aftermath of the 1986 suspensions, impeded the identification and development of a set of national issues from among the evolving positions of various candidates and political groups. The suspension of the ban on public meetings in March cleared the way for public campaigning, until then mostly confined to the private space of diwaniyyas. Press censorship also was suspended in the spring of 1992.[5] However, most candidates continued to be circumspect in their public criticisms. A few told me that they wanted to avoid provoking the government into canceling the election. Others recalled how the regime's critics had been arrested in the spring of 1990 during the lead-up to the election for the Majlis al-Watani. However, as the campaign season continued without arrests or other government disruptions, the participants became more open and more active in presenting themselves to the electorate.

Campaign headquarters were established by declared candidates and their supporters, generally in one or more tents erected on vacant land along the streets in or near their districts. Candidates used these large outdoor spaces to house a variety of campaign activities. Candidate 'Abbas al-Khodary was an experienced campaigner, having been elected both to the 1985 parliament and to the Majlis al-Watani. His campaign in District 13, covering the heavily Shi'i suburb of Rumaithiya, boasted the largest tent in Kuwait. This green-and-white-striped extravaganza—'Abbas al-Khodary employed his name as a pun on "green" ('akhdar) in his campaign materials—had been ordered months in advance from tentmakers in Pakistan. In addition to the giant striped tent where carpets were laid and chairs set up for formal speeches, 'Abbas's staff presided over another tent housing kitchen facilities, large areas lined with comfortable seating for informal talks, and an "office" complete with extensive files of information about every voter in his district, cross-referenced by name, block, and family. That tent also was the home of the campaign's computer, used to record data and run analyses and projections.[6]

The candidates' tent headquarters were the sites of scheduled meetings and other campaign events, some featuring guest speakers in addition to the candidate himself. Their kitchens supplied food, tea, and coffee to guests. On nights when no formal events were on the calendar of a particular campaign, staff members sat in these temporary diwaniyyas and chatted with anyone who might drop by. Usually the candidate himself stopped in late on such evenings, after having attended events elsewhere. So many tent headquarters were clustered along one boulevard in the suburb of Mishref that the area quickly reclaimed its old nickname, "Democracy Street," first coined during the 1985 parliamentary election campaign. Reporters wanting to interview candidates and campaign officials could talk to several on the same evening on Democracy Street, perhaps one reason why candidates from this area were so often featured in stories appearing in the foreign press.

Campaign diwaniyyas are protected spaces for ideas and their public expression. The large numbers of people who come to formal meetings are more than just an audience. They also are witnesses. For example, I attended a diwaniyya on September 22 where candidate Ahmad al-Khatib, running in District 9, al-Rawdha, made his second major campaign speech. Following his formal presentation, Ahmad answered a number of questions, including several about incidents of harassment against him in which he referred explicitly to members of the family of the crown prince as having been involved. Ahmad al-Khatib, like other members of his political group, the Kuwait Democratic Forum (KDF), was a target of smear campaigns impugning his loyalty during the occupation. During the September 22 meeting, he challenged his attackers to prove their charges that he had been an Iraqi sympathizer and offered to make available to local television stations a video tape of the TV interview on which the allegations about him were based.

Thousands of persons attended the meeting, and Kuwaitis talked about it for days afterward. This ensured that many people who had not been present were aware of Ahmad's response to the charges. Political scientist Shafeeq Ghabra believes that this event transformed Ahmad al-Khatib into a victim and earned him sympathy, support, and eventual election.[7] However, I believe that Ahmad's discussion of specific occasions of harassment, along with his offer to provide the video tape, shifted the burden to his critics to prove the allegations—a put-up or shut-up gesture publicly made. The failure of government-controlled television stations to accept his offer and show the tape added to the candidate's credibility and undermined government efforts to discredit him.

Public speech and assembly were not visibly impeded during the campaign, but, as the story just recounted shows, the government did limit some forms of campaign communication. There was virtually no campaign coverage by state-controlled electronic media. The most frequent answer to my questions about this was that there were too many candidates to cover even one major address by each, and that if all were not covered equally, critics would charge the government with favoritism. However, group events were not covered either, such as the two sets of debates, one sponsored by the Kuwait Graduates Society and the other by the political science department at Kuwait University. These debates were the first independently organized mass events featuring multiple candidates ever held during a Kuwaiti election campaign. They provided novel and fascinating opportunities to observe policy differences among candidates as well as to see how effectively each performed.

The print press did cover the independent debates, along with many of the events held at individual campaign diwaniyyas all over Kuwait. Still, the publication of newspaper stories was frequently delayed because of printing schedules. Occasionally the placement and content of stories were affected by events occurring during these delays. In my experience, qualities inherent in print-press reporting also make it difficult to associate a news story with an event that one has witnessed personally. Whether this is due to systemic influences, such as professional folkways or pressures from powerful elites, or to mundane decisions such as the number of column inches to be devoted to a particular event, few newspaper stories convey the flavor of personalities, the composition and comportment of audiences, and the peculiarities of the spaces in which they come together. This is why electronic coverage, which does highlight such qualities, is a useful supplement to the analytical coverage at which newspapers excel. A vivid example of information loss related to single-medium coverage is reflected in press reports about a meeting sponsored by another District 13 candidate, Saleh al-Yasin, at his campaign headquarters on Democracy Street.

This was the first time in a political campaign in Kuwait that women were the featured speakers. The announcement of the event drew a large crowd that gathered in the diwaniyya itself, along with scores of male-female couples who listened from their cars to the speeches, which were broadcast over loudspeakers. The diwaniyya space was divided by a physical barrier separating the audience area into men's and women's sections. The men's side was much larger, open to the street, and had better physical facilities. Its active and noisy population included many little boys who often accompany their fathers on such excursions. The women packed into the smaller side were quieter and far less mobile than the men. Most sat in rows in as many folding chairs as could be squeezed in, and scores of latecomers stood against a wall. I saw only two little girls. The women's section was separated from the street by walls, the speakers' facilities, and a parking lot. The crowding and the walls hemmed the women in, making movement in this space difficult and disruptive. In consequence, the women were not only physically uncomfortable but also could not assemble and reassemble into various small groups as the men could do, to discuss and comment on what they were seeing and hearing. The women's conversation was limited to persons seated or standing immediately by.

The speakers were both prominent women. Moudhi al-Hmoud is a former dean of the faculty of commerce at Kuwait University and an associate professor of business management; attorney Badria al-'Awadhi is Kuwait's representative to the United Nations International Labor Organization and an official of the Regional Organization for the Protection of Marine Life. Both women spoke forcefully about issues affecting families, such as problems faced by working women and the plight of Kuwaiti women married to non-Kuwaitis. The groups on both sides of the gender barrier listened respectfully and, after the speeches were over, hands went up throughout the audience as the question-and-answer session began. Suddenly, during the second question, a firecracker was flung from a passing automobile. Its loud report startled the crowd and the woman who was speaking. Recovering herself, the questioner scorned what she interpreted as an attempt to frighten women from the gathering. Within moments, the meeting continued as though nothing untoward had happened.[8] Little of the texture of this event, and nothing about the firecracker, appeared in press accounts.

Issues

A former speaker of the U.S. House of Representatives, the late Thomas P. O'Neill, was fond of saying that all politics is local. This is as true in Kuwait as it is in the United States. But the 1992 election in Kuwait also was run on a number of national issues. Indeed, one of the most striking aspects of the campaign was the high level of comprehensiveness and coherence evident in so many candidates' analyses of the overall situation of the country. These are the main issues of the campaign as they were reflected in news reports, candidate debates, and the interviews I conducted with candidates, campaign staffs, and other observers.

The top campaign issue in 1992 was security. Even before the invasion, Kuwaitis felt a tremendous insecurity in all too many aspects of their lives. International concerns included fear of Iraqi border violations, economic and social pressures from Saudi Arabia, and continuing anxiety about militant Shi'i Islamism in Iran. During the 1992 campaign, the primary focus was on the Iraqi threat and charges of government incompetence leading up to "August second." Opposition candidates talked frequently about the need to "open the files" on the period prior to the invasion to expose who was responsible for the government's missteps and the military's failure.

Economic fears also absorbed Kuwaiti candidates and voters. Particular concerns included investment policy and imported labor, both of which were seen as threatening the long-term stability of the economy. The rapidly growing proportion of foreigners in the Kuwaiti population had reignited fears about cultural integrity, a prominent concern among many of the Kuwaitis I had talked to in 1990. The opposition was less united than government supporters with respect to these issues, perhaps because the economic interests of core members of the various opposition groups differed. However, virtually all among the opposition agreed that government corruption had degraded Kuwait's overseas holdings—on this point, news of disasters connected to the Kuwait Investment Office's Spanish holdings were uppermost in people's minds. Along with suspicions that authorizations to import foreign labor were awarded as political favors rather than as the result of a rational policy, fears about Kuwait's future economic security united candidates across the spectrum of opposition groups.

A number of candidates called for structural reform of the political system. Many suggested introducing additional institutional checks and balances by creating an independent judiciary and separating the position of crown prince from the prime ministership. There were many calls to reform the bureaucracy and to increase the accountability of ministries. Chief among the ministries criticized were Education and Oil. The large number of university faculty among the candidates may have had something to do with the prominence of education as a campaign issue, but another spur was the growing perception that many Kuwaiti graduates were poorly prepared for employment. With regard to oil, investment policy disagreements and charges of corruption dominated this discussion. Another prominent issue was the status of laws passed during the parliamentary suspension. Under article 71 of the constitution, amiri decrees promulgated when the parliament is not in session have the force of law. However, such laws must be referred to a sitting parliament within fifteen days after it reconvenes or, in the case of a new parliament, "at its first sitting," in order for them to be confirmed. Without such legislative confirmation, interim laws presumably become invalid (see chapter 7). Decrees imposing censorship and forbidding public assembly were the most frequently discussed during the campaign as needing to be canceled by the new parliament.

Citizenship and human rights issues were far less prominent than the others mentioned here, with the exception of women's political rights. The salience of women's rights may have been related to the high degree of foreign interest in the campaign and was certainly connected to the increased pressure for political rights from Kuwaiti women's groups. The visibility of women in the Resistance and among activist exiles strengthened the position of women's rights advocates, whose public involvement in the campaign was extensive and widely covered in the press. The political rights of second-category Kuwaitis were of minor concern during the campaign but gained in prominence after the election. Second-category men were still denied the right to vote and run for office in 1992, although they were not barred from other citizenship benefits. The number of persons at issue was relatively small—"several thousands"—as opposed to the more than 100,000 adult women who would be eligible to vote and run for office should women's rights be granted, or to the even larger number of *bidun* who would suddenly receive economic as well as political rights should their petitions for Kuwaiti nationality be granted. Thus, it is not surprising that the first citizenship issue decided by the 1992 parliament was to confer first-category status on sons born to naturalized Kuwaitis.[9] Problems such as mistreatment of domestic servants and the status of the *bidun* gained virtually all the attention they acquired on Kuwait's postelection political agenda as the result of external pressures from domestic and international human rights groups and from the foreign press. Most Kuwaitis were not very interested in these issues in the fall of 1992.

Cutting across the divide between candidates running as part of the political opposition and those supporting the government were issues arising from the ideological division between Islamists and secularists. Prominent among these was the Sunni Islamist call to amend article 2 of Kuwait's constitution to make Kuwaiti law conform to the Islamic Shari'a. This highly contentious and problematic issue joined tribal candidates from the outlying area with members of the Sunni opposition political blocs. I discuss it further below, along with the influence of sectarianism on the campaign and election.

Districts, Candidates, and "Parties"

Kuwait is divided into twenty-five election districts, each of which sends two representatives to the National Assembly (see table 6.1). These districts were created prior to the February 1981 election, which marked the close of the period of parliamentary suspension initiated in 1976 by the then-amir, Sabah al-Salim.[10] The present amir, Jabir al-Ahmad, acceded to his position in 1977. He presided over the resumption of formal political life in 1981 as well as in 1992. Compared to 'Abdullah al-Salim, the amir under whom the 1962 Kuwaiti constitution was written and ratified, Jabir al-Ahmad is far less tolerant of the constitution and the legislature for which it provides, although he is not so hard-line as his designated successor, Crown Prince Sa'd al-'Abdullah. As part of the political settlement leading up to the 1981 election, the amir tried to curb the powers of the parliament. In early 1980 he set up a commission to amend the constitution. The commission completed its work in four months. The amend-ments it proposed were supposed to be submitted to the new parliament, but they became the center of attention during the 1981 campaign and the result-ing popular outcry forced the amir to rethink the wisdom of a frontal assault on the constitution.[11] His second strategy was two-pronged and more discreet. Large numbers of *badu* were given first-category citizenship which includes, for men, the right to vote and run for office. The new voters were geographi-cally concentrated. This was a result of intentional and epiphenomenal settle-ment patterns that have produced significant, though far from universal, resi-dential segregation in Kuwait, not only by tribe but also by sect, income group, age cohort, nationality, and marital status.[12] As you may recall, the *badu*, along with the Shi'a, were historic allies of the Sabah family.[13] Increasing the number of tribal voters was expected to marginalize the regime's mostly *hadhar* critics and produce a less oppositional legislative body.

The political impact of tribal voters on the composition of the National As-sembly was heightened by changes in election districts. In 1980, Law no. 99 was issued which set out new election districts. Under this law the old system of ten districts each electing five representatives was replaced by a new system of twen-ty-five districts each electing two. The largest single change from redistricting was the division of the old tenth district, Ahmadi, already heavily tribal, into five districts. This effectively doubled tribal representation from that area, raising it from five to ten members. The enlargement of the voter base by selective enfran-chisement of tribal Kuwaitis, together with the strategy that guided drawing new district lines, reduced the proportion of *hadhar* in the 1981 parliament. Redis-tricting readjusted voting margins among other groups by shifting neighbor-hoods from one constituency to another. The biggest losers here were the Shi'a. However, the largest impact of redistricting was to shift representation from the *hadhar* population to the *badu*, most of whom live in the outlying areas.

Tribal gains at *hadhar* expense resulted not only from doubling representa-tion from the Ahmadi area but also from reorganizing city districts such as old Shuwaikh and old Kaifan into smaller, more socially homogeneous districts, and enfranchising new clan groupings, adding substantial numbers of *badu* to voter rolls in urban districts. Together, these measures ensured the election of a parliament dominated by tribal representatives. At the same time, it also im-peded the formation of cohesive tribal blocs by altering the distribution of vot-ers from different tribes. Different clans and branch clans dominated new tribal districts, and some large tribes were distributed across several districts.[14] This forced the tribes to develop new strategies for maximizing clan power in the parliament, the most important of which was the tribal primary. Devised to counter the negative electoral impact of the redistricting on formerly dominant tribes, tribal primaries, first conducted by the 'Ajman in 1975 in the old tenth district,[15] were adopted by other tribes in several different districts in

Table 6.1   Voters, Turnout, and Election Districts in Kuwait, 1992

District Number and Name	Registered Voters	Voters Voting	Turnout (in %)
1. Sharq	1,898	1,615	85.1
2. al-Murqab	1,728	1,445	83.6
3. al-Qiblah	1,666	1,346	80.8
4. al-Da'iya	2,927	2,506	85.6
5. al-Qadisiya	2,549	2,173	85.2
6. al-Faiha'	2,630	2,221	84.4
7. Kaifan	2,120	1,774	83.7
8. Hawali	4,595	4,025	87.6
9. al-Rawdha	2,536	2,189	86.3
10. al-'Adeliya	3,729	3,235	86.8
11. al-Khaldiya	2,409	2,070	85.9
12. al-Salmiya	2,912	2,542	87.3
13. al-Rumaithiya	5,000	4,100	82.0
14. Abraq Khaittan	3,146	2,588	82.3
15. al-Farwaniya	4,277	3,451	80.7
16. al-'Umariya	4,962	4,283	86.3
17. Julib Al-Shiyoukh	3,389	2,876	84.9
18. al-Sulaibikhat	3,370	2,867	85.1
19. al-Jahra' al-Jadida	2,643	2,188	82.8
20. al-Jahra' al-Qadimi	4,313	3,557	82.5
21. al-Ahmadi	7,130	6,039	84.7
22. al-Riqa	3,301	2,682	81.2
23. al-Subahiya	4,148	3,403	82.0
24. al-Fahaheel	3,166	2,696	85.2
25. Um al-Haiman	896	552	61.6
TOTAL VOTERS	81,440	68,423	84.0

Sources: State of Kuwait, Ministry of Interior, Office of Elections, Registered voters by district, 1992. Typescript with ink corrections. (Received September 1992.) 1992 election results by candidate and district. Typescript. (Received September 1995.) Turnout calculated.

1985. Nicolas Gavrielides calls tribal primaries the functional equivalents of nominating procedures mediated by political parties, then as now illegal in Kuwait, and also sees them as normative trendsetters, introducing populist democratic principles into the electoral process.[16] *Hadhar* Kuwaitis are less impressed by the democracy of tribal primaries, which have proven to be most effective in ensuring the election of members of the largest tribes to parliament, where they have worked assiduously to promote clan interests.[17] As I discuss below, some "new men"[18] from the tribes also are unimpressed by tribal primaries, criticizing them precisely for their lack of democratic qualities.

Finally, the 1981 redistricting increased the number and influence of parliamentarians who, in today's terms, would be called Islamists. This happened in two ways. Representatives from the outlying areas, though seldom members of Islamist political groups, tend to agree with Islamists on social issues, guided by traditional values which, not entirely coincidentally, confer legitimacy on their own leadership. Another boost to Islamists comes from the effects of adjusting the urban districts, especially the change from electing five members from a large district to electing two from a smaller one. The result has been to improve the electoral chances of new men of all types, including Islamists, over members of the old elite. Members of Islamist political groups won election to the parliament for the first time in 1981. The consequences of these shifts for policy were evident immediately. For example, the 1981 parliament imposed a total ban on alcohol which, until the measure passed in 1983, had been legal for use by foreigners. Over the longer run, redistricting handed the future Islamist movement a structural advantage in mobilizing a parliamentary base. Although the intention behind redistricting was to hobble what at that time was a predominantly secularist political opposition, among the unforeseen outcomes was to privilege urban as well as tribal Islamists as a political force.

The 1992 election was run in the same districts as the elections in 1981 and 1985, and it brought out large numbers of candidates representing newly prominent social bases. Perhaps the least noted outside Kuwait was the change in the type of person running from tribal areas.

> What we have seen this time is something we have never seen before, not only many candidates but many different kinds of people running. There is a difference between the inner and outer areas. In the inner city, the inhabitants are people who have been out of the nomad system for a long time. The outer areas are dominated by the tribal system until now. In the past, the quality people came from the inner areas. We see this time that high-quality people are also running from the outer areas—PhDs, lawyers, and teachers. They come from a very healthy background and cultural experience.[19]

Sa'd Ben Tafla al-'Ajmi, a young professor at Kuwait University, ran as an independent in District 20, Old Jahra.' Sa'd turned down the opportunity for endorsement by a tribal primary.

> There are clan elections. We want somebody to run for the whole tribe. Anybody who is a member of the clan has the right to run. I refused that. I thought it was arbitrary—some sort of segregation. You should run as a Kuwaiti and not as a member of a clan. It is also discrimination. Those who do not have a big clan don't have a chance. Each clan has its own branches, subclans. If yours is not so big, you don't have a chance. Mine represents 70 percent of the tribe in the area and provided a good chance of my winning, but I refused [tribal endorsement] out of principle.[20]

Sa'd al-'Ajmi was a prominent campaigner outside his district, appearing in both the Kuwait Graduates Society debate series where he talked about human rights, and in the Kuwait University debate series where he spoke on a number of issues including problems arising from the dominance of tribal and Islamist tendencies among Kuwaiti political groupings.[21] Although Sa'd lost the election in his district, his campaign won him recognition nationally as a rising political star, and he was subsequently invited to become a political consultant to the 1992 parliament.[22]

The ranks of new men running in the urban areas also swelled in 1992. Occupation activists, both insiders and exiles, were well represented among this group. They ran even though few believed they could defeat better known or better bankrolled opponents. One of them put it this way, "I will probably not win. Here we have standard candidates from a long time. But you will see me again." Activists ran to bring some sense of closure to their wartime experiences and to share what they had learned from these experiences with their fellow Kuwaitis. Two campaigned as independents in District 10, 'Adaliya. One was an attorney and insider, Saleh al-Hashem; the other was a professor and exile, Saif 'Abbas 'Abdulla.

Saleh al-Hashem, like many insiders, was horrified at the postliberation exacerbation of social divisions among Kuwaitis, divisions that had virtually disappeared inside Kuwait during the occupation.

> Before the invasion there was no equality among the Kuwaiti people regarding their loyalty to the country. They were not equal in front of the law. . . . But during the invasion we experienced equality and the true spirit of liberation. . . . After the liberation I was shocked at how Kuwaitis hated other Kuwaiti men. We don't feel secure among ourselves so I try to do something about it. When I speak, I make it clear that this is not the time to divide the

Kuwaitis. When Saddam Hussein came, he treated us equally. He did not kill Shi'a or Sunna: he killed Kuwaitis.[23]

Like most *hadhar* candidates, Saleh was critical of the regime's handling of foreign policy immediately prior to the invasion, and also of its management of the country's finances. He advocated a reorganization of the government to increase transparency and political participation, and endorsed the Kuwait Democratic Forum's suggestion that the office of prime minister be separated from the position of crown prince. The rationale for this change is that monopolization of both positions by the same person serves to keep the top political leadership in the hands of the ruling family. It also inhibits the behavior of the opposition, which sees the visage of a future amir in every face-off against the current leader of the government.

Saleh also advocated a greater degree of direct involvement by average citizens in political affairs. He had tough words for Kuwaiti women.

The main problem is that Kuwaiti women don't believe in women's rights. Older women are more stubborn about their rights than younger ones—they don't want the responsibility. You cannot fight for someone else. If they believe in equality, they must start, but instead they ask the man to do it for them. I will take their case free of charge if a woman goes to the court for their rights.[24]

This candidate's emphasis on responsibility carried throughout his analysis of Kuwait's situation. Saleh al-Hashem was consistent in advising the Kuwaiti people and their government to be more open, more direct, and more involved.

Saif 'Abbas 'Abdulla is a former diplomat and was chair of the department of political science at Kuwait University when he stepped down to campaign for the parliament in 1992. The Iraqi invasion occurred when he, his wife, and three of their children were in the United States. They rushed immediately to augment the staff at the Kuwait embassy in Washington, focusing their initial efforts on aiding stranded refugees. Shortly after, Saif was one of the group of Kuwaitis who set up Citizens for a Free Kuwait. He spent most of the occupation on radio, on television, and making speeches to live audiences all over the United States, pleading Kuwait's case before the court of public opinion. After Saif returned to Kuwait following liberation, he began to consider running for parliament. He was slow to make up his mind because of his family and work responsibilities, his residence outside the district where the bulk of his family lives, and the fact that other family members also were likely to run. Their candidacies would not dilute his vote because they would be running in a different district. However, they would draw on the same family pool of human and financial resources. These and other concerns prevented Saif from declaring until September.

Saif's positions reveal some of the complexity of political allegiances in Kuwait. Like Saleh al-Hashem, Saif advocates greater responsibility for citizens, but he sees the impact of this lack of responsibility on government policy differently from most other middle-class Kuwaitis. Perhaps because he is a Shi'a and because he spent so much of his life representing Kuwait abroad, Saif has more sympathy for the government's point of view. He says that the political opposition is critical of the government not because the government is bad but because the critics are angry with themselves for being so dependent on it. This minority viewpoint is reflected in Saif's analysis of the situation leading up to the Iraqi invasion, which he approached from a longer time perspective than most Kuwaitis ordinarily take, and in which he included the parliament as well as the government among the responsible agents.

How can the ones who are running now justify their silence [i.e., their lack of protest at giving aid to Iraq during the first Gulf War]? Will they appeal to Arab nationalism? To emotionalism? . . . Even if the government requested the aid, why didn't the parliament object?[25]

On other issues, Saif's positions were similar to those of most other *hadhar* candidates. On education, for example, he was critical of Kuwait's education policy, particularly as it affects the university.

There are no clear education plans. They change according to politics. . . . There are too many dropouts. Graduates do not work in the fields they were trained for. This is because of social pressure and politics. The degree is a license and not a background.[26]

Saif's campaign was most interesting for its procedural innovations. An expert in American politics, Saif tried to run an American-style campaign in Kuwait. At the outset, he invited all the other candidates running in his district to debate the issues at his headquarters. Several came privately to complain about the rules but only one—Saleh al-Hashem—showed up for the event itself. Willing debaters were not the norm in Kuwait in 1992. Few candidates running in any district were prepared to subject themselves to public questioning in an uncontrolled environment. The participants in the two independent debate series were nearly all new men with good educations and highly developed public-speaking skills. Many also were first-time candidates and probably saw the debates as opportunities to become more widely known. The highly educated and articulate Khaled Sultan, an experienced candidate, an Islamist, and a member of a prominent merchant family, decided at the last minute to cancel his appearance at one of the university debates because

> it was not a balanced panel, directed toward our way. The members of the panel represented a specific ideology, more in the liberal and leftist type, and the issues that are likely to come up were directed toward a specific area. . . . Second, the mechanism of question-and-answer does not give the respondent the opportunity to respond to the question.[27]

Saif's proposed debate was even more alarming because it imposed a territorial disadvantage on his opponents along with the fear of uncontrolled questioning—a candidate would have to be very sure of himself to debate in an open forum on his opponent's home turf.

Saif encountered other problems grafting American tactics onto a Kuwaiti campaign. Family involvement in his campaign extended beyond his brothers and nephews—standard practice—to include his wife and daughters—not standard practice at all. The daughters and their friends worked on Saif's advertising and offered a steady stream of suggestions about campaign tactics. They wanted him to invite women to speak at his diwaniyya even before the Yasin diwaniyya with its two female speakers had been announced, and pressed him strongly to go on record immediately in support of women's political rights. Saif's brothers were uncomfortable with the girls' involvement, especially the role of Lubna, Saif's eldest daughter. Lubna's energy, activism, and self-confidence horrified her uncles and challenged their authority. They applied strong pressure to get all the girls out of the campaign. Their position was reinforced by critical comments regarding the propriety of a feature story on the candidate and his family—with photographs—published in one of the Arabic dailies. This far-from-conventional incorporation of the private into the public sphere simultaneously obscured the candidate's message about women's rights and estranged him from more traditionally minded constituents, including some in his family. Family solidarity is important in Kuwaiti elections because family resources—everything from money to voting relatives— are the mainstay of most campaigns.

In countries where political parties take responsibility for nominating candidates and providing campaign resources, they also mobilize voters from different social groups into voting coalitions. Government intervention in the electoral process in Kuwait is designed to thwart nonfamily coalition-building, not simply by making parties formally illegal but also by direct in-

terference. One way is to provide under-the-table financial assistance to selected campaigns. Many of the Kuwaitis I interviewed in 1992 and 1996
thought the government was funneling money to particular candidates. The
logic behind such a tactic is to add to the number running, thereby diluting
the votes of antigovernment candidates, and also to introduce distractions
that take attention away from issues. People making such charges pointed to
the modest means of some candidates as compared to highly visible evidence—like lavish refreshments for audiences at speeches, or the prolifera-
tion of expensive, professionally produced campaign materials—that their
campaigns were spending a lot more money than could be accounted for by
family resources alone.

Some well-heeled campaigns countered charges of covert financing by
openly soliciting resources from their potential voter base. This was the tack
taken by ʿAbbas al-Khodary, whose campaign staff stressed that the candidate's
friends were donating time, materials, and services to ʿAbbas's campaign. The
campaign manager called attention to these donations as evidence of the candidate's effectiveness as a district representative. Friends contributed to ʿAbbas
because "we like him." But demonstrating obligations to friends may pose
problems too, because it is likely that at least some friends give assistance with
the expectation of favors in return.

Favors for favors, measured in votes as well as in direct campaign contributions, are the province of the "service candidate" who acts both as ombudsman
and benefactor to individual constituents in his district. The government is a
silent partner in this patron-client system, helping to entrench service candidates by channeling favors through parliamentarians who prove themselves to
be the kind of men the government prefers. Constituents who approach service
candidates find it easier to obtain scarce and selective benefits ranging from
permits to import labor to authorizations to seek medical care abroad—for
which travel as well as medical expenses are paid—than if they were to apply
through regular bureaucratic channels. ʿAbbas al-Khodary was well known as a
service candidate—the Alphonse D'Amato of Kuwait—and details about favors he had done for his constituents were included in the impressive computerized voter files at his headquarters.

Many party functions are carried out by the most highly developed of the
"political groups," Kuwait's substitute for political parties. The names of these
groups sometimes change from election to election, usually after particular organizations are banned by the government and members reorganize under a
new banner. The 1992 election revealed institutionalization of the dominant
political trends embodied in what Shafeeq Ghabra refers to as "public political
blocs." Six of these quasi-parties operated in Kuwait in 1992.[28]

1. The Kuwait Democratic Forum (KDF), a secular opposition group with Arab nationalist roots. Many of its members are active in the Graduates Society and some are former members of the Istiqlal Club, which was banned in 1986.
2. The Islamic Constitutional Movement (ICM), a Sunni Islamist group in which the Muslim Brotherhood (the Ikhwan) is prominent, along with members of al-Islah al-Ijtama'i, an Islamist association.
3. The Islamic Popular Alliance (IPA), a Sunni Islamist group popularly known as al-Salafin. The Salafin are part of the Wahhabi movement and are generally more conservative than the Ikhwan on social issues, though more liberal on economic issues.
4. The Islamic National Alliance (INA), a Shi'i Islamist group, many of whose members come from al-Jamiyyah al-Thaqafiyyah, an organization incorporating several factions among the Shi'a. INA candidates supported the expansion of most political rights to women and opposed using Shari'a law to govern Kuwait.
5. The Constitutional Bloc (CB), whose constituency is concentrated among the old merchant families.
6. The Former Parliamentarians (85P), not an issue grouping per se, but a status grouping. Its institutional base was the twenty-six-member rump of the 1985 parliament. It was a strong secular proponent of constitutionalism and opponent of the government. Some among this group ran under a second, issue/ideology-oriented designation.

Despite the number and variety of political groups, most candidates in Kuwait run as independents. This choice reinforces the factionalization of Kuwaiti politics and the persistence of family and quasi-family alliances and allegiances that retard the development of representative political institutions.

Tribal identification as a primary source of factionalism is actively promoted by the government. For example, the government follows a procedure in listing candidates that emphasizes clan affiliation. Many Kuwaitis, especially those from prominent families, are already known by a family marker in addition to their personal names and the names of their fathers. For others, official documents such as candidate lists included tribal markers in the names of Kuwaitis who did not customarily use them. For example, Saif 'Abbas 'Abdulla acquired a "last name," Dehrab, in addition to the three names—his own (Saif), his father's ('Abbas), and his grandfather's ('Abdulla)—by which he had identified himself since he was a young man. The inclusion of tribal identities is a strategy for managing reflexivity because it keeps "traditional" tribal designations socially prominent despite the efforts of new men to overcome tribalism in their bid for larger, more socially comprehensive constituencies.[29]

Political parties and political groups emphasize issues and ideologies over family and tribal identities and even over candidates' personalities. The functional correspondence between Kuwaiti political groups and political parties is clear with respect to a number of activities. For example, the KDF worked out a platform long before the 1992 campaign began—some of the KDF planks, most notably the demand to separate the positions of crown prince and prime minister, were developed during the occupation. The KDF also ran a candidate slate—eight persons, the largest of any of the political groups. Candidates were recruited to run in urban districts where the KDF anticipated a voter base sympathetic to its positions. However, only two KDF candidates were victorious, 'Abdullah Nibari, in District 2, and Ahmad al-Khatib in District 9. Both were strongly identified with the KDF in 1992. 'Abdullah Nibari was the KDF's secretary general then as he had been in the group's earlier incarnations, and both men had been elected to previous parliaments.

How the KDF fared is indicative of some of the contrary pulls that make party-formation difficult in Kuwait irrespective of government actions. For example, entrepreneurs who see themselves as stronger than a political group are seldom willing to lend their luster to others by running under the group's designation. The KDF was particularly vulnerable to a drop-off in support from voters and candidates in 1992 because of smear campaigns, such as the one targeting Ahmad al-Khatib, and because of widespread (and long-standing) perceptions that the group as a whole was doctrinaire and inflexible. Ahmad al-Khatib was able to turn the tables on his attackers and win in his district, but the KDF as a whole could not shake its rumor-driven reputation as a group of people whose loyalty to Kuwait was questionable and who, in any event, were out-of-step with the mass of the population.

This vulnerability played out in an interesting way in District 8, Hawali. The KDF named Ahmad al-Rub'i to run under its banner in District 8, but he held them off for some time and chose finally to run as an independent. Scrambling at the last minute to find a substitute, the KDF chose a first-time candidate, Ahmad Dayin, an insider during the occupation who had participated in the Resistance.[30] His campaign was based entirely on the KDF platform, which featured a list of proposals for government reform and a promise to investigate the events leading up to the Iraqi invasion. In line with the KDF platform, which advocated full political rights for women, Ahmad Dayin named a woman, Iman al-Bidah, to run his campaign, and also tried to run a gender-integrated campaign headquarters.

I started out wanting a mixed diwaniyya, but the men complained and I had to have a second tent. We did this because we go according to the social

norms. . . . Even though some liberated women come, housewives, we go by
the social norms and keep them in a separate place. The women who come
to the headquarters watch events through closed-circuit TV. They [also attend mixed] meetings in private houses. On nights when there is an announced meeting, about sixty or seventy women come.[31]

Ahmad Dayin was not expected to win, but he did attract a respectable number of votes, some likely to have come from Kuwaitis committed to the KDF
and its platform.

Meanwhile, the charismatic and politically experienced Ahmad al-Rub'i ran
an aggressive campaign as an independent, tied to no platform or political
group though he endorsed most of the KDF's positions. Having broken with
the KDF, Ahmad al-Rub'i was able to maneuver freely to mobilize a diverse and
impressive base of support for himself.[32] Another charismatic independent in
District 8 was a newcomer, Husain 'Ali al-Qallaf, a young Shi'i mullah with a
large and passionate following.[33] On election day, Husain came in third. The
story of his electoral fate features a complicated interaction between two patterns of group identification in Kuwait: sectarianism and diwaniyya voting.

"Diwaniyya" is a term used to describe a room in a house, a campaign tent
headquarters, and the meetings that go on in both as well as in places such as
the Fatima Mosque in 'Abdullah al-Salim neighborhood where one of the
Monday special diwaniyyas was held during the pro-democracy campaign (see
chapter 4). But when a person talks about "his" diwaniyya, he usually means
the regular weekly meetings that he hosts in his own house or attends regularly at the home of a relation, a friend, or a patron. These meetings center around
a core group whose association extends back for years and sometimes for generations. A diwaniyya like this resembles a family, an intimate group conscious
of its shared interests and common history.

In District 8 a few diwaniyyas were said to have voted strategically to defeat Husain al-Qallaf. Several persons I discussed this with stressed that diwaniyya voting is not unusual in Kuwait. It is a strategy that works like a tribal primary or a family council where participants agree ahead of time on one
or two candidates as a way to concentrate their votes and improve the likelihood that their choices will win.[34] Shortly before the 1992 election, the members of a diwaniyya in Mishref are said to have decided that each would cast
only one vote for Ahmad al-Rub'i and not choose a second candidate. Ahmad
had spent a lot of time talking with them and was seen as deserving their support. Casting one vote would increase the likelihood that Ahmad would win
a seat by avoiding adding to the totals of rival candidates. Most of the diwaniyya members were indifferent about the other candidates anyway, and

the single-vote tactic reflected their actual preferences as well as constituting an electoral strategy.

According to what I have been able to piece together from several informants, the ICM mounted a sophisticated campaign to undermine the strength of Husain 'Ali al-Qallaf. They feared Husain's chances would be boosted by the "one-eyed votes" of those whose only candidate was Ahmad al-Rub'i, and concentrated their efforts on diwaniyyas whose members were known to have decided to cast only one vote for Ahmad. In one of them, an ICM member objected to the single-vote strategy, saying that unless the group voted as a bloc for a second Sunni candidate, "the mullah" would win. This comment played off sectarian rivalry, what another informant called a "scare campaign" against Husain and still another interpreted as a reaction to a Sunni belief that Shi'i voters would pick Husain because they "choose as a religious matter." After some persuading, the diwaniyya members agreed and pledged to vote for the same two candidates, Ahmad al-Rub'i and ICM candidate Isma'il al-Shati.[35] Other Sunni diwaniyyas were said to have made a similar decision. A fourth informant told me that on the night before the election, "People stayed until three in the morning; in certain cases even until light," trying to convince small groups of voters to support Isma'il al-Shati. The spread of this kind of behavior from diwaniyya to diwaniyya also is not unusual. It is an example of how the bandwagon phenomenon, also visible in other electoral settings, works in practice. In Kuwait, a carefully timed and targeted effort like this one can change the outcome of an election because of the small number of voters in each district and the large number of candidates running—winning margins often are very small (see appendix 6.1).

Observers of the 1992 election disagree about the impact of sectarianism on the results. Shi'i winners and their supporters insist that sectarianism was a minimal factor in their own elections. However, several persons I talked to who had information about ballot counting in districts with prominent Shi'i candidates reported that votes for Shi'a were more likely to be paired with votes for other Shi'a than with votes for Sunni candidates. Kuwaiti attorney and author Mohammad al-Jasim obtained a vote tally matrix from District 4, al-Da'iya, showing that only thirty-five of the votes for Shi'i candidate 'Ali al-Baghli, who came in first with 919 votes, were paired with votes for non-Shi'i candidates—not even 4 percent.[36] The diwaniyya voting described above indicates that sectarianism remains an important mobilizing force for Sunni Kuwaitis also. An openly sectarian campaign was run by Sunni candidates in District 4 in 1996, and included a "Sunni primary," conducted in a number of Sunni diwaniyyas shortly before the election. I discuss this further in subsequent chapters.

The salience of sectarianism as an electoral issue is connected to the policy positions of explicitly Islamist candidates. As in other countries where Islamists run for electoral office, a standard "plank" in most Islamist platforms is a promise to make the country's laws conform to Islamic law, the Shari'a. In virtually all cases of Islamist propagandizing for Shari'a, the assumption is that there is one Islamic law that simply can be slotted into place. In reality, however, there are multiple interpretations, beginning with the primary division of Islam into Sunni and Shi'i variants. Within Sunni Islam, there are four major schools of doctrinal interpretation—the Maliki school is the one followed by most Sunni Kuwaitis. Other sources of doctrinal divergence are *fatwas*, which are formal opinions issued by individual religious authorities; interpretations of laws made by Islamic councils and courts; and the interpretation that each individual finds in the Qur'an. The assertion that there is one right way to interpret Islamic law—a fundamentalist assumption—is contradicted by an even more fundamental tradition in Islam, which is that the individual bears personal responsibility for her or himself before God.

Some Islamists talk as though Islamic law is uniform and self-evidently so to any diligent reader of the Qur'an, but this is not reflected in actual practice. In most Muslim countries, personal status laws regulating such things as divorce, child custody, and inheritance are adjudicated in sectarian courts, according to communally based interpretations of the Qur'an, rather than in secular courts applying a single legal standard.[37] Kuwait provides for religious adjudication, but state courts go beyond the already-liberal Maliki standards in areas such as child custody, where they have introduced the "best interests of the child" concept into Kuwaiti family law. This provides a morally defensible legal alternative that is especially attractive to Shi'i mothers seeking custody of their children.[38]

In Kuwait the sectarian distribution in the population is approximately 30 percent Shi'a and 70 percent Sunni Muslims. As I noted earlier, since the 1981 redistricting, the Sunni majority among elected officials is larger than it was before. Sunni Islamist candidates in 1992 routinely included a call to amend article 2 of the Kuwaiti constitution. This article already states that Shari'a is a major source of Kuwaiti law, but Sunni Islamists wish to change it to say that Shari'a is the *only* source of Kuwaiti law. Shi'i candidates, conscious of their status as members of a minority group and the likelihood that any interpretation of Shari'a chosen to guide Kuwaiti law would discriminate against their tradition, did not support amending article 2.

Kuwaiti standards for political correctness in 1992 required candidates to avoid sectarian issues in public forums. On the few occasions where sectarianism was part of a debate, the wisdom of this convention was more than apparent. During the first Kuwait University debate, for example, a comment from 'Abd al-Latif Du'aij, a columnist on the panel posing questions to the candidates, brought up potential problems with other parts of the constitution should article 2 be amended as Sunni Islamists were advocating. The columnist offered his opinion that an amended article 2 would be incompatible with the article giving the Sabah family the right to rule in Kuwait (because they are not descended from the prophet Muhammad) and also would violate several constitutionally protected civil liberties. In response, ICM candidate Isma'il al-Shati said that the perspective of the questioner reflected a minority (i.e., Shi'i) viewpoint within Islam and that such an amendment would not interfere with the article making the Sabah the ruling family—the Sunni position. Another respondent, Yacoub Hayati, openly accused 'Abd al-Latif Du'aij of trying to embarrass Sunni candidates. Yacoub, a Sunni, was running as an independent in Sharq, a district with a large Shi'i population. Disparaging remarks about Shi'a were made by several others, and the discussion got nastier as more people joined in, both from the panel and from the floor. The argument grew so heated that university officials discussed canceling the remaining debates to prevent similar confrontations in the future.[39]

Sectarian concerns underlie other differences on issues between Sunni and Shi'i Islamists in addition to the conflict over whether to amend article 2. Perhaps the most significant of these is women's rights, an issue usually regarded as dividing Islamists from secularists. In Kuwait, where Shi'a are too few to aspire to dominance but too many to be marginalized—even in the parliament—women's rights cut across the Islamist-secularist division during the 1992 campaign. This twist reveals not only sectarian differences in interpreting the boundaries of separate spheres for men and women as mandated by the Qur'an but also hints that the Shi'a could have been positioning themselves to seek and be allies of secular liberals on issues where their interests coincided, including on some issues involving women's status.

The manipulation of women's rights as a marker of political rather than religious principles in the 1992 campaign was not always easy for candidates to orchestrate successfully, whether they ran under a religious designation or not. Consider, for example, the desire of KDF secularist Ahmad Dayin to preside over a gender-integrated diwaniyya and how he was thwarted by the refusal of the presumably secularist men attending his events to tolerate the presence of women in the same tent. Similarly, Husain 'Ali al-Qallaf, the young Shi'i mullah, along with his campaign staff, were uncomfortable with the reality of women attending the candidate's rallies, but their principles demanded that they provide facilities for any who might actually present themselves. Shi'a such as Nasir Sarkhou, an IPA candidate running in District 13, Rumaithiya, along with members of his campaign staff, took pains to distinguish their positions supporting women's rights as distinct from the positions on women's rights taken by Sunni Islamist candidates. In Nasir's case, this position included a formal recognition of women's equality to men, and their right under Islam to occupy public space, vote and run for office, and hold leadership positions in the government other than those putting them in charge of a religious or judicial body.[40] In contrast, Salaf candidates such as Khaled Sultan (District 3), ICM candidates such as Mohammad al-Basiri (District 20), and Sunni Islamist independents such as Khaled al-'Adwa (District 21), made a point of their opposition to women's participation in politics other than voting—about which they were not very enthusiastic either. The Sunni Islamists I encountered were especially adamant against women's attendance at public meetings and any changes in the law that would give women the right to hold public office.[41]

The Sunni Islamist political groups may have noted the positioning of Shi'i rivals as potential coalition partners with secularists and wanted to proclaim the similar availability of their candidates on issues other than women's rights or amending the constitution. They also may have wanted to increase their visibility in the campaign and their clout after the election. For whatever reasons, shortly before election day, both the ICM and the IPA gave public endorsements to lists of candidates who were not running under their designations. (See appendix 6.1.) These endorsements, like the two independent debate series and female speakers at diwaniyyas, constituted another 1992 campaign innovation. I interviewed several candidates who were endorsed by one or both groups; all denied having solicited the endorsements though none repudiated them. One noted that because he had not sought the endorsement he was not obligated to do anything in return for it, while the fact of the endorsement might shift a few votes his way and help him win. However, such an eventuality would cut both ways, as the endorsing political group could increase its status and assert an obligation by claiming that its endorsement had provided the margin of victory.

The strategic conception of the endorsements as enhancing the authority of the Sunni Islamist groups in the new parliament may be inferred from the fact that the endorsements were concentrated among apparent front-runners. For example, in only three districts (2, 14, and 24) did anyone receive an endorsement who finished in less than fourth place.[42] Interestingly, there were cross-endorsements—IPA endorsements of ICM candidates and vice versa—and double endorsements—both Sunni Islamist political groups endorsing the same outside candidate. Thus, the two Sunni groups behaved less as rivals than as partners, though this was not universally true. The ICM refused to endorse Khaled Sultan or Fahad al-Khanah (who ran as an IPA candidate in District 6), and the Salaf were said to have refused to endorse Ikhwan candidates elsewhere. Among the nine cases where both the ICM and the IPA sponsored or endorsed the same candidate, seven won.

While much was made of the endorsements during the last few days of the campaign, their importance faded quickly after the election. Even so, the endorsements marked an organized effort to counter political fragmentation. As such, along with the preparation of coherent platforms and compatible candidate slates, they demonstrate the growing political sophistication of Kuwaiti political groups and their ability to compensate for some of the effects of the regime's divide-and-rule approach to Kuwaiti electoral politics.

The Election

Prior to election day, Kuwaitis as well as foreigners expressed many doubts about the likely honesty of the electoral procedure itself. As a result, I devoted some time to learning about the standard Kuwaiti techniques for cheating in elections as well as about measures election officials were taking to foil them. On election day I traveled to six polling stations and observed for more than an hour at each one. While I noted substantial divergences from the recommended procedures at two polling stations, my overall impression is that, on the whole, the election procedures in five of those districts were carried out conscientiously, in large part because most officials, including judges and poll watchers representing candidates, conducted themselves in a highly professional way. Most manipulations of Kuwaiti elections occur prior to the polling rather than on election day itself, though vote-buying continues to be a problem.

There is no indication that voters were prevented from casting their ballots. In fact, the voter registration system in Kuwait is permissive rather than restrictive, and there are many formal and informal arrangements available to help the infirm as well as those who are incapacitated in other ways, to vote. Although qualified citizens have only a brief period in which to register—for the 1992 election, twenty days in February—this is not a time when many Kuwaitis are out of the country.[43] If a voter moves to another district after registration is closed, he can vote in his old district, where he is officially registered.[44] Registration is closed early in the cycle so the names of all the voters can be published—and potentially challenged. According to 'Ali Murad, the Interior Ministry employee in charge of electoral procedures, one person challenged seven hundred registrants in 1992. After investigation, one hundred were eliminated from the list. One went to court asking to be reinstated, but "the judge decided they should drop him."[45]

The electoral process in Kuwait can be corrupted by registering the un-qualified and loading candidate slates in key districts, matters already touched on. One also can "buy" votes and tamper directly with ballots. When I de-scribed diwaniyya voting earlier in this chapter, you might have wondered why diwaniyya members would keep their word and vote as they had promised—and how anyone could tell whether they had or not. The same thought crossed my mind with respect to vote-buying. Prior to the adoption of the "Australian" or secret ballot in the United States, parties could assure that "their" voters were voting as they should simply by watching them. A voter entered the public polling place and requested a "ticket" for a particular party. He then dropped this ticket into a visible receptacle, also a public act. Anyone buying a vote could see exactly what he was paying for. But when the secret ballot came in, all voters received identical ballots listing every candi-date, ballots they were to mark privately. They could vote for candidates from different parties in the same election—this is where the term *split ticket* comes from—and they could vote for candidates other than the ones they might have been paid to vote for without anyone being the wiser. The level of "party voting" dropped sharply after the Australian ballot was adopted, and soon even the "honesty" of bribed voters was called into question as results verged from vote-buyers' expectations.[46]

Kuwait also has a secret ballot, so I was at first mystified at how vote-buying could be accomplished with any confidence. One of the first people I asked said that buyers simply marched their voters to the mosque and had them swear be-fore God that they would vote as they had promised. I had some doubts about the reliability of this method and, inquiring further, learned of others. The old-est depends on the number of illiterate voters or voters who can pass them-selves off as illiterate. This practice is dying out, especially in the city, along with the Kuwaitis who grew up before education became free and widespread. A voter who cannot read is permitted to vote aloud, before a judge and anyone else who might be present, including representatives of the candidates who are there to observe the judge's conduct as he questions voters and marks their bal-lots. A voter may be challenged by an observer who knows he really isn't illit-erate, and the judge can decide to disqualify him. A judge also can disqualify a voter without an external challenge if he thinks the voter is pretending to be il-literate or is purposely revealing his vote to observers.

The standard method for vote-buying before 1992 was the ballot switch. A vote-buyer sends in his first voter, who pretends to vote by dropping a blank paper provided by the vote-buyer into the ballot box. The "voter" takes the real ballot he received from the judge to the vote-buyer to get his money. The next voter goes in with this ballot already marked. He gets his money when he comes back with a second blank ballot, having "voted" with the premarked ballot. This process continues until all the paid voters cast ballots. The success of this method depends on being able to switch ballots without being seen, easy to do in a standard voting booth.

To combat the ballot-switch scam, 'Ali Murad and his staff prepared a new voting space, a lectern with a four-inch rim around three sides. The idea is to place the lectern in the open in such a way that the judge can watch the voter's back and see whether his hands go into his pockets, while casual observers from the sides and front cannot see how he marks his ballot. The effect of this simple but ingenious innovation was remarkable. In the first days after the 1992 election, grumbling that voters had not voted for candidates they had been paid to vote for was heard in several diwaniyyas and not a few government offices.

My experience watching voting in the six districts I had chosen to observe confirms the success of properly applied procedures in limiting obvious fraud. For example, the judge supervising illiterates voting in Ahmadi revealed both firmness and compassion in dealing with the elderly men he was assisting, one quite befuddled by his prior instructions from a family member. The official poll watchers, one from the ministry and the others representatives of the candidates, unfailingly supported the judge, who was remarkably patient, gentle, and, like so many Kuwaiti judges, very young. Not all the judges whom I observed in their various capacities as election monitors and referees were equally conscientious. Procedures at District 14, Abraq Khaittan, were slipshod at best, and I was not surprised to learn a few days later that the election in that district was being contested on the grounds that disqualified persons had been permitted to vote. In these six districts as a whole, however, most of the judges were reasonably good about following procedures.

The security of the ballot boxes was ensured by the number and interests of the persons observing them at all times, but depended most heavily on the probity of the judges. Ballot boxes were always in the sight and custody of the judges. When a polling place was closed, the chief judge in the district locked the ballot box and sealed it with red sealing wax. Then he dropped the voter tally and the unused ballots, along with the list of voters registered in that precinct, the pens used by the judges during the polling, and the remaining sealing wax sticks, into the box. This was all done before witnesses. The ballot boxes have windows so their contents are visible from outside and observers can see what is and is not inside each box at any time.

In 1992 all the ballots from each district were counted in the first precinct of that district. Boxes from the other precincts were carried by each presiding judge as he was escorted to a waiting police car. Judge and box together were driven to the first precinct where the judge continued to carry the box as he was escorted into the polling place. All the boxes and all the judges were present when the votes were counted. The boxes were not opened until every box was in and certified by the chief judge of the first precinct. The count itself was done by all the judges together, working before a large crowd consisting of candidates and their staffs, friends, voters, reporters, television crews, the odd professor studying the election, and security personnel with machine guns to keep them all in order.

The boxes were unlocked, one at a time. All the ballots were removed, counted by the judges, and the sum compared to the official total that had been compiled during the balloting by each presiding judge. Then each ballot was read and tallied. A judge unfolded it and read the marked names. He held the ballot up so everyone could see that it had been correctly read and properly marked—a ballot with more than two candidates marked was disqualified, as was any ballot with a write-in vote.[47] In consequence, the several voters who wrote in "George Bush" sacrificed their second vote as well as the write-in. The judges and the people sitting close to the front of the room also could check the special watermark on the ballot, a device to detect ballot substitution in order to prevent variations on the vote-and-switch scam. The ballot was passed down the row of judges, one of whom compiled the official vote total. Running tallies were kept by candidate representatives also, most of whom marked them in a matrix so as to record vote pairs. This keeps a record of the ballots, not merely a tally of the vote, preserving more information about voting choice. (Examples collected in 1996 can be found in appendix 6.2.) A big tally was recorded on poster board with Magic Markers by members of the Interior Ministry staff. Every now and again the judge in charge halted the count to read from the official tally to be sure that everyone had recorded the same figures.

With the very first box of votes counted in Hawali, it was apparent that strategic voting had been widespread. About 10 percent of the ballots in that box had only one candidate marked. People who watched the count in other districts reported that some had produced even higher proportions of single-vote ballots. In District 7, for example, observers I questioned estimated that single-vote ballots made up more than a quarter of the total cast. Such large numbers of single-vote ballots in a precinct or district is more likely to reflect diwaniyya voting than strategic choices made by individuals. If the former, their concentrated support strengthens the clout of the diwaniyya if its candidate wins.

What goes on in diwaniyyas is not considered to be privileged information, and diwaniyya members are quick to use stories about what people said and did there for a whole range of purposes. In her book on the Palestinian village of Ein Houd, anthropologist Susan Slyomovics recounts reports from her informants that Iraqi security forces searching Kuwaiti diwaniyyas during the occupation had found listening devices they said were planted by the Kuwaiti government.[48] The idea that the government might be listening to diwaniyya conversations does not perturb Kuwaitis. Diwaniyya members are aware that whatever they say is likely to find its way into the rumor mill and into the ears of the rulers. This is one of the principal ways that the rulers can estimate the tolerance of the population to whatever they might be doing. Consequently, in most people's minds, a diwaniyya is a sounding board and what someone says there is supposed to be overheard, especially if the news that gets around could benefit diwaniyya members. When diwaniyya members concentrate their vote for a winner, they are sure to be among the first to inform him of that fact.

While the count was still in progress in Hawali, I went to the first precinct in Kaifan to see the end of the count in a very close election there. When I arrived, the last box was about to be opened. The intensity of the crowd watching the neck-and-neck race for second place between 'Abd al-'Aziz al-'Adsani, the brother of a member of the 1985 parliament, and ICM-endorsed 'Adil Khaled al-Subieh made the judge reading the ballots increasingly nervous. After it became clear that 'Abd al-'Aziz would win, the judge ejected the noisiest observers and had the security forces lock the doors. The counting and tallying were completed before the remaining witnesses.

The procedure I have described is cumbersome and takes a long time. Some districts were not fully counted until daybreak. However, close scrutiny by observers of deliberate behavior by judges gives confidence in the reported results. In 1996 the ballot-counting procedure was changed so that individual tallies were made in each precinct in order to have the results available as quickly as possible. The shortage of competent judges to conduct the counting was more than evident where I witnessed it, in the first precinct of District 13. The chief judge finally had to give up on one colleague who could neither read accurately nor record the marks on the tally board properly when others called out the names of the candidates marked on the ballots. It took hours to count the vote in this single precinct because of the problems caused by that one individual. Meanwhile, results from other precincts and districts arriving over cell phones and television feeds were constant sources of distraction to and disruption of an already chaotic process. Later, when one of the losers in District 4 insisted that the judges had mixed up the tallies from the different precincts and added votes belonging to him to someone else's, the charge did not seem far-fetched given what I had seen in District 13. Most of the election results were available before 11:00 P.M. on election evening, the goal of the change in procedures, yet much of what was gained in speed was lost in dignity and to some degree in confidence in the reported results, even though all the ballots were preserved and recounts were run where requested. There were four legal challenges by losers in 1996 as opposed to only two in 1992.

The Results

The 1992 election produced a parliament in which more than half of those elected had run on platforms opposing the government. Even proven vote-getters like 'Abbas al-Khodary, whose entire raison d'être seemed to be *wasta* ("connections," patronage), were edged out by opponents promising reform. The exact number of opposition members elected differed slightly depending on who was counting, particularly with respect to the many newly elected independents whose political antecedents were not fully known. Shafeeq Ghabra put the number of opposition members at thirty-five, and he called these results a victory for the middle class: "Twenty-three seats went to formal opposition groups. . . . The remaining twelve went to eight independent candidates affiliated with the opposition . . . tribal candidates with opposition sympathies took four seats."[49] More than half of the elected members of the 1992 parliament, twenty-seven, were newcomers, and most of them, nineteen, came from tribal districts (see table 6.2 and appendix 6.1).

Table 6.2   Experienced Members in Kuwaiti Parliaments

Year	Oldtimers	Incumbents
1967	19 (38%)	19 (38%)
1971	27 (54%)	22 (44%)
1975	27 (54%)	25 (50%)
1981	18 (36%)	11 (22%)
1985	23 (46%)	22 (44%)
1992*	23 (46%)	19 (38%)
1996	32 (64%)	25 (50%)

Notes: "Oldtimers" = members who served in one or more previous parliaments. "Incumbents" = members who had served in the immediately preceding parliament.
*New members from urban districts = 8; new members from tribal districts = 19.

Sources: Arab Times, October 9, 1996, 6–7; voter tallies for 1981, 1985, and 1992 from the Kuwait elections office (photocopy); Nicolas Gavrielides, "Tribal Democracy: The Anatomy of Parliamentary Elections in Kuwait," in Linda Layne, ed., *Elections in the Middle East: Implications of Recent Trends,* 187–213 (Boulder: Westview, 1987).

The 1990 election of the Majlis al-Watani had produced an even larger proportion of newcomers among the winners because so many veterans had refused to run. However, the 1992 election reflected a different hierarchy of values and produced legislators from different segments of the middle class than
had been elected in 1990. Candidates and political groups worked hard in 1992
to nationalize the campaign. They developed platforms, built coalitions, and
emphasized issues rather than identities. This was most marked in the newspaper coverage of the campaign and was reflected also in the decision to organize the two debate series. Yet the great diversity in individuals' backgrounds
and interests make the Kuwaiti middle class, like its counterparts elsewhere,
difficult to designate as "the" winner of an election, as well as a difficult base on
which to organize a coherent and politically effective opposition to an entrenched regime.

Shafeeq Ghabra's identification of the "middle class" as the winner of the 1992
election encourages us to think about what that term means in Kuwait. I believe
that in Kuwait, as elsewhere, "middle class" often is a synonym for "modern" as
this concept was developed in chapter 2. Modern persons are individualistic:
inner-directed, competitive, and oriented toward personal achievement.[50] The
tendency to read "middle class" as an economic designation defining particular
relations of production is why I prefer the term "new men"—and, where appropriate, "new women" or "new persons"—which conveys the sense of modernity
I intend without requiring resolution of definitional conflicts and categorical exclusions associated with the term "class."[51] The new man in Kuwait sees himself
as constructing personal and professional identities from his own efforts rather
than receiving them as a consequence of family membership. In this sense, a
merchant or a tribe member also may be a new man (another reason why "middle class" is such a confusing designation), although others may have difficulty
seeing such persons as individuals independent of their family backgrounds.

The conceptual incompatibility of the two halves of new-men-as-middle-
class is one reason why strong class interests such as those pulling Kuwaiti merchants together to fight time and again against the power of the Sabah are difficult to find among members of this group. In Marxian terms, it is the
merchant class and not the middle class that is the analogue to the bourgeoisie.
Unlike the merchant class, Kuwait's middle class is an economic group defined
by income level. It is highly varied even though its members share a number of
vulnerabilities, the chief of which is their dependence on salaries, nearly all
coming from the government.[52] The economically marginal are especially conscious of the generous perquisites of their offices and work hard to hold onto
them. Even so, as many observers have pointed out,[53] such persons do not constitute a "working class" in the Marxian sense, a class position that, in Kuwait,

is occupied by foreign, mostly south- and east-Asian contract workers. Other members of the middle class, such as professionals and technocrats, are economically better off in the present and more confident in the future than low-skilled and unskilled Kuwaiti workers. Although they too are nearly all dependents of the state in terms of the source of their income, they are more visible socially and politically. Many are willing to take risks and exercise autonomy, and they see themselves as active contributors to present and future Kuwaiti life.

Increasingly, merchant interests also work against the coherence of the opposition, not only because the opposition includes larger numbers of new men but also because the merchant class itself is becoming modern. Merchant exclusivity and the strongly strategic orientation of the old merchant families placed class and family interests above those of the individual. Such merchants today find it difficult to understand, much less applaud or even tolerate, the individualistic strategies and goals of ambitious new men. This was evident in ambivalent responses by merchants well before the 1992 election to the electoral and popular successes of Ahmad al-Rub'i. Yet the merchant class too is internally divided. Sociologist Khaldoun al-Naqeeb calls opposition merchants "traditionals." Traditionals coordinate their strategies in the Chamber of Commerce, an institution they continue to dominate though no longer monopolize.[54] In contrast, the merchant allies of the Al Sabah, like the rulers themselves, are primary beneficiaries of state resources. Merchant allies front for ruling family investments and are rewarded handsomely with lucrative contracts and agencies. Some, such as members of the Behbehani, were small merchants before the 1970s but grew very large as the result of their connections to the government. Others, such as members of the Marzouk, were already rich and powerful but increased their wealth and reach through similar favors. An example is the awarding of the postwar oil field reconstruction contract to Bechtel as the sole contractor rather than to all five of the firms chosen by the KPC group. Faisal al-Marzouk was the agent for Bechtel.[55]

Growing divergence within the merchant class complicates the contending myths describing the merchants, the ruling family, and their respective positions in the state as both elites compete for allies from the middle class. Interclass conflicts tend to paper over divisions within classes, but they add to the power of the ruling family by deepening the gulf between classes. For example, financially pressed members of the middle class, even those who are critical of the government, more often speak of themselves as disadvantaged competitors in an economy dominated by greedy merchants than as potential allies of merchants who suffer economic retaliation for their prominence in the political opposition.

Class, status, and ideological differences among members of the 1992 parliament were aggravated by the proportion of newcomers among them. Part of what enables legislatures to conduct their business is the socialization of members to respect and follow the institution's norms and folkways. During their socialization, newcomers are supposed to observe and learn—be seen and not heard—and take their cues from the oldtimers. As table 6.2 shows, in the 1992 parliament newcomers outnumbered oldtimers. Most newcomers were elected as independents and came from the outlying area. Many saw themselves not merely as new men but as self-made men. They had run populist campaigns, sometimes as tribal candidates, and were closely tied to their electoral constituencies. Like the large "class" of Republican first-termers who came to Washington after the 1994 U.S. congressional elections, many among Kuwait's new parliamentarians in 1992 came to change the system, not accede to its demands.

Members of the ruling family to whom I spoke were openly disappointed (perhaps disgusted is a better word) at the results of the election, but they were far from daunted. Pressed by a chorus of demands from the new parliament, along with citizens' expectations, the rulers realized that the new cabinet would have to include more than the one or two tokens from among the elected parliamentarians that had been a characteristic of Kuwaiti cabinets since the 1981 election. But their analysis of the likely weaknesses of the new parliament was acute, and in their choice of cabinet members, as in their governing strategy, they manipulated these weaknesses with great skill to undermine the effectiveness of the opposition in its attempts to reduce the hold of the ruling family on national power.

1. Sharq

'Adnan 'Abd al-Samad	**81**	85	*	**INA**	695
Yacoub Hayati	81	**85**	*	**85P**	642
Ahmad al-Malafi	*	*	*	IPA	460
Salman al-'Alowan	*	*	*	**T**	450
'Ashour al-Sabagh	*	*	**MW**	*	272
Qasim al-Serraf	*	85	*	*	182
Khaled al-Mas'oud	*	*	*	*	155
Kathim Bu 'Abbas	*	*	**MW**	*	76
Faisal al-Jazaf	*	*	*	*	64

2. Al-Murqab

Hamad al-Jou'an	*	**85**	*	**85P/IPA**	681
'Abdullah al-Nibari	**81+**	**85+**	*	**KDF**	470
Jarallah al-Jarallah	*	*	*	**ICM**	320
'Ali al-Ghanim	*	*	*	**CB**	311
Saleh al-Nafisi	*	*	*	IPA	216
Faisal al-Waqyan	81	*	*	*	201
'Abd al-'Aziz al-'Andalib	*	*	*	*	125
Badir al-Bashir	*	*	*	*	120
'Abdullah al-Yacoub	*	*	*	*	86
Mohammad al-Roumi	*	*	*	*	85
'Abd al-'Aziz al-Majid	*	*	*	*	75
'Abd al-Wahhab al-Tammar	*	*	*	*	69
Mahmoud al-'Adsani	*	*	*	*	14
Subahi al-Hindi	*	85	*	*	9

+ From al-Qaidisya
+ From al-Faiha'

3. Al-Qiblah

Ahmad al-Nasir	*	*	*	*	635
Jasim al-Saqr	**81**	85	*	**CB/ICM**	619
Khaled Sultan	**81+**	**85+**	*	**IPA**	566
Jasim al-Qatami	81	**85**	*	**85P/KDF**	392
Barjis al-Barjis	*	*	*	*	160
'Abd al-'Aziz al-Fulaij	*	*	*	*	40
'Abdullah al-Khatib	*	*	*	*	38
'Abdullah al-Shayeji	*	*	*	*	36
Zahr al-Sharhan	*	*	**MW**	*	23

+ + From al-Murqab

4. Al-Da'iya

'Ali al-Baghli	*	*	*	*	919
'Abdullah al-Roumi	*	85	*	85P/ICM	899
Jasim al-Mudhaf	*	*	*	ICM	599
Hasam al-Roumi	*	*	MW	*	386
'Abd al-Wahed al-'Awadhi	*	*	*	*	377
Saqr al-'Anizi	*	*	MW	*	324
'Eisa Ahmad	*	*	*	*	296
Majid Mousa al-Ustath	*	*	*	*	189
Shakr Sayid Isma'il	*	*	MW	*	152
Mubarak al-Mutawa'	*	*	*	*	121
Isma'il al-'Awadh	*	*	*	*	119
Mohammad al-Qadhibi	*	*	*	*	111
'Abdullah Mohammad Shahab	*	*	*	*	103
'Abd al-Latif Malala	*	*	*	*	94
Salim Yousef Saleh Akhil	*	*	*	*	58
Hasan 'Ali 'Emran	*	*	MW	*	32
'Abd al-Hamid Malala	*	*	*	*	28

5. Al-Qadisiya

Ahmad Baqr	*	85	*	IPA/ICM	839
'Abd al-Mohsin Jamal	81	85	*	*	626
'Abd al-'Aziz al-Mutawa'	*	85	*	85P/ICM	575
'Abd al-'Aziz al-Mukhled	*	85	*	*	473
Ahmad Behbehani	*	*	MW	*	462
Ibrahim al-'Abd al-Mohsin	*	*	*	KDF	373
Khaled al-'Abdullah al-Fares	*	*	*	*	304
'Alla' al-Din al-Salimi	*	*	*	*	261
Matr Sa'id Salman Matr	*	*	*	*	121
Jowwad Mubarak Sa'ud Hasan	*	*	*	*	25
'Eid al-Salidi	*	*	*	*	12

6. Al-Faiha'

Mishairy al-'Anjari	81	85	*	85P	1,182
Mishairy al-'Osaimi	81	*	*	*	935
Fahad al-Khanah	*	*	*	IPA	870
Hmoud al-Roumi	81	85	*	ICM	579
Mohammad al-Barazi	*	85	*	*	230
Turki al-Anbu'i	*	*	*	*	182
Mohammad al-'Otaibi	*	*	MW	*	148
'Abd al-'Aziz al-Duwaish	*	*	*	*	32

7. Kaifan

Jasim al-'Aoun	81	85	*	IPA	877
'Abd al-'Aziz al-'Adsani	*	*	*	*	810
'Adil Khalid al-Subieh	*	85	*	ICM	765
Sa'ud al-Samaka	*	*	*	*	413
Ahmad Yousef al-Sa'id	*	*	*	*	226

8. Hawali

Ahmad al-Rub'i	*	85	*	*	1,669
Isma'il al-Shati	*	*	*	ICM	1,265
Husain 'Ali al-Qallaf	*	*	*	*	1,047
Ahmad al-Takhim	81	85	*	*	563
Hmoud al-Habini	81	*	*	T	553
'Abd al-Hadi al-Salah	*	*	*	*	509
'Umar al-Gharir	*	*	*	*	441
'Abd al-Karim 'Abbas Husain	*	*	*	*	397
Jawwad 'Ali Hmoud Maki	*	*	MW	*	341
Mohammad al-Hajri	*	85	MW	*	214
Ahmad 'Ali 'Abdullah Dayin	*	*	*	KDF	205
Mustafa 'Abbas M'arafi	*	*	*	*	153
'Abd al-Rahman al-'As'ousi	81+	85+	*	*	142
'Abd al-'Aziz al-Mutawa'	81	85	*	*	63
Yousef al-Toura'	*	*	*	*	48
Mohammad al-Mousoui	*	*	*	*	45
Mohammad al-Hafiti	*	*	*	*	43
Mohammad al-Jabar	*	*	*	*	32
'Abd al-Rahman al-Rifa'i	*	*	*	*	21

+ From al-Adeliya

9. Al-Rawdha

Nasir Jasim al-Sana'	*	*	*	ICM	1,070
Ahmad al-Khatib	81	85	*	KDF	886
Jasir al-Jasir	81	85	MW	*	783
Yacoub al-Fadhala	*	*	*	*	347
'Adil al-Zowawi	*	*	MW	*	315
Sulieman al-Thowikh	81	*	*	*	199
Jum'a al-Yasin	*	*	*	*	84
'Abd al-Hamid Bu al-Banat	*	*	*	*	42
Yousef 'Ali al-Mana'i	*	85+	*	*	40
'Abkil M'ijil al-'Abkil	*	*	*	*	32

+ From Da'iya

10. 'Adeliya

Saleh Yousef al-Fadhala	**81**	**85**	*	**85P/ICM/IPA**	1,434
Ahmad Khaled al-Kulaib	*	*	*	ICM/IPA	963
Sami al-Munayes	*	**85**	*	**KDF**	803
'Ali Husain al-'Umar	*	*	**MW**	*	608
Hasham al-Mou'min	*	*	*	*	511
Mohammad 'Eisa al-Bloushi	*	*	*	*	356
Hamad al-Tuwejri	*	*	**MW**	*	337
Walid Khaled Boursali	*	*	*	*	225
'Abdullah 'Abd al-Ghafour	*	*	*	*	201
Ibrahim 'Abdullah Deshti	*	*	*	*	191
Mutlaq Muzid al-Mos'oud	**81+**	85+	*	*	160
Yousef al-Ghanim	**81**	85	*	*	149
Habib Ibrahim Sh'aban	81	85	*	*	52
Saif 'Abbas 'Abdulla	*	*	*	*	40
Saleh al-Hashem	*	*	*	*	21
Nasr 'Abd al-Majid Idris	*	*	*	*	6

+ + From Jahra' al-Jadida

11. Al-Khaldiya

Ahmad al-Sa'doun	**81**	**85**	*	**85P/ICM**	1,403
Mohammad Sulieman al-Marshad	**81**	**85**	*	**85P/ICM**	919
Khalaf Hamad al-Tamimi	81	85	**MW**	*	583
Badir Nasir al-'Ubaid	*	*	*	**IPA**	487
Mohammad Mubarak al-Fajir	*	*	*	*	405
Walid Ahmad al-Wazzan	*	*	*	*	57
'Abdullah Rashid al-Hajri	*	*	**MW**	*	23
Badr Nasir al-'Asalawi	*	*	**MW**	*	14
Sa'ud 'Abd al-'Aziz al-Hajri	*	*	*	*	13

12. Al-Salmiya

'Abd al-Mohsin al-Mud'ej	*	*	*	IPA	1,047
Salim 'Abdullah al-Hamad	**81**	**85**	*	**85P**	605
Ahmad Nassar al-Hariti	*	*	*	ICM/IPA	584
'Abdullah Jarragh Isma'il	*	85+	*	**INA**	572
Rashid 'Awadh al-Jowisri	**81**	**85**	**MW**	*	442
Tarad Sulieman al-Tarad	*	*	*	*	395
Jam'an Mohammad al-Hariti	81	85	**MW**	*	313
Thuniyan 'Ali Thuniyan	81	85	MW	*	254

'Abd al-Redha 'Abd al-Razzak	*	*	*	*	170
Ahmad Mousa al-Hadiya	*	*	*	*	168
Yousef Khalaf al-Hamad	*	*	MW	*	100
Mohammad 'Eisa Mohammad	*	*	*	*	30
'Ali Darwish Hasan 'Abbas	*	*	*	*	13
'Ali 'Eisa Mohammad 'Ali	*	85	*	*	12

+ From Hawali

13. Al-Rumaithiya

Nasir 'Abd al-'Aziz Sarkhou	81	85	*	INA	1,822
Jamal Ahmad al-Kandary	81	85	*	ICM	1,516
'Abbas Husain al-Khodary	*	85	MW	*	1,471
'Abd al-Hamid Deshti	*	*	MW	*	840
Khaled al-Wasmi	81	85	*	KDF	758
'Abbas Khourshid	*	*	MW	*	732
Jasim Qabazard	*	*	MW	*	284
Ahmad Jamid al-Gharib	*	*	*	*	205
'Abd al-Rahman bin Saleh	*	*	*	*	161
Nabeel 'Abd al-Hadi Mudhahi	*	*	MW	*	144
Saleh al-Yasin	*	*	*	*	109
'Abdullah Yacoub al-Wazzan	*	*	*	*	108
Talal Ahmad 'Abbas 'Abdullah	*	*	*	*	45

14. Abraq Khaittan

'Ali Salim Abu Hadida	*	*	*	*	610
Hmoud Nasir al-Jabri	*	85	MW	*	562
'Abd al-Salam al-'Osaimi	*	*	*	*	553
Nasir Fahad al-Banai	81	85	MW	85P/ICM	476
Fahhad Mohammad al-'Eriman	*	*	*	IPA	458
Ahmad Ghazi al-'Otaibi	*	85	*	*	385
Zibin Sa'ijir al-'Otaibi	*	*	*	ICM	333
Khaled Ibidah Bu Reden	*	*	*	*	303
'Ali 'Abdullah al-'Otaibi	*	*	MW	*	284
Fahad 'Ali al-Jabri	*	*	*	*	258
Nasir 'Ali al-Hadi al-'Ajmi	*	*	*	*	190
Riyyadh 'Abdullah Mulla	*	*	*	*	110
Usama Khaled al-Fahid	*	*	*	*	104
Khaled Khalaf al-'Otaibi	*	*	*	*	73
Yousef Mohammad al-Bedah	*	*	*	*	48
Jasim Mohammad al-Shihab	*	*	*	*	27

15. Al-Farwaniya

'Abbas Habib al-Musailim	81	**85**	*	**85P/ICM**	1,350
Ghannam 'Ali al-Jamhour	81+	85+	MW+	**T**	1,165
Mohammad Mufrej al-Musalim	81+	**85**	**MW**	*	931
Sa'ud Urushaid al-Rushaidi	*	85	MW	*	849
Khaled Nazzal al-Mu'asub	**81**	85	*	*	723
'Abd al-Hadi al-Mutairy	*	*	*	**T**	487
Fayez Hamad al-Rushaidi	**81**	85	**MW**	*	433
Mohammad Nasir al-Rushaidi	*	*	*	*	379
Salim Sulieman al-Rushaidi	*	*	*	*	20
Dhafi Mohammad al-'Anizi	*	*	*	*	19

+ From al-'Umariya

16. Al-'Umariya

Mubarak Fahad al-Duwailah	*	**85**	*	**ICM/IPA**	2,193
Mubarak Binaia al-Khrainej	*	*	**MW**	*	1,351
Mosalim Muhammad al-Barrak	*	*	*	**T**	1,341
Barrak Nasir al-Noun	81	**85**	**MW**	*	1,276
Fahad Khaled Fahad 'Elaj	*	*	MW	**T**	630
Mubarak Sultan al-'Adwani	*	*	*	**KDF**	307
Sa'd 'Abbas Husain Sawarej	*	*	*	*	280
Fahad 'Abdullah al-'Adwani	*	*	*	*	127
Jasim Mohamad al-Qattan	*	*	*	*	26

17. Julib Al-Shiyoukh

Mohammad Khalaf Umhamel	*	85	**MW**	*	577
Mohammad Dhaif al-Sharar	*	*	**MW**	*	466
Yousef Khaled al-Mekhled	81+	**85**	*	**85P**	456
Faisal Bandar al-Duwaish	**81**	**85**	*	*	435
Rajja Hijilan al-Mutairy	81	*	*	*	434
Falah 'Aqil al-Mutairy	*	*	*	**ICM**	428
Husain 'Umar Thiyab	*	*	*	*	404
Mahdi 'Abdullah al-Mutairy	**81**	*	*	*	394
Sa'aran Fahad al-Mutairy	*	*	*	*	376
'Abd al-Karim al-Jihaidly	**81**	85	**MW**	*	354
Nashy al-Hamidy al-'Adwani	*	85	*	*	345
Sa'd Mohammad al-'Mutairy	*	*	*	*	321
'Aqqab 'Awadh al-Mutairy	*	*	**MW**	*	155
'Aloush Lafi al-Mutairy	*	*	*	*	101
'Ali Sa'd Mos'ad al-Mutairy	*	*	*	*	90

Sa'd Salim Sa'id al-Rukhimi	*	*	*	*	31
Fadhil Fahad al-'Enizy	*	*	*	*	23

+ From al-'Umariya

18. Al-Sulaibikhat

Khalaf Dimethir al-'Enizi	81	85	MW	*	1,296
Rashid Salman al-Hubaida	*	*	MW	*	1,054
Hamad Saif al-Harshani	81	85	*	T	882
'Abdullah 'Arboud al-Bithali	*	85	MW	T/ICM	740
'Abdullah Mut'ab al-'Urada	*	*	*	*	672
'Abd al-Amir al-Turki	*	*	*	*	234
Sha'ib Shabab al-Muwaizri	*	*	*	*	221
Khaled Ibrahim al-Muthin	*	*	*	*	103

19. Al-Jahra' al-Jadida

Mufrej Nahhar al-Mutairy	*	*	*	IPA/ICM	760
Ahmad Nasir al-Shriyan	*	85	*	85P	757
Munaizel al-'Enizi	*	85 MW	*		644
Mutlaq Sa'ud Bu Thihir	*	*	MW+	*	354
Mutlaq Mohammad al-Shilimi	81	85	MW	*	347
Bader Mohammad al-Mutairy	*	*	*	*	289
Fahad Nasir al-Dhafiry	*	*	MW	*	195
Naf'a Mohammad al-Fahid	*	*	*	*	159
Bandar Sou'an al-'Anizy	*	*	MW	*	165
Mufrej al-Khalifa	81	85+	MW+	*	108
'Abd al-'Aziz al-Rushaidi	*	*	*	*	101
Khashman Minoukh al-Dhafiry	*	*	*	*	89
'Ali Marzouq al-Rushaidi	*	*	*	*	28

+ From al-Jahra' al-Qadimi

20. Al-Jahra' al-Qadimi

Talal Mubarak al-Ayyar	*	*	MW	*	1,382
Talal 'Uthman al-Sa'id	*	85	MW	*	963
Mohammad Mohsin al-Basiri	*	*	*	ICM/IPA	883
'Ali 'Abdullah al-Sa'id	*	85	MW	*	619
Jaza' Fahad al-'Anizy	*	*	*	*	605

Mohammad Haif al-Hijref	*	*	MW	*	564
Sa'd Mohammad al-'Ajmy	*	*	*	*	454
Salim Mubarak al-Shamiri	*	*	*	T	441
Hadi Mohammad al-'Anizy	*	*	*	*	386
Mohammad Salaf al-Hraishy	*	*	*	*	372
'Ali Ferraj al-Shamri	*	85	*	*	61

21. Al-Ahmadi

Khaled al-'Adwa al-'Ajmy	*	*	*	T/ICM/IPA	2,736
Shari' Nasir S'ad al-'Ajmy	*	*	*	T/ICM	1,900
Rashid 'Ali al-'Azemy	*	85	*	T	1,380
Hmoud Sa'ud al-'Azemy	*	*	*	T	1,290
Du'aij Khalifa al-Jary	*	85	*	*	971
Jasim Mohammad al-Hamdan	*	85	*	*	932
Sa'doun Hamad al-'Utaibi	*	*	MW	*	718
'Ali Bijad al-Mutairy	*	*	*	*	352
'Abd al-Karim al-Rahim	*	*	*	*	280
'Ayad 'Ali 'Ayad al-Hajry	*	*	*	*	217
'Abd al-Husain al-Kazimy	*	*	*	*	143
Mohammad Munif al-'Utaibi	*	*	*	*	140
Rakkan 'Abisan al-Harabi	*	*	*	*	64
Saleh Sa'ud al-Mejibel	*	*	*	*	19

22. Al-Riqa

'Ayedh 'Aloush al-Mutairy	*	*	*	T/ICM/IPA	1,274
Hadi Hayef al-'Ajmy	81	85	MW	T	1,101
Marzouq Faleh al-Habini	*	*	MW	T	1,036
Sultan Salman Sultan al-'Ajmy	81+	85	*	T	854
Qalifis Nasir al-'Akshani	*	*	*	*	637

23. Al-Subbahiya

Jam'an Faleh Salim al-'Azemy	*	*	*	ICM/T	2,265
Fahad Dahisan al-'Azemy	*	*	*	T	1,835
Fahad Hamad Rakan al-Mekrad	*	*	*	T	1,361
Bayan Salmy Faleh al-Mutairy	*	*	*	T	993

24. Al-Fahaheel

'Abdullah Rashid al-Hajri	*	*	*	T/ICM	1,381
Turki Mohammad al-'Azmy	*	*	*	T	993
Husain Barrak al-Dosary	*	*	*	*	769
Hmoud 'Abdullah al-'Utaibi	*	*	*	*	741
Sa'd Mohammad al-'Ajmy	*	*	*	ICM	705
Mubarak 'Abdullah al-Jasim	81	85	*	*	315
Sami 'Ali Ghanim al-Jasim	*	*	*	*	237
Mubarak 'Ubaid al-Dosary	*	85	*	*	46
Nahidh Nasir al-Hajry	*	*	*	*	18

25. Um al-Haiman

Sa'd Biliq Q'am al-'Azemy	*	*	*	T	525
Musaleh Hamijan al-'Azemy	*	*	*	T	522
'Abdullah Rashid al-Hajry	81	85	MW	*	22
Mohammad Wahash al-Za'iby	*	*	*	*	10
Jasim Mohammad al-'Eraifan	*	*	*	*	6
Hasan 'Abd al-Malik Bahman	*	*	*	*	6
Yacoub Hashem Mohammad	*	*	*	*	2

Notes: **81**/81: **won**/lost election to parliament in 1981

85/85: **won**/lost election to parliament in 1985

MW/MW: **won**/lost election to Majlis al-Watani in 1990

* = did not run in that election

Bloc affiliation/endorsement by bloc

        KDF: Kuwait Democratic Forum

        ICM: Islamic Constitution Movement

        IPA: Islamic Popular Alliance

        INA: Islamic National Alliance

        CB: Constitutional Bloc

        85P: Member of the Group of 26 in the 1985 parliament

Where no affiliation is listed, the candidate ran as an Independent.

Footnotes (+) to entries within districts refer to other districts from which a candidate ran in one or more previous elections.

Sources: State of Kuwait, Ministry of Interior, Office of Elections, 1992 election results by candidate and district. Typescript. *Al-Qabas* (Kuwait), September 29, 1992, 21.

District 2

	AN	AWH	SJ	JJ	IS	AAT	SN	AAA	MA	NW	total
AN	34	247	44	40	193	59	17	12	4	4	654
AWH	247	16	127	87	48	48	20	0	6	3	602
SAJ	44	127	21	168	24	6	51	4	19	8	472
JJ	40	87	168	23	29	9	20	2	13	6	397
IS	193	48	24	29	11	8	15	0	3	0	331
AAT	59	48	6	9	8	73	2	79	1	5	290
SN	17	20	51	20	15	2	7	0	3	1	136
AAA	12	0	4	2	0	79	0	2	0	0	99
MA	4	6	19	13	3	1	3	0	0	1	50
NW	4	3	8	6	0	5	1	0	1	0	28
TOTAL	654	602	472	397	331	290	136	99	50	28	

Abbreviations: AN = 'Abdullah al-Nibari
  AWH = 'Abd al-Wahhab al-Haroun
  SJ = Saleh al-Jadr
  JJ = Jarallah al-Jarallah
  IS = Imad al-Saif
  AAT = 'Abd al-Amir al-Turki
  SN = Saleh al-Nafisi
  AAA = 'Abd al-'Aziz al-'Andalib
  MA = Mahmoud al-Adsani
  NW = Nasir al-Wuqyan

Notes: Registered Voters: 1,959
  Number voting: 1,635
  Turnout: 83.4%
  Single-vote ballots: 187

Source: 'Abd al-Rahman R. al-Haroun, October 19, 1996

District 4

	HQ	JM	AWA	AB	AR	ALU	EA	total
HQ	103	7	38	548	33	207	84	1,020
JM	7	21	628	9	271	7	4	947
AWA	38	628	30	19	182	20	7	924
AB	548	9	19	59	47	49	69	800
AR	33	271	182	47	228	10	2	773
ALU	207	7	20	49	10	4	7	304
EA	84	4	7	69	2	7	0	173
TOTAL	1,020	947	924	800	773	304	173	

Abbreviations: HQ = Husain 'Ali al-Qallaf
JM = Jasim al-Mudhaf
AWA = 'Abd al-Wahid al-Awadhi
AB = 'Ali al-Baghli
AR = 'Abdullah al-Roumi
ALU = 'Abd al-Latif al-Ustath
EA = 'Eisa Ahmad

Notes: Registered voters: 3,194
Number voting: 2,711
Turnout: 84.9%
Single-vote ballots: 483

Source: 'Abd al-Rahman R. al-Haroun, October 19, 1996

Back to the Future:
The Return of Normal Politics

The 1992 campaign in Kuwait was like a wedding feast, a gigantic party celebrating the reunification of Kuwaitis with their country and their history. The 1992 election was generally seen as a victory for popular government, the constitution, and much of what Kuwaitis value in themselves and their political traditions. However, it also brought back the long-running conflict between the government and a sitting parliament, always more difficult for the opposition to manage to its advantage than the conflict between the government and "the people," which is how politics in Kuwait tends to be framed when the parliament is suspended.

The Kuwaiti parliament is both subject and object of contending myths and conflicting interests. Despite how deeply it is embedded in Kuwaiti mythic history, the parliament remains an insecurely rooted organ of practical governance. Ever since the 1981 redistricting which made cultural conflict between *hadhar* and *badu* understandings of citizenship and loyalty a constant feature of legislative decision-making, the parliament's internal culture has been unstable. Interpersonal relations have become more contentious and, as a result, institutional autonomy has suffered. Yet even though the parliament is a fragile governing institution, it remains the primary base upon which constitutional democracy in the country can be constructed and maintained. In Kuwait, voluntary associations and the highly institutionalized and protected network of diwaniyyas are important arenas for direct political participation—populism; the parliament is the embodiment and guarantor of constitutionalism and the rule of law.

The Prime Minister and the Cabinet

Kuwait's political system incorporates aspects of parliamentary regimes and systems where the executive and the legislature are separate institutions. The Kuwaiti system also has a number of unique features affecting the separate and joint operations of the parliament and the cabinet. Led by the prime minister, the cabinet sets much of the political agenda and directs the work of government agencies. However, unlike what happens in parliamentary systems such as Britain's, the Kuwaiti parliament cannot bring the cabinet down, get rid of the prime minister, or force new elections. The Kuwaiti cabinet is not an extension of the parliament but rather is a fusion of the executive and the legislature.[1] Without parties to connect programmatic leadership and government policy, and without an electoral or a parliamentary role in choosing the prime minister, the head of Kuwait's government often is the chief antagonist of the National Assembly.

In the Kuwaiti system, the cabinet is an arm of the rulers. If elected members move too far away from the cabinet's positions, the arm tightens in a choke-hold, giving parliament the unhappy choice of retreating or being throttled. Sitting parliaments have been so throttled three times in Kuwaiti history, yet the ethos of the institution demands an independent role for elected representatives. The cabinet and parliament are both weakened by the blending of these two institutions caused by including cabinet members as members of parliament and appointing parliamentarians to the cabinet.

Every cabinet minister automatically becomes a member of parliament, whether he was elected to the National Assembly or not. Consequently, Kuwait's rulers prefer to minimize the number of elected parliamentarians appointed to the cabinet, leaving more places to fill with their supporters, who then become full members of the National Assembly. This shifts the balance between the opposition and the supporters of the regime in parliament toward the latter, and dilutes the power of all the elected representatives. Another reason for keeping the number of elected parliamentarians in the cabinet as small as possible is to reduce demands for accommodation from within the cabinet, a much easier prospect when those most likely to make such demands are excluded. A third objective is to keep key ministries—Foreign Affairs, Interior, and Defense, and one or more among Information, Finance, and Oil—in the hands of members of the ruling family.[2] Although the proportion of cabinet offices held by ruling family members has declined since the constitution first went into effect, the first three of these key ministries have been monopolized by ruling family members.

The crown prince in his role as prime minister is the linchpin of this system. Together with the amir and their close advisers, he chooses the cabinet, leads the government, and exerts continual psychological and political pressure on the parliament as an institution and its members as individuals to surrender their limited autonomy to the demands of the ruling family. The Kuwaiti constitution does not require the crown prince to be the prime minister. As a result, the KDF-led campaign to separate the prime ministership from the crown princeship constituted a potent threat to the architecture of ruling family control of Kuwait's political system. Their desire to defuse this demand prompted the rulers to orchestrate an elaborate charade to undermine the movement by Kuwaiti constitutionalists to formalize an institutional separation between rulers and parliament. It also provided an opportunity for the rulers to pull off a smaller coup with respect to the assignment of cabinet portfolios. This scenario was played out so rapidly that the opposition could not open a political space quickly enough to take the issue of the prime ministership into the public arena.

In the midst of speculation and maneuvering regarding the choice of ministers for the new cabinet, the crown prince made a sudden and unexpected move. On October 10 he told a number of people that he was giving up the post of prime minister because he didn't have the unanimous support of the Kuwaiti people. The announcement fell like a bombshell on the political opposition. The newly elected parliamentarians were exhausted from the campaign and from fulfilling the social obligations of winners to receive the congratulations of supporters and constituents.[3] At the time, they were meeting in daily strategy sessions aimed at maximizing the number of potential cabinet ministers from among themselves. Meanwhile, the lack of unity among the new members had already begun to make itself felt in rumblings against the reelection of Ahmad al-Sa'doun to the speakership. As a result, there was no ready-made "game plan" on hand to respond to the apparent capitulation by the crown prince to what had been, up to that time, a theoretical argument opposing his monopoly over the prime ministership.

The novelty and timing of the crown prince's offer created a situation similar to the amir's 1990 speech outlining the plan for the Majlis al-Watani. The opposition was caught flat-footed, without an alternative ready in the wings. Into the vacuum created by the rulers' challenge and the opposition's lack of a comeback, supporters of the regime moved from behind the scenes to create an illusion of a popular endorsement of the crown prince that was even less grounded in democratic formalities than the illusion of parliamentary elections that had produced the Majlis al-Watani. This began immediately after reports of the "resignation" appeared in the press. A stream of individuals and groups from among the regime's supporters paraded to the palace, reportedly to beg the amir to persuade the crown prince to change his mind. Recalling the traditional custom of *shura*, consultation, stories about the petitioners made the rulers' choice of the crown prince to be prime minister appear to be the people's choice. The populist mood was intensified that night when, at nearby diwaniyyas, men were urged to go home and mobilize their wives. Soon a crowd of shouting women, some of them weeping, converged on the Bayan Palace in a "spontaneous" demonstration against the resignation of the crown prince. The next day, citing "popular demand," the crown prince announced that he would stay on as prime minister and form a new government.[4] Some said that the crown prince had demanded that Shaikh Sabah al-Ahmad al-Jabir return to head the foreign ministry, the post he had held at the time of the invasion.[5] Whatever the role of the crown prince in his rehabilitation, the appointment of Sabah al-Ahmad was a warning to members who had campaigned against the incompetence of the preinvasion leadership and were threatening to "open the files on August second" as soon as parliament convened. It let them know that any attempt to extend their investigations all the way to the top would meet with resistance.[6]

It was difficult for the opposition to criticize the rapidity of the resolution of this minicrisis, which came and went in something like twenty-four hours (though news coverage was spread out over several days, making it appear to have taken longer). Kuwait's constitution requires that the new National Assembly convene two weeks after an election (article 87). Choosing a new prime minister, even one from the ruling family, would have required delicate negotiations among competing claims.[7] This may have been impossible given the time constraints. The end result was that the crown prince's coup delegitimated the movement to free the prime ministership from its bondage to Kuwait's rulers, keeping the Sabah's chief mechanism for parliamentary penetration intact.

The opposition had not considered alternative candidates for the prime ministership, but it did devote a great deal of time and effort to devising a strategy to strengthen its position in the cabinet. On the same day that the crown prince withdrew his promise to resign, the Group of Forty-five named a ten-member committee, including two of the four men being mentioned for the speakership, to ask the amir to broaden the "popular platform in the formation of the new cabinet."[8] The delegation reportedly went to the amir armed with the names of seven parliamentarians who had agreed to serve in the government and whom the group had agreed to support.

According to Hamad al-Jou'an (85P), a member of the core leadership of the opposition, the crown prince had approached members individually to ask if they would accept ministerial appointments. Those who answered yes then went to the Group of Forty-five, which had begun to see itself as the coordinating organization for all the opposition groups in parliament, to ask for the group's endorsement. The Forty-five asked prospective ministers seeking its endorsement to get the prime minister to agree that parliamentarians would be given half the seats in the cabinet, and that appointees would have a say about which portfolios they would accept. The Forty-five also wanted a pledge that the crown prince would not appoint ministers from outside the parliament who had been associated with antidemocratic activities—that they "will be from non-corrupted backgrounds."[9]

The decision to send a delegation from the Forty-five to the amir reflected the group's desire to assert its authority to speak for the opposition and also its understanding that aspiring ministers would need help putting forward the collective demands of the group, given the intensity of each aspirant's private desire for cabinet office. In addition, as parliamentarian 'Adnan 'Abd al-Samad (INA) was quick to point out, by dealing with members as individuals rather than going through the political blocs, the crown prince could sidestep even these much smaller organizing institutions and help perpetuate personality politics in Kuwait.[10] Hamad al-Jou'an confirmed this, also noting that after the crown prince had refused the demands of the Forty-five, the ministerial candidates did not withdraw their names.[11] In the end, the rulers refused to appoint half the cabinet from the parliament, but they did agree to hold the cabinet to fifteen members and thereby limit the relative weight of the "government vote." This was a significant concession to opposition forces.[12]

Newspaper articles predicted that as many as eight of the new ministers would be from the parliament, and other predictions were offered regarding the portfolio each would hold. Ahmad al-Rub'i (I = Independent), a member of the ten-man Group of Forty-five delegation and also on the list as a potential minister, was reported as being considered for the Information portfolio; Jasim al-'Aoun, an ICM delegate with IPA backing, was touted as the next minister of either Oil or Housing. The incumbent oil minister, Hmoud 'Abdullah al-Ruqbah, also was seen as a strong contender for the oil portfolio, and there was a great deal of speculation regarding which ruling family members would get cabinet positions and which one each might hold.

The "slate" supported by the Group of Forty-five is reported in table 7.1. It includes Islamists as well as secularists, reflecting an effort to balance the interests of the major factions among the opposition. 'Ali al-Baghli is a Shi'a (though he ran as an independent). Two others were from the outlying areas and one of them, 'Abdullah al-Hajri, had won a tribal primary and been endorsed by the ICM. Of the two experienced parliamentarians, only one, Mishairy al-'Anjari (85P), had had prior cabinet experience. All were new men and ambitious, and their backers expected great things of them.

TABLE 7.1   Cabinet Formation, October 1992

Group of 45 Delegates and Delegate-Nominees	Touted For	Post Received
Ahmad al-Sa'doun (85P)[a]	—	—
Ahmad al-Rub'i (85P)[b]	Information	Education
Ahmad al-Khatib (KDF)	—	—
Jasim al-'Aoun (IPA)[b]	Justice or 'Awqaf	Social Affairs and Labor
Khaled al-'Adwa		
(T = Tribal primary/ICM/IPA)	—	—
'Abd al-Mohsin al-Mud'ej (IPA)	—	—
'Ali al-Baghli[b]	Transportation	Oil
Ghanim al-Jamhour al-Mutairi	—	—
Mubarak al-Duwailah (ICM/IPA)	Oil or Housing	—
Mohammad Sharar	—	—

Nondelegate Nominees from Parliament		
Ismail al-Shati (ICM)	Oil or Housing	—
'Abdullah al-Hajri (ICM)[b]	Education	Commerce and Industry
Mishairy al-'Anjari (85P)	Commerce	Justice

Non-Nominees from Parliament		
Jam'an Faleh al-'Azemy (ICM/T)[b]	—	'Awqaf

Nonparliamentarians		
Sabah al-Ahmad al-Jabir[c]	—	Foreign Affairs
Dhari al-Othman[d]	—	Cabinet Affairs
Ahmad al-Hmoud al-Jabir	—	Interior
Ahmad Mohammad Saleh al-'Adsani	—	Electricity and Water
Habib Jowhar Hayat	—	Communications
Sa'ud Nasir al-Sabah[b]	—	Information
'Abd al-Wahhab al-Fouzan	—	Health
'Ali Sabah al-Salim	—	Defense
Nasir al-Roudhan	—	Finance and Planning

[a] = Speaker of the National Assembly
[b] = First-time minister
[c] = First deputy prime minister
[d] = Second deputy prime minister
(group affiliation)/(group endorsement)

Source: *Arab Times*, various issues.

The rulers picked and chose from this list, destabilizing the balance of the slate endorsed by the Group of Forty-five in several ways. 'Ali al-Baghli and the IPA's Jasim al-'Aoun received portfolios, but neither of the ICM hopefuls, Mubarak al-Duwailah and Isma'il al-Shati, was picked for a ministry. The lack of Sunni Islamist opposition representation in the cabinet reduced opposition cohesion, a situation aggravated by the distribution of portfolios. Ahmad al-Rub'i was chosen to head Education. This was taken very badly by supporters of Mubarak al-Duwailah (ICM), whose star as the top challenger of Ahmad al-Sa'doun (85P) for the speakership had begun to dim.[13] Education is a critical political arena for Kuwaiti Islamists. They controlled the student union at Kuwait University and, in the previous parliament, had succeeded in blocking what they said were anti-Islamic policies advanced by another professor-minister, Hasan 'Ali al-Ebraheem, who had held this portfolio before the 1985 parliament was dissolved.[14] Finally, an ICM parliamentarian not endorsed by the Forty-five, Jam'an Faleh al-'Azemi, was given the Ministry of 'Awqaf and Islamic Affairs. His appointment was a subtle jab at the Sunni Islamist opposition and also undermined the emerging role of the Group of Forty-five as a forum where parliamentary ministers could work out common positions. As a result of these maneuvers, headlines proclaiming the parliament's victory in gaining six seats in the cabinet, although technically correct, were misleading; meanwhile, the authority of parliament was diminished by a distribution of portfolios different from what prospective ministers and their supporters had hoped for. To professor Ahmad al-Rub'i, Education was a wasps' nest. Despite the authority conferred by professional expertise, Ahmad's secularist positions were resisted from the outset by powerful Islamists in the upper echelons of Education's bureaucracy. These conflicts soon spilled over into the parliament. There, battles over Islamist proposals, such as a bill to permit female medical students to wear veils during clinical and laboratory work, and an education bill that included a provision to end gender-integration in the university, widened the division in the opposition between secularists and Islamists and contributed to the rapid erosion of the initial commitment of members on both sides to work together.

A slightly different but similarly unhappy situation greeted 'Ali al-Baghli at the Oil Ministry. Oil is another wasps' nest, notoriously corrupt and a key channel directing financial rewards to the high rollers in and out of the ruling family who form the backbone of the regime's support. The ministry's rejection of accountability and its resistance to external controls had become legendary during the long reign of 'Ali al-Khalifa as oil minister. Oil would have been a challenge to any of the men seeking it and presented formidable obstacles to the man it eventually was handed to. The natural allies of the new oil minister were the technocrats at KPC, equally hostile to corruption in the ministry and very anxious to halt the policy drift that had characterized the hydrocarbon sector since liberation. However, 'Ali al-Baghli was associated with that segment of the opposition most hostile to KPC. In chapter 5, I noted that KPC technocrats were equally hostile to the opposition, a result of the rulers' manipulations during the occupation and the early days of the liberation. Many of the oil technocrats I interviewed in 1992 were at first cautiously optimistic about the new minister. However, his words and actions—for example, he did not begin his tenure by visiting affiliate managers or inviting them to see him at his office, a disregard of their expertise, authority, and interests that they noted and resented—reinforced the negative impressions of the opposition they had acquired during the tense days of 1990 and 1991. This mutual ill will prevented the formation of a coalition that might have been useful to both sides.[15]

While the parliamentary ministers struggled to get a grip on their new responsibilities, the parliament as a whole struggled to put itself in order and cope with the enthusiasm of individual members eager to follow through on the issues that had been prominent in their campaigns. Judicial reform had many supporters in the parliament and the population, though Islamists were conspicuous by their absence among them. Veteran legislators Mishairy al-'Anjari and Hamad al-Jou'an each submitted proposals to make the judiciary an independent branch of government rather than part of the Ministry of Justice, a course of action that had engendered fierce government opposition when it was proposed during the 1985 parliament.[16] Other initiatives provided clearer evidence of ideological and policy differences among parliamentary factions. Even before the new parliament convened, Mufrej al-Mutairy (IPA), from District 19 in the outlying area, called for amending article 2 of the constitution to make Shari'a "the source of legislation."[17] Soon the parliament was full of proposals, but few attracted the broad support that could have transformed them into laws.

Parliamentary Institutions

The outcome of elections for speaker and members of parliamentary committees is emblematic of the impact of intraparliamentary factionalism on the effectiveness of the Kuwaiti legislature. The speaker is elected by the body as a whole. Candidates for the speakership may run on the basis of an agenda setting out their legislative priorities,[18] but their peers vote for them because of their personalities, a desire to honor them for past achievements, or because they share an ideological outlook or a cultural base.

Of the three most prominent candidates for speaker in 1992, Jasim al-Saqr (CB) was the least enthusiastic about running. He had already enjoyed a long and illustrious career that had included a policy-making position in the oil sector, election to two previous parliaments, and work in his family's private-sector enterprises.[19] Jasim would take the job if it was offered but was reluctant to compete for it. He withdrew from the speaker's race shortly after the election when he realized that he did not have the support of members from the outlying areas. Such support was critical if he were to win over Ahmad al-Sa'doun, the favorite of most urban-based opposition groups.

Mubarak al-Duwailah was keen to become speaker and ran as the candidate of the outlying areas. Mubarak had previous political experience as a member of the 1985 parliament. He ran a strong race in 1992, coming in first by a very wide margin over the second-place winner in his district. Mubarak's supporters emphasized his having avoided confrontations with the government, stressing this quality as a guarantee that the 1992 parliament would be accommodating if he were elected.[20] Mubarak's campaign for the speakership was viewed by some as an embarrassment to the ICM, formally part of the opposition which nominally was united in support of Ahmad al-Sa'doun.[21] However, as Hamad al-Jou'an points out, the ICM had its own agenda, part of which was to create a separate constituency for itself by playing up the division between *hadhar* and *badu*.[22] This was the crux of Mubarak's campaign strategy; together with his ICM affiliation, it indicated that his election would exacerbate already troublesome tensions within the parliament. Observers in and out of the assembly expected that Mubarak would use the speakership to push the ICM's Islamist agenda.

The man who was elected speaker, Ahmad al-Sa'doun, was backed by most opposition members. Although he has programmatic and issue preferences, Ahmad's primary loyalty—perhaps obsession is not too strong a word—is to the parliament and its role as *the* democratic institution of Kuwait. From a long interview with him in February 1990, and interviews before and since with his associates, a portrait emerges of Ahmad al-Sa'doun as the quintessential constitutionalist. His uncompromising stand against the amir's July 1986 violation of Kuwait's political pact included using his position as speaker of the 1985 parliament to keep the large remnant represented by the Group of Twenty-six together. Ahmad also led the Group of Forty-five, which coordinated the pro-democracy movement and took its battle for political liberalization into the streets of Kuwait. Ahmad's leadership throughout this time was grounded on his strong advocacy for the return of constitutional government in Kuwait, including basic civil rights guarantees and the resumption of parliamentary life.

Ahmad al-Sa'doun's election sent a very different signal from the one that would have resulted from the election of Mubarak al-Duwailah. No one expected Ahmad to be accommodating to the regime, least of all the appointed representatives among the cabinet whose candidate for speaker was 'Abd al-'Aziz al-'Adsani (I), the former head of the Kuwait municipality. Forty-six of the fifty-nine votes cast were for Ahmad al-Sa'doun, who received the gavel from the hand of the temporary speaker and his nominal rival, Jasim al-Saqr.[23] However, this apparent victory for the opposition also was deceptive. Most of the opposition had in fact united behind Ahmad al-Sa'doun, but elections for other assembly positions highlighted the Islamist-secularist split that cut across so many other cleavages in the parliament. Saleh al-Fadhala, a member of the 1985 parliament who was endorsed in 1992 by both the ICM and the IPA, was reelected deputy speaker. To every formal post other than speaker, including membership on parliamentary committees, all those elected were Islamists or sympathetic to Islamist positions with the sole exception of Hamad al-Jou'an.[24] The dominance of the Islamists in the 1992 parliament guaranteed the prominence of religion in National Assembly politics.

The National Agenda

The cleavages separating various parliamentary factions interfered with the ability of the National Assembly to pass needed legislation, and none was more destructive of parliamentary cohesion than the antagonism between secularists and Islamists. The government became progressively dismayed at rising hostility among members and the consequent paralysis of policy-making on a wide spectrum of issues. This was especially serious where broadly based coalitions were needed to support initiatives requiring economic sacrifices from key constituency groups, sacrifices urged by the regime to compensate for the heavy expenses arising from occupation, liberation, and reconstruction. Even addressing such issues was difficult because neither the government nor the opposition spoke with one voice on any of them.

One example is imported labor. As I noted in the previous chapter, a desire to minimize imported labor was articulated by many candidates during the 1992 election campaign. However, the postcampaign reality brought the opposite, a rapid increase in labor imports. This is because labor is a no-win issue for both the government and the opposition. Virtually every Kuwaiti benefits from foreign unskilled labor, and curtailing labor imports requires making distinctions among workers and employers. For example, any substantial reduction in foreign labor by necessity implies the employment of more domestic labor, a shift known locally as "Kuwaitization." However simple and sensible this might sound as a process, however, Kuwaitization as an outcome is not unproblematic. Kuwaitization of household help would effect an immediate drop in living standards and leisure time because Kuwaitis would have to do all their own housework, childcare, driving, gardening, and the myriad other jobs that in most families are done by foreign labor.

Work outside the household is difficult to Kuwaitize for other reasons. Under article 41 of the constitution, "Every Kuwaiti has the right to work and to choose the type of his work. . . . The State shall endeavor to make [work] available to citizens and to make its terms equitable." In practice, this translates into a system of wage differentials that favor Kuwaiti over foreign labor and confirms the role of the state as employer of last resort.[25] Worker discipline is another problem, one heightened by comparison to the excessive amount of control that Kuwaiti law permits employers to exercise over foreign workers.[26] Kuwaiti nationals are protected legally from what would be violations of their civil rights, and the concentration of Kuwaiti workers in public-sector jobs reflects additional protections. Supervisors are reluctant to discipline Kuwaiti workers in an environment suffused by *wasta*, or political influence. Workers denied promotions they believed themselves ready for, and some fired from government jobs for what their supervisors say was extreme provocation, have been successful in appealing to a cabinet minister or even the crown prince for intervention on their behalf. In one of the many cases I heard about during my fieldwork studying the Kuwait Petroleum Corporation, the supervisor who had dismissed a problem worker was himself disciplined for this action after the worker was reinstated on order of the crown prince.

Kuwaiti elites are equally, though differently, implicated in the nation's labor problem. "Visa merchants," individuals with rights to import contract labor, often are political allies of the government. In 1990, I interviewed members of one merchant family who said that identification with the opposition constrained their ability to obtain foreign workers, while merchant allies of the regime could import far more labor than they needed for their own operations. Foreign workers are lucrative not only because the wage differential makes them cheaper to employ but also, for the visa merchant, because foreign labor is a commodity he can sell to others. Trade in contract labor is profitable because of the differential between domestic and foreign wages—buying someone else's labor contracts is still cheaper than employing Kuwaitis.

The traffic in foreign labor in Kuwait is highly political. It is part of the same system of payoffs that gives Kuwaitis economic privileges in the form of agency contracts, monopolies, and jobs as "service MPs," candidates who, once elected, become professional conduits for *wasta*. Dealing with the "labor problem" in Kuwait would mean dealing seriously not only with citizen education, training, salary schedules, and worker discipline, all implicated in the foundation of regime support among Kuwaiti workers and their families, but also the system of favors underpinning elite support for the regime. This is one reason why it was easier for the government and a majority of the parliament to fold the labor issue into education policy, as I discuss below.

Structural adjustment is similarly treacherous to effect. In everyday terms, structural adjustment involves reducing or ending subsidies, pruning redundant workers from state and private payrolls, and privatizing state-owned enterprises, including services such as utilities, education, and health care that are provided free or at subsidized prices, to increase the international competitiveness of one's economy. Achieving structural adjustment in Kuwait conflicts with building support for the regime. An example can be found in the large increase in salaries and benefits for Kuwaiti government employees instituted following liberation, a situation that the government hoped to recoup by instituting broadly based taxes and user fees.

Subsidized food prices, state employment, and a high level of social services are only a part of the welfare package offered to Kuwaitis by the state. The other part involves subsidies going almost entirely to wealthy Kuwaitis. Such wealth transfer schemes go back to the Land Acquisition Program, which transferred huge sums from the state to ruling family members and merchants. Today these schemes include agency commissions, monopoly privileges, and the permission to import labor mentioned earlier, along with government bailouts of failed corporations, collapsed stock markets, and bad debts. Islamists in particular are strong opponents of structural adjustment policies that concentrate on low- and middle-income Kuwaitis, conflating religious and class conflicts in government and parliament. Yet an across-the-board strategy would be difficult from the government's point of view because it would mobilize multiple constituencies against what each would interpret as its social contract with the regime. In consequence, while a few new user fees were approved and others already on the books were collected more systematically, devising an acceptable fiscal policy including taxes on Kuwaitis and limits on government bailouts proved to be an impossible task for the 1992 parliament.

A third complex of contentious issues centers on investment. Kuwait's position as a rentier state is based both on the state's reliance on oil income and, from the mid-1980s until liberation, on an even greater reliance on returns to portfolio investment in Western markets.[27] State oil income itself has become diversified as Kuwait acquired holdings in exploration, production, processing, and marketing overseas. In consequence of its multinational vertical integration, KPC now can claim a significant share of the value added to its oil production by processing and marketing. Critics are concerned that oil investment other than in Kuwait itself raises national dependence on this single industry to dangerous levels. Yet there is no consensus on investment outside of oil. Some want the state to invest in non-oil domestic industries; others prefer that the state reduce its presence in all Kuwaiti industries and leave more opportunities for the private sector. In 1993 the World Bank completed a study of the Kuwaiti economy that included a privatization strategy which recommended extensive divestiture of oil industry investments, including the state's monopoly of the domestic industry.[28] However, the absence of consensus in the parliament or in the government on an investment strategy made it impossible for either one to propose a coherent strategy for privatization. Instead, privatization on a limited scale has been the province of the Kuwait Investment Authority (KIA).[29] KIA is a public authority in the Ministry of Finance which is charged with managing the state's domestic and foreign investments. The state's domestic equity holdings were nonexistent until the 1950s, when oil income began flowing into the country and the government started investing in economic development projects. For example, KNPC (Kuwait National Petroleum Company), along with several other companies that presently are subsidiaries of KPC, started out as a joint venture among the state and private-sector investors. The state acquired equity in other Kuwaiti companies as the result of a drop in the stock market in 1976, and it bought even more shares in even more companies following the 1982 collapse of the illegal Suq al-Manakh. These purchases were made at above-market prices, both to support stock prices and to indemnify investors who wanted to get out with at least some of their capital intact.[30] The state also bought private-sector holdings in the oil industry when it consolidated the properties it had nationalized from foreign companies under KPC. While some of these purchases were voluntary—the Kuwait Oil Tanker Company (KOTC) and the Petrochemical Industries Company (PIC) had been major money-losers prior to the buyout of private-sector holdings at very favorable prices—others were not. KNPC investors still refer to the government's assumption of their holdings as the "nationalization" of the company.[31]

Shortly before the Iraqi invasion, KIA began selling small lots of shares from its non-oil holdings and continued this practice after liberation. The aim of these small transactions was to "help put these companies back on track so they could more efficiently resume their operations."[32] In 1994, perhaps because there had been no action on the World Bank's recommendations, KIA stepped up its asset sales, calling its activities "privatization." KIA's stated aims included providing opportunities for small investors to acquire holdings in "large, well-managed and financially sound companies." However, in practice, it transferred shares through two kinds of open market auctions rather than through vouchers or some other program aimed at small investors.[33] Stimulated by the sale of large numbers of shares in going concerns, the Kuwait Stock Exchange became the most active stock market in the Middle East. KIA's asset sales also fostered repatriation of private capital.[34] The initial success of KIA's program, reflected in good prices for assets and a booming stock market, reduced pressure on the government and parliament to take a comprehensive approach to investment and privatization. However, it also left the government open to criticism on equity grounds, particularly after the boom faltered and stock values plummeted, events that also prompted new demands for yet another investor bailout.

Avoidance of difficult issues by the 1992 parliament was the fault both of the government and the parliament. The government failed to lead on policy and instead spent its political capital on warfare against the parliament as an institution. Unfortunately, the opposition was neither large nor cohesive enough to offer alternative leadership. Some of the most articulate members of the opposition were stifled by their positions in the cabinet. But the most serious problem for the opposition came from ideological warfare between Islamists and secularists, which blocked formation of interest-based coalitions strong enough to take a systematic approach to the economy and a balanced view of pressing social problems such as the shocking postliberation increase in violent crime. The parliament's repeated failures to accomplish badly needed reforms, together with disgust at the behavior of a few individual members (see below), eventually turned the Kuwaiti people against the 1992 parliament.

Islamist Politics in the 1992 Parliament

Some theories explaining the rise of fundamentalist movements associate these movements with modernism. Explanations differ according to whether Islamism is seen as part of the modernizing wave—that is, as an outsiders' attack on traditional power monopolies in society[35]—or as a reaction to that wave— indicating that activists see modernization as having gone too far.[36] A somewhat different construction of fundamentalist Islam casts it as a recurrent feature of Muslim societies experiencing economic crises, and thus a phenomenon whose origins predate the modern period. Fatima Mernissi, for example, argues that Islamism is independent of modernity, appropriating whatever is useful and condemning whatever seems threatening to its leaders and their agendas. Now, as in the past, she says, Islamic fundamentalism is a vehicle for justifying male gender interests in pushing otherwise legitimate female competitors out of public life.[37]

Fundamentalist movements have unique advantages as political forces. One is their capacity to mobilize large numbers of followers from their bases in religious institutions. Also, they claim divine legitimacy to challenge the state and its representatives by whatever means they choose, including violence. Such challenges directly contradict constitutionalism, the principle that all citizens are entitled to equal treatment and protection. They also undermine the legitimacy of the nation-state which claims both supreme authority and a monopoly over the use of violence on its territory. Consequently, fundamentalist movements seem revolutionary, and their populist potential alarms not only governments but also secularists committed in principle to the rule of law. Fearing a religious war in an arena where they feel themselves vastly outnumbered, secularists also depend on the law to ensure their corporal and material survival.

Gender issues are a major axis of conflict between secularists and fundamentalists of all kinds.[38] High on most fundamentalist social agendas is to achieve an authoritatively enforced system of gender relations that subordinates women to men. For Muslim fundamentalists, whose ideologies also are influenced by a history of manipulation of gender relations by colonial administrators, politics and religion converge on what Leila Ahmed calls "the discourse of the veil" and Deniz Kandiyoti "the politics of authenticity."[39] Veiling in this context is more than a costume denoting religious propriety. It is a symbolic position marking preferences on an entire range of policies drawing lines between women and men and also between the community of the faithful and those it sees as its opponents.

Despite the unanimity of Muslim fundamentalists with respect to the inferiority of women, the actual status of women in individual Islamist organizations varies such that the position of women is a bellwether of the political thrust of particular Islamist social movements and groups. As I noted earlier, both Ellis Goldberg and Olivier Roy point to the integration of women in Islamist movements as characteristic of what Roy calls "political Islam."[40] Political Islam challenges the legitimacy of traditional Muslim political and religious elites who monopolize power and authority by virtue of lineage, tradition, and learning. Arguing on the basis of Islamic tenets such as that the individual is the sole judge of whether she or he is a Muslim, and is responsible before God but not before men for what she or he does and believes, political Islamists are actively revolutionary, offering themselves and their ideas as alternatives to religious and secular leaders whose ideas and actions they condemn.

Goldberg sees a resemblance between some types of Islamist and Christian fundamentalism. Drawing on Michael Waltzer's analysis of Puritanism, Goldberg argues that Puritanism and political Islam both are reactions against rising state authoritarianism. He shows convincingly that political Islamists, like the Puritans before them, are hostile to all but the narrowest conception of the private sphere. They prefer a system of intellectual and emotional support amounting to collective surveillance of virtually every aspect of life likely to give rise to individualism and independent thought, both abhorred as violations of God's will and thus as dangers to the soul.[41] Yet, at the same time, unlike activists Roy calls "neofundamentalists," political Islamists argue that a woman is more than a toy for a man to enjoy in the privacy of the harem. Rather, she is a partner (albeit a junior one) in a joint enterprise dedicated to achieving God's will on earth and an afterlife in heaven. For political Islamists, women's roles can include political and economic labor outside the home (although from inside gender-segregated spaces and enveloping costumes that protect vulnerable men from temptation by female charms). In contrast, neofundamentalist claims to political authority inhere almost entirely in religious idioms focused on female subordination. Roy regards only political Islamists as modern but notes that all Islamists unite on the issue of coeducation.

> It is true [for both types of Islamism] that the position of women is still secondary: Islamists always speak of the weakness of women as inherent in their nature ("her sensibility is greater than her reasoning power; she is physically weaker"); similarly, they insist that family and motherhood are the natural spheres of women. But the true taboo is that of coeducation (*ikhtilat*). Remember that in Iran women vote and drive cars, which would be unthinkable in traditionalist fundamentalism of the Saudi variety. Those most radical in their politics are often the least inegalitarian.[42]

The centrality of coeducation as an Islamist preoccupation (and one of the few points on which neofundamentalists and political Islamists can agree) explains some of the reasons why education policy is such a point of contention and the one most likely to bring Islamists of all stripes together into a single bloc. In Kuwait secondary schools and postsecondary institutions are primary venues for recruitment into the movement. Islamism claims the student body at Kuwait University as one of its strongest bases; Islamist discourse, whether conducted by adults or adolescents, is saturated with sex. Gender issues at the university, therefore, naturally attract the attention of Kuwaiti Islamist leaders. Unlike proposals to amend article 2 or extend political rights to women, questions of personal status in the setting of the university have the power to unite neofundamentalists and political Islamists, Sunni and Shi'i, in their common pursuits of political dominance over Kuwaiti secularists and new adherents to

Islamist movements. The university is a focal point of both concerns because it is an economic gatekeeper—university degrees are passports to higher-paying and higher-status jobs—and, even more, because the university is the place where large numbers of young Kuwaiti men first discover how poorly prepared most of them are to compete and win in a system that is not rigged in advance in their favor.

Gender politics in Kuwait is an arena where many contradictory trends initiated by modernization collide.[43] Haya al-Mughni argues that the merchant class uses gender in a long-range strategy for defending class interests: merchants mobilize "their" women to occupy positions in a partially gender-integrated economy that otherwise would go to new men. Meanwhile, from within the separate world of Kuwaiti women, these same elite women restrain the autonomy and upward mobility of the new women of the middle class.[44] When gender is a weapon in class competition, it is aimed by and at both women and men. However, in struggles for upward mobility where interclass rivalries are less relevant, gender becomes an axis of intraclass conflict because of the disjunction between cultural values and economic and social demands imposed or intensified by modernization.

Modernity requires self-discipline that rarely is found among the male children of Kuwait's new middle class. At the same time that traditional patterns of child-rearing place few demands and restraints on the behavior and performance of boys and male adolescents, they place many on girls and young women.[45] This translates into better work habits and superior academic performance by girls, a pattern that persists at the university where young women competing for admission to technical, high-status majors in medicine and engineering have an edge over young men if grades and performance are the primary criteria for selection and retention.[46] Interestingly, the academic achievements of young women are considered to have been unjustly earned, not only by the young men they leave in the dust but also by their own parents, professors, and peers. "Girls have to stay at home," said a father of a high-achieving daughter and a son who left the university because of bad grades. "What else can they do but study? It's not fair."[47]

Islamism finds ready adherents among the angry young men at Kuwait University and in Kuwait's secondary schools. They are present admirers of and future voters for Islamist politicians who appeal simultaneously to their religious idealism and their self-interest. The Islamist agenda in parliament attracts them with highly publicized initiatives whose effects would improve young men's chances of success at the university and eventually in the job market. Many are couched in terms of tradition and religion; they promise to redraw a system widely perceived as unfairly biased toward women to bring it back into conformity with what most Kuwaitis believe that God and nature intended it to be. Even though the family lives of several prominent Kuwaiti Islamists fall short of conforming to the picture of male supremacy they themselves advocate as the Muslim ideal, it is the image they project of female subordination and its translation into policies erecting barriers to women's academic and economic advancement that attract large numbers of young men to support Islamists politically.

The strength of Kuwaiti Islamists in parliament does not rely entirely on the admiration of the young or the popularity of Islamism among voters.[48] Islamists also get help from the regime. Electorally favored by the 1981 redistricting, Islamists in the 1992 parliament were assisted organizationally by a commission established to encourage the implementation of Islamic law in Kuwait. The commission was inaugurated in December 1991 in response to demands by the Islamist-dominated student council at Kuwait University to restrict women's access to classes.[49] The university is thereby implicated in both parts of the Islamist agenda in parliament: to amend article 2 of the constitution with results that are implicit rather than articulated, and to ensure that personal-status legislation continues to place explicit limits on women's social, economic, and political autonomy.

As in other Muslim countries where Islamists constitute a large segment of potential and actual opposition to ruling regimes, Kuwaiti rulers are widely believed to be supporting particular Islamists. Their chosen allies are most often identified by Kuwaiti observers as the Muslim Brothers (the Ikhwan). However, ruler support of neofundamentalist, generally tribal, independents seems to me to have been the more consistently pursued strategy in Kuwait, with support thrown to other Islamists when expedient. Among the assumptions supporting such a government-Islamist alliance is that tradition and religious prescriptions predispose Islamists to respect the ruling family's authority more than secularist opponents tend to do, implying that powerful Islamists are less dangerous to the regime than powerful secularists. A related assumption is that pan-Islamism is less dangerous to the regime—less revolutionary—than the pan-Arabism with which prominent Kuwaiti secularists sympathize.[50] Both assumptions might usefully be reconsidered in the light of a successful Islamist revolution in Iran, an Islamist counterrevolution in Afghanistan that toppled the secularist regime of Najibullah, and pan-Arab Iraq's invasion of Kuwait, which was applauded by movement Islamists such as non-Kuwaiti Ikhwan groups and Algeria's Islamist political party, the Islamic Salvation Front (FIS).

A different kind of assumption is that the large Shi'i minority provides enough of a check within the Islamist trend to prevent even a united Sunni segment from leading a successful popular movement against the regime. This assumption may have had some validity prior to the 1981 redistricting which cut Shi'i political representation in half; now it seems dubious. All those assumptions in turn depend on another one, which is that the government is clever enough to manipulate Islamist allies without weakening its position vis à vis Islamist rivals—Algeria's mistake and perhaps Egypt's as well; or without making such a hash of things that the entire opposition, Islamist and secularist, unites against it—as happened in Kuwait itself in 1986 and again in 1989–90. Thus, while I agree that the regime has done many things to favor Islamists in politics, I do not see its strategy as effective for ensuring the long-term survival of the Sabah as the rulers of Kuwait.

Islamist politics dominated the 1992 parliament. The first skirmish came in January 1993, when Islamists proposed a law to prevent the university from forbidding female medical students to wear veils during clinical and laboratory sessions. The university's policy on veiling, which permitted women to veil at all other times, had the support of the faculty and the new education minister, Ahmad al-Rub'i. The minister's disagreement with the demand of Islamist students that women be allowed to veil even when faculty believed it was potentially dangerous enraged parliamentary Islamists who spearheaded the introduction of the veiling bill over his opposition.[51] The proposed law had the backing of Islamist parliamentarians and the legislative committee to which it was referred.[52] Debate dragged on for weeks, embroiling the university administration, bureaucratic factions in the Education Ministry, the minister, and the cabinet in acrimonious wrangling. Meanwhile, other Islamist initiatives also were put forward, including several proposals for amending article 2 and one to create an Islamic television channel.

The secularists were ultimately successful in fending off the law on veiling at the university,[53] but this did not end Kuwait's culture war. Both at the university and in parliament, Islamists continued to demand policies that kept the battle for the allegiance of the young going strong. Their next attempt was a bill jointly sponsored by Shi'i and Sunni Islamists to end coeducation at the university. Introduced as part of a larger bill to build a new university campus, the entire measure sailed through committee. It was defeated in a tie vote because one of its supporters, Shari' al-'Ajmy (T = Tribally endorsed), failed to arrive in time to vote on the motion for final passage. Shari' promptly introduced a new gender-segregation bill, but assembly rules forbid reconsideration in the same legislative session of a bill that already has been voted down.[54]

Supporters of gender segregation insisted that the measure was widely supported throughout the country and had been defeated by government pressure and a smear campaign spearheaded by the press.[55] Government intervention also was charged as a reason why Islamists were ousted from a number of committee slots when the assembly reorganized for its second session in October 1994. But these setbacks failed to dampen Islamist enthusiasm for bills aimed at the university. In December 1995 another proposal to segregate the university was announced by Mubarak al-Duwailah, and a new idea was floated, to require female university students to wear some type of Islamically correct uniform.[56] These initiatives ensured that the university-Islamist controversy would come to the boiling point shortly before the 1996 parliamentary campaign.

The recurrent uproars pitting Islamists against secularists in the National Assembly took their toll in many ways. The ability of members to hammer out compromises on complex and difficult issues was gravely impaired by the lack of good faith across the Islamist-secularist divide. One example involved policies and procedures to resolve the bad debts crisis, one of the longest-running soap operas in Kuwaiti politics. A debt-resolution schedule was finally passed in 1993, but every repayment deadline since then has attracted vociferous opponents among the remaining debtors, who continue to be able to find allies in the government or the parliament to offer deadline-extending amendments to get them off the hook.[57] Opposition Islamists such as Ahmad Baqr oppose these amendments on equity grounds but cannot mobilize a broadly based coalition able to stop them once and for all.

Institutional Conflicts in the 1992 Parliament

As the first assembly session entered its second year, playing politics with serious economic issues like the debt crisis and defense budgets spilled over into members' willingness to face one another in the assembly. On March 8, 1994, for example, the speaker was forced to cancel the week's session for lack of a quorum.[58] Public complaints about inaction on critical issues concentrated on the behavior of the National Assembly, while parliamentarians insisted that the real problem was the government's "passive strategy," designed to make the legislature look bad. In the spring of 1994, many Kuwaitis expressed hopes that the cabinet would be reshuffled, arguing that the existing cabinet was ineffective because it included too many elected members. The reshuffling took place on April 13, and three parliamentary ministers were dismissed. 'Ali al-Baghli was replaced at Oil by 'Abd al-Mohsin al-Mud'ej, an independent delegate from District 12. 'Abdullah al-Hajri, who had headed Commerce and Industry, and Jaman Faleh al-'Azemi, who had headed the 'Awqaf, were replaced by nonparliamentarians. Parliamentary representation on the cabinet thus was reduced from six to four.

Issues involving the integrity of parliament as an institution also played a part in the contentious politics of the 1992 National Assembly. Paling into insignificance amid brawls over religion, bad debts, corruption, defense, and whether, how, and when to privatize which state-owned industries, these were problems whose publicly visible manifestations looked like personality politics but actually were clashes over principles. I discuss two of them here, both complicated by their overlap with the Islamist agenda. One, the principle of parliamentary immunity, was trivialized by a pair of inconsistent votes in the assembly. The other, a dispute over the authority of the parliament as a governing institution, was the focal point of a struggle that came close to precipitating a crisis of the same order of magnitude as the parliamentary investigations of four cabinet ministers, which had triggered the suspension of the 1985 parliament.

The immunity issue turned on the alleged behavior of two members of parliament that threatened to bring each of them into court if their immunity were to be lifted. One case stemmed from the conflict over student veiling at Kuwait University. It began with a 1993 public speech by Khaled al-ʿAdwa (T) that allegedly slandered four university professors for their opposition to the Islamist position on the veiling law. Khaled accused all four of being "secularists and infidels," and referred to the one woman among them, Farida al-ʿAwadhi, in sexually explicit derogatory terms. The speech was distributed on cassette and provoked the four professors to file a lawsuit charging Khaled with defamation and slander. His friends prevailed upon Khaled to apologize, which he did, finally, in a February 22, 1994, speech in the National Assembly. However, the professors, with the support of their colleagues, refused to accept the apology and vowed to continue their lawsuit. The attorney general then requested that the National Assembly lift parliamentary immunity so that Khaled al-ʿAdwa could be questioned. If sufficient cause were found, he would be required to meet his accusers in court. However, the request was rejected by the full assembly on the recommendation of the Islamist-dominated Legal and Legislative Affairs committee, which opposed it on the grounds that the suit was a "conspiracy" to punish Khaled for his prominence among the parliamentary advocates of the proposed law on veiling.[59]

In the second case, assault charges against another parliamentarian, Ahmad al-Shriyan (85P), for resisting arrest for alleged sexual improprieties, brought calls for the suspension of parliamentary immunity not only from the public but also from the accused.[60] Rumors and suggestive stories, along with large color photographs of Ahmad's automobile, were plastered all over the newspapers for weeks. Ahmad al-Shriyan was a tribal representative from New Jahraʾ, a member of the Group of Twenty-six, and an organizer of the pro-democracy

Monday diwaniyyas in 1989–90. The meeting called at his home in Jahra' was attacked by the police and Ahmad himself was arrested (see chapter 4). Given this history, there was widespread speculation when the scandal broke that the charges against Ahmad had been manufactured to discredit him among his predominantly tribal constituents. The request to suspend parliamentary immunity, which Ahmad supported to enable him to clear his name, was reviewed and voted on only a week before the request to lift the immunity of Khaled al-'Adwa. Ahmad al-Shriyan's request was approved by the Legal and Legislative Affairs committee. The full assembly passed it one week following the denial by both of these bodies of the same request in Khaled al-'Adwa's case.

The results of the two votes diminished further the already-damaged reputation of the parliament as a responsible body. A number of Kuwaitis who talked about these votes with me in March 1994 pointed to the Khaled al-'Adwa vote as evidence of parliamentary bad faith and irresponsibility. Khaled's taped performance had circulated widely and no one doubted that he had said what he had been accused of saying. The vote against suspending his parliamentary immunity was seen as an example of parliament closing ranks to protect a member from having to vindicate truthful accusers. Kuwaitis also drew unfortunate conclusions from the pair of cases: a member of parliament who probably was innocent of charges made against him would request that his immunity be lifted, while one who probably was guilty would hide behind his immunity. The principle of parliamentary immunity as a civil liberty and a mechanism for protecting the separation of powers was lost in the fortuitous juxtaposition of these two votes on highly publicized scandals. Like invoking the Fifth Amendment has become in the United States, recourse to parliamentary immunity in Kuwait now is assumed by the politically naive to be tantamount to an admission of wrongdoing.

The second controversy was even more dangerous to parliament as an institution. Its outline came into focus during the lawsuit brought against five men accused of embezzling an estimated $200 million from the Kuwait Oil Tanker Company, one of the Kuwait-based affiliates of KPC. The Kuwaitis accused were KOTC's former managing director, 'Abd al-Fattah al-Badr, who fled the country to avoid prosecution, and two defendants who remained within the jurisdiction of the court. One, Hasan Qabazard, KOTC's former deputy managing director for financial affairs, repaid about $7 million on the assumption that this would keep him from going to jail. Instead, he was arrested and jailed until the trial began a year later, on January 18, 1994.[61] The other defendant, former oil minister Shaikh 'Ali al-Khalifa al-Sabah, denied all charges and remained free throughout.[62] Parliament's involvement in the KOTC scandal turned on the legality of trying the former minister in the regular criminal court.

In 1990, during the parliamentary suspension, the government authorized a law mandating special proceedings for trying cabinet ministers accused of crimes committed in connection with their government service. This measure was one of some five hundred amiri decrees handed down during the suspension. As such, it was required under article 71 of the constitution to be reviewed and approved by the National Assembly in order to remain in effect after parliament was restored. On January 11, 1994, one week before the start of the KOTC trial, the assembly struck down the Ministers' Trial Law by a vote of thirty-nine against it, with thirteen members abstaining. All who abstained were cabinet ministers and included the six parliamentarians then in the cabinet who refused a direct appeal by the speaker to vote against the decree.

An official opinion from the minister of justice, Mishairy al-'Anjari, affirmed that the assembly vote had nullified the 1986 amiri decree. However, 'Ali al-Khalifa's lawyers insisted that it was the nullification that was invalid, organizing their defense around the alleged illegality of the trial court.[63] The attorneys asserted that the trial court was incompetent to decide an issue of such complexity, and that the charges against the former minister were politically motivated rather than supported by facts. The defense also argued on procedural grounds, insisting that in order for the decree to be repealed properly, another law would have to be passed in its place.[64] But when a replacement Ministers' Trial Law was passed in September 1995,[65] 'Ali al-Khalifa's lawyers shifted their position. They argued that the new law was unconstitutional and that the "previous" Ministers' Trial Law, the one that had been nullified in the parliament, was still effective because the new law did not include explicit wording stating that the old one had been abrogated.[66] The nullified law had required that suits against a minister be initiated by the amir at the request of the cabinet, an effective procedure for squelching any proceeding that might prove embarrassing to the regime. The assembly-passed substitute leaves the initial decision to bring charges against a minister up to the public prosecutor, who presents evidence before a special committee which makes the final decision regarding whether to prosecute.[67]

A public trial of 'Ali al-Khalifa promised to embarrass the ruling family profoundly. 'Ali al-Khalifa was said to have threatened to name names if he were convicted—presumably the names of other family members also engaged in siphoning money out of the state treasury.[68] The imminent prospect of an even wider financial scandal implicating even more members of the ruling family prompted the amir to become involved. Rather than dealing with the KOTC case directly, however, the amir framed his attack on the National Assembly by appealing the rejection of another suspension decree, a 1986 grant of authority to the government to halt the publication of newspapers.[69] This decree, a revival of one passed during the 1976–1981 suspension and later nullified by the 1981 parliament, was part of the press censorship apparatus imposed following the 1986 suspensions.[70]

The nature of the amir's appeal set the stage for a constitutional crisis. Rather than requesting a ruling specifically on the press censorship nullification, the amir asked the Constitutional Court for an interpretation of article 71 regarding the right of the assembly to repeal any decree adopted during a suspension.[71] The scope of his appeal violated a prior agreement between the amir and the parliament whereby the parliament had agreed to abide by the ruling of the Constitutional Court on any government appeal of a specific law which it might invalidate.[72] In February 1995 the Constitutional Court ruled that assembly approval was not necessary to keep suspension-passed decrees in force. Then the amir forced a showdown on article 71 by asserting his authority under the already-nullified 1986 press law to suspend a local newspaper (see below).

Meanwhile, the Islamist connection came into play with yet another attack on the education minister. At the end of February 1995, following his interpellation on the floor of the assembly, parliamentary Islamists succeeded in getting a majority to support placing a motion of no-confidence against Ahmad al-Rub'i on the agenda. The motion charged the minister with changing textbooks to reduce the Islamic content of the public school curriculum. A second crisis was provoked when the Islamists in the parliament split. Jasim al-'Aoun (IPA), who had been moved during the 1994 cabinet reshuffle to the Ministry of Electricity and Water, said that a second interpellation of the education minister would damage national unity. Polarization increased further in response to rumors that the crown prince, whose wife heads both an Islamist women's organization and an umbrella organization which advertises itself as the collective voice of Kuwaiti women, would institute his own investigation of the textbooks at issue.[73]

When a parliamentary vote is taken on whether a minister should be censured, no minister, elected or appointed, is permitted to vote. The motion passes only if a majority of nonministerial parliamentarians votes for it, and the Islamists were unable to mobilize a large enough number against Ahmad al-Rub'i. Four parliamentarians who had earlier declared their intention to vote against him abstained at the last minute, reportedly as the result of intense pressure from the government.[74]

Shortly after the failure of the motion of censure, the regime's assault on article 71 escalated with the five-day suspension of the Kuwaiti daily, al-Anba', reportedly for printing interviews with opposition members advocating the separation of the crown princeship from the speakership. After a pause during which the crown prince threatened in public to resign with his cabinet while the speaker engaged in behind-the-scenes efforts to calm the members down, a full-throated outcry arose from a dozen opposition members. These secularist critics, led by Hamad al-Jou'an, found themselves in a difficult dilemma. On the one hand, the crown prince's intervention had just turned back the Islamists' assault on one of their number; on the other, the amir's assault on the parliament threatened to destroy completely the already-tenuous rule of law in Kuwait.

Hamad al-Jou'an led the fight on the floor on behalf of article 71 from his wheelchair, charging that the government was attacking the fundamental idea of democracy in Kuwait and, in effect, was "turning the constitution into Kleenex paper."[75] Before and during the debate, the government's opponents in the assembly linked the regime's press-suspension challenge to article 71 to the controversy over the trial of 'Ali al-Khalifa.[76] During the debate on the propriety of the amir's request that the meaning of article 71 be addressed by the Constitutional Court, the entire cabinet, including the four parliamentary ministers,[77] supported the amir's request unanimously. Hamad al-Jou'an appealed by name to each of the three parliamentary ministers formally associated with the opposition, Ahmad al-Rub'i, Mishairy al-'Anjari, and Jasim al-'Aoun, asking them to tell the Kuwaiti people whether they had turned their backs on the pro-democracy movement.[78] But so recently reminded of the government's power either to remove them from office or save them from ouster by their opponents in the parliament and, regardless of which, to be able to mobilize a majority on almost any issue whether they defected or not, the parliamentary ministers held firm against his entreaties. However, the magnitude of the threat to parliament as an institution did mute conflicts among the other members. Charging the elected ministers with participating in a "coup against the constitution," the opposition mobilized a thirty-two-vote majority in favor of asking the Constitutional Court to rule on the constitutionality of the amir's request to interpret article 71.[79]

The constitutional impasse thus created was sidestepped by a government announcement a month later that the amir would withdraw his request for a ruling on article 71 from the Constitutional Court.[80] The struggle would not be over, however, until the main event, the issue of 'Ali al-Khalifa's trial, could be resolved. The passage of the new Ministers' Trial Law in September 1995 increased the pressure on the ruling family to come up with a solution before the by-then threadbare arguments of 'Ali al-Khalifa's lawyers were completely reduced to tatters. An effort was made in October to settle the case out of court by offering $55 million to the KOTC board in return for dropping the charges. The newspaper report about the deal carefully avoided naming the defendants in whose name the offer had been made, but it also noted separate offers made on behalf of the Jordanian and the British defendants, leaving readers to surmise that it had been made on behalf of one or more of the Kuwaitis.[81] On October 17, 1995, another session of the trial was held, but despite attorney Salman al-Du'aij's colorful appeal that the court treat 'Ali al-Khalifa as generously as O. J. Simpson had been treated, the court stood firm in its claim that it had proper jurisdiction to try the case.[82]

The court changed its mind shortly afterward. In November a publication of Al-Shall Economic Group reported that the court had agreed to the separation of 'Ali al-Khalifa's case from the other four and sent it to the new Ministers' Court provided for under the September 1995 law. As part of the deal, twelve of the thirteen charges pending against 'Ali al-Khalifa were dropped. "The former minister has been referred to the special court to face one charge and that is allowing the other four defendants [to carry out] transactions which are believed to have enabled them to make $200 million in illegal profits."[83] In June 1996 the trial court found 'Abd al-Fattah al-Badr and Hasan Qabazard guilty as charged. Their respective punishments were thirty-five and forty years in prison, and fines of $49.2 million and $65.7 million.[84] But by that time, Hasan Qabazard, like 'Abd al-Fattah al-Badr, had slipped out of the country, beyond any Kuwaiti court's jurisdiction.[85]

Meanwhile, wrangling continued over the legality of trying 'Ali al-Khalifa in a court other than the one outlined in the nullified Ministers' Trial Law. This dispute moved closer to resolution when the Constitutional Court ruled on December 23, 1996, that the regular court was competent to try the case against 'Ali al-Khalifa but that the case should be moved to the new Ministers' Court anyway.[86] The new Ministers' Court handed down its first decision on the matter in April 1997. It rejected the case as it had been presented for failure to conform to procedural requirements of the law in effect at the time of the initiation of the case—the old Ministers' Trial Law—an outcome that at first had 'Ali al-Khalifa's supporters jubilant. But in a subsequent clarification of its decision, the court noted that the new law had superseded the old one.[87] I shall return to this contentious issue in chapter 8.

The Pathology of Normal Politics

The restoration of the constitution and parliamentary life in Kuwait had brought back a future too much like the past. The government and the parliament remained at loggerheads throughout the lifetime of the 1992 parliament. Although the amir did not dissolve it, thinly veiled threats by the prime minister that he might do so dangled like Damoclean swords over its deliberations. The opposition was hamstrung in most of its efforts to move Kuwait closer to the rule of law, and confusion about what actually *was* the law given the still-unresolved conflict over article 71 made this task even more difficult. The difficulties were compounded by the division between opposition secularists and Islamists, and the tendency of individuals within each group to sacrifice principles for political glory or personal gain. Meanwhile, neofundamentalists like Khaled al-ʿAdwa brought disrepute on the whole parliament by their outrageous behavior; by failing to take a stand against such it, more moderate Islamists tarnished their own reputations.

Secularists also sacrificed principles for popularity, most notably by acquiescing to a government-backed version of the Islamists' gender-segregation measure shortly before the 1996 parliamentary election campaign got under way. Charges that leading members of the opposition had sold out their principles, their constituents' interests, or both, dominated campaign discourse in 1996, and the most frequently cited example was the vote on the gender-segregation bill. In its final version, this measure netted only one dissenting vote, from ʿAbdullah Nibari (KDF).[88] With the exceptions of Ahmad al-Khatib (KDF) and Jasim al-Saqr (CB), who were out of the country when the vote was taken, and ʿAli al-Baghli (I) and Yacoub Hayati (85P), who abstained, secularists either ducked the vote by failing to show up or leaving the floor before the vote was taken, or else they voted with the Islamists. Academic observers noted that, given overwhelming support from members representing the outlying areas, cabinet support ensured the bill's success. Votes against it would not have changed the outcome but might well have angered devoutly religious constituents. To many, secularist support for the compromise bill seemed like the only way to get beyond the culture war to more substantive issues prior to the campaign. Instead, the gender-segregation vote dominated the campaign, particularly after foreign journalists arrived to cover the election,[89] and it was repeatedly cited as evidence of the secularists' perfidy among Kuwaitis themselves.

Disenchantment with parliamentarians rested on more than this one vote, however. Most opposition secularists and even some Islamists had managed to alienate significant portions of their core constituencies by the time the 1996 campaign season rolled around. Some saw the writing on the wall and simply retired, but others were not so prescient. When the ballots were counted in 1996, fifteen incumbent candidates were turned out of office by the voters (see table 7.2). At the same time, the sectarian upsurge during the campaign helped to ensure that the balance among Islamists and secularists did not shift appreciably. "Official" Islamists, those formally associated with organized political groups, continued to make up a minority of members of the 1996 parliament just as they had in the 1992 body. However, as I noted above, the voting weight of Islamism in Kuwait's legislative process comes from issue coalitions among official Islamists, tribal representatives (particularly winners of tribal primaries who are defending social patriarchy as much as religious patriarchy), and the large pool of pro-government parliamentarians, many of them service candidates. Table 7.3 shows the affiliations and issue orientations of incumbent and/or winning candidates in the 1996 election.

Disordering and discrediting the parliament did not bring unalloyed benefits to the rulers, however. Islamist politics proved to be politically and economically costly, preventing the government from mobilizing allies to support and therefore share the blame for unpopular measures such as economic rationalization. Academic analysts argue that such blame-sharing is a primary impetus behind political liberalization elsewhere in the region.[90] However, parliament's weakness coupled to government ineptitude blocked consensus on such issues as how to raise revenues from Kuwaitis and how to privatize which state-owned holdings. Especially in view of the fact that the government did go ahead with limited privatization coordinated by KIA, the failure to arrive at even general guidelines or procedures left the regime open to charges of corruption (see the discussion in the next chapter).

Kuwait's governance problems coincided with multiple small-scale border violations by Iraqis and a couple of well-publicized incidents of Iraqi troop movements just north of the border. Such incidents probably helped the parliament in that they kept Kuwaiti rulers painfully aware of the need to avoid antagonizing the United States by any blatantly antidemocratic move against the National Assembly. Even so, rulers and opposition both were impaled on the horns of Kuwait's political dilemma. To end the policy paralysis required a degree of trust and cooperation that was impossible to achieve.

Table 7.2   The Fates of Incumbents in the 1996 Parliamentary Election

Member and District	Previous parliaments			1996 results
1. Sharq				
'Adnan 'Abd al-Samad	81	85	92	won
Yacoub Hayati	85	92		retired
Hmoud al-Ruqbah				won
2. Al-Murqab				
Hamad al-Jou'an	85	92		retired
'Abdullah al-Nibari	71	75	92	won
'Abd al-Wahhab al-Haroun				won
3. Al-Qiblah				
Ahmad al-Nasir				won
Jasim al-Saqr	75	81	92	retired
Jasim al-Khorafy	75	81	85	won
4. Al-Da'iya				
'Ali al-Baghli	92			lost
'Abdullah al-Roumi	85	92		lost
Husain al-Qallaf				won
Jasim al-Mudhaf				won
5. Al-Qadisiya				
Ahmad Baqr	85	92		won
'Abd al-Mohsin Jamal	81	85		lost
'Abd al-'Aziz al-Mutawa'	85			won
6. Al-Faiha'				
Mishairy al-'Anjari	81	85	92	lost
Mishairy al-'Osaimi	92			won
Fahad al-Khanah				won
7. Kaifan				
Jasim al-'Aoun	81	85	92	retired
'Abd al-'Aziz al-'Adsani	92			won
Walid al-Tabtaba'i				won

Table 7.2   The Fates of Incumbents in the 1996 Parliamentary Election, cont.

Member and District	Previous parliaments					1996 results
8. Hawali						
Ahmad al-Rub'i	85	92				lost
Isma'il al-Shati	92					lost
Hasan Jawhar						won
Ahmad al-Mulaifi						won
9. Al-Rawdha						
Nasir Jasim al-Sana'	92					won
Ahmad al-Khatib	63	71	75	85	92	retired
Jasir al-Jasir	75	81	85			won
10. 'Adeliya						
Saleh Yousef al-Fadhala	81	85	92			lost
Ahmad Khaled al-Kulaib	92					won
Sami al-Munayes	63	71	75	85		won
11. Al-Khaldiya						
Ahmad al-Sa'doun	75	81	85	92		won
Mohammad Sulieman al-Marshad	81	85	92			lost
'Ali al-Khalaf al-Sa'id	MW					won
12. Al-Salmiya						
'Abd al-Mohsin al-Mud'ej	92					won
Salim 'Abdullah al-Hamad	81	85	92			lost
Mekhled al-'Azemi						won
13. Al-Rumaithiya						
Nasir 'Abd al-'Aziz Sarkhou	81	85	92			lost
Jamal Ahmad al-Kandary	92					lost
'Abbas al-Khodary	85	MW				won
Saleh Khorshaid						won
14. Abraq Khaittan						
'Ali Salim Abu Hadida	92					lost
Hmoud Nasir al-Jabri	85	MW	92			lost
'Abd al-Salam al-'Osaimi						won
Badr al-Ji'an						won

Table 7.2   The Fates of Incumbents in the 1996 Parliamentary Election, cont.

Member and District	Previous parliaments				1996 results
15. Al-Farwaniya					
'Abbas Habib					
al-Musailim	81	**85**	92		lost
Ghannam 'Ali al-Jamhour	92				won
Sa'ud al-Qafidi					won
16. Al-'Umariya					
Mubarak Fahad					
al-Duwailah	85	92			won
Mubarak Binaiah					
al-Khrainej	MW	92			won
17. Julib Al-Shiyoukh					
Mohammad Khalaf					
Umhamel	MW	92			retired
Mohammad Dhaif					
al-Sharar	92				won
Musalem al-Barrak					won
18. Al-Sulaibikhat					
Khalaf Dimethir					
al-'Enizi	81	85	MW	92	won
Rashid Salman					
al-Hubaidah	MW	92			won
19. Al-Jahra' al-Jadida					
Mufrej Nahar al-Mutairy	92				won
Ahmad Nasir al-Shriyan	85	92			lost
Munaizel al-'Enizi					won
20. Al-Jahra' al-Qadimi					
Talal Mubarak al-Ayyar	MW	92			won
Talal 'Uthman al-Sa'id	92				won
21. Al-Ahmadi					
Khaled al-'Adwa al-'Ajmy	92				won
Shari' Nasir Sa'd al-'Ajmy	92				retired
Walid al-Jari					won

Table 7.2   The Fates of Incumbents in the 1996 Parliamentary Election, cont.

Member and District	Previous parliaments						1996 results
22. Al-Riqa							
'Ayidh 'Aloush al-Mutairy	92						won
Hadi Hayef al-Huwailah	75	81	85	MW	92		won
23. Al-Subbahiya							
Jam'an Faleh Salim al-'Azemy	92						
Fahad Dahisan al-'Azemy	92						won
Mohammad al-'Olaim							won
24. Al-Fahaheel							
'Abdullah Rashid al-Hajri	92						won
Husain al-Dosari							won
25. Um al-Haiman							
Sa'd Biliq Q'am al-'Azemy	92						retired
Musaleh Hamijan al-'Azemy	92						retired
Jam'an Faleh al-'Azemy	92						won
Marzouk al-Habini	MW						won

Note: In Districts 23 and 25 an asterisk (*) denotes a parliamentary incumbent who ran in District 23 in 1992 and in District 25 in 1996.

Sources: Arab Times, October 9, 1996, 6–7; voter tallies for 1981, 1985, 1992, and 1996 from 'Ali Murad at the Kuwait elections office, photocopy; Nicolas Gavrielides, "Tribal Democracy: The Anatomy of Parliamentary Elections in Kuwait," in Linda L. Layne, ed., *Elections in the Middle East: Implications of Recent Trends,* 187–213 (Boulder, Colo.: Westview,1987).

TABLE 7.3
Bloc Affiliations and Political Leanings of Incumbents and Winners, 1996

Member and District	Political leanings	1996 results
1. Sharq		
'Adnan 'Abd al-Samad	Shi'a, opp	**won**
Yacoub Hayati	Secular, opp	retired
Hmoud al-Ruqbah	Pro-gov, Cab	**won**
2. Al-Murqab		
Hamad al-Jou'an	Secular, opp	retired
'Abdullah al-Nibari	Secular, opp	**won**
'Abd al-Wahhab al-Haroun	Secular, opp	**won**
3. Al-Qiblah		
Ahmad al-Nasir	Issue opp	**won**
Jasim al-Saqr	Secular, opp	retired
Jasim al-Khorafy	Pro-gov, Cab	**won**
4. Al-Da'iya		
'Ali al-Baghli	Secular, Cab, opp, Shi'a	lost
'Abdullah al-Roumi	Secular, opp	lost
Husain al-Qallaf	Shi'a, opp	**won**
Jasim al-Mudhaf	Pro-gov, pro-Islamist, SP	**won**
5. Al-Qadisiya		
Ahmad Baqr	Salaf, opp	**won**
'Abd al-Mohsin Jamal	Shi'a, issue opp	lost
'Abd al-'Aziz al-Mutawa'	Pro-gov, pro-Islamist	**won**
6. Al-Faiha'		
Mishairy al-'Anjari	Secular, opp, Cab	lost
Mishairy al-'Osaimi	Secular, opp	**won**
Fahad al-Khanah	Salaf	**won**
7. Kaifan		
Jasim al-'Aoun	Salaf, Cab	retired
'Abd al-'Aziz al-'Adsani	Issue opp	**won**
Walid al-Tabtaba'i	Salaf	**won**

TABLE 7.3
Bloc Affiliations and Political Leanings of Incumbents and Winners, 1996, cont.

Member and District	Political leanings	1996 results
8. Hawali		
Ahmad al-Rub'i	Secular, opp, Cab	lost
Isma'il al-Shati	Ikhwan, opp	lost
Hasan Jawhar	Shi'a, opp	**won**
Ahmad al-Mulaifi	Pro-Islamist	**won**
9. Al-Rawdha		
Nasir Jasim al-Sana'	Ikhwan	**won**
Ahmad al-Khatib	Secular, opp	retired
Jasir al-Jasir	Pro-gov	**won**
10. 'Adeliya		
Saleh Yousef al-Fadhala	Pro-Islamist	lost
Ahmad Khaled al-Kulaib	Pro-gov, pro-Islamist, Cab	**won**
Sami al-Munayes	Secular, opp	**won**
11. Al-Khaldiya		
Ahmad al-Sa'doun	Secular, opp	**won**
Mohammad Sulieman al-Marshad	Secular, opp	lost
'Ali al-Khalaf al-Sa'id	Pro-gov	**won**
12. Al-Salmiya		
'Abd al-Mohsin al-Mud'ej	Issue opp	**won**
Salim 'Abdullah al-Hamad	Secular, opp	lost
Mekhled al-'Azemi	Pro-gov, T	**won**
13. Al-Rumaithiya		
Nasir 'Abd al-'Aziz Sarkhou	Shi'a, opp	lost
Jamal Ahmad al-Kandary	Ikhwan, pro-gov	lost
'Abbas al-Khodary	Shi'a, Pro-gov	**won**
Saleh Khorshaid	Pro-gov	**won**
14. Abraq Khaittan		
'Ali Salim Abu Hadida	Pro-gov.	lost
Hmoud Nasir al-Jabri	Pro-gov	lost
'Abd al-Salam al-'Osaimi	T	**won**
Badr al-Ji'an	Pro-gov	**won**

TABLE 7.3
Bloc Affiliations and Political Leanings of Incumbents and Winners, 1996, cont.

Member and District	Political leanings	1996 results
15. Al-Farwaniya		
'Abbas Habib al-Musailim	Secular, opp	lost
Ghannam 'Ali al-Jamhour	Pro-gov, pro-Islamist, T	**won**
Sa'ud al-Qafidi	Pro-gov	**won**
16. Al-'Umariya		
Mubarak Fahad al-Duwailah	Ikhwan	**won**
Mubarak Binaiah al-Khrainej	Pro-gov	**won**
17. Julib Al-Shiyoukh		
Mohammad Khalaf Umhamel	Pro-gov	retired
Mohammad Dhaif al-Sharar	Pro-gov, pro-Islamist	**won**
Musalem al-Barrak	Issue opp	**won**
18. Al-Sulaibikhat		
Khalaf Dimethir al-'Enizi	Pro-gov	**won**
Rashid Salman al-Hubaidah	Issue opp	**won**
19. Al-Jahra' al-Jadida		
Mufrej Nahar al-Mutairy	Salaf	**won**
Ahmad Nasir al-Shriyan	Secular, opp	lost
Munaizel al-'Enizi	Pro-gov	**won**
20. Al-Jahra' al-Qadimi		
Talal Mubarak al-Ayyar	Pro-gov	**won**
Talal 'Uthman al-Sa'id	Pro-gov	**won**
21. Al-Ahmadi		
Khaled al-'Adwa al-'Ajmy	Salaf, T	**won**
Shari' Nasir Sa'd al-'Ajmy	Pro-gov	retired
Walid al-Jari	Ikhwan, T	**won**

Bloc Affiliations and Political Leanings of Incumbents and Winners, 1996, cont.

Member and District	Political leanings	1996 results
22. Al-Riqa		
'Ayidh 'Aloush al-Mutairy	Ikhwan, T	**won**
Hadi Hayef al-Huwailah	Pro-gov, pro-Islamist, T	**won**
23. Al-Subbahiya		
Jam'an Faleh Salim al-'Azemy	Ikhwan, Cab	*
Fahad Dahisan al-'Azemy	T	**won**
Mohammad al-'Olaim	Pro-gov, pro-Islamist, **T**	**won**
24. Al-Fahaheel		
'Abdullah Rashid al-Hajri	Pro-gov, Ikhwan, **T**	**won**
Husain al-Dosari	Pro-gov	**won**
25. Um al-Haiman		
Sa'd Biliq Q'am al-'Azemy	Pro-gov	retired
Musaleh Hamijan al-'Azemy	Pro-gov	retired
Jam'an Faleh al-'Azemy	Pro-gov, Ikhwan, Cab *	**won**
Marzouk al-Habini	Pro-gov, T	**won**

Notes: In Districts 23 and 25 an asterisk (*) denotes a parliamentary incumbent who ran in District 23 in 1992 and in District 25 in 1996.

Abbreviations: Cab: former cabinet member
   Ikhwan: affiliated with Muslim Brothers (Sunni)
   Issue opp: opposes the government on some issues
   Opp: opposes the government on constitutional issues
   Pro-gov: supports the government most of the time
   Pro-Islamist: supports Islamist agenda but is not affiliated with an
      Islamist group
   Salaf: affiliated with Islamic Heritage Society (Sunni)
   Secular: opposes Islamist agenda
   Shi'a: religious affiliation
   SP: winner of the Sunni primary in Da'iya
   T: winner of a tribal primary
   T: primary winner representing a tribal alliance

TABLE 7.3
Bloc Affiliations and Political Leanings of Incumbents and Winners, 1996, cont.

Clarification: In 1996, unlike 1992, political blocs were less important, particularly for Islamists. The Shi'i group was disbanded and did not endorse candidates. The ICM (Ikhwan) and IPA (Salafin) did not follow consistent rules on endorsements, so I have listed affiliation rather than endorsements in this table as more informative regarding the policy placement of the candidates. "Pro-Islamists" endorsed one or more major Islamist issues, the most important of which is amending article 2. "Secular" candidates may be religious persons, but they do not promote a religious agenda. Some candidates who are members of tribes refused to participate in tribal primaries and are not shown as tribal candidates.

Sources: Arab Times, various issues; voter tallies for 1996 from 'Ali Murad at the Kuwait elections office, photocopy; interviews with Sa'oud al-'Anezi and others in Kuwait, 1996.

Analyses of political and economic hurdles blocking the
pathways of "late developers" such as Kuwait are staples
of the political economy literature, though some analysts are less pessimistic than others, stressing the "advantages of backwardness" and the opportunity for late
developers to learn from the mistakes of their predecessors.[1] On balance, however, especially during periods
characterized by widespread financial insecurity and
commodity price collapse, pessimism dominates. A few
writers have stopped believing that economic development in late-developing countries is even possible.[2] A
related literature on "dependent development" concentrates on the situation of states that depend on a single
exported commodity for the bulk of their national in-
comes.[3] The rentier state is a privileged member of this
group but, like the others, is subject to economic forces
over which it has little or no effective control. I discussed some of the theoretical literature on this topic in
chapter 3; similar concerns also are reflected in empirical and policy studies of oil exporting states.[4]

The politics of late development could very well be
called "dependent politics." Examined in the context of
imperialism and the Cold War in Africa,[5] Asia,[6] and
the Middle East,[7] this literature shows in detail how
external intervention has selected in favor of authori-
tarians among contenders for power in late-developing countries. Charles Tilly's lament about the difficulties of political development in the modern age finds
plenty of support in these studies.

States that have come into being recently through
decolonization or through reallocations of territory by dominant states have acquired their military
organization from outside, without the same inter-

nal forging of mutual constraints between rulers and ruled [as occurred in early developers]. To the extent that outside states continue to supply military goods and expertise in return for commodities, military alliance or both, the new states harbor powerful, unconstrained organizations that easily overshadow all other organizations within their territories.[8]

The message of the literature on dependent politics stresses the damage done by external actors and an external environment that distorts the evolution of domestic political structures just as incorporation into global capitalism distorts the economies of late developers. However, the message of this chapter comes from a different perspective.

As a political economist and something of a structuralist, I must confess that I tend to be pessimistic about prospects for development. Even so, as someone who also believes in human agency and ingenuity, I am drawn to examine cases through lenses that focus on more than simply systemic qualities defining imperialism, globalization, and other totalizing orders so often cast as Satanic mills grinding helpless human beings into atoms. Throughout this volume, I have tried to show how individuals exercise agency—power: autonomous capacity to transform if not always to control. As Anthony Giddens puts it, "What is at issue is the capability even of the most dependent, weak and the most oppressed to have the ability to carve out spheres of autonomy of their own."[9] In Kuwait, where people are blessed with social, economic, and personal resources not only in their individual capacities but also in their collective capacities as families, neighborhoods and congregations, and professional and business groupings, we have seen that the ability of citizens to carve out spheres of autonomy is extensive. The interplay between pacts and populism which, in the Kuwaiti case, is mass politics of a particularly resourceful kind, reflects the unusually rich resources available to Kuwaiti elites and Kuwaiti "masses."

In this chapter I revisit the interdependence between pacts and populism in an enlarged context that includes international, transnational, and global actors and networks. The city-state today is, like its ancient and medieval predecessors, a nexus of the larger world. It is a port of trade, a locus of diversity, and a center of culture. City-state politics is an arena in which ideas of civic culture and civil society find a variety of concrete expressions, and what some see as new forms of social organization stimulated by globalization are developing most rapidly. Roger Keil argues that such communities are "world cities," places where pasts and futures are articulated in a lively and contested present far more complicated—and interesting—than the nation-states he sees them as replacing.[10] Kuwait is such a world city, one whose "local" politics is connected to persons, movements, and institutions worldwide. Such connections support political development by providing protected spaces for resistance and by offering alternative sources of power and authority for nonviolent social change.

New Social Movements and Old Institutions

Social movement theory seeks to explain why and how people mobilize against institutional forces that oppress them and the conditions under which their movements succeed or fail.[11] Social movements themselves incorporate participation by mass publics in activities intended to expand their rights. These include collective bargaining by labor and the extension of civil identity and protection to formerly subject groups such as women and ethnic minorities. So-called new social movements are defined as those featuring highly participatory leadership and action styles, and participants who are younger, more middle class, and more likely to be female than old-style, centralized, and hierarchical movements. Another quality of new social movements is their fluidity. Activists come together over specific issues and for limited purposes, disperse, and then reform as a somewhat different cast of characters depending on events and how they intersect individual and collective interests.[12]

New social movements are fluid horizontal mobilizations that combine the efforts of issue activists with those of persons in sympathetic government agencies and established voluntary associations, both of which tend to be structured and hierarchical. In Kuwait voluntary associations are formally regulated by the state. Consequently, new social movements are doubly important as one of the few indicators of institutionally unmediated popular will, including the will of citizens with formal government responsibilities. New social movements everywhere are boosted by the ability of members and leaders to communicate directly by telephone, fax, and the Internet. This contributes to their growing capacity to mobilize on short notice and to initiate and maintain international linkages to sister movements and other supporters based abroad. The fluidity of these movements and their international connections contribute to their civic efficacy by allowing activists to elude surveillance controls and providing them with protected spaces constructed from publicity and protest.[13] In this regard, international linkages become "transmission belts" for external pressure on domestic regimes with respect to movement issues and activist protection.

In addition to assistance from international and transnational groups, external support for activists and institutions also is available from the judicial bodies of international organizations and foreign countries. Illustrated recently in the effort by Spain to extradite former Chilean dictator Augusto Pinochet for trial on alleged human rights violations, international treaties increasingly are being used by activists in and out of government to bring criminals to courts abroad when the courts in their home countries refuse or are blocked from hearing cases against them. Even before this trend in human rights protection became a general matter of public knowledge, citizens and organizations long had sought civil redress in foreign courts for a wide variety of reasons.

> Foreign parties suing for redress in the courts of other countries is a HUGE area of the law—it happens all the time. There are, [in the United States] for example, whole courses in law school devoted to various aspects of this— courses like conflict of laws, private international law, public international law, transnational litigation, international human rights law, international business transactions, international trade, international finance, international banking and development finance, plus [the status and role of] foreign parties in . . . areas of the law like corporations [and] tax.[14]

The availability of legal redress overseas is a crucial support for social activists in countries whose courts enjoy no or only limited independence. Here I look at two sets of issues variously involving Kuwaiti government organizations, voluntary associations, and new social movements. These are the protection of public funds and human rights. In both areas, extra-national assistance was crucial to making significant progress on national movement goals.

Public Funds

The limited constitutional leverage afforded the parliament includes its institutional responsibility for oversight of public finances, and this is a role that Kuwaiti parliaments have struggled very hard to fulfill in the face of government evasion and secrecy.[15] Contemporary assertions of parliamentary oversight rights were stimulated by discoveries of embezzlement of public funds, such as in the Kuwait Oil Tanker Company (KOTC) case discussed in the previous chapter and below, and in consequence of a long parliamentary investigation chaired by Ahmad Baqr (IPA) into the events leading up to the Iraqi invasion. This inquiry by the 1992 parliament disclosed financial irregularities in how defense contracts were awarded and managed, along with political and military failures by leaders in charge of managing the crisis which ended in the invasion and occupation of Kuwait. The 1992 parliament had little time to act on all the committee's recommendations, but legislation was passed tightening auditing requirements and establishing a new standing committee, the Protection of Public Funds Committee (PPFC), to monitor expenditures by ministries, including Defense. The PPFC also was charged with supervising state investments, including oil industry investments and the portfolio investments in Kuwait's Reserve Fund for Future Generations (RFFG) which, by law, receives 10 percent of annual government revenue.

The PPFC provided the platform on which members of the 1996 parliament mounted a vigorous campaign to halt what they termed the theft of public funds. A major role in this campaign was played by the Audit Bureau, a government agency established in Law no. 30 of 1964. The Audit Bureau works for the parliament, which appoints its chair, but until recently this agency was not noted for its energy. After the 1992 election, the Audit Bureau came under scrutiny from parliament and was urged by the speaker to be more aggressive in monitoring appropriations and expenditures. In December 1994 the Audit Bureau chief announced his resignation in a letter to the crown prince in which he complained about the speaker's "attempts to interfere in the bureau's internal affairs followed by continuous pressures to quit."[16]

Early in the 1995 fiscal year, the Audit Bureau reported large budget overruns for fiscal 1994. The government said it would close the budget gap by the year 2000, though no one expected that this could be done without a serious overhaul of fiscal policy.[17] Meanwhile, the alliance between the Audit Bureau and the parliament was strengthened by popular approval of the bureau's exposure of unlawful financial dealings by the government. Shortly after the 1996 parliament convened, the Audit Bureau reported that the government had made unauthorized withdrawals from the RFFG, and the PPFC's chair, 'Adnan 'Abd al-Samad, made an immediate request that this action be halted. When the request was made at the end of January 1997, the sum of unauthorized withdrawals already had reached KD 0.24 billion.[18]

Under the legislation setting up the RFFG, no withdrawals are permitted. Despite that, many in and outside Kuwait believe that the government has routinely moved investments among reserve accounts, including the RFFG, and that it has used the RFFG as a screen for other investments.[19] During the occupation, this blue-chip fund, which at that time was estimated as amounting to more than $100 billion, was stripped of more than two-thirds of its assets and reduced to a reported $30–35 billion.[20] Some of this money was used to sustain Kuwaitis during the occupation; a much larger sum, approximately $26 billion, went to pay Kuwait's share of the formal and informal costs of military operations Desert Shield and Desert Storm.[21] However, that leaves quite a large amount unaccounted for. One rationale for establishing stricter oversight procedures and calling for investigations of particular instances where abuses were suspected was to find out what had happened to the rest.

The Audit Bureau confirmed everyone's worst suspicions when it sent a formal letter to National Assembly speaker Ahmad al-Saʿdoun stating that the government had withdrawn more than $80 billion from the RFFG since the invasion. An emergency amiri decree made on August 3, 1990, had authorized withdrawals to deal with the crisis, but this decree was canceled a week after liberation. The subsequent unauthorized withdrawals were made despite two formal warnings from the Audit Bureau, the first issued in November 1995 and the second a year later. When the government failed to halt its illegal withdrawals and return the money it had taken without authorization, the Audit Bureau wrote to the speaker. The finance minister responded by submitting a request to the parliament for retroactive legalization of the unauthorized withdrawals.[22]

Even before the uproar over unauthorized withdrawals from the reserve fund, the PPFC had notified the government that the entire cabinet might be questioned in parliament because ministers had failed to respond to the committee's many requests for information on spending as well as on the government's failure to collect fees such as rents for industrial and recreational property. Meanwhile, at a December 1996 press conference, the managing director of KOTC, ʿAbdullah al-Roumi, charged that he had been threatened, offered a bribe, and then falsely implicated in a drug charge because he had refused to halt his investigation of the KOTC embezzlement (see below). Shortly afterward, oil minister ʿEisa al-Mazidi referred ʿAbdullah al-Roumi and several other KOTC board members to the public prosecutor for having accepted "illegal bonuses" for the overtime they had put in on the KOTC investigation. The allegation later was found to be without foundation, but when parliamentarians asked questions about ʿAbdullah al-Roumi's charges they were criticized for bringing these issues before the public instead of allowing them to be handled behind closed doors.[23]

This new conflict between the government and parliament provoked the by-then usual intimations that parliament might be dissolved. This time, Kuwaiti activists mobilized to head off the suspensions they feared might be imposed to cover up the misuse of public funds. They formed a citizens' watchdog group whose members pledged to raise public awareness of how the government was spending public money by writing articles about the use of public funds and publicizing Audit Bureau reports. Over two hundred persons attended the group's first meeting in early March 1997, including prominent pro-democracy activists and several present and former members of parliament. A board of eleven members was elected at this meeting and, despite warnings about the dangers of operating without state sanction, the group, chaired by Mohsen al-Mutairy, decided to begin work without waiting for a government license.[24]

Within a month, cabinet ministers were pledging government support for any parliamentary proposal to strengthen procedures to stop the misuse of public funds. The PPFC produced a wide-ranging report at the end of April that called for the government's secret service organization to investigate charges of embezzlement and other irregularities in the use of public funds, including any such crimes committed abroad.[25] In early May, Ahmad al-Sa'doun, whose entitlement to the speakership in the 1996 parliament had been affirmed by the Constitutional Court just a short time before,[26] attacked the Kuwait Investment Authority's (KIA) privatization program, charging that the government was "privatizing without controls or regulation, and is simply selling its assets to a select number of Kuwait's elite."[27] The already dangerously overheated political pot was stoked further by charges that four members of the public prosecutor's office had accepted money from KOTC to conduct their investigations of the embezzlement charges.[28]

The pot exploded on June 6 in an assassination attempt against 'Abdullah Nibari which wounded him seriously and also injured his wife. The speaker blamed the thieves of public funds for the tragedy. "The shooting at Nibari was not directed against his person, but because he was one of those who defended public funds and stood against those playing in the future of the country."[29] The conviction that there was some connection between the funds scandals and the assassination attempt was strengthened by the discovery that the person who had organized and led the assault had been cited by a parliamentary committee as having "allegedly benefited from illegal profits through dubious catering contracts with the Ministry of Defence."[30] A prominent feature of contemporary news coverage of the event was the fact that this man also was a relation of the finance minister, Nasir al-Roudhan. 'Abdullah Nibari, who had been publishing articles and making speeches about the misuse of public monies since November 1993, himself believed that the assassination attempt had been motivated by his investigations of persons involved in the theft of public funds.[31]

Shock at the assassination attempt on 'Abdullah Nibari, along with concerns that the violence would continue,[32] increased popular support for the opposition. Meetings were held by various groups, and opposition newspapers called for a thorough investigation. Some critics intimated that the rulers were involved in the shooting and the opposition immediately was taken to task for its "language," a euphemism that refers to public mention of possibly shady behavior by Kuwait's rulers.[33] However, as is often the case in Kuwaiti politics, opposition ascendency was short-lived, confounded by the sheer magnitude of suspected wrongdoing, a strategic error in choosing the primary target to investigate, and disagreement among opposition Islamists.[34]

The opposition decided to question only one minister "to preserve the unity of the National Assembly."[35] The man they chose to interpellate was the finance minister, Nasir al-Roudhan, but the list of issues to be covered did not include anything about the assassination attempt on ʿAbdullah Nibari. The minister already had been called by the public prosecutor to testify about his knowledge of the shooting. However, the topics for questions did include the minister's alleged failure to implement laws and procedures regarding accountability for public money, and his conduct as the ex officio head of several government corporations.[36] That opposition Islamists might be weak allies in this confrontation became evident when ICM deputies complained that they had not been consulted in advance about the issues appearing on the list. When July 15, the day of the "grilling," finally arrived, the minister was well prepared. He denied every allegation made by the three signers of the request for the session, Sami al-Munayes (KDF), Mishairy al-ʿOsaimi (I), and Ahmad al-Mulaifi (I).[37] And although he did admit that some irregularities had occurred, the minister was far from contrite. He attacked the questioners for their immoderate language and accused them of using the interpellation as a ploy to bring down the government. By the end of the thirteen-hour session, the minister and his supporters clearly had emerged as the victors. The three challengers proved unable even to come up with the ten signatures necessary to offer a motion of no-confidence.[38]

Although the minister's performance allowed him to escape with his position secured and his reputation enhanced, the opposition did not give up on the issues. Members continued to insist on a more rigorous implementation of the laws governing the spending of public money. In one of the last parliamentary sessions before the 1997 summer recess, a majority of twenty-three out of the thirty-four members present approved a request that the government not sign any new exploration or production agreements with foreign oil companies before consulting the National Assembly. An additional request, approved by only eighteen members, requires prior notification before any contracts for new projects for KPC are signed and also that a separate central committee for tenders at KPC be established to handle all contracts. After this measure passed, the finance minister claimed it was unconstitutional. The members then passed unanimously a third recommendation asking that KPC coordinate all its investment activities with KIA.

These initiatives to tighten parliamentary control over state finances complemented a new "transparency law" governing public-sector contracts issued by the 1992 parliament in August 1996. All government agencies, the Kuwait Municipality, public organizations and institutions, and companies owned one half or more by the state or any "juridical personality" must report to the Audit Bureau the names of anyone receiving special fees or commissions in connection with government contracts, along with those who authorize such payments. The law covers all goods and services, including arms purchases. Following any agreement to pay and any transfer of payment, the recipient and the payer are required to provide to the Audit Bureau a detailed written description of the nature of the commission—whether it is cash, goods, or services—its value, where it was or will be paid, and the names of the parties involved. Failure to report a commission is punishable by a fine of twice its value, and submitting a false statement about a commission incurs a risk of up to three years of imprisonment.[39] The law is an attempt to control corruption by making agency personnel as well as third parties culpable for failing to report commissions.

The manipulation of commissions to embezzle funds was exposed in the KOTC investigations, which began in a very small way following the resignation of the company's managing director, 'Abd al-Fattah al-Badr, in February 1992. His successor, 'Abdullah al-Roumi, was formerly the assistant managing director for marketing at KPC and a nonexecutive director of KOTC. 'Abdullah was alerted to possible irregularities in the company's finances when Nader Sultan, then deputy chairman of KPC, mentioned in passing that a KOTC subsidiary had paid a higher-than-market price for a charter some time in 1988 and that his attempts to investigate why this had happened had been stifled. Shortly afterward, a Kuwaiti bank official called 'Abdullah al-Roumi to inquire why KOTC suddenly had stopped purchasing large quantities of traveler's checks.[40] These and perhaps other anomalies stimulated 'Abdullah al-Roumi's initial investigation of KOTC. As he went on, he encountered strenuous efforts to close off the investigation, such as the bribery attempts referred to above in the discussion of events leading up to the attempted assassination of 'Abdullah Nibari.

The investigations of KOTC's finances soon produced criminal indictments of three Kuwaitis: former oil minister Shaikh 'Ali al-Khalifa, former managing director of KOTC 'Abd al-Fattah al-Badr, and former deputy managing director of KOTC, Hasan Qabazard, along with two foreigners. The inclusion of 'Ali al-Khalifa as a defendant in the criminal case triggered the series of clashes between the parliament and the amir described in the preceding chapter. As I recounted there, repeated challenges by 'Ali al-Khalifa and his representatives of the legitimacy of trying him in any court other than the one provided for in the amiri decree passed during the second constitutional suspension succeeded in gradually whittling down the number and severity of the charges against him.

Although I believe that a strong effort was made to intimidate the judges in the Kuwaiti criminal court case, I must agree with Nathan Brown that the systemic problems of all Kuwaiti courts and judges are more serious than individual instances of intimidation whether or not they succeed. Kuwaiti courts lack the institutional independence that could provide them even the limited protected space that the constitution offers to the National Assembly and its members.

> The minister of justice is involved in the appointment of almost all senior judicial officials. . . . The Supreme Judicial Council is devoid of budgetary independence, and all the administrative support for the courts is part of the Ministry of Justice. . . . [A] proposed law [to give the judiciary greater independence may have been] one of the causes of the government's decison to dissolve the parliament indefinitely [in 1986]. . . . [A] new law was introduced by several members of [the 1992] parliament. . . . When a complex dispute between the parliament and the government erupted over the legal status of legislation enacted in the absence of parliament . . . however, the proposed law became a victim of an agreement between parliamentary leaders and the government.[41]

The lack of judicial independence is clearly shown in the KOTC case. Even though the criminal court found the nonministerial defendents guilty in June 1996, after 'Ali al-Khalifa had been separated from the case the Court of Cassation threw out the conviction the following year on the grounds that the verdict had not been dated.[42] Both the long prison sentences imposed and the requirement for restitution of the stolen funds were thereby overturned.

However, KOTC was not solely dependent on Kuwaiti courts for redress. The company brought a civil suit against 'Abd al-Fattah al-Badr, Hasan Qabazard, and Timothy St. John Stafford, former fleet operations manager for KOTC, in the Queen's Bench Commercial Court in London. Six weeks of court argument began in February 1998. It laid out four schemes by which the defendants and others, including 'Ali al-Khalifa, had embezzled millions of dollars from KOTC beginning in 1985, the year before the second parliamentary suspension. After eight months of deliberation, the judge in the case handed down his draft judgment on November 16, finding the three defendants guilty and asking for complete restitution, including interest, of the money they had stolen.[43]

The decision itself was only part of the victory achieved by Kuwaiti activists. Even more important was the detailed reconstruction of the crimes from testimony and documents, and the evaluations of the credibility of the various witnesses by the judge, reconstructions and evaluations which, when suggested by Kuwaitis, had been dismissed as immoderate language and baseless charges. Report of the draft judgment touched off a firestorm of popular protest in Kuwait. Prominent opposition members of parliament, including 'Abdullah

Nibari (KDF) and Mubarak al-Duwailah (ICM),[44] and other respected critics of the regime's financial policies, spoke at public gatherings about the necessity to reclaim Kuwaiti agency in the KOTC case. According to Ghanim al-Najjar, "a vigorous campaign led by *al-Qabas* newspaper, and [featuring] scores of public rallies organized by MPs demanding that 'Ali al-Khalifa be charged" forced the government to resubmit the case to the public prosecutor. But the critics did not have the field to themselves. Head-to-head with *al-Qabas*, the newspaper owned by traditionals in Chamber of Commerce, was *al-Watan*, the daily owned by a consortium headed by 'Ali al-Khalifa. Perhaps desirous of demonstrating his own extra-national bona fides, 'Ali al-Khalifa, "as owner of *al-Watan*, announced in a huge celebration his partnership with *Newsweek* as the sole publisher of [the magazine's] Arabic edition."[45]

Resistance by the government and members of the ruling family to submit to demands for financial accountability has been constant and multifocal. Another recent example is the regime's attempt to take over the PPFC. When the third session of the 1996 parliament began in October 1998, parliamentary committee members were reelected. Prominent Islamist critics of the government's fiscal policies were defeated in bids for seats on powerful committees. Examples include Mubarak al-Duwailah, a fierce opponent of arms purchases who was kept off the Legal and Legislative Affairs committee, and even more telling, Ahmad Baqr, the parliament's greatest proponent of cooperative health insurance that would require employers to pay a share of employees' premiums, who lost his bid for a seat on the Health and Labor committee. Secularist critics, most notably 'Abdullah Nibari, who was kept off Finance and Economy, also were defeated for key committee posts.[46] Charges that the government had interfered in the committee elections were made by several Islamist members.[47]

The appearance of interference in elections for the PPFC was even clearer. The PPFC is selected from two other standing committees—Finance, and Legal and Legislative. The members chosen from the latter committee were three "service MPs," 'Abbas al-Khodary, Khalaf al-'Enizi, and Mubarak al-Khrainej. The Finance Committee members included veteran watchdog 'Adnan 'Abd al-Samad, 'Abd al-Wahhab al-Haroun, a secularist independent, 'Abdullah al-Hajri, ICM member and tribal representative, and 'Ali al-Khalaf al-Sa'id, a service MP whose previous experience in elected office had been as a member of the Majlis al-Watani. 'Ali al-Khalaf had been imported from Old Jahra' to run in Khaldiya in 1996, where his defeat of the popular Mohammad al-Marshad took many by surprise. 'Ali al-Khalaf's election to the PPFC enraged 'Adnan 'Abd al-Samad, who resigned from the committee, vowing to take his crusade to protect public funds to the floor of the National Assembly.[48]

The conflict over public funds in Kuwait is far from resolved. Indeed, the May 1999 dismissal of the 1996 parliament can be read as part of the regime's counterattack against parliamentary watchdogs of the public purse. It is true, of course, that the 1996 parliament was marred by behavior every bit as self-centered and disruptive as any that tarnished the reputation of the 1992 body. However, it also is true that the suspension of a parliament removes both the government's most visible critics and the institutional procedures impeding its freedom to make economic policy as it wishes. The subsequent preoccupation of parliamentarians, citizens, and media with the impending election reduces attention paid to what the government is doing about important issues at the same time that the absence of the parliament allows the amir to govern by decree.

The 1999 parliamentary suspension also opened an opportunity for the government to incorporate extranational friends of its own in the struggle to dominate economic policy-making. If successful, this could spill over into the conflict over the balance of power between the legislature and the executive. An article 71 already weakened by the amir's actions during the 1992 parliament (discussed in the previous chapter) would be gutted further if external pressures could be mobilized successfully against parliamentary cancellation of amiri decrees issued in its absence.

Key oil policy and restructuring decisions lie at the heart of this conflict. During the past several years, and along with most of the rest of OPEC, Kuwait has edged toward inviting international oil companies (IOCs) back in as partners in the upstream[49] phases of its hydrocarbon industry. Reprivatization would go a long way toward negating the nationalizations of the early 1970s, which allowed OPEC members to set their own crude prices and production levels and also to keep the entire margin between costs and prices for themselves rather than having to share it with foreign corporate owners. Production control per se was an important goal of oil exporters in the 1960s and 1970s. When Kuwaitis were debating whether to nationalize completely or reclaim their hydrocarbon resources through a phased-in participation plan, oil-field management was one of the deciding factors in their decision to nationalize.[50] Oil production at rates higher than necessary to meet current income needs were criticized by the parliament as damaging to ultimate recovery levels and, in response, production was cut by a third between 1972 and 1974.[51] Also at that time most Kuwaiti gas was being flared. Repeated company rejection of proposals for higher levels of gas utilization in secondary recovery and as an industrial raw material had been a point of contention between the government and its concessionaires for some years. Nationalization gave Kuwait both full control of oil production and resources for investments, enabling it to exploit its natural gas as it chose.[52]

The owner of a substantial proportion of the world's hydrocarbon re-sources, Kuwait after nationalization opted for multinational vertical integration of its corporate holdings. This strategy opened a space within which Kuwait could seek to maximize jointly its national autonomy and security, and its hydrocarbon revenues.[53] However, the government and the parliament had very different views of how oil policy should be made and also what its methods and goals should be. To the government, oil revenues are the backbone of the state economy and the foundation of citizen support for the regime. To the parliament as well, hydrocarbon revenues are the state's income mainstay, but parliament sees oil and gas as the patrimony of the Kuwaiti people, and members are equally concerned about policies that appear inconsistent with this image. These perspectives clash with regard to oil revenue stability which, however you look at it, is an elusive goal. Although the government can control its own oil production, it cannot control production from other sources and thereby regulate oil prices. As a result, major oil producers like Kuwait have to balance their needs for income and even for control over their key domestic industry to meet equally pressing needs to avoid extreme price fluctuations either up or down. A price collapse brings immediate budget deficits, but sustained high prices are problematic too because they cause consumers to shift to alternative fuels and reduce income over the long term.

Kuwait is a pivotal actor in oil market management because of the relative size of its production and reserves. As a result, its actions matter to the market as a whole and it approaches oil policy from a long-term and highly strategic perspective. This viewpoint rarely is shared by domestic interests represented in the parliament and, since the early 1970s, the government has tended to avoid making major oil policy decisions when the parliament is in session. As I noted in a previous chapter, corporate reorganization under KPC was initiated in 1980, during the first parliamentary suspension. During the second parliamentary suspension, KPC conducted all its business out of the sight of Kuwaiti citizens and, by the end of the decade, was routinely producing oil over Kuwait's OPEC quota.

Prior to the 1999 dismissal of parliament, government oil-policy makers had published a detailed plan for upstream privatization, a policy that had attracted sharp parliamentary criticism since its first inception. Government interest in altering the ownership basis of Kuwaiti hydrocarbons was first expressed early in the 1990s, when upstream privatization was framed as part of a national defense policy—Kuwait would seek foreign participation in its northern oil fields on the theory that foreign oil company personnel and equipment might serve as potential hostages against another Iraqi invasion. Kuwaiti oil industry managers also cited capital shortages and a desire for access to frontier technologies as reasons to reprivatize, rationales which had shaped their decision to invite Union Carbide to become a partner in the new facility constructed by KPC's Petrochemical Industries Company subsidiary. However, I believe these latter reasons are not so crucial for Kuwait as for some other producing countries, such as the successor states of the former Soviet Union. In fact, it is those successor states and their desperate bids for hydrocarbon investment on almost any terms that have frightened the established producers, Kuwait among them, into considering the surrender of some of the fruits of nationalization by inviting the IOCs back in on a limited basis. They hope privatization will preempt production capacity expansion in the successor states and thereby forestall the deleterious impact of a flood of oil from new and uncontrollable sources on an already weak market.

In the early 1990s, there was little interest from IOCs in investing in projects in northern Kuwait. Kuwait did sign controversial contracts with BP and with Chevron for consultation services with respect to oil field development. However, the privatization scheme seemed to have been abandoned, despite World Bank encouragement of privatization throughout the Kuwaiti economy, including in its hydrocarbon industry.[54] In 1997, however, Kuwait's Supreme Petroleum Council, the country's chief oil-policy decision-making body, reiterated the state's interest in privatization and once again targeted the "northern fields" as the first to be offered for participation deals.[55] Again, some in parliament objected, saying this would violate Kuwait's constitution which forbids foreign ownership of Kuwaiti resources. Despite these concerns, the government announced a privatization plan that included procedures for selecting partners and a timetable for the new policy's implementation.[56] When the plan was released in April 1999, it was widely assumed that privatization would not go forward before the parliament had agreed it was constitutional and had approved the terms under which IOCs would be invited to participate in upstream projects.[57]

Meanwhile, the government continued to press the parliament to agree to its positions not only on oil privatization but also on a series of measures to restructure Kuwait's domestic economy. Many restructuring proposals, such as those which advocated cutting subsidies for utilities; limiting the number of children entitled to a family allowance; increasing taxes on housing, airport departures, and large appliance purchases; and introducing worker contributions to social security,[58] all were resisted because they would impose disproportionately higher living costs on low-income groups. Even a fairly modest proposal to increase retail fuel prices was attacked without mercy for weeks in the parliament. Some years earlier, KPC managers told me that resistance even to marginal adjustments in domestic gasoline prices was at the root of the company's decision to introduce lead-free gasoline in Europe but not in Kuwait because KPC would not be permitted to recoup the higher cost of production in the domestic market.

Budget manipulation has been a favorite government technique for mobilizing parliamentary support for restructuring. Kuwait's budgets (like the budgets of other states) are political documents as much as economic blueprints. For one thing, they do not reflect all the government's income and expenditures: in Kuwait, dividends and capital gains from investments held in state reserve accounts such as the RFFG, along with profits from KPC activities other than the sale of crude oil (examples would be oil refining and product sales), are not counted as income in the state's budget; on the other side of the ledger, defense expenditures are all off-budget. Another distortion whose result is to make the budget a less-than-transparent mechanism for assessing the fiscal health of the state is the practice of the government to forecast crude oil prices and thereby estimates of its anticipated income at a level well below what outside experts and perhaps even finance ministry officials themselves believe will be the case. In January 1999, for example, the finance minister announced that his next budget would be based on an oil price assumption of US $8/bbl., two dollars under the previous year's price.[59]

The government's deficit projections based on these exclusions and assumptions were challenged by independent estimates from sources such as Moody's.[60] They also were challenged by members of the National Assembly who objected not only to the estimation methods but also to questionable expenditures arising from government corruption and what they charged was fiscal irresponsibility in off-budget purchases of foreign-made weapons systems.[61] Consequently, prior to the suspension of the parliament in May 1999, domestic economic restructuring, weapons system purchases, and upstream privatization all were on the table, and each had garnered significant opposition among secularist and Islamist members.

What Aristotle would term the "efficient cause" of the dismissal of parliament was the parliamentary interrogation of the minister of justice, 'Awqaf, and Islamic affairs, Ahmad al-Kulaib, for having distributed defective copies of the Qur'an. Although no one seems to have believed that his error was intentional, many were convinced that the minister would fail to win a vote of confidence in the parliament.[62] But there are reasons to doubt that the efficient cause was the actual reason—in Aristotelian language, the "final cause"—for the amir's action. As I discuss in the next section of this chapter, only the year before two other ministers faced parliamentary questioning. Because both were ruling family members, these cases were more directly challenging to the regime than the interpellation of Ahmad al-Kulaib. In spite of this, both conflicts were resolved short of a dissolution.

An even more telltale sign that the government might have collaborated in the events leading up to the 1999 dismissal of parliament is the identity of the man leading the charge against Ahmad al-Kulaib. This was 'Abbas al-Khodary, a Shi'a who is neither a member of the Islamist opposition nor someone normally associated with Islamist positions. Indeed, 'Abbas as a service MP maintains close relations with the government to ensure continuation of the stream of favors he can dispense to his constituents in return for their support at the polls. As I noted earlier in this chapter, 'Abbas probably owes his membership on the PPFC to his political reliability, and his prominence in the attack on Ahmad al-Kulaib supports suspicions that this was a government-approved production rather than a genuine reflection of offended religious sensibilities. However, that a religious issue triggered the dismissal of parliament also had its uses because it focused negative popular attention on Islamist deputies. Opposition Islamists such as Mubarak al-Duwailah, the most visible critic of the government's weapons purchases, and issue Islamists such as Nasr al-Sana', were high on the list of members said to have been targeted by the regime for defeat in the July 1999 elections.[63]

Threats to investigate allegations of corrupt business deals by ruling family members and conflicts over oil and finance policies—the same issues that triggered the two earlier parliamentary dissolutions[64]—are the most likely final causes of the dismissal of the 1996 parliament. Immediately following the amir's announcement, members of the opposition suggested that the planned questioning of finance minister and ruling family member 'Ali al-Salim al-Sabah for irregularities associated with the privatization of the Kuwait Investment Company was the actual reason for the suspension of the parliament.[65] Other fortuitious events created opportunities that could be opened by a parliamentary suspension at this particular time. One indication was a signal of the government's intention to ignore the 1997 measures discussed earlier in this chapter which demanded closer coordination between itself and the parliament on oil and investment issues. In a statement the day after the amir's decree dismissing the parliament, oil minister Sa'ud Nasir al-Sabah said publicly that upstream privatization did not require the passage of a new law,[66] although he also said that "the government would not try to finalise the [oil privatization] plan with oil majors in parliament's absence. . . . 'We will discuss this matter with the brothers in the new parliament and see what will be decided upon in this project.' "[67] Shortly afterward, the amir issued a decree granting permission for foreign ownership of up to 100 percent of Kuwaiti firms,[68] a significant reversal of a series of policies going back to 1960 which had protected domestic, primarily merchant-class, interests from foreign competition in Kuwait itself.[69] This direct attack on the merchants' heretofore protected domestic economic stronghold marks a departure from the ensemble of pacts between these two political forces that Jill Crystal identified as integral to the social contract between rulers and merchants in Kuwait.[70] Not coincidentally, it also signaled the rulers' intentions of providing a hospitable climate for foreign investment.

Some Kuwaitis were encouraged by the decision of the amir to call for new elections at the same time that he dismissed the 1996 parliament, believing that his action indicates the growing responsiveness of the regime to the demands of democratic governance.[71] Others are less optimistic that the decision to follow constitutional procedures this time signals a real sea change in the attitudes of Kuwaiti rulers.[72] All would do well to recall the words of economist Walter J. Levy who, more than twenty years ago, cautioned policymakers in oil-exporting countries not to ignore the long-term interests of their countries in their euphoria at the rivers of revenues flowing to them from the oil revolution.[73] Despite its many failures, Kuwait did better than most in this regard, particularly during the period when rulers and parliaments kept one another in check.[74] If these checks and balances can be strengthened, many of what now appear to be intractable economic and social problems could find constructive amelioration and resolution.

Human Rights

While many would argue that economic entitlements to national resources are human rights,[75] in Kuwait as elsewhere human rights are more conventionally seen as civic, civil, and property rights. With respect to these issues, Kuwait's human rights record was harshly criticized following liberation, when news of mistreatment of household servants and abuse of prisoners subject to State Security Court procedures were brought to the attention of the world community by international human rights groups.[76] The first domestic human rights group organized following liberation was the Kuwaiti Association to Defend War Victims, established in March 1991. Chaired by Ghanim al-Najjar, the group applied twice for a license but was denied both times.

> We concentrated on human rights work during the dangerous and chaotic period after liberation. We cleaned prisons because there was no staff to do that. We appointed lawyers for the prisoners and, with the [cooperation] of prison authorities, we were able to arrange visits for prisoners' families. . . . We had a membership of more than 900 Kuwaitis, all insiders.[77]

Following the 1992 election, on November 17, the association, along with another group working on prisoner-of-war issues, organized a large demonstration in front of the parliament building. The demonstration drew the members outside to listen, and its size and intensity convinced the government that it needed to exercise greater control over human rights groups operating in Kuwait. The government tried to persuade the activists to form a united organization under its aegis, a strategy similar to what had been used in the co-optation of Citizens for a Free Kuwait during the occupation. In the case of the human rights groups, however, activists felt that the government's terms were "too political to accept," and they continued to work on their own. The government then asked the parliament to pass a law banning unlicensed groups. The measure passed by one vote and the decree to dissolve all unlicensed voluntary organizations was published in the summer of 1993.[78]

The Kuwaiti human rights community is large and varied, and carries on extensive relations with similar groups abroad. For example, the Kuwait Society for Human Rights (KSHR), organized in 1993 under the leadership of former parliamentarian Jasim al-Qatami, is affiliated with the Cairo-based Arab Organization for Human Rights. KSHR also was denied a license to operate legally. Most Kuwaiti human rights groups are unlicensed, a few by choice. The Pro-Democracy Committee did not seek a license because it wanted to avoid government interference in its activities. The League of Families of Prisoners of War did not register because members saw the group as temporary. However, the unlicensed status of virtually all the rest of the voluntary associations Kuwaitis have established to work on human rights, including an Islamist group that concentrates on POW issues, is not a result of design but rather of government denial of their legal status to operate. These groups irritated the government, not only because they were more effective than state organizations charged with overseeing efforts to deal with the same problems—for example, the Kuwaiti Association to Defend War Victims and the League of Families of POWs actually carried out the investigations that resulted in detailed information about Kuwaiti POWS, including biographical information and testimony from Iraqi prisoners who had been released as to the last date each one had been seen alive—but also because they were so effective in building international channels of communication and playing a role independent of the government in international arenas.[79]

When the cabinet published the order to dissolve all unlicensed voluntary organizations, only human rights groups were mentioned by name although the ban was to apply to societies of every type.[80] The government justified the ban as nothing more than an attempt to enforce a 1985 moratorium on new voluntary associations. That moratorium had been augmented by a 1988 amendment to the then twenty-six-year-old basic law governing voluntary associations which gave the cabinet complete authority over licensing.[81] Here it should be noted both that the moratorium was, in practice, selective—it was not applied to groups such as the Islamist women's organization headed by the wife of the crown prince, for example, which received a license in 1991—and that the amendment to the 1962 law on associations was one of the more than five hundred pieces of legislation passed during the 1986/1992 parliamentary suspension. As I discussed in the previous chapter, the amir has fought the right of the National Assembly to overturn any of these nonparliamentary decrees. Thus, the showdown over human rights activism was and continues to be embedded in the larger struggle of the regime to limit the power of parliament and the civil rights of Kuwaiti citizens.

In spite of the risks of operating without a license, the banned human rights groups have remained active, supporting their work through donations and member dues. Meanwhile, the parliament created a new standing committee on human rights. This initiative is another illustration of the interdependence between populism and pacts in Kuwait. The parliamentary human rights committee, like the PPFC during its heyday, provides a protected space within which the concerns of citizen activists can be articulated and pursued. It also moves issues identified by the popular groups into the National Assembly for consideration, and serves as an official channel through which international pressure can be applied to support both the local activists and their human rights initiatives.[82]

Following the establishment of the parliamentary committee, Kuwait's human rights community succeeded in promoting a rapid expansion of formal human rights protections. A major step forward was taken in a July 1995 decision by the government to abolish the much-hated State Security Court. Citizen pressure also stimulated a modest reorganization of priorities in government ministries such as Interior and Labor. The consequence was to strengthen regulation and supervision of visa authorizations, foreign labor recruitment practices, and conditions of employment for domestic workers. In addition, the staff of the Dasma police station, the main center for dealing with complaints about employer abuses, was upgraded.[83] Other concerns include protecting the due process rights of foreigners. For example, the KSHR adopted the cause of a foreign teacher who was shot by a disgruntled Kuwaiti student.[84]

Citizens also organize spontaneously to halt particular instances of abusive behavior. A "milestone" case occurred in 1995. A shopowner in 'Abdullah al-Salim neighborhood fired a non-Muslim worker because the shopowner thought his employee's religion was "putting customers off." Within twenty-four hours, as the result of a stream of faxes and letters of condemnation, the shopowner was given a notice of eviction by the cooperative society for violating his employee's human rights. 'Ali al-Baghli, then the chair of the parliamentary human rights committee, said of this episode, "When it happened . . . many aware citizens sprang up at this irresponsible act and they redressed the situation. This is the kind of support we also hope to get, the kind of strong popular support."[85]

The parliamentary committee allows the National Assembly to initiate action on human rights issues via normal parliamentary procedures. Following the abolition of the State Security Court, the parliament ratified three pending human rights conventions, although it has yet to rescind reservations that were attached to its February 1994 ratification of the Convention to End Discrimination Against Women.[86] A related popular initiative is a campaign to incorporate human rights issues and the Universal Declaration of Human Rights in school curricula.[87] The pattern of human rights activities in Kuwait reveals an informal division of labor between the voluntary associations and the parliamentary committee. Responding to a charge that his group concerned itself only with the rights of expatriates, Jasim al-Qatami replied that the KSHR was ready to respond to any charge of human rights violations in Kuwait, but that Kuwaiti nationals have multiple venues for such complaints, including the courts and the parliamentary committee. "Our society mostly receives complaints relating to human rights from expatriates who face more violations than citizens."[88] The society's efforts on behalf of the teacher mentioned earlier, and on behalf of Kuwaiti prisoners of war, Jordanian prisoners in Kuwait, and the group's participation in international conferences such as the 1995 Beijing meeting on women's human rights, a 1996 human rights conference in Lebanon, and the 1997 National Organization for Human Rights Workshop in Mexico, are other indications of its role as an integral element in the vigorous and highly developed new social movement to promote human rights in Kuwait.

Citizen activists and parliamentary bodies have made progress in extending human rights protections, but Kuwait has much more to do in this regard. The U.S. State Department's report on human rights in Kuwait in 1997 notes that, despite improvement in the country's overall human rights record, many serious problems remain.

> Citizens cannot change their head of state. The Government bans formal political parties. . . . The government restricts freedom of assembly and association, and places some limits on freedom of religion. Journalists practice self-censorship, and the Government uses informal censorship. The Government prevents the return to Kuwait of stateless persons who have strong ties to the country. Deportation orders may be issued by administrative order, and hundreds of people are being held in detention facilities pending deportation. Many have been held for up to 6 years. Discrimination and vio-

lence against women are problems. Domestic servants are not protected by labor law, and unskilled foreign workers suffer from a lack of a minumim wage in the private sector, and from failures to enforce labor law.[89]

Many of the problems recounted in the State Department's list are intertwined together, but perhaps the predominant cause of human rights abuses in Kuwait is the problem at the top of the list, the lack of government accountability. A brief review of one recent example shows this well.

The spring of 1998 can only be described as politically turbulent. It included a forced cabinet reshuffle in April to avoid a vote of no-confidence against the information minister, Shaikh Saʿud al-Nasir al-Sabah, for failing to halt the sale at a book fair of literature to which parliamentary Islamists took objection.[90] However, calls for interpellations of ministers did not halt with the formation of a new government. Other ministers complained of "threats" that they would be hauled up for a grilling by service MPs out to gain stature among their constituents, and by Islamists who wanted to put pressure on the education minister to speed up gender segregation.[91] These attacks on ministers came on top of continuing pressure from parliamentarians and citizens about the misuse of public funds. Harsh parliamentary criticism of government initiatives ranging from revenue-raising measures such as the proposal for a 50 percent increase in motor gasoline prices to revenue-depleting measures such as contracts to purchase British missiles and American howitzers, were among many that drew the ministers' ire.[92] The resulting government disarray provoked feelings of schadenfreude in some columnists writing for the independent Kuwaiti press, who saw it as poetic justice.

> In *al-Qabbas*, Saud al-Samaka . . . says that the government is largely to blame for parliament's failure to act on various pressing national issues that have been put to it. Its legislative sessions and meetings of its various committees are often without a quorum because of the absence of "service MPs"—the term used to refer to apolitical legislators who used their posts primarily to secure government patronage—who stay away because they are busy soliciting official favors for their constituents. And those MPs, who constitute a large proportion of the total, were helped to win their mandates by the government itself, which provided them with the "facilities" needed to defeat their rivals at the ballot box.[93]

However, rather than accepting some of the responsibility, the government chose to castigate parliament as an institution for the problems it was encountering. With great publicity, the crown prince sent invitations to a reported 1,200 public figures to attend a gigantic banquet on June 1. He invited "hundreds of ministry undersecretaries, assistant undersecretaries, heads of government and other official bodies, businessmen, academics and journalists," along with the members of the Majlis al-Watani whose ostentatious inclusion made some parliamentarians nervous. "These are not representatives of the people, and no one should assume that together they make up an enlarged parliament for the Kuwaiti people."[94] The dinner was expected to produce a definitive public statement about the government's current difficulties but, in the end, the crown prince offered little more than platitudes about Kuwait's "family spirit" and the need to adopt measures to make Kuwait a leading commercial center in the region.[95]

On the day of the crown prince's dinner, Husain 'Ali al-Qallaf produced its most significant event. He submitted a request to question interior minister Shaikh Mohammad al-Khaled al-Sabah "over increased violence, rampant human rights abuse, and a pervasive drugs problem." Citing an "unprecedented deterioration in security performance," Husain denounced rising rates of violent crime; routine escapes from Kuwaiti prisons by prisoners convicted of violent crimes; a rapidly growing drug problem exacerbated by the apparent ease with which police officers and other highly connected traffickers had been able to use their connections to escape arrest and prosecution; and human rights abuses of persons arrested and in detention, including two Kuwaiti Shi'a whom the ministry allowed to be extradited to Saudi Arabia for questioning with regard to the bombing of a U.S. military installation there.[96] The two detainees had been held for a year and a half but eventually were sent home without being charged. They reported that during their incarceration they had been tortured, and so contacted Husain, a member of the parliamentary human rights committee, to ask him to seek restitution. Husain's motion to question the minister touched so many nerves that he was able to demand to cross-examine Shaikh Mohammad about his overall performance rather than having to specify particular grievances to which he might have been limited during the interpellation.

The crown prince responded the next day by saying that it was not in Husain's interests to make such accusations and that he hoped that the request would be withdrawn.[97] Shortly afterward, the cabinet proclaimed its full confidence in the minister and made pointed reference in its announcement to how highly he was valued by the amir.[98] But Husain failed to withdraw his interpellation request, prompting the crown prince to send a request of his own, to the amir, to dissolve the parliament. The regime was praised for the impending dissolution by its supporters in the Kuwaiti press including *al-Watan* (owned by Shaikh 'Ali al-Khalifa—see above), and *al-Siyassa* (its English-language version is published as the *Arab Times*), whose editor, Ahmed al-Jarallah, has been a vociferous opponent of parliamentary independence virtually since the rein-statement of the National Assembly in October 1992.[99] The crown prince's re-quest initiated a series of negotiations with parliamentary leaders in which the threat of dissolution was used to wring concessions out of the parliament.[100]

Following these negotiations and the settlement which allowed the parlia-ment to continue, the negotiators from the parliament were criticized for hav-ing caved in to pressures from the government.[101] However, as I discussed above, there was mounting evidence that the theft of public funds had reached crisis proportions despite massive efforts by parliament and citizen watchdogs to halt it.[102] This may have contributed to the parliamentary negotiators' deci-sion to go along with "the deal" pushed by the government. The closure of par-liament in 1998 not only would have cut off all official sources of information about government fiscal policies but also all legislative avenues for limiting both new taxes and new spending.

The deal also involved substantial losses in parliamentary power. It entailed the staging of a vote on a proposal to conduct the grilling of the interior min-ister *in camera*. Its adoption prompted Husain 'Ali al-Qallaf to walk out and then to withdraw his request.[103] Other elements in this "gentlemen's agree-ment" included pledges by members to moderate their criticism of ministers, reduce the number of critical responses to ministerial statements "with or without good cause," and minimize their use of parliamentary devices such as points of order to influence the course of debate.[104] *Al-Qabbas* was particular-ly concerned that the deal would make any future attempt to interpellate a minister impossible.[105] These fears were justified. As I have noted, both previ-ous dissolutions were preceded either by parliamentary requests to interpellate ministers who were members of the ruling family or by severe disagreements between the government and the parliament on financial issues and oil policy. The 1999 dissolution also preceded a request to interpellate a ruling family member at a time when the government and the parliament were at odds over economic restructuring and a significant shift in oil policy. Even though the third dismissal of a sitting parliament followed constitutionally mandated pro-cedures, the strong family resemblance among the various political circum-stances surrounding all three dissolutions suggests caution in equating this one instance of constitutionality with a new commitment to democratic life.

How Long?

The constitutionality of the procedures governing the 1999 parliamentary dis-solution might well be another example of Kuwaitis getting by with the help of their friends. The restless international spotlight has shifted to many other trouble-spots since invasion, war, liberation, and the restoration of normal political life drew the eyes of the world to Kuwait. But the events of the early 1990s, along with the normal processes associated with modernity, have enlarged the boundaries of the Kuwaiti political arena. Democracy constituencies in states that Kuwait depends on for its strategic security are among the external actors for whom Kuwait is a sector of the world stage on which they operate. Expatriates, international oil companies, British courts, transnational human rights organizations, and many other individual and corporate bodies are active participants in Kuwaiti life and link that life to other people and issues in other places.[106] For most of these external actors, constitutionality—clear rules and governments that abide by them—are bottom-line requirements.

The world city is embedded in an international public life; meanwhile, the city-state is the product of a domestic public life that seems all too often like life in a large and contentious family. The 1992 parliament was widely regarded as overly contentious. Whether the government interfered as extensively in the 1996 election as so many Kuwaitis insisted to me that it had, the outcome of the vote brought defeat to key opposition critics. These results were touted as a popular reaction against the opposition, an electorate opting for cooperation over contention. But the 1996 parliament was even more contentious than its predecessor, and even less inclined to follow the government's lead on critical issues. What the 1996 election demonstrates to me is the aptness of the adage, "Be careful what you wish for." The same advice holds true for the 1999 election.

Since 1980 the rulers of Kuwait have manipulated constituencies and elections to change the character of the parliament. Their aim was to get rid of the merchant traditionals who felt themselves entitled to a strong voice in public affairs, and to replace them with "new men" and tribal representatives who, because they would owe their social prominence and their private benefits to the regime, would know their places and act accordingly. To do this, they promoted what Shafeeq Ghabra calls the "desertization" of Kuwait, the incorporation of massive numbers of tribesmen, along with traditional tribal values, into the politics and society of the country.[107] They shaped election districts to improve the chances of religiously oriented candidates whom they saw, I believe mistakenly, as additional sources of "traditional" support for the regime. The amir's 1999 bid to enfranchise women reflected the regime's expectation that including women as voters would shift election results in its favor. However, woman suffrage, when it comes, may lead to as many unforeseen and unwanted results as has the naturalization of *badu*.

Kuwaiti rulers have long interfered in elections, both to defeat their opponents and to help their friends. The parliaments that resulted should have been far less critical of the rulers' autocratic ways than pre-1981 Kuwaiti parliaments had been. However, I argue in the last chapter that this calculation was incorrect. The desertization strategy was costly financially and in terms of social cohesion. It also didn't work. Most new men saw their preferments as entitlements and quite a few came to parliament with their own agendas. Many willing to go along with the government in exchange for personal perks and constituent benefits proved to be unreliable allies and expensive to boot. Enfranchised women may be similarly uppity and resistant to control.

Meanwhile, the myriad outcomes of modernity continue to fragment Kuwaiti society and support autonomy and agency among members of every social group, including the ruling family itself. In the last chapter, I look at some of the hopeful outcomes of modernity, particularly those centered on Kuwaitis engaged in improving old institutions, creating new ones, and staking out innovative positions on the issues of the day. It is difficult to imagine that current political antagonists could put their bitter memories of the past twenty years far enough behind them to move on. However, they are not the only ones involved in shaping the future of Kuwaiti politics.

In the days following the opening of the 1992 National
Assembly, I talked with a number of Kuwaitis about
the future of parliamentary democracy in their country. Two of them, 'Eisa al-Serraf and Hasan al-'Eisa, are
secularist democrats.[1] 'Eisa al-Serraf is a strong believer in the power of civil society to reform autocratic
regimes. Although he was pessimistic in the short
term, 'Eisa was optimistic overall about Kuwait's future as a democratic state.

> I see this parliament as similar to the 1981 parlia-
> ment. In this parliament, the liberal opposition is
> rather weak. In 1996 the people will correct this im-
> balance as they did in 1985. In 1981 there was only
> one democrat in the parliament. The others were
> not liberal. They were just independent and sympa-
> thetic with the Islamists. In 1985 the Islamists were
> reduced to their just representation. . . . When we
> have a suspension, the committed democrats are the
> most vocal. They get chopped, harassed, and give
> the Islamist groups the chance to rise up. . . . As com-
> mitted democrats we feel pissed. *We* fight for the
> restoration of the constitution. *We* get the beatings.
> *We* get the tear gas. And *they* get the benefits. . . .
> [But] they are part of the civic groups and influence
> the regime with continued democratic life. With
> continued democratic life we can make a difference.
> In a twist of things, events, they also can have a role
> in changing people's minds.

Hasan al 'Eisa was far less sanguine because he sees
Kuwaiti culture as resistant to the slow forces of democratization that his friend puts so much faith in.
Hasan also is profoundly mistrustful of the Islamist
trend and the way its brand of politics and its message

damage the confidence of the public in democratic institutions and practices. He does not see civil society as inherently liberalizing but rather as capable of altering the balance between democratic and authoritarian forces in either direction, depending on the programs and actions of its various components.

> The Islamists will be dangerous in 1996. They are controlling everything on the street. They are allied with the regime. . . . The people of Kuwait are unaware of liberal democracy. They say, "We are Muslim and we should vote for another Muslim. Human rights is not such a big issue. We should enforce Islamic laws." These people know nothing of the decline in human rights. The government itself is betting with the Ikhwan because the people are ignorant and do not see them as a threat to the future. . . . Liberal democracy is not deeply evolved in this country, in spite of the bullshit that we have been democratic for thirty years.

"Liberal democracy is not deeply evolved in this country." "We have been democratic for thirty years." These observations are the bookends bracketing a long shelf of stories about democracy in Kuwait. In between are many volumes of varying lengths and genres, from grand narratives of the evolution of political institutions to romances and adventure stories describing individuals and groups pushing forward their own visions of the good society. Scattered throughout the ups and downs of Kuwait's grand narrative there are short stories and vignettes that reflect the active engagement of thousands of Kuwaitis in political life.

Plurality in the City-State

I begin my less than firm conclusions about the prospects for democracy in Kuwait with some vignettes; in Kuwait, vignettes are not trivial. The size of the community; its integration via social networks, national news media, and the ubiquitous telephone; and the centrality of politics to everyday life in a city-state all contribute to the dissemination of information about the opinions and actions of individuals in a way that amplifies their political effect. Kuwaiti political myths and popular institutions are based on a fundamental notion of the right of Kuwaiti men, and increasingly Kuwaiti women as well, to participate directly in the public life of the nation. Kuwaitis engage in this arena not simply as candidates or occupants of political offices; many speak to a national audience from other professional points of view such as business or the arts. "Public intellectuals" regularly offer their opinions on a wide variety of issues, persons, and events. The inclusion of so many who are not formally politicians as opinion leaders and role models explains why, even before the amir decreed that women should have formal political rights, they had begun entering this grand national arena in ever larger numbers. Women and men and their multiple overlapping discourses are like a chorus made up of many parts—singing together, though rarely in unison. In Kuwait the legitimacy of the voice that speaks and answers for itself is one of the mythic values underlying cultural support for protected spaces, and constitutional protections for free speech, a free press, and the right to meet together in public.

This myth is challenged by others depicting Kuwait as a mass society divided by sect, education, residence, gender, family, and class. Their stories feature noble/thieving princes, magnanimous/rapacious merchants, ethical/depraved secularists, holy/crazed Islamists, oppressed/uppity women, along with a large cast of city slickers, bedouin bumpkins, and other stock characters. Their message is that listeners should understand the voice as representative of an interest, and interests as inherently in conflict. Such a perspective in the West is associated with the ideology of possessive individualism and the rise of mass politics.[2] The pattern in Kuwait appears to be similar. Mass politics appeals to large numbers of Kuwaiti *attentistes* to whom the service candidate tells a story of himself as the defender of the interests of constituent victims in need of political protection—a Kuwaiti version of the organized crime that Charles Tilly describes as integral to state formation (see chapter 2). At the same time, some Kuwaitis from virtually every social group aspire to and achieve an individual public identity, thanks to the scale of public life in a city-state and the fast transition to modernity made possible by the country's oil wealth and the unusually egalitarian formula that guided its distribution in Kuwait as compared to most other oil-exporting countries.

Because of the salience of the individual to politics, the overall trend of any political group is matched in importance by variability within it. The relative weight given to each depends on the ideology and experience of the observer. For example, in the two analyses above, both 'Eisa and Hasan talked about Islamism as a political force, but each understands and evaluates its contributions differently. To the democratic populist, Islamist movements are ideologically problematic but, even so, enhance the authority of civil society as a whole. They provide protected, if unreliable, platforms for attacking an autocratic state, and the actions of their individual members contribute to changing people's minds about political participation—Islamists also engage in political action whose outcomes cannot be controlled. They, like other activists, contribute to democratization by the fact of their engagement and the example it sets, not merely by what they say they are trying to accomplish through their programs.

To the democratic constitutionalist, the individual is less salient as a political force and, consequently, Islamist movements are more threatening. Sunni Islamism in particular advocates discrimination against women and minorities, and Islamists of both sects advocate the imposition of significant, though somewhat different, constraints on everyone's civil liberties. Even worse, the numeric dominance of neofundamentalists among Kuwaiti Islamists ensures the persistence of attacks on democracy as an alien doctrine that Kuwait should expel from its body politic. Rather than sheltering democratic life, the mosque of the neofundamentalists is another citadel of autocratic authority.[3]

However they are judged, Islamists are the pivot of the balance of power between autocrats and constitutionalists in Kuwait today. Islamism's attacks on civil liberties are real assaults on the rights of women, children, and minorities of every kind. However, this far-from-monolithic movement is rife with competing agendas. The fearsomeness of Kuwaiti Islamism today revolves around its surprising success at imposing gender segregation at postsecondary schools in Kuwait. This victory is interpreted as a reflection of Islamism's hegemonic power. However, there are few other issues capable of mobilizing most or all of Kuwait's Islamist political forces on the same side. As the "easy" issues are used up, Islamist cohesion and Islamism's political base are likely to erode. Neofundamentalist attacks on civil liberties already have begun to edge into danger zones for Islamist leaders, few of whom seem to appreciate the degree to which modernity has penetrated Kuwaiti life. Demands to prohibit mixed-gender public gatherings such as concerts and lectures stimulate backlash among students. Calls to ban books and films are resented by middle-class intellectuals. Proposals to outlaw satellite dishes might even mobilize housewives angry to lose access to their favorite foreign programs. One of the most interesting among such developments in Kuwait is the growing prominence of people whom Haya al-Mughni calls "independent Islamist women" speaking in "new voices of protest."[4] The fragmentation characteristic of modernity disrupts Islamist plans for social control by diminishing the number of citizens who share their monadic worldview, even from within the Islamist movement itself.

The significant community of interests shared by Islamists and the regime is not the only story here. Islamist leaders also have real conflicts with the government and its policies. One example is the lack of a serious government response to the results of the three-year investigation headed by the IPA's Ahmad Baqr that had looked into Kuwait's defense and foreign policy before and after the Iraqi invasion. The committee found strong evidence of corruption in defense procurement and faulted the government for Kuwait's failure to perform better militarily when Iraq invaded. Despite the discretion of the committee throughout its proceedings, however, the crown prince refused to attend parliamentary sessions when the report was scheduled to be discussed, convincing the chair that the rulers not only oppose reform but feel safe in ignoring the appeals of those who want to clean up corruption in Kuwait. The Salafin are not the only Islamists with a strong anticorruption agenda. Mubarak al-Duwailah of the ICM is among the most energetic critics of wasteful expenditures on defense.

Another little-noted development in Islamist politics in Kuwait is that leaders who do throw in their lot with the government may weaken their popular appeal. Secularists attracted the most vociferous criticism during the 1996 campaign for having sold out the interests of their constituencies, but Islamist Jasim al-'Aoun (IPA) also

> had problems with his constituency. People said he betrayed the values of the group. It was very clear. Originally he was Minister of Electricity and Water, but in the cabinet he did not stand up to support the voters. He is pro-government. He goes along with whatever the government wants. He has no strong beliefs of his own.[5]

Although Jasim cited reasons of health for deciding not to run in 1996 (he had donated one of his kidneys to his daughter and experienced complications from the surgery), his chances for reelection were poor given his support for utility user fees and his statement opposing the no-confidence motion on Ahmad al-Rub'i. Following the election he continued as a cabinet member and thus as an unelected member of parliament, a sign that his health probably was not the primary motivation for his decision not to run in 1996.

Islamist successes themselves plant seeds that undermine future political victories. For example, the Islamists' insistence that gender segregation was supported by everyone but the press and a few government ministers, though it was not accurate, was persuasive enough to convince the government to support a modified gender-segregation proposal. When government support ensured its passage, the resulting uproar prompted candidates from across the 1996 political spectrum, from Shi'i Islamists like Husain 'Ali al-Qallaf to service candidates like 'Abbas al-Khodary, to put themselves forward as advocates of women's rights, although most Sunni Islamists remained firm in their opposition. Kuwaiti women used the opportunity created by the spotlight on gender politics to bring their demands for political rights to the attention of the members of the future 1996 parliament, and to attract new allies from a public absorbed in the campaign.

In 1996 feminist efforts were more broadly based and differently organized than in 1992, part of the trend in new social movement activism noted elsewhere in Kuwaiti society (see chapter 8). Rather than being associated primarily with formal voluntary associations such as the elite Women's Cultural and Social Society (WCCS), some demonstrations, including a one-day women's strike,[6] were organized by an ad hoc group of young working women. Organizers went out to the grass roots, including to women's tents at campaign diwaniyyas, to explain their positions and ask women and men to wear blue ribbons signifying the wearer's support for women's rights. These novel activities capitalized on the salience of the gender issue and attracted political newcomers such as students and middle-class working women to events promoting women's rights.

The mobilization of interest and support from social groups formerly not very prominent in women's rights activism in Kuwait continued after the election and contributed to the normalization of the idea that women's involvement in public life was natural. This shift supported expectations that women's achievement of full political rights was merely a matter of time. The 1999 election in Qatar in which women not only voted but also stood as candidates was embarrassing to Kuwaitis who thought that their country would be the first on the Arab side of the Gulf to give women political rights. Consequently, the amir's attempt later that year to give women the right to vote and run for office did not seem particularly radical or ideologically motivated, but rather a reasonable and pragmatic way to deal with a reform that was long overdue.

Middle-class activism in Kuwait as elsewhere tends to be pragmatic and issue-oriented rather than ideological, another mark of new social movements and further evidence of their growing importance in Kuwaiti politics. The greater appeal of this style of activism may partly explain why the old secular political blocs have had limited success in attracting new candidates and voters. Another problem for the old groupings is a negative result of personal politics: an accumulation of personal animosities that reflect on the entire group. Perceptions that the old groups are too doctrinaire and too dominated by individuals whom one might dislike—or simply be tired of—are helping to set the stage for a different approach to Kuwaiti "quasi-party" politics, as well.

A potentially important step was taken following the 1996 election, when twenty Kuwaitis got together to talk about how politics might be done differently.[7] In April 1997 the first announcement that a new political group was on the horizon appeared in local newspapers.[8] According to founding member Shamlan al-'Eisa,

We aspire to greater democratic freedoms, be it at the economic or social level. [Our group] is not against the government . . . or against [already existing] parties. We seek to be independent and attract the silent majority of the people.[9]

The new organization, called the Nahdha (Renaissance) Party by the *Arab Times* and the National Democratic Rally by the *Mideast Mirror*, includes women among its founding members—Moudhi al-Hmoud, the Kuwait University professor who was one of the two female speakers at the 1992 campaign rally sponsored by Saleh al-Yasin (see chapter 6), is one of them.[10] Before it had even selected a governing board, the group applied for and received a licence to publish a weekly journal. It also attracted the attention of members of parliament, several of whom are reported to have asked to join but were turned down "for the time being."[11] By June 1997 about two thousand citizens had stated their interest in joining. If there is to be a renaissance in Kuwaiti politics, efforts to organize the center will be a crucial element in bringing it about.

> The emergence of the Grouping has created fresh hope in Kuwait that political life can become more institutionalized and geared to policies rather than individuals. It is a political party in the Kuwaiti style, in a country whose constitution bans parties but not informal political groups. . . . It seeks to promote respect for political and intellectual pluralism, give national interests precedence over factional considerations, and champion openness and tolerance.[12]

'Abdullah Nibari thinks the "silent majority" that Shamlan al-'Eisa identifies as being attracted to the new group includes those middle-class professionals among Kuwaiti *attentistes* who want to be involved in politics but have been afraid that public activism would draw them into confrontations with authority.[13] Such a group as he describes is the liberal antithesis of Islamism. It is made up of a collection of persons whose preferred antidote to the autocratic state is a very large private sphere in which they can carry on, unmolested by the state or by religious radicals, those aspects of their lives that they choose to move into that protected space. As such lifestyle liberals enter the public arena, Islamist puritans will encounter strong competition for their voter bases.

Nonviolent political change in Kuwait also depends on changes in the attitudes of members of the ruling family. Some will occur automatically as the older members, with their own lifelong antagonisms toward participatory politics and its irritating gadflies, exit the political scene. Crown Prince Sa'd al-'Abdullah went to England in March 1997 for cancer surgery. His long absence from the parliament during his illness and recovery is probably a major reason why the rulers' exasperation with the 1996 National Assembly was expressed more frequently as calls to change the cabinet than as threats to dismiss the parliament. Although his stand-in as prime minister, Shaikh Nasir al-Ahmad, is not exactly a democrat, he was significantly more accommodating in his public behavior than Shaikh Sa'd as well as less provocative with regard to playing the "religious card." As I noted in chapter 8, after Shaikh Sa'd returned, threats to dissolve the parliament resumed. Meanwhile, the cordial reception by the crown prince of the "spiritual leader" of the Palestinian Islamist group HAMAS in May 1998 was perhaps intended to reestablish his authority over another cousin and potential rival, foreign minister Shaikh Sabah al-Ahmad, who resigned in protest but withdrew his resignation two days later at the request of the amir.[14]

It is conventional among a number of analysts to explain Kuwaiti ruling family politics as a rivalry for power between the descendents of Mubarak's two sons, Jabir and Salim. Such an approach seems overly simplified, ignoring as it does how modernity has affected the ruling family itself. Modernity as a worldview alters the ambitions of ruling family members just as it alters the ambitions of merchants and members of the middle class, and reflexivity enlarges the strategic repertoires of all of them. One example can be found in the attempts of younger members of the Sabah to run for parliament. Two declared their interest in 1992 and one in 1996. The 1996 contender, Shaikh Ahmad al-Fahad, then head of Kuwait's Olympic Committee, said that he wanted to run to shake up the parliamentary routine by introducing a member of the ruling family in the same capacity as other elected members. Insisting that other family members as well as citizens had urged him to run, he cited among the reasons for his action the need for strong leadership and the importance of the government's enforcing the laws if it wants to preserve its power.[15]

These ventures into electoral politics by younger family members were squelched by the amir. He asked them to withdraw their candidacies on the grounds that the constitution establishes the relationship between the rulers and the people, a subtle way of saying not only that the Sabah are a race apart from the rest of the Kuwaitis but also that the amir and his close advisers are the only members of the family who ought to be involved directly in politics.

This euphemistic slap to the ambitious young is not likely to reconcile them to decorative roles as the family grows larger at the same time that the number of powerful positions in the state that the family can continue to monopolize is under pressure to shrink. I have speculated elsewhere that Shaikh 'Ali al-Khalifa's intensely competitive behavior is driven in part by his exclusion from the family's center of power because he is not a direct descendent of the amir Mubarak.[16] A similar desire for individual status and recognition is revealed by the decisions of young Sabah to engage in public life on the same basis as all but their senior relations enjoy. Even when public expressions of dissent by young Sabah can be interpreted as an extension of the conflicts between the two "entitled" branches of the family, such as the statement issued by Shaikh Nasir al-Sabah al-Ahmad blaming the prime minister for the standoff between the cabinet and the parliament setting off the June 1998 crisis,[17] it also signifies an assertion of the self by a subordinate male family member. This desire by the ambitious and able young to achieve for the self rather than to act as an instrument of a clan also marked the aspirations of Sa'd Ben Tafla al-'Ajmy, who ran for parliament on his own without seeking a primary endorsement from his tribe. Both examples mark modern desires and behaviors and indicate a growing hollowness at the center of traditional tribal social formations.

Modernity enlarges the individual and increases the attractiveness of private life;[18] it also enlarges the public sphere and provides opportunities for new political men to mobilize constituencies.[19] Among the most powerful of these venues are the mass media.[20] New men in the ruling family have superior resources for a relatively independent engagement in public life through newspapers and magazines. 'Ali al-Khalifa, as I discussed in chapter 8, is now an owner of a leading Kuwait daily, *al-Watan*. Another example is *al-Zaman*, a magazine run by Nasir al-Sabah al-Ahmad. Shortly before the attempt on 'Abdullah Nibari's life, *Al-Zaman* ran an editorial advocating more decisiveness and innovation in government. Complaining that that "the government had no program or vision . . . and was . . . continuing to run the country as a rentier state,"[21] it concluded by calling for "an effective and lively political administration which possesses vision and decisiveness."[22] Few in the opposition would disagree with this assessment which, perhaps not surprisingly, echoes closely the statements of the aspiring Sabah parliamentary candidate, Shaikh Ahmad al-Fahad. It also foreshadowed the comments Nasir al-Sabah al-Ahmad made during the parliamentary crisis of 1998 (see above) which emphasized the superiority of representation of the parliament over the cabinet and the constitutional authority of the parliament to question ministers about their actions.[23]

To be able to continue to manage Kuwaiti politics in the style of the old imagining depends not only on politicians who follow the norms of traditional life but also on a continued supply of voters who see their electoral role as following the leadership of a patron or family head. The selective enfranchisement of new, mostly *badu*, voters reflects an appreciation by Kuwaiti rulers of their dependence on citizens who behave like subjects. A young Kuwaiti who lives in the district of Old Jahra' recounted some childhood memories of post-1981 elections in Kuwait.

They used to go around with pickup trucks and pack bedouins in the back like so many sheep. Then they'd get them to the [polling station] and march them in to vote. Most of them [the *badu*] didn't even know what they were doing. They just did what the organizers told them to.[24]

The voter-as-subject continues as a potentially decisive presence in Kuwaiti political life as long as there are enfranchisable Kuwaiti residents who live in the old imagining. Three friends accompanied me to the school that served as the Old Jahra' polling station near the end of election evening in 1996. We two women went into several "precincts," classrooms built around a central court-yard, to observe the balloting. Meanwhile, the two men meandered around the crowded courtyard, observing negotiations between vote buyers and tribal leaders and watching the subsequent herding of silent men into the various rooms to vote. We did not know who these men were, or whether they were among the newly enfranchised second-category citizens who were voting for the first time in 1996.[25] My assumption in telling this story is that persons who lead traditional lives are more vulnerable to having their votes suborned than those from the modernizing elements of the population. However, this is not a unanimous assumption, and the reality is probably far more complicated than I can show it here.

> Vote-buying has nothing to do with illiteracy. There are a lot of old men here [in District 13] but they have principles. In Kaifan, there are 'Awazim and 'Ajman and *hadhar*. The city people are a minority so there, *hadhar* be-come desirable votes to buy. An associate of the candidate [a potential vote seller] is in the area where he goes to vote. He [a bought voter] comes back into a car and says he voted for [the candidate] and then they pay him. There is only one bad paper. We have calculated [that the candidate buying votes] will give up ten votes [if he has ten cars working the ballot-switch scam in the district].[26]

Demographic trends are shrinking the relative number of illiterate tradi-tional voters as compared to educated modern voters but, as the young cam-paign worker quoted above has noted, this is not to say that vote buyers find no sellers among the literate or among the modern. However, it does change the process and also the results. In the situation he describes, there is no inter-mediary such as a tribal patron to negotiate on behalf of his clients. Vote sellers increasingly have to be dealt with on the retail level rather than in the whole-sale patterns common to the old imagining. The new pattern is evident even in the outlying areas. "My uncle sold his vote last time [in 1992]," a young woman told me about a relation who lives in District 14. "They paid him KD 1000 and he bought a satellite dish. I think he sold it twice because the first election was canceled and they had to vote again." At the same time, selling your vote as an independent entrepreneur who is making his own deal brings consequences that must be weighed against the value of the immediate quid pro quo. "An MP who had purchased votes and goes into parliament, those who had sold votes came to him for *wasta*. He says, 'No, I bought your vote, and now we are even.'"[27] Thus the shift to a dependence on expert systems as opposed to patron-client networks undercuts the incentives—or raises the ante—for corrupt practices, and the corruption itself might be corrupted, as vote buyers complained in 1992 (see chapter 6).

The politics of selective enfranchisement forces decision-makers to consider carefully the likely effects that each new group of potential voters may have. Such assessments are not easy because none of these groups is monolithic in its orientation or behavior. Whether a new group is enfranchised depends on assessments of how "controllable" their votes are—from the perspective of the rulers, how much confidence one can have that traditional methods of social control will dictate their actions. And there is a second question: if a particular group of votes is relatively controllable, which among the various political forces is most likely to be in the driver's seat. Responding to a question at a press conference for foreign reporters covering the 1996 election, political scientist Ghanim al-Najjar explained the situation this way:

> The government has a vested interest in knowing who are the voters. When the base opens—adding women will be more than a 100 percent increase—it makes it harder to control. If the government wants women, external pressure will not matter. The issue is whether or not to open democracy. The government calculates on the political base. The government knows and can predict what the base will do. If you add women, this becomes extremely unpredictable and may change the political equation. The government is extremely careful and does not want to open the system too much. Like for second-class citizens: when they realized there were only twenty or twenty-five thousand, it wasn't so scary.[28]

This thoughtful analysis encourages a careful look at the May 1999 amiri decree extending political rights to women. I believe that the amir's action reflected two partially contradictory impulses. On the one hand, the amir demonstrated that patriarchy can be equitable regarding an important category of human rights, setting himself apart from the democratic parliament which, as an institution, never had shown itself to be hospitable to women's reasonable political aspirations.[29] On the other hand, the rulers undoubtedly saw practical benefits to themselves from this change. The loudest critics of the amiri decree were Sunni Islamists, who offered a variety of proposals to reduce its scope and impact during the 1999 campaign season. Shi'i Islamists took the other side; consequently, by his decision the amir divides Sunni from Shi'i Islamists and reduces Islamist cohesion. Also, many Kuwaitis—religious and secular and perhaps including the amir and his advisers as well—believe that women are more likely to support traditional values than men, and therefore to support candidates presenting themselves as champions of such values.

From this perspective, women might look to the regime like the "last *badu*," the last traditional force whose enfranchisement would strengthen its position. Thus, the amir's apparently radical departure from Kuwaiti tradition might be just another "between-parliaments adjustment" to the electoral system whose purpose is to shift the balance of domestic political forces away from parliament and toward the ruling family.[30] However, as Hannah Arendt cautioned, political action always has consequences that are unforeseen by its initiators. Like the "desertization" strategy underlying the government's alteration of the political system prior to the 1981 election, the 1999 "feminization" strategy also produced unexpected results.

Institutions and Rules

The grand narratives of democratization look at constitutions and the development of institutions that mediate political life. The grand narratives of parliamentary life in Kuwait are, as we have seen, bitterly contested, a function of one of the fundamental processes of modernity which is to orient one toward the future—toward a *desired* future—via a selective appropriation and interpretation of the past.[31] Such narratives tell two interdependent stories: each formal narrative comes with a subtext that signals what the narrative is about. The subtext reflects the dependence of choice and outcome on constraints arising from institutions and rules, and on attempts to legitimate some institutions and rules while delegitimating others. The narrative process itself becomes a manipulation of systems that carries with it a great potential to injure or to build trust.[32]

Since the late nineteenth century, the drama of Kuwaiti politics has been played out in a series of attempts by rulers to carve out a space for autonomous action for themselves and countervailing attempts by elites outside the ruling family to limit the public activities in which the rulers can engage without their explicit consent. Kuwaiti rulers strove to elude merchant control by reducing their dependence on merchant financing. They looked for private sources of income, first from their date gardens in Iraq and then from Ottoman and

British subventions. The inauguration of the oil era in Kuwait freed the rulers from their remaining financial dependency on merchant wealth,[33] but it did not free them from the merchants' insistence that rulers held their positions not because of royal entitlement but only insofar as they retained the consent of the governed: in Kuwait, although taxation no longer was practiced, the expectation of representation continued undiminished.

The 1962 constitution can be viewed as an attempt to manage conflicts in interests and expectations between Kuwaiti rulers and prominent citizens by formalizing the relationship of the ruling family to the rest of the nation. In the process, it also created independently legitimated institutions such as the National Assembly, and a set of rules under which differences between the rulers and other Kuwaiti social groups which might be represented in that assembly could be bargained out. Despite the highly favored position of the ruling family under this constitution, rulers continued to long for fewer restraints on their authority. At the same time, the institutionalization of a popular assembly, however limited its formal representation might be, created a permanent legitimate check on the parameters of any narrative told from the ruling family's perspective. The rulers attempted to achieve a freer hand first by dismissing the parliament, but the parliament's legitimacy could not be denied and by trying to deny it, the rulers jeopardized their own. When the insistence that parliament be restored grew too strong prudently to ignore, the rulers were forced to move the struggle to preserve and extend their autonomy to one centered on changing the rules of engagement, that is, by changing the rules by which members of the National Assembly were elected and thereby what sort of person—which set of interests—the rulers would have to accommodate.[34]

Managing elections depends both on controlling who gets to vote and on controlling the rules for choosing candidates and allocating representatives. As I described in previous chapters, changes in all these rules, including the 1981 redistricting and the selective enfranchisement of increments of mostly tribal voters, altered the internal culture of the parliament and the balance of forces in society as a whole. Merchants, city dwellers, and Shi'a lost representation while nonurban and tribal groups, along with Sunna, gained; secularists lost representation as compared to Islamists. As a result, former concentrations of countervailing political power were both shrunken and fragmented across constituency groups with the result that opposition power, cohesion, and effectiveness were damaged. At the same time, Islamist forces, particularly those I have described as neofundamentalist, gained political power. Both the large tribes and urban secularist political forces developed new strategies to reclaim some of their former power, the most successful of which was the tribal primary. But the splintering of districts made it easier to change the outcome of elections illicitly, by financing additions to candidate slates, manipulating the group dynamic at diwaniyyas, and outright vote-buying in key districts. Consequently, even where political forces managed to reorganize coherently, it still was possible to deny a particular man his seat in parliament through careful planning and judicious spending. Thus, it is clear that rules have significant effects on outcomes, not only through their normal operation but also by how, how easily, and by whom these rules are most likely to be circumvented.

The increasing ease of manipulating electoral outcomes following the 1981 redistricting was clearly evident to the opposition, which asserted such manipulation as lying behind their lost ground. It also suggested using redistricting in the future as a strategy to benefit other groups, such as to bring districts closer to the one-man-one-vote ideal which would increase representation from the outlying areas. Observers from across the political spectrum have been calling for a redrawing of constituencies in the name of reform.[35] Some of the people I talked to about this in 1990 and 1992 wanted to go back to the ten five-member districts of the pre-1981 era, which they felt represented their interests more fairly than the twenty-five two-member districts of today; others wanted to redraw the lines defining the post-1981 two-member districts so that they would be more equally populated.

The present system violates fairness both by reducing interest representation and by violating one-man-one-vote standards. For example, since 1981 direct representation of Shi'i Kuwaitis in the parliament has fallen to half of the already underrepresented proportion of the population they managed to elect prior to the redrawing of districts. At the same time, a review of table 6.1 shows how disparate the populations of the various districts were in 1992, ranging as they did from fewer than nine hundred persons to more than seven thousand. The populations of election districts in 1996 and 1999 were similarly diverse. Direct representation of persons defined by their residence also is highly disproportionate under these rules.

In April 1997 a proposal to create a single election district covering all of Kuwait was submitted by Ghannam al-Jamhour (T, Farwaniya) to the parliamentary committee on Interior and Defense Affairs. Advocates of the proposal said it would "put an end to buying votes during electoral campaigns, put an end to by-elections, and ensure national unity."[36] The reference to "by-elections" is to tribal primaries, which supporters of the single-constituency plan would like to see ended. The single-district proposal that emerged from the committee six weeks later provided for a two-step process. Each voter could choose up to five candidates from a single list. Any candidate obtaining 15 percent of the total votes cast would be elected automatically. A second round of voting from a list of those who had received at least 7 percent but less than 15 percent of the votes in the first round would be used to fill the remaining seats.[37]

Advocates of the single-district plan seek to satisfy a number of goals simultaneously with its adoption, not only to discourage vote-buying and wring out frivolous candidacies but also to eliminate the vexing though technically soluable problem of unequal populations across districts and the far less tractable problems of extra-district voting, the tribal primary, and the troubling implications of its spread to nontribal factions. As I noted above, vote-buying has not gone away with the ebbing of illiteracy; it merely has changed its social character. The small district makes vote-buying of all types more manageable, and it also is more vulnerable than a large one to manipulation of election results by flooding it with frivolous candidates. Both kinds of tampering become more expensive and less effective under a single-district system, not only because of the district's larger size but also because of its more varied interests and the change in electoral dynamics that would result from putting the entire country into a single constituency. Some kinds of diwaniyya voting also would become less effective, such as the strategy used against Husain al-Qallaf in 1992—see chapters 6 and 7.

A regular redrawing of the present number of twenty-five district boundaries to accommodate population shifts would be technically feasible in Kuwait. However, it would generate its own corrupt practices, just as it has in the United States where the term *gerrymandering* was coined to describe how election districts were drawn to suit the taste of Massachusetts governor Elbridge Gerry in the late eighteenth century. Complicating redistricting in Kuwait is the increasing number of persons who claim legal residence in one area and actually live somewhere else. A few do this for political reasons—a Kuwaiti variation of carpetbagging—but most do it because they have moved their residences to districts in the outlying areas.[38] Since liberation, the process of obtaining a new civil identity card has become almost impossibly arduous, and most people with family members in their old neighborhoods do not subject themselves to it. Some also prefer to receive services, such as medical care, from their old city neighborhoods, where facilities are more familiar and less crowded than they are in the newer suburbs. An additional residency problem arose following the Iraqi invasion, which generated internal "refugees." These are persons whose homes were destroyed, some of whom continue to live in other districts. There is a large tolerance for extra-district registration,[39] and the names of former residents and current refugees are seldom challenged when the lists are published. Following the 1996 election, 'Ali al-Baghli challenged the results on the grounds that close to three hundred refugees from Failaka Island had voted in his district. However, the judge dismissed his suit because he had not asked that they be struck from the voter rolls beforehand. The legitimacy of the extended family as a corporate body, along with tolerance for refugees whose current residence is not necessarily a matter of their own choosing, makes a concerted attempt to "regularize" residency requirements in Kuwait problematic.

The tribal primary was criticized by many urban Kuwaitis in 1992 and, as I indicated in chapter 6, also by some in the outlying areas. In this regard, it is significant that the sponsor of the single-district plan is himself a tribal representative from the outlying areas. But there is a new intensity in urban opposition to the tribal primary which arises from its use in 1996 by another kind of "tribe," religious sectarians. In District 4, Da'iya, a Sunni primary was cobbled together shortly before the election to oppose two very strong Shi'i candidates, an incumbent parliamentarian, 'Ali al-Baghli, and Husain 'Ali al-Qallaf, the man whose strong run in District 8 in 1992 had been stymied by sectarian diwaniyya voting for Isma'il al-Shati (see chapter 6). Nine organizers got the Sunni candidates to agree to a "Sunni primary," a poll to be taken at selected diwaniyyas to choose the two strongest Sunni candidates. All the candidates agreed in advance to withdraw from the race should they lose the primary, improving the winners' chances of taking the district. However, shortly before the primary was run, the Sunni incumbent backed out of the agreement. The primary went on as scheduled and the winners, 'Abd al-Wahed al-'Awadhi and Jasim al-Mudhaf, campaigned as a team until the election.

To close off further use of the primary by sectarian groups, several bills to end all primaries held in conjunction with elections to national or municipal offices were submitted to the 1996 parliament. Like pushing for a single district as opposed to a reapportionment of voters across twenty-five geographically defined districts, this proposal appears to be antitribe. The tribes developed the primary strategy and (with the exception of the single Sunni primary run in 1996—which in practice was more like diwaniyya voting than like the primaries run by the tribes) are the only ones who have used it. The chair of the parliamentary committee charged with reviewing the bill, Fahad al-'Azemy (T, Subbahiya), stated publicly that the committee could not support a ban that targets a particular segment of the community—i.e., the tribes—and that if the proposal could not be worded to apply uniformly to all groups for all elections to any office, including offices in unions, cooperative societies, and voluntary organizations, it would be rejected in committee.[40] In 1998 the parliament came up with an acceptable compromise, passing an amendment to the election law that made all primary elections, whether held by tribes or by sects, illegal.[41]

During the 1999 campaign season, more than a dozen tribal primaries were held, most of them organized by the seven large tribes that had held a majority of the elected seats in the 1996 parliament.[42] The tribes attempted to evade the ban by gathering in small groups called "coordinating meetings," limited to random samples of about one hundred members selected by computer.[43] But to the surprise of tribal leaders and meeting participants, the public prosecutor arrested and questioned hundreds of tribesmen, including members of the dismissed parliament, about the primaries. One of them, Khaled al-'Adwa, was reported to have won the 'Ajman primary in his district (Ahmadi). He was arrested for his participation in an illegal primary during the campaign, put under a travel ban, and released only on payment of a KD 2000 bond, which just happens to be the maximum fine for this offense.[44] Whether the government deals as harshly with other tribe members found guilty of violating the primary ban or simply allows the issue to fade away, primaries as ad hoc grassroots institutions that simultaneously reflect and entrench the power of geographically concentrated ascriptive groups will continue to be undermined by growing perceptions of their inherent unfairness. Helped along by the dismay engendered by the Sunni primary in 1996, as well as by the refusal of some young tribe members to participate in them even when they were legal, the change in the electoral law adds to the declining legitimacy of self-regarding interference by any single political force in Kuwaiti elections.

Even though the unregulated primary has become a formally illegitimate institution, the single-district plan finds support among Kuwaitis for reasons in addition to whatever virtues it might have as an anticorruption measure. Political scientist Lani Guinier has written extensively on "the tyranny of the majority." By this she means the ability of a numerical majority to use electoral rules to deny representation of the interests of minority groups in policy-making bodies.[45] The tyranny of the majority operates in Kuwait as as it does in the United States and other majoritarian winner(s)-take-all systems constructed on narrow, geographically based constituencies, particularly where there are no effective political parties to create communities of interest among members of a district.

In Kuwait the interdependence of these factors is revealed in a number of ways. One is opposition to tribal primaries from members of smaller clans. Members of a small clan have little chance of achieving direct representation whether they hold a tribal primary or not. They also see themselves as denied interest representation because, without being able to put a member of their own group into office, they are not confident that their interests will be taken into account. They have no trust in the system and perhaps little reason to feel otherwise. Some Kuwaiti Shi'a also feel disenfranchised, as do Sunni residents of the few districts that are predominantly Shi'i, one reason for the hysteria in both groups over the 1996 Sunni primary in District 4. Guinier argues that an electoral system that denies not only direct representation (that is, one that denies members of minority groups the possibility of being elected) but also interest representation (that is, one that denies minority groups the power to affect the results of elections) is unfair.[46] Of the two, Guinier believes that interest representation is by far the more important, both in terms of normative principles and with regard to the function of representation as a support of the legitimacy of a political regime. In fact, as she points out, direct representation is no guarantee of interest representation. Even a member of a voter's own nominal group could fail to represent her or him on issues that do not relate directly to the particular dimension of group construction. Also, any individual or group whose ownership of an office cannot be contested successfully under whatever rules may be in effect is likely to be deaf to unwanted demands from any segment of her or his nominal constituency. Fair representation, minimally defined as a situation in which it is possible for a coherent interest of reasonable size to win at least some of the time, depends less on electing a representative who shares specific attributes with a majority of the voters than on electing someone who has to depend on multiple elements of a mixed constituency to win. These same principles would contribute to a dampening of intergroup conflict in Kuwait.

The complicated procedures of the single-district plan have their critics and others dislike it because of its effects. For example, some say it would deny them representation by their neighbors, people they know. At-large electoral systems do favor candidates whose appeal transcends local concerns. In consequence, at-large elections tend to be biased against newcomers and individuals whose situations are such that their views and talents are less well known than those of more famous persons. Single districts also favor candidates capable of putting together a broadly based voter coalition over those who rely on particular attributes such as sectarian affiliation or clan membership. Thus, the automatic primacy of the largest plurality based on personal attributes like religion and family membership would disappear, engendering opposition from persons for whom these are electoral plusses under the current system. A single-district system also has the potential to redistribute offices among the set of persons affiliated with a political bloc. This attracts individual opposition and support depending on how each potential candidate assesses his chances under each system.[47]

It is clear from this discussion that electoral rules affect more than the distribution of representation. They also constitute grounds for the reflexive process that shapes political attitudes and behaviors in the future. This is particularly true in Kuwait where urban legends cluster around issues where there is a lack of faith in the reliability of expert systems and a lack of trust in existing institutions. It is these issues that provoke the strongest desires in average citizens to return to the stability of tradition. Yet modernization cannot simply be turned off or turned back. As Giddens implies and Polanyi insists, modernization is not merely a path toward modernity but is itself, as a process, something that disassembles the material, social, and psychological supports for traditional life. It is this aspect that makes the association of Islamism with modernization and modernity most troubling.

Islamism uses religious symbols to mobilize people for political action. In doing so, it taps into emotions that are so powerful and deeply embedded in the human brain that we cannot comprehend them rationally except through mythic stories such as family romances, or bring them under our conscious control except through exemplary rituals such as the Catholic Mass or the Muslim ram sacrifice.[48] All religions have at their disposal a repertoire of myths and symbols whose effects can be benign or horrible depending on how they are used.[49] Such myths and symbols rationalize powerful negative emotions like anger, fear, insecurity, and dread, and one way they do this is by demonizing enemies to explain their power to harm and hurt. Symbolic violence and real violence are connected through action undertaken in spaces of appearance,[50] where the politics of religion has a special power to unleash violence that the initiators of action find themselves unable to control because religion is so intimately connected to primordial human emotions. Religion informs cognition and behavior by giving shape to these emotions such that human beings can continue to live in the presence of pain and the imminence of death. Ideally, religion strengthens individual and collective capacities to reconcile desire to necessity; when such a reconciliation is not possible, religion has an enormous capacity to inflict harm.

Islamist movements appeal most strongly to those who are left out of the benefits of modernization, not only the transitional generation(s) who have "paid their dues" and yet are deprived of the customary authority and privileges of age, but also people of all ages facing acute insecurity, and those who must compete for positions that they believe tradition entitles persons of their status to receive automatically. Like other fundamentalisms, neofundamentalist Islamism promises to restore tradition by reinstituting the subjection of women and minorities, entropy-resistant persons who can serve as scapegoats and, by their subjection, reaffirm the premodern social order. But to say or even imply that tradition is recoverable in a simple, direct, and nonviolent way is untrue. An even bigger lie is the representation of Islamism, a movement that attacks political authority and proposes radical revisions in religious norms as well, as compatible with tradition.[51] Islamism uses gender politics to attest to its traditionality[52] but, as Fatima Mernissi among others notes, Islamists do not hesitate to appropriate those aspects of modernity that suit their political purposes, particularly technologies that speed reflexivity.[53]

Inasmuch as Islam provides a principled and coherent set of values under which one can live a moral life, it is not religion but rather the co-optation of religious symbols by political entrepreneurs that is the crux of arguments against Islamist politics. However, it is difficult for people to disentangle religious and political claims, especially where religious traditions are complex, on the one hand embracing values compatible with pluralism and democracy and on the other enjoining obedience to authority, including clerical authority, to control significant aspects of a believer's personal life.[54] This complexity allows both liberal and fundamentalist movements to claim religious sanction for their goals and, in Kuwait, helps to explain why many Islamists share some liberal values, just as many liberal "secularists" are devoutly religious. Even so, the dangers of neofundamentalism to peaceful political change are acute, and among my greatest problems in assessing whether democratization in Kuwait can proceed comes from the conundrum with which I began this chapter: an inability to decide whether Islamism is building civil society through new social movements and coalition politics faster than it is destroying civil life by acquiescing to the rulers and mobilizing the street. Another question for Islamists is whether they can be both populists and institutionalists. Among the lost opportunities that have marred Kuwaiti politics since liberation are those caused by the repeated failure of Islamists and secularists to hammer out unified and principled positions that both groups can support wholeheartedly. The 1999 parliament marks what could be the last opportunity to achieve democratic politics in Kuwait based on this nationalist vision.

Turning the Kaleidoscope: Plus ça change . . .

The 1999 parliamentary election shifted the positions of key actors in Kuwaiti national politics. The unprecedented constitutionality of the 1999 dissolution, along with the amir's decision to force the issue of political rights for women, added new dimensions to old political divisions. Yet the perennial twin dilemmas of Kuwaiti domestic politics remain to be resolved. The first is a problem of agency for the regime. Does it accept the necessity of democratization and therefore the legitimacy of the parliament as a partner in making national policy, or will it continue to undermine the operation and effectiveness of all of Kuwait's representative institutions? The second is a problem of agency for the parliament. Does it have the collective capacity to make itself the legitimate representative of the highly varied collection of constituencies that make up the Kuwaiti nation, or will it continue to allow primordial loyalties and private desires to impair its capacity to act in the national interest?

Despite their novel aspects, the dissolution procedure and the election that followed are very much part of the Kuwaiti political tradition that I have traced throughout this volume. As I noted in chapter 8, the 1999 dissolution, like its predecessors in 1976 and 1986, was preceded by conflict over economic policy and a threatened parliamentary investigation of fiscal malfeasance by a member of the ruling family. In addition, the 1996 parliament, which had sat for nearly three years, had managed to pass very few laws. The dissolution allowed the amir both to take full control of policy-making and to draft much-needed legislation.

Between the dismissal of parliament on May 4 and the election on July 3, the amir issued some sixty decrees. The decree on housing tackled a critical long-standing domestic problem. The decree conferring full citizenship rights on women also was long overdue. Most of the decrees dealt with economic issues. These ran from routine housekeeping measures such as the national budget and annual accounts for state institutions, to new policies on contentious subjects such as upstream privatization and domestic economic restructuring. Both the intermingling of issues and the absence of the emergency conditions which article 71 requires for amiri decrees to be promulgated legitimately during a parliamentary recess, complicated the parliament's response.

The lack of an overriding necessity might have been used as grounds for the wholesale cancellation of all the decrees as unconstitutional. This hard-line position was argued strongly by Ahmad al-Sa'doun even before the July election, and contributed to the determination of the rulers to prevent his re-election as speaker in the 1999 parliament. The defeat of Ahmad al-Sa'doun (see below) and the commencement of the new fiscal year in the interim between the dissolution and the election persuaded members to treat the budget bills as necessary and deal with them immediately. Discarding the option of voting all the decrees up or down at one time opened a window for possible compromise on several measures. These were bound over for consideration in the session due to begin in October, leaving more than two months for negotiations among members of parliament and the government. Even in the absence of a fiscal exigency, the inclusion of the women's rights proposal among the decrees blocked their wholesale cancellation. Cancellation without debate would have been castigated by foreign observers and by Kuwaiti feminists as just one more instance of masculinist obstruction by the parliament of Kuwaiti women's achievement of their legitimate rights. As he did with his proposal for the Majlis al-Watani, the amir once again succeeded in drawing attention away from unconstitutional actions by himself and his government by clothing them in superficially democratic garb—an election in 1990 and women's rights in 1999.

However, as Shaikh Ahmad al-Jabir discovered during his confrontation with the 1938 parliament, dismissing a sitting parliament and calling for new elections do not always bring in the desired results. A listing of the 1999 winners and their political affiliations can be found in table 9.1. A brief inspection reveals that many of the regime's most vociferous opponents were returned by the voters in 1999, along with a large number of members who are designated as "independent liberals," a term that signifies, in addition to a lack of affiliation with an organized political group, a strong commitment to constitutionalism. The press described the result as a victory for "Islamists and liberals,"[55] shorthand for a parliament in which the regime's opponents are heavily represented. Equally important is that less than a quarter are first-time winners, so the 1999 parliament has an unprecedented proportion of experienced members (please refer back to table 6.2).

The rulers tried to deal with this by offering cabinet positions to prominent members of the opposition.[56] As I discussed in chapter 7, the structural position of the cabinet is a serious impediment to parliamentary independence. The cabinet serves at the will of the crown prince in his role as prime minister. The joining of these two positions is sanctified by recent custom but is not supported by law and theoretically could be changed. In addition, appointed members of the cabinet vote as members of the parliament while elected cabinet members find their hands tied by two other informal customs—the practice of bloc voting by cabinet members and the norm forbidding cabinet members to speak against a government position once it has been taken. Even though neither is required by law, these customs would be difficult to violate regardless of who is prime minister.

The consequences of these informal systems were highlighted in chapter 7, in the discussion of the 1992 parliament which, like the 1999 parliament, also had an ostensible opposition majority. Following its impressive victory in the 1992 election, the opposition saw its majority as a ticket to dominate the cabinet. However, the ride was a bumpy one. Although as many as six elected MPs held cabinet portfolios during the tenure of the 1992 parliament, all—Islamists and liberals—found themselves bound by the custom of bloc voting and gagged by the custom dictating no dissent. Equally galling, the voices of these members not only were lost to the parliament but also were submerged in the cabinet where opposition parliamentarians were outnumbered by pro-government appointees. While it is easy to say that parliamentarians who do not like the restrictions imposed by cabinet rank should resign their portfolios, the resistance of Ahmad al-Rubi' to such a solution despite great pressure indicates

TABLE 9.1   Results of the 1999 Parliamentary Election

---

1. Sharq

'Adnan 'Abd al-Samad   INA, Shi'a
* Saleh Ashour   Independent Islamist, Shi'a

2. Al-Murqab

'Abd al-Wahhab al-Haroun   Independent liberal, M
'Abdullah al-Nibari   KDF

3. Al-Qiblah

* Muhammad Jasim al-Saqr   Independent liberal, M
Jasim al-Khorafy   Independent

4. Al-Da'iya

'Abdullah al-Roumi   Independent, M
'Abd al-Mohsin Jamal   Independent Islamist, Shi'a, io

5. Al-Qadisiya

Ahmad Baqr   IPA, Sunni
'Abd al-'Aziz al-Mutawa'   Independent

6. Al-Faiha'

Mishairy al-'Anjari   Independent liberal, M
Mishairy al-'Osaimi   Independent liberal, M

7. Kaifan

Walid al-Tabtaba'i   IPA, Sunni
* Ahmad al-Duaij   IPA, Sunni

8. Hawali

Hasan Jawhar   INA, Shi'a, io
'Abd al-Mosin al-Mudej   Independent liberal, M

9. Al-Rawdha

* Faisal al-Shaye'   Independent liberal, M
Nasir al-Sane'   ICM, Sunni

10. 'Adeliya

Saleh al-Fadhalla   Independent, io
Sami al-Munayes   KDF

TABLE 9.1   Results of the 1999 Parliamentary Election, cont.

11. Al-Khaldiya

Ahmad al-Sa'doun	Independent, M
Ahmad al-Rub'i	Independent liberal, M

12. Al-Salmiya

Mekhled al-'Azemi	ICM, Sunni
Salim al-Hamad	Independent, M

13. Al-Rumaithiya

Husain 'Ali al-Qallaf	Independent Islamist, Shi'a
Saleh Khorshaid	Independent, Shi'a, pg

14. Abraq Khaittan

Walid al-'Osaimi	Independent, pg
Hmoud al-Jabri	Independent, pg

15. Al-Farwaniya

* Mubarak al-Haifi	Independent
* 'Eid al-Rashidi	Independent (cabinet minister)

16. Al-'Umariya

Mubarak al-Duwailah	ICM, Sunni
Mubarak Khrainej	Independent, pg

17. Julib Al-Shiyoukh

Musallem al-Barrak	Independent liberal, M
* Husain Mazyad	Independent

18. Al-Sulaibikhat

Khalaf Dimethir	Independent, pg
* 'Abdullah Aradah	ICM, Sunni

19. Al-Jahra' al-Jadida

* Muhammad al-Khalifah	Independent
Ahmad Nasir al-Shriyan	Independent, M

20. Al-Jahra' al-Qadimi

* Muhammad Busairi	ICM, Sunni
Talal al-'Ayar	Independent, pg

TABLE 9.1   Results of the 1999 Parliamentary Election, cont.

21. Al-Ahmadi

Walid Jari	Independent
* Sa'doun 'Otaibi	Independent

22. Al-Riqa

Sa'd Tami al-'Ajmi	Independent, M
* Mubarak al'Ajmi	ICM, Sunni

23. Al-Subbahiya

Khamis Talaq	Independent, M
Fahad Lumaia	Independent, pg

24. Al-Fahaheel

Rashid Saif al-Hujailan	Independent
* Fahad Hajri	Independent

25. Um al-Haiman

* Mashan al-'Azmi	Independent
Marzouk al-Habini	Independent

Notes:

   *   Denotes a newcomer to the Parliament

   Organized political groups
       ICM: Islamic Constitution Movement
       INA: Islamic National Alliance
       IPA: Islamic Popular Alliance
       KDF: Kuwait Democratic Forum

   Other leanings
       M: Movement activists, including but not limited to members of the National
          Democratic Rally
       pg: pro-government
       io: issue opposition

   Cabinet member: in the Council of Ministers appointed on July 13, 1999.

Sources: In addition to the sources listed for other tables, Kuwait Information Office, Washington, D.C. <www.kuwait-info.org>; and personal communications from Ghanim al-Najjar and Haya al-Mughni. Haya supplied the list of movement activists which was published by *Al-Tali'a*, July 7–13, 1999, 1.

that this option is not so easy to choose in practice. It is simpler to refuse a portfolio than to resign one.

With its single elected member, the first cabinet—Council of Ministers— appointed during the tenure of the 1999 parliament is, in one sense, a return to the past when the rulers' objectives included keeping elected members out of the government. But the lessons of postliberation cabinets were learned by both sides. The rulers sought to immobilize key opponents by offering them portfolios. The opposition chose to retain its independence by refusing them. Consequently, a third of the ministerial portfolios went to members of the Sabah. Signifying the continued if uneasy alliance between the regime and the mosque, three portfolios, two of which (Electricity and Water, and Housing Affairs) oversee the distribution of significant social benefits, went to a strong Islamist. Opposition trends clearly evident in the election results also are represented in the cabinet. From the Chamber of Commerce, 'Abd al-Wahhab al-Wazzan, who is a Shi'a, holds two portfolios: Trade and Industry, and Labor and Social Affairs. Two founding members of the new National Democratic Rally also received portfolios: linguistics professor Sa'd al-'Ajmy, who had made two unsuccessful bids for a parliamentary seat, was named Minister of Information; another professor, economist Youssef al-Ibrahim, is the new Minister of Education. All three men are liminals, persons who occupy two worlds and can bridge differences between them—if the other occupants of the two worlds only will allow it.[57]

The elected members of parliament bear an equal responsibility with the government for political outcomes, but the government's initial moves reduced the 1999 parliament's capacity to act in the collective interests of the body. The openly antigovernment stance of Ahmad al-Sa'doun, along with the unexpectedly large majority of opposition candidates elected in 1999, prompted government intervention in the election for speaker between Ahmad and his rival, Jasim al-Khorafy. To ensure their success in defeating Ahmad al-Sa'doun, the government is reported to have made a deal with ICM members. In exchange for the government's agreement to overlook the activities of what the *Kuwait Times* calls the ICM's "illegal committees hiding under charity work,"[58] ICM members were to vote for Jasim al-Khorafy. The illegal activities included "diverting several million dollars missing from funds raised for Kosovar Albanian refugees to run election campaigns."[59] Out of a total of sixty-four valid votes, Ahmad al-Sa'doun received only twenty-seven; Jasim al-Khorafy won thirty-seven and the speaker's chair. Had the six ICM members maintained solidarity with the opposition in this instance, the vote for speaker would have gone the other way, as it had in 1996.[60]

In spite of the cynicism that infuses this story (a story that has been denied by none of the alleged participants), there are reasons to believe that it is possible for the parliament to build coalitions strong enough to command a constructive role for the nation's elected representatives in making the policies that shape Kuwaiti citizens' lives. One is the evidence that growing numbers of independents with national political orientations are coming into the parliament. As long as the rulers can portray the parliament as nothing more than a collection of (to use the favorite term of the pro-government *Arab Times*) "mouthpieces" who speak only for the interests of a particular clan, class, or sect, they can paint themselves as the only representatives of the nation as a whole. This neat partition is disintegrating on both sides. The position of the ruling family as selfless representatives of the national interest continues to be eroded by revelations of financial peculations by its members. Meanwhile, the capacity of the parliament to claim that it too can represent the nation is growing as the result of two populist trends. One is the election of members based on their positions on national issues rather than on their connection to a particular sect or tribe, and the other is the growth of a new nationalist social movement advocating constitutionalism, democratization, and human rights. Shiʻi members are prominent supporters of women's rights and have a strong interest in blocking any alliance between the rulers and Sunni Islamists who are working to amend article 2. The latter has loosened the bond between the rulers and the Shiʻa that goes back to the 1930s. Meanwhile, growing diversity among Kuwaiti Shiʻa reduces pressures for bloc voting and contributes to the capacity of Shiʻa to participate as individuals in issue-oriented coalitions.

Rising issue-oriented independence among Kuwaiti Shiʻa is mirrored by a similar trend among secularist-"liberal" forces. Many independents who won election in 1999 are part of the growing political center whose members can vote either way depending on the issues involved. The National Democratic Rally is a key association in the movement, but movement activists include many Kuwaitis in addition to NDR members. Known movement activists among the winners of the 1999 election are noted in table 9.1. Even parliamentarians with traditional loyalties and preferences face pressures from modernizing constituencies that occasionally lead to independent votes.

"Independent" is a description which many members [of parliament] and candidates prefer. . . . [It] means . . . within the Kuwaiti political context, that the person is capable of taking independent stands against the government. . . . As for the general platforms, they vary immensely. Pro-government [members] are more likely to support the government on certain sensitive issues, but not necessarily all the way because they have to attend to their voters.[61]

The need to "attend" to one's voters is an outcome of the shift from wholesale to retail politics. This shift impairs not only the government's ability to mobilize support from the tribes but also the ability of the organized political groups to trump demands from other constituents.

The machinations behind the election for speaker have damaged chances for accommodation between the parliament and the government on the tabled decrees. Economist Jasim al-Sa'doun believes that those measures initiating major departures in current economic policy are likely to be the chief casualties of the renewal of conflict between the parliament and the government.

> Some of these decrees [dealing with economic reform] are unconstitutional decrees and very sensitive and therefore might be opposed by the parliament. . . . The government now expects perhaps more confrontation from the parliament rather than collaboration, and the victims might be some of those decrees. . . . With the government just formed we are closer to confrontation rather than collaboration. Without collaboration neither side will be willing to take responsibility for unpopular reforms.[62]

It was a surprise to many observers that among the first casualties was women's rights. The regime's Sunni Islamist allies were predictably among the first to react negatively to the amiri decree conferring political rights on Kuwaiti women. Less predictable was the reaction of opposition liberals, several of whom followed Ahmad al-Sa'doun's lead in condemning all the decrees as an encroachment on the constitutional authority of parliament. Throughout the period between the issuing of the decree and the time it was voted on in late November 1999, however, Islamists were the vanguard of the attack against it. The Islamist campaign was directed not only against the decree but also what Islamists alleged were other examples of foreign-inspired moves to denigrate Islam and secularize Kuwaiti society. The most prominent of these collateral attacks was the accusation by an Islamist leader against an article written by the chair of Kuwait University's political science department. The accused, Ahmad al-Baghdadi, was arrested, tried, and convicted of blasphemy in October 1999. Despite a bad heart, Ahmad began a hunger strike in prison to protest his conviction. Meanwhile, his cause was taken up by an ad hoc human rights group, the Committee to Protect Freedom of Expression, which put on a series of public events warning of the danger to all Kuwaitis that convicting an observant Muslim for blasphemy on such flimsy grounds represented. In response to these pressures, the amir quickly pardoned Baghdadi. Meanwhile, the Islamists who had accused the government of caving in to foreign influence were taken in for questioning.

By late November, when the women's rights decree finally came up for a vote in parliament, the atmosphere was highly charged. The decree itself was voted down, forty-one to twenty-one, reflecting a confluence of interests between Islamist opponents of women's rights and parliamentary opponents of legislation by decree. A new bill was introduced immediately by parliamentary supports of women's rights but, less than a week later, it too was voted down, though very narrowly. Thirty members supported the bill while thirty-two voted against it and two members abstained.

In a regretful communication to Gulf2000 members that evening, political scientist Ghanim al-Najjar called November 30, 1999, a "sad day for women's political rights in Kuwait . . . and for human rights in general," although some comfort should be taken from the narrowness of the Islamist victory and the strong likelihood that another bill will be introduced in the next session. Interestingly, Ghanim numbered among the reasons for the failure of the measure to pass a lack of government "enthusiasm" for it. There were "no serious government proposals to talk to the 'hard-liners' " who, in consequence, both decided on their own and then announced their decisions publicly, making it virtually impossible to persuade them to change their minds.

The lack of active government lobbying until shortly before the vote was scheduled is likely to have been connected to the regime's growing dependence on Islamist votes in the parliament. As I noted earlier, the government had had to agree to ignore illegal activities by ICM committees in order to guarantee Islamist votes for its preferred candidate for speaker, a reflection of the ideological shift in the composition of membership from tribal areas that formerly had supplied a bedrock of reliable support to the rulers. Yet the boldness of Islamist leaders in attacking the amir on the issue of women's rights highlights the risks to the regime of regarding this alliance with the same assurance it had felt toward tribal traditionalists.

To avoid these political risks requires initiative from the center and a willingness of the government to allow the parliament to have more than a rubber-stamp role—that is, to allow the parliament to do what the constitution envisions. This might require old enemies to hold their noses in order to deal with one another. Even so, the ensemble of characters in parliament and on the Council of Ministers includes men who have both hands available for hammering out compromises. The 1999 election may be the first page in a new story rather than just a continuation of the old one. Stay tuned.

Stories of Democracy

The example of Kuwait is a constant challenge to the myths of Arab and Muslim exceptionalism promulgated by governing coalitions and aspiring dictators
throughout the Middle East. The myth that Arabs and Muslims are intellectu-
ally and culturally unsuited to democratic life also is embraced by prominent
scholars and policymakers in the West, lending credence to the claims of local
counterparts that authoritarianism is the only alternative to anarchy. Kuwaiti
democracy, though imperfectly realized and seriously flawed, is a direct refuta-
tion of these myths. Kuwait's democrats also refute the myth that democrats
and monarchs are fundamentally incompatible. Like the British and the Scan-
danavians, whom few would accuse of being antidemocratic, Kuwaiti democrats have demonstrated again and again that they are in no hurry to dismiss
their rulers, preferring that the Sabah be their partners in a constitutional system and accept legal controls on their power and authority.

The pro-democracy movement in Bahrain that burst into public view in
December 1994 displayed many parallels to the Kuwaiti movement of 1989–90.
Perhaps because these parallels were so apparent to Bahrain's government, it
resisted taking any responsibility for the conflict between citizens and the state,
choosing rather to blame the situation on outsiders and seeking scapegoats
among Bahrain's Shi'i population. It moved quickly and ruthlessly, if not entirely successfully, to suppress the movement and punish its leaders.[63] Pressures
for democratization elsewhere in the Gulf also continue and in Qatar have
been met with positive responses indicating that populism as a political force
is percolating outside as well as inside Kuwait.

The Kuwaiti example also has relevance to countries beyond the Arab Gulf
and the Middle East. What is so striking about Kuwait is how populism is expressed as compared to our expectations and perceptions of populist movements in "adversary democracies."[64] Even though Kuwaiti populism is not an
unambiguously positive force with respect to democracy and democratization,
it is a force whose positive effects still outweigh the negative. By themselves and
as part of a broad array of new social movements, Kuwaiti populists have
demonstrated more than once their ability to restore their constitution and to
continue the process of institution-building that improves their prospects of
achieving a stable democracy in the future. As the movements described in
chapter 8 illustrate, populism and constitutionalism are interconnected strategies for democratization. Human rights activists move easily among populist
and constitutional courses of action. The coordination of efforts between government and voluntary organizations that is such a large task in Western countries is hardly a task at all for human rights activists in Kuwait. Similarly, pop-

ular pressure increases the effectiveness of the sometimes less-than-diplomatic efforts of parliamentarians to curtail abuses of public funds.

Part of the ease in blending these two approaches to democratization lies in what some view as a defect of civil society in the Middle East: the interpenetration of government and civil bodies.[65] Understanding this interpenetration as a defect results from looking at it as though one partner, the state, is always dominant. The story of such a state is the myth represented in the frontispiece to Hobbes's *Leviathan*. There is the king, holding his mace, his large crowned head topping a body within which his subjects float like tiny corpuscles. As Patricia Springborg reminded us in chapter 2, this is the story of a tradition in which the king is not only the "head" of his country but also its only "person."

Yet as we have seen over and over in this volume, civil bodies—citizens meeting together and defining themselves in speech and action—are more than capable of moving the state. Kuwaiti myths and political practices spring from such an ideal, one whose legends have been recounted for millennia by storytellers as different in time, place, and situation as the Greek philosopher Aristotle and the American suffragist Carrie Chapman Catt. The stories they tell us say that if the state is virtuous, it is citizens who can take the credit; if the state is unjust it is citizens who must be ashamed. They say that the state is not an enemy: rather, citizens and the state are part of a single whole. Although Kuwaitis have far to move before they arrive at a working model of citizenship that reflects modern democratic ideals, many of the political stories they tell about themselves acknowledge Kuwait's shortcomings and some are tales of actions taken to bring state and society closer to these ideals.

Kuwaiti political myths are legends of a state and a civil society that envision both together as a shared enterprise. However much the fruits of this enterprise might be fought over, a sense of joint, if not yet equal, entitlement to an autonomous life is part of their message. That the myths and the reality are still far apart does not negate the reality of what Kuwaitis already have achieved, or the aspirations of those who persist in their attempts to shrink the remaining gap. Democrats everywhere have much to learn from the stories Kuwaitis tell about themselves and their politics. As they listen, they should imagine how these stories would sound if they were telling them about themselves.

Notes

1. Introduction

1. Ghassan Salamé, "Small Is Pluralistic: Democracy as an Instrument of Civil Peace," in Salamé, ed., *Democracy Without Democrats? The Renewal of Politics in the Muslim World*, 87.

2. Mary Ann Tétreault, "Kuwait: The Morning After," *Current History* 91 (January 1992): 9.

3. Throughout this volume, I use "citizen" to describe a legal status based on nationality. Haya al-Mughni and I discuss the ambiguity of this term generally and in the Kuwaiti context in "Gender, Citizenship, and Nationalism in Kuwait," *British Journal of Middle Eastern Studies* 22 (1995): 64–80. One ambiguity of relevance here is the overlap between "citizen" and "subject," discussed at greater length in chapters 2 and 3. In this context, citizenship in Kuwait has been achieved only partially. The impact of Kuwait's large population of foreign workers on citizenship is not dealt with explicitly in this volume. Interested readers should consult Anh Nga Longva, *Walls Built on Sand: Migration, Exclusion, and Society in Kuwait.*

4. Mary Ann Tétreault, *The Kuwait Petroleum Corporation and the Economics of the New World Order.*

5. The distinction I wish to emphasize here is that, unlike an "international" economy, a "global" economy is not mediated significantly by state institutions, thus exposing the domestic economy directly to uncontrolled market forces. The disintegration of national economies that is the natural consequence of globalization was analyzed by Jane Jacobs in *Cities and the Wealth of Nations: Principles of Economic Life*, and Susan Strange, *Casino Capitalism* (London: Basil Blackwell, 1986), although each saw the mechanics of the process somewhat differently, Jacobs emphasizing trade relations and Strange the uncontrolled operation of international finance. Kuwaitis hold their government responsible for bad outcomes such as erratic national income levels and capital losses, both heavily influenced by global market forces.

6. Patricia Springborg, *Western Republicanism and the Oriental Prince*; Edward Said, *Orientalism*. For a perfect illustration of polarity reversal in Western conceptions of the East, see Lucette Valensi, *The Birth of the Despot: Venice and the Sublime Porte*.

7. The place of the Balkans on the mental maps of Westerners is particularly illustrative of the fluidity of identity boundaries and some of the factors that influence their construction. An independent Bosnia and its cosmopolitan capital, Sarajevo, were off the map for European and American policymakers in the early 1990s. By the end of the decade, inspired in part by guilt for having abandoned Bosnia to territorial dismemberment and its population to genocide, an obscure province of Yugoslavia, Kosovo, was deemed to be part of "Europe." Members of the North Atlantic Treaty Organization (NATO) declared Kosovars to be entitled to NATO military protection against their own state government and its army.

8. Salamé, "Small Is Pluralistic," 100.

9. I have written about this in "Formal Politics, Meta-Space, and the Construction of Civil Life," in Andrew Light and Jonathan M. Smith, eds., *Philosophy and Geography* 2:81–97.

10. For examples of how and why this is done, see the essays in George C. Bond and Angela Gilliam, eds., *Social Construction of the Past: Representation as Power*.

11. Anthony Giddens, *The Consequences of Modernity*.

12. Mary Ann Tétreault, "Kuwait's Democratic Reform Movement," *Middle East Executive Reports* (October 1990).

13. See, for example, Michael Hudson, "After the Gulf War: Prospects for Democratization in the Arab World," *Middle East Journal* 45 (1991): 407–26; Paul Aarts, "Democracy, Oil, and the Gulf War," *Third World Quarterly* 13 (1992): 525–38; Tétreault, "Kuwait: The Morning After."

14. Examples include Bernard Lewis, "Islam and Liberal Democracy," *Atlantic Monthly* 271 (February 1993): 89–94; and Samuel P. Huntington, "The Clash of Civilizations?" *Foreign Affairs* (Summer 1993).

15. See, for example, Hisham Sharabi, *Neopatriarchy: A Theory of Distorted Change in Arab Society*. Sharabi points to culture as the cause of Arab authoritarianism. Others offer more structural analyses. One of the best comes from Kuwait University sociologist Khaldoun Hasan Al-Naqeeb, *Society and State in the Gulf and Arab Peninsula: A Different Perspective*. He argues that imperialism and then, for some Arab states, oil money, transferred resources to the state that enabled it to quash indigenous checks on its power and to create a new state class that, in return for its livelihood, supports the state against its democratic critics. Sharabi also nominates this new class as an element in *neopatriarchy*, but his argument is essentially cultural rather than structural. Lewis and Huntington come to the same conclusion based on different mixes of cultural and structural arguments. See Lewis, "Islam and Liberal Democracy," and Huntington, "The Clash of Civilizations?"

16. See Simon Bromley, *Rethinking Middle East Politics*; or Aziz al-Azmeh, "Populism Contra Democracy: Recent Democratist Discourse in the Arab World," in Salamé, ed., *Democracy Without Democrats?*, 112–29.

17. Fatima Mernissi, *Islam and Democracy: Fear of the Modern World*. See also Charles Lindholm, "Quandaries of Command in Egalitarian Societies: Examples from Swat and Morocco," and Ellis Goldberg, "Smashing Idols and the State: The Protestant Ethic and Egyptian Sunni Radicalism," both in Juan R. I. Cole, ed., *Comparing Muslim Societies: Knowledge and the State in a World Civilization*; and Mary Ann Tétreault, "Individualism, Secularism, and Fundamentalism," paper presented at the annual meeting of the British Society for Middle Eastern Studies, Birmingham, UK, July 1998. That multiple interpretations of Islam are characteristic rather than exceptional is well illustrated in Jonathan E. Brockopp, "Early Islamic Jurisprudence in Egypt: Two Scholars and Their *Mukhtasars*," *International Journal of Middle East Studies* 30: 167–82.

18. Patricia Springborg, "Politics, Primordialism, and Orientalism: Marx, Aristotle, and the Myth of the Gemeinschaft," *American Political Science Review* 80 (March 1986): 185–211; Germaine Tillion, *The Republic of Cousins: Women's Oppression in Mediterranean Society*; Ann Elizabeth Mayer, "Reform of Personal Status Laws in North Africa: A Problem of Islamic or Mediterranean Laws?" *Middle East Journal* 49 (Summer 1995): 432–46.

19. Charles Tilly explores some of the connections between the strength of the state and its institutions vis-à-vis society and its institutions in "War Making and State Making as Organized Crime," in Peter B. Evans, Dietrich Rueschemeyer, and Theda Skoçpol, eds., *Bringing the State Back In*, 168–91.

20. Irving Louis Horowitz, *Taking Lives: Genocide and State Power*, 6.

21. Both Hobbes and Locke were concerned more with the potentially devastating actions of individuals and disadvantaged groups than they were with overreaching by the state: see C. B. MacPherson, *The Political Theory of Possessive Individualism: Hobbes to Locke*. The power of "society" rather than "the state" is the focal point of John Stuart Mill's critique in *On Liberty*, first published in 1859. Today many fear the activities of militias, death squads, youth gangs, and other terrorist groups more than the states where these groups operate with such apparent freedom, and "mafias," international banks, and multinational corporations that evade state regulation as they exploit the vulnerable.

22. The notion that governments negotiate with populations in such circumstances is reflected in Tilly's discussions of state-building in Europe, for example, in "War Making and State Making as Organized Crime." This point is made throughout Salamé, ed., *Democracy Without Democrats?*, particularly in the case studies. I have examined this phenomenon in the context of social movements in "Spheres of Liberty, Conflict, and Power: The Public Lives of Private Persons," *Citizenship Studies* 2 (July 1998): 273–89.

23. The argument that such differences create possibilities, even imperatives, for change is made by Eric R. Wolf, *Europe and the People Without History*, 387–90.

24. Hannah Arendt, *The Human Condition: A Study of the Central Dilemmas Facing Modern Man*, 177.

25. Arendt, *The Human Condition*, 179.

26. Virtual space is necessarily truncated by the limitations of various media, and never reproduces the full scope of even the individually limited experience of a single person. It

also is distorted by the particular qualities of each medium of transmission. For example, television enhances the power of visual images over other kinds of information even when the other information explicitly contradicts the message of the picture.

27. Mary Ann Tétreault, "Civil Society in Kuwait: Protected Spaces and Women's Rights," *Middle East Journal* 47 (Spring 1993): 275–91.

28. The continuities between old regimes and postrevolutionary regimes often are cited in support of this point. See, for example, Alexis de Tocqueville, *The Old Regime and the French Revolution*, or Theda Skoçpol, *States and Social Revolutions*.

29. Tétreault, "Spheres of Liberty."

30. Henry Shue, *Basic Rights: Subsistence, Affluence, and U.S. Foreign Policy*; see also Carol C. Gould, *Rethinking Democracy: Freedom and Social Cooperation in Politics, Economy, and Society*.

31. See, for example, Bromley, *Rethinking Middle East Politics*.

32. Attorney Saleh al-Hashem, in an interview with the author, September 29, 1992, in Kuwait.

33. For the importance of imagination of this kind as a matrix for nationalist identity and emotions, see Benedict Anderson, *Imagined Communities: Reflections on the Origin and Spread of Nationalism*, and Liah Greenfeld, *Nationalism: Five Roads to Modernity*.

34. Lawrence J. Hatab, *Myth and Philosophy: A Contest of Truths*, 29.

35. Harold Bloom and David Rosenberg, *The Book of J*, 178–80.

36. Elaine Pagels, *Adam, Eve, and the Serpent*.

37. See Garry Wills, *Lincoln at Gettysburg: The Words That Remade America*.

38. Jean Leca, "Democratization in the Arab World: Uncertainty, Vulnerability, and Legitimacy. A Tentative Conceptualization and Some Hypotheses," in Salamé, ed., *Democracy Without Democrats?*, 56–57.

39. An example of this perspective that asserts a global reach can be found in Huntington, "The Clash of Civilizations?"

2. Citizens and States

1. Alexis de Tocqueville, *The Old Regime and the French Revolution*.

2. Anthony Giddens, *A Contemporary Critique of Historical Materialism* 1:31–34. See also Karl Polanyi, *The Great Transformation*; Daniel Lerner, *The Passing of Traditional Society: Modernizing the Middle East*; Abdelrahman Munif, *Cities of Salt*.

3. Charles Tilly, "War Making and State Making as Organized Crime," 169–91. The impact of traditional culture, structures of resistance, and the accidents of timing, events, and personalities on how different states made the transition to modernity is nicely revealed in Liah Greenfeld, *Nationalism: Five Roads to Modernity*.

4. The definition of revolution used by Samuel Huntington is one such conventional understanding: "a rapid, fundamental, and violent domestic change in the dominant values and myths of a society, in its political institutions, social structure, leadership, and government activities and policies." See Samuel P. Huntington, *Political Order in Changing Societies*, 264.

5. These models, of *Gemeinschaft* and *Gesellschaft*, were formally developed by Ferdinand Tönnies, *Community and Association*. A similar conceptualization of modern civil society can be found in John Keane, "Despotism and Democracy: The Origins and Development of the Distinction Between Civil Society and the State, 1750–1850," in Keane, ed., *Civil Society and the State*, 35–37.

6. Springborg, "Politics, Primordialism, and Orientalism," 185–211.

7. The use of ideal types as analytical models comes from Max Weber. For an examination of the utility of ideal types for social analysis, see Ahmad Sadri, *Max Weber's Sociology of Intellectuals*, 11–22. The ideal types describing "positive" and "negative" liberty are developed in Isaiah Berlin, "Two Concepts of Liberty," in *Four Essays on Liberty*, 118–72, and Berlin, "The First and the Last," *New York Review of Books* 45 (May 14, 1998): 52–60.

8. I use the term *problematique* here in the sense meant by Robert Cox—that is, a historically conditioned awareness of certain problems and issues that guide the translation of reality into theory. See Robert W. Cox, "Social Forces, States, and World Orders: Beyond International Relations Theory," *Millennium* 10 (Summer 1981): 126–55.

9. Springborg, "Politics, Primordialism, and Orientalism," 200.

10. Tétreault, "Formal Politics, Meta-Space, and the Construction of Civil Life," 81–97.

11. Springborg, "Politics, Primordialism, and Orientalism," 199.

12. Otto Hintze, "The Formation of States and Constitutional Development: A Study in History and Politics," in *The Historical Essays of Otto Hintze*, 163.

13. Salamé, "Small Is Pluralistic," 84–111.

14. Ibid., 86.

15. The role of pacts as guarantees for minority rights is explored in Jean Leca, "Democratization in the Arab World," 48–83.

16. Michael Walzer, *The Revolution of the Saints: A Study in the Origins of Radical Politics*, 4–5.

17. Jürgen Habermas, *The Structural Transformation of the Public Sphere: An Inquiry into a Category of Bourgeois Society*, 6.

18. Ibid., 7 (emphasis in the original). Clifford Geertz describes the classical civilization of Bali in very similar terms—see Geertz, *Negara: The Theatre State in Nineteenth-Century Bali*.

19. Charles Tilly, "Reflections on the History of European State-Making," in Tilly, ed., *The Formation of National States in Western Europe*, 22–23.

20. Keane, "Despotism and Democracy," 35–77.

21. Material in the following section is taken from Tétreault, "Spheres of Liberty, Conflict, and Power," 273–89.

22. Walzer, *Revolution of the Saints*, 12–13.

23. Not only Roman Catholicism, but also Arminianism, an extremely high-church variant of Anglicanism.

24. John Stuart Mill, *On Liberty*, 15.

25. Elaine Pagels, *Adam, Eve, and the Serpent*, 9–14, 32–36, 40–56.

26. Berlin, "Two Concepts of Liberty," 131.

27. Cynthia Farrar, *The Origins of Democratic Thinking: The Invention of Politics in Classical Athens*, 94–95.

28. Ellis Goldberg, "Smashing Idols and the State," 195.

29. See, for example, Max Weber, *The Protestant Ethic and the Spirit of Capitalism*, ch. 2; and Lawrence Stone, *The Family, Sex, and Marriage in England, 1500–1800*, 168ff. Stone notes that the decline in religion accompanied an "increasing stress laid on personal privacy" (169), a relationship whose development in Kuwait I reflect in the text.

30. Nazih N. Ayubi, *Over-stating the Arab State: Politics and Society in the Middle East*, 439–40.

31. T. H. Marshall, "Citizenship and Social Class," in *Citizenship and Social Class and Other Essays*, 10–11.

32. Marshall, "Citizenship and Social Class," 12–13.

33. Ibid., 18. Marshall uses "men" advisedly, paying careful attention to the status of women as a separate issue.

34. Marshall, "Citizenship and Social Class," 19. See also Polanyi, *The Great Transformation*, ch. 19. A similar argument is made by Tilly with respect to elite entitlements in "War Making and State Making as Organized Crime."

35. Marshall, "Citizenship and Social Class," 32, 54.

36. Ibid., 58.

37. A number of participants in a conference held at the University of Oslo noted shortcomings in that regard. See especially Inga Brandell, "North Africa: From Social to Political Citizenship?" and Atle Hommersannd, "Citizenship and Levels of Political Organisation in the Middle East: A Normative Approach," papers presented at the Conference on Citizenship and the State in the Middle East, University of Oslo, November 22–24, 1996.

38. Bryan S. Turner, "Contemporary Problems in the Theory of Citizenship," in Turner, ed., *Citizenship and Social Theory*, 6–9.

39. Barry Hindess, "Citizenship in the Modern West," in Turner, ed., *Citizenship and Social Theory*, 25.

40. Hindess, "Citizenship in the Modern West," 32–33.

41. Anthony Giddens, *Modernity and Self-Identity: Self and Society in the Late Modern Age*, 14–15.

42. Giddens, *The Consequences of Modernity*, 36–38.

43. The four institutional dimensions of modernity identified by Giddens are capitalism, industrialism, surveillance, and military power. Although there is substantial overlap in the management of these characteristics by various individual and collective actors and agents, Giddens nominates the development and spread of nation-states as primary among them, in large part because of the key role of violence in the establishment of the modern order. See *A Contemporary Critique of Historical Materialism*, vol. 1, *The Nation-State and Violence*.

44. Much of the analysis that follows is derived from Mary Ann Tétreault, "Gender, Citizenship, and the State in the Middle East," in Nils Butenshøn, Uri Davis, and M.

Hassassian, eds., *Citizenship and the State in the Middle East: Approaches and Applications* (Syracuse: Syracuse University Press, 2000).

45. Anderson, *Imagined Communities*, 19.

46. See, for example, Sandra Mackey, *The Iranians: Persia, Islam, and the Soul of a Nation*, and David G. Marr, *Vietnamese Tradition on Trial, 1920–1945*.

47. Anderson, *Imagined Communities*, 24.

48. The apparently odd coupling of singularity with essential sameness and uniformity with individuality is reproduced through costumes. Writing about the variability in women's clothing during the romantic period, Anne Hollander observes that " 'woman' became a sort of single primitive force, encountered by individual men in the form of dramatically varied samples which were nonetheless believed to be only superficially different, sisters under the differently colored skin. . . . The faces might as well be all the same, just as if the same doll were dressed in many different ways. [At the same time, men's clothing was becoming more uniform with the result that] the individual character of each man is made more important." See Anne Hollander, *Sex and Suits: The Evolution of Modern Dress*, 98. This identification of what we might term "authentic" individuality with similarity in costume is particularly interesting in the context of Kuwait, where traditional clothing has a high symbolic value throughout the culture, and female veiling has become a major axis of political conflict over the past two decades. These issues will be discussed in subsequent chapters.

49. Ernest Gellner, *Nations and Nationalism*, 37.

50. Ibid., 65.

51. Anh Nga Longva, "Kuwaiti Women at a Crossroads: Privileged Development and the Constraints of Ethnic Stratification," *International Journal of Middle East Studies* 25 (August 1993): 448.

52. Carole Pateman, "The Fraternal Social Contract," in Keane, ed., *Civil Society and the State*, 101–27.

53. The construction of "the devil" in Jewish and Christian cosmology is a paradigm for the psychological role of "the enemy within" in political and social bodies. See Elaine Pagels, *The Origin of Satan*.

54. This pattern has been noted in virtually every modern study of nationalism. See, for examples, Anderson, *Imagined Communities*; Gellner, *Nations and Nationalism*; Greenfeld, *Nationalism*; Anthony Smith, *Theories of Nationalism*.

55. Anthony Smith, *National Identity*, 14.

56. Giddens, *The Consequences of Modernity*, 55–63.

57. Ibid., 21–36.

58. See, for example, Marshall, "Citizenship and Social Class"; Peter J. Katzenstein, ed., *Between Power and Plenty: Foreign Economic Policies of Advanced Industrial States*, a Special Issue of *International Organization* 31 (Autumn 1977); Peter B. Evans, Dietrich Rueschemeyer, and Theda Skoçpol, eds., *Bringing the State Back In*; Barbara Geddes, *Politician's Dilemma: Building State Capacity in Latin America*, esp. ch. 1.

59. The views of Marx and Engels on the subject can be found in "The Communist Manifesto." Examples of liberal views can be found in David B. Truman, *The Governmen-*

tal Process, and Theodore J. Lowi, *The End of Liberalism: Ideology, Policy, and the Crisis of Public Authority.* This issue is discussed in Ayubi, *Over-stating the Arab State,* ch. 1.

60. Tilly notes that the relative proportion of state financing coming from the bourgeoisie depended on whether the state could take most of what it needed through engaging in military violence against its rivals ("war making": military action against rivals outside the territories of the state; and "state making": military action against rivals inside the territories of the state), or had to earn its keep by selling its capacity for violence in the form of "protection" paid by bourgeois and other clients for state neutralization or elimination of the clients' enemies. See Tilly, "War Making and State Making as Organized Crime," 181–82.

61. Albert O. Hirschman, "Exit and Voice: An Expanding Sphere of Influence," in *Rival Views of Market Society, and Other Recent Essays,* 77–79.

62. Giddens, *The Consequences of Modernity,* 83–88. See also Leca, "Democratization in the Arab World."

63. Tétreault, *The Kuwait Petroleum Corporation,* 163–64.

64. Giddens notes that trust differs from faith in that faith is confidence that things which human beings cannot help are in the care of a beneficent deity. Trust is confidence in expert systems which are creations of human beings rather than elements of nature. These systems involve risk which is assumed to be at least partially calculable, unlike the dangers of living in nature which are not. See *The Consequences of Modernity,* 83–92.

65. Geddes, *Politician's Dilemma,* 83. Geddes's argument about the propensity of "special interests" to triumph over latent interests is based on the model first developed by Mancur Olson to explain the free rider problem in the provision of collective goods. See Olson's *The Logic of Collective Action: Public Goods and the Theory of Groups.*

66. Some authors, notably Nazih Ayubi for Middle East politics (and, to some extent, Karl Polanyi for Europe), elaborate types of mass political mobilization in ways that are useful in examinations of states characterized by mass politics but less so for the politics of city-states. See Ayubi's *Over-stating the Arab State,* esp. ch. 6; Polanyi, *The Great Transformation,* chs. 19–20.

67. Leca, "Democratization in the Arab World," 56–57.

68. Polanyi, *The Great Transformation;* Walter Dean Burnham, *Critical Elections and the Mainsprings of American Politics;* Ellen Meiksins Wood, "Labour and Democracy, Ancient and Modern," and "The Demos Versus 'We, the People': From Ancient to Modern Conceptions of Citizenship," both in *Democracy Against Capitalism: Renewing Historical Materialism,* 181–203 and 204–37, respectively.

69. I use this term in an Aristotelian sense. In *The Politics,* where Aristotle defines regimes as a function of the number of rulers (the one, the few, and the many), he also describes stable democracies functionally, as a variable mixture of popular rule combined with protections of property rights (1316b–1323a).

70. Aziz al-Azmeh, *Islams and Modernities.*

71. For example, ibid. See also Goldberg, "Smashing Idols and the State"; Dale F. Eickelman and James P. Piscatori, *Muslim Politics;* Olivier Roy, *The Failure of Political Islam.*

72. Fatima Mernissi is scornful of those who think that Islamism is premodern in either its theories or its practices, noting particularly the skillful utilization of modern technology by political clerics. See Mernissi, *Islam and Democracy*, 52.

3. Stories of State and Society

1. In a talk at Rice University in March 1975.
2. Hasan 'Ali al-Ebraheem, *Kuwait: A Political Study*, 25.
3. B. J. Slot, *The Origins of Kuwait*, 185n99. This volume compares contemporary writings with Kuwaiti legends about the founding of Kuwait. It also reproduces contemporary maps of Kuwait and the Gulf region.
4. Alan Rush, *Al-Sabah: History and Genealogy of Kuwait's Ruling Family, 1752–1987*, 2.
5. Robert Stephens, *The Arabs' New Frontier*, 30.
6. H. R. P. Dickson, *Kuwait and Her Neighbours*, 27.
7. Ibid., 28.
8. Peter Mansfield, *Kuwait: Vanguard of the Gulf*, 5–6.
9. Dickson, *Kuwait and Her Neighbours*, 32.
10. Ahmad Mustafa Abu-Hakima, *The Modern History of Kuwait, 1750–1965*, 1.
11. Al-Ebraheem, *Kuwait*, 26.
12. Lynn Hunt, *The Family Romance of the French Revolution*. Hunt takes Freud's conception of the family romance as a fable of an individual's desired place in the social order to mean the "political—that is, the collective—unconscious" made up of "images of the familial order that underlie revolutionary politics" (xiii). I believe that Kuwaiti political myths serve a similar function and thus also are family romances, arising from a collective unconscious structured by myths and experiences of family life.
13. A fascinating description of living conditions for average citizens in Kuwait town in the 1930s and after can be found in Mary Bruins Allison, M.D., *Doctor Mary in Arabia*.
14. Jacqueline S. Ismael, *Kuwait: Social Change in Historical Perspective*, 46, 56–57.
15. Frederick F. Anscombe, *The Ottoman Gulf: The Creation of Kuwait, Saudi Arabia, and Qatar*, 114, 155, 224n.
16. Ismael, *Kuwait*, 60.
17. Abu-Hakima, *Modern History of Kuwait*, 92–106.
18. Al-Ebraheem, *Kuwait*, 101; also Ismael, *Kuwait*, 61–64. The sailors' debts were not canceled by their deaths. Captains could claim the services of the relatives of sailors who had died owing them money. Similarly, the ship captains, *nakhodas*, were tied to the merchants who financed them. If a ship was lost at sea, the *nakhoda* lost his investment and also was required to repay cargo losses. "The ships belonged to the nakhodas and the debts to the merchants" (Alan Villiers, *Sons of Sinbad*, quote from 377).
19. Villiers, *Sons of Sinbad*; see also M. W. Khouja and P. G. Sadler, *The Economy of Kuwait: Development and Role in International Finance* (London: Macmillan, 1979), 16.
20. Quoted in Stephens, *The Arabs' New Frontier*, 30.
21. Khouja and Sadler, *The Economy of Kuwait*, 12–16.

22. Interviews with Kuwait University political scientist Saif 'Abbas 'Abdulla, spring 1990.

23. Rush, *Al-Sabah*, 3, 175. The story of the date gardens and how they complicated Kuwaiti-British relations is told very well in David H. Finnie, *Shifting Lines in the Sand: Kuwait's Elusive Frontier with Iraq*.

24. From a secret report written by S. Hennel for the Court of Directors of the East India Company, quoted in Rush, *Al-Sabah*, 174.

25. Rush, *Al-Sabah*, 154.

26. Interviews in Kuwait, spring 1990.

27. Anscombe, *The Ottoman Gulf*.

28. Ismael, *Kuwait*, 42.

29. Anscombe, *The Ottoman Gulf*, 93.

30. Rush, *Al-Sabah*, 140. Rush notes that this new relationship between the Kuwaiti ruler and the Ottomans strengthened the family's title to its date gardens in Iraq, and allowed 'Abdullah significant policy independence from the merchants. 'Abdullah was said to have used much of his income to entertain lavishly, not to suit his personal tastes but, in Rush's words, "to enhance his prestige and the strength of his position when negotiating with tribal leaders and foreign governments" (139).

31. Anscombe, *The Ottoman Gulf*, 21.

32. Ibid., 92.

33. Rush, *Al-Sabah*, 120.

34. Jill Crystal, *Oil and Politics in the Gulf: Rulers and Merchants in Kuwait and Qatar*, 23.

35. Anscombe, *The Ottoman Gulf*, 94.

36. Mubarak received income from the Ottomans as a dependent of the Porte, and from the British in return for a series of secret agreements giving Britain special privileges in Kuwait. See ibid., 114, 116.

37. Al-Ebraheem, *Kuwait*, 122.

38. Khouja and Sadler, *The Economy of Kuwait*, 14.

39. Rush, *Al-Sabah*, 103.

40. Finnie notes that, technically, the British-Kuwaiti relationship was not a protectorate. Still, throughout his book he makes it very clear that Britain dominated the relationship and frequently supported the Kuwaiti ruler against internal and external threats. (See Finnie, *Shifting Lines in the Sand*.) Anscombe agrees, reporting analyses from contemporary British officials making the same point. He notes that the primary difference between a protectorate and a "bond," the term used to describe the British-Kuwaiti relationship, lies in the secrecy of the latter, an important qualification both for London and for Kuwait. (See Anscombe, *The Ottoman Gulf*, 111.)

41. These agreements are reproduced in appendix 4 of Abu-Hakima's *Modern History of Kuwait*.

42. Mary Ann Tétreault, "Autonomy, Necessity, and the Small State: Ruling Kuwait in the Twentieth Century." *International Organization* 45 (Autumn 1991): 572–74.

43. Dickson, *Kuwait and Her Neighbours*, 258.

44. Al-Ebraheem, *Kuwait*, 133.

45. Crystal, *Oil and Politics in the Gulf*, 58. Crystal is referring to the parliaments of the 1930s, but these parliaments themselves were seen by contemporaries as direct descendants of the council.

46. Interviews with Ghanim Hamad al-Najjar and others, spring 1990, in Kuwait.

47. Economist Intelligence Unit (EIU), "Kuwait: Country Profile, 1990–91" (London: Business International, 1990), 10.

48. Tétreault, "Autonomy, Necessity, and the Small State," 576–77.

49. Frank Stoakes, "Social and Political Change in the Third World: Some Peculiarities of Oil-Producing Principalities of the Persian Gulf," in Derek Hopwood, ed., *The Arabian Peninsula: Society and Politics*, 196.

50. Abdul-Reda al-Assiri and Kamal al-Monoufi, "Kuwait's Political Elite: The Cabinet," *Middle East Journal* 42 (1988): 48–58.

51. This opinion was widespread among businessmen and members of the political opposition whom I interviewed in the spring of 1990 and in September and October 1992 in Kuwait.

52. This conclusion is based on many interviews of Kuwaitis conducted over more than fifteen years in and outside of Kuwait.

53. Al-Ebraheem, *Kuwait*, 133–41.

54. For example, see Nicolas Gavrielides, "Tribal Democracy: The Anatomy of Parliamentary Elections in Kuwait," in Linda L. Layne, ed., *Elections in the Middle East: Implications of Recent Trends*, 165; and Kamal Osman Salih, "Kuwait's Parliamentary Elections: 1963–1985," unpublished paper. See also chapters 6 and 7, this volume.

55. Crystal, *Oil and Politics in the Gulf*.

56. See Ralph H. Magnus, "Societies and Social Change in the Persian Gulf," in Alvin J. Cottrell, ed., *The Persian Gulf States: A General Survey*, 399–402; also several 1990 interviews with Saif 'Abbas 'Abdulla. Nazih Ayubi argues that oil income has retarded modern class-formation throughout the gulf region, including in Kuwait (see *Over-stating the Arab State*, 225–30). Ayubi calls groups occupied by Kuwaiti government workers "intermediate classes," created by capitalist modernity but not yet either classes in themselves or classes for themselves. I discuss Kuwait's middle class further in subsequent chapters.

57. Khaldoun Hasan al-Naqeeb, *Society and State in the Gulf and Arab Peninsula*, 129. This is not to say that all Kuwaiti state employees are indifferent workers, but dedicated workers are exceptions and even persons in elite positions such as university professors have told me that they work much less than they would if they were not state employees.

58. Crystal, *Oil and Politics in the Gulf*, 75–78.

59. Ibid., 76–77; Michael E. Bonine, "The Urbanization of the Persian Gulf Nations," in Cottrell, ed., *The Persian Gulf States*, 250; Ghanim Hamad al-Najjar, "Decision-Making Process in Kuwait: The Land Acquisition Policy as a Case Study," Ph.D. diss., University of Exeter, 1984.

60. Al-Najjar, "Decision-Making Process in Kuwait"; Khouja and Sadler, *The Economy of Kuwait*, 45; interviews with 'Abdullah Nibari, spring 1990.

61. Khouja and Sadler, *The Economy of Kuwait*, 44–45.

62. Crystal, *Oil and Politics in the Gulf*, 76.

63. Interviews in Kuwait (spring 1990, September-October 1992, September-October 1996). For an excellent treatment of agency relationships and the role of migrant workers in the creation of Kuwaiti citizenship, see Longva, *Walls Built on Sand*.

64. See, for example, Timothy W. Luke, "The Discipline of Security Studies and the Codes of Containment: Learning from Kuwait," *Alternatives* 16 (1991): 315–44.

65. See, for example, Theodore Draper, "The True History of the Gulf War," *New York Review of Books* (January 30, 1992): 38–45 (quote on 44).

66. According to Phebe Marr, writing in the mid-1980s, "It is not yet possible to speak of an Iraqi nation." See Marr, *The Modern History of Iraq*, 5.

67. Anh Nga Longva, "Citizenship in the Gulf States: Conceptualisation and Practice," paper presented at the Conference on Citizenship and the State in the Middle East, University of Oslo, November 22–24, 1996.

68. Quoted in Longva, "Citizenship in the Gulf States."

69. Ibid.

70. Zahra Freeth, *A New Look at Kuwait*, 141.

71. In December 1915, Salim had allowed members of the 'Ajman tribe, then at war with Ibn Sa'ud, to take refuge in Kuwait. "This enraged 'Abd al-'Aziz [Ibn Sa'ud] . . . [and] marked the beginning of the enmity between the two men, an enmity which led later to the siege of al-Jahra town by the forces of the fanatic Wahhabi Ikhwan (brothers) under the command of Faisal al-Duwaish in 1920." Abu-Hakima, *Modern History of Kuwait*, 132.

72. Ibid., 133; H. V. F. Winstone and Zahra Freeth, *Kuwait: Prospect and Reality*, 83–84.

73. Jill Crystal, *Kuwait: The Transformation of an Oil State*, 15.

74. Freeth, *A New Look at Kuwait*, 139. The old *hadhar* families also originated in Najd.

75. Winstone and Freeth, *Kuwait*, 84.

76. Abu-Hakima, *Modern History of Kuwait*, 132.

77. Winstone and Freeth, *Kuwait*, 84.

78. Ibid., 84–85.

79. Longva, "Citizenship in the Gulf States."

80. Ibid.

81. Freeth, *A New Look at Kuwait*, 140–41.

82. Crystal, *Oil and Politics in the Gulf*, 88–89; and chapter 6, this volume. Among the results of this policy is what Shafeeq Ghabra refers to as the "desertization" of Kuwaiti political life. See Ghabra, "Kuwait and the Dynamics of Socio-economic Change," *Middle East Journal* 51 (Summer 1997): 358–72; and chapter 6, this volume.

83. The status of the *bidun* is of staggering importance to Kuwait today, not only because of internal and external pressures to resolve the issue but because of the myriad effects of that resolution on the state—who will be the policemen and soldiers when *bidun* become full citizens, for example; and on the economy—how will the incorporation of what is estimated to be more than 125,000 Kuwaiti *bidun* affect the provision and distribution of social rights, including housing, services, and jobs?

84. Longva, "Citizenship in the Gulf States."

85. Lindholm, "Quandaries of Command in Egalitarian Societies," 63–94.

86. Ghassan Salamé, " 'Strong' and 'Weak' States: A Qualified Return to the *Muqaddimah*," in Giacomo Luciani, ed., *The Arab State*, 32.

87. Sharabi, *Neopatriarchy*.

88. Habermas, *Structural Transformation of the Public Sphere*, 7.

89. Mary Ann Tétreault and Haya al-Mughni, "Modernization and Its Discontents: State and Gender in Kuwait," *Middle East Journal* 49: 407.

90. Gavrielides, "Tribal Democracy," 158–63.

91. Lonva, "Citizenship in the Gulf States."

92. Tétreault and al-Mughni, "Gender, Citizenship, and Nationalism in Kuwait," 75–77.

93. Ibid., 71–72. I discuss Islamism in Kuwait further in subsequent chapters.

94. Anthony Giddens, *The Transformation of Intimacy: Sexuality, Love, and Eroticism in Modern Societies*. Benedict Anderson envisions the spread of alternative life models as an outcome of print capitalism and the widespread distribution of newspapers and novels (which today would be augmented by television and films)—see *Imagined Communities*.

95. Eqbal al-Rahmani, "The Impact of Traditional Domestic Sexual Division of Labor on Women's Status: The Case of Kuwait," *Research in Human Capital and Development* 9 (1996): 79–101.

96. Roy, *The Failure of Political Islam*, 58–59. See also Tétreault, "Individualism, Secularism, and Fundamentalism"; and Haya al-Mughni, "Women's Movements and the Autonomy of Civil Society in Kuwait," in Robin L. Teske and Mary Ann Tétreault, eds., *Feminist Approaches to Social Movements, Community, and Power*, vol. 1, *Conscious Acts and the Politics of Social Change*.

97. Tétreault and al-Mughni, "Gender, Citizenship, and Nationalism in Kuwait," 69, 74.

98. On May 16, 1999, the amir issued a decree granting full political rights to female citizens. These included both voting rights and the right to run for parliament. Under the decree, women could not vote in the July 1999 election, in part because there would not have been time to get them registered properly but, more importantly, because amiri decrees promulgated during parliamentary recesses must be approved by the new parliament when it reconvenes. As I describe in chapter 9, this decree was rejected in November 1999.

99. Longva, *Walls Built on Sand*, 131.

100. One example can be found in Charles F. Doran, *Myth, Oil, and Politics: Introduction to the Political Economy of Petroleum*, 161–62.

101. Hazem Beblawi, "The Rentier State in the Arab World," in Luciani, ed., *The Arab State*, 86–88 (emphasis in the original).

102. Beblawi points out that the implicit normative judgment carried by the imputation of "rentier" to anyone has generally been negative ever since the concept was first developed by the classical economists (ibid., 86).

103. See, for example, Paul Aarts, "Democracy, Oil, and the Gulf War," 525–38. Two morally divergent examples of earlier versions of this myth, extended to the region as a

whole, can be found in Joel S. Migdal, *Strong Societies and Weak States: State-Society Relations and State Capabilities in the Third World*, and al-Naqeeb, *Society and State in the Gulf and Arab Peninsula*. A differently focused and highly sophisticated analysis of rentier status and political development can be found in Kirin Aziz Chaudhry, *The Price of Wealth: Economies and Institutions in the Middle East*.

104. Tilly, "War Making and State Making as Organized Crime."

105. Jonathan Nitzan, "Differential Accumulation: Toward A New Political Economy of Capital," paper presented at the annual meeting of the International Studies Association, Toronto, March 1997, emphasis in the original. Another version of this paper can be found in the *Review of International Political Economy* 5 (Summer 1998): 169–216. See also Jonathan Nitzan and Shimshon Bichler, "Bringing Capital Accumulation Back In: The Weapondollar-Petrodollar Coalition—Military Contractors, Oil Companies and Middle-East 'Energy Conflicts,' " *Review of International Political Economy* 2 (Summer 1995): 446–515.

106. See, for example, Bruce W. Jentleson, "Kruschev's Oil and Brezhnev's Natural Gas Pipelines," in Robert J. Lieber, ed., *Will Europe Fight for Oil?*, 33–69. An example of Soviet disruption of oil markets can be found in Mary Ann Tétreault, *Revolution in the World Petroleum Market*, 80–81.

107. Those who admit the existence of domestic resources in the generation of rentier wealth discount their importance by assuming that the opportunity cost of these resources approaches zero. For an example of this kind of reasoning, see Paul Hallwood and Stuart Sinclair, *Oil, Debt, and Development: OPEC in the Third World*.

108. Mary Ann Tétreault, "Independence, Sovereignty, and Vested Glory: Oil and Politics in the Second Gulf War," *Orient* 34 (March 1993): 96–98.

109. Doran, *Myth, Oil, and Politics*. See also Stephen D. Krasner, *Structural Conflict: The Third World Against Global Liberalism*.

110. George Tomeh, "Interdependence: A View from the Third World," in Peter Dorner and Mahmoud A. El-Shafie, eds., *Resources and Development: Natural Resource Policies and Economic Development in an Interdependent World*, 359–84.

111. For two interesting discussions of urban legends, see Patricia A. Turner, *I Heard It Through the Grapevine: Rumor in African-American Culture*, and Roger Angell, "True Tales—Well, Maybe," *The New Yorker*, January 22, 1996, 37–43.

112. In her book *Poetic Justice: The Literary Imagination and Public Life*, philosopher Martha C. Nussbaum looks at injustice as a function of the denial of intersubjectivity and the imputation of malevolence to the unknown. Patricia Turner sees it more as the reflection of the fears that members of one group have about members of another (see *I Heard It Through the Grapevine*).

113. For examples see al-Ebraheem, *Kuwait*; Khouja and Sadler, *The Economy of Kuwait*; and Abdul-Reda al-Assiri, *Kuwait's Foreign Policy: City-State in World Politics*.

114. Tétreault, "Autonomy, Necessity, and the Small State."

115. Al-Ebraheem, *Kuwait*, 46–50; Edith Penrose and E. F. Penrose, *Iraq: International Relations and National Development*, 16–17; Anscombe, *The Ottoman Gulf*, 116–17.

116. Quoted in Abu-Hakima, *Modern History of Kuwait*, appendix 4, 185.

117. Ibid., 197.

118. Finnie, *Shifting Lines in the Sand*, 17.

119. Anscombe, *The Ottoman Gulf*, 132–42.

120. Quoted in Finnie, *Shifting Lines in the Sand*, 32.

121. Finnie, *Shifting Lines in the Sand*, 118.

122. Ibid., 35. The issue was described by British contemporaries as the difference between "sovereign" and "suzerain," with the presumption that the Ottomans might have been suzerains over Kuwait but never sovereigns.

123. Extract from the "Report on the Negotiations with Hakki Pasha on the Baghdad Railway and the Persian Gulf, 3 May 1913," reprinted in E. Lauterpacht, C. J. Greenwood, Marc Weller, and Daniel Bethlehem, eds., *The Kuwait Crisis: Basic Documents* (Cambridge: Grotius, 1991), 32; "Press Release by the Press Office of the Embassy of the Republic of Iraq, London, 12 September 1990," in ibid., 75. Finnie also points to the Anglo-Ottoman Convention as the basis for Saddam's claims to Kuwait (*Shifting Lines in the Sand*, 37) and its role in the very first such claim proposed in 1938 by Iraq's foreign affairs minister, Taufiq Suwaidi (Finnie, ibid., 99ff.).

124. David Fromkin, *A Peace to End All Peace: The Fall of the Ottoman Empire and the Creation of the Modern Middle East*.

125. The story of the boundary talks is told in Dickson, *Kuwait and Her Neighbours*, 270–80. Finnie does not share Dickson's perspective that Kuwait was entitled to the territory transferred to Saudi Arabia. Most of it fell between the so-called red and green lines in the Anglo-Ottoman Convention and thus had been recognized as early as 1913 as tribal lands rather than areas clearly under the control of the Kuwaiti ruler. Finnie, *Shifting Lines in the Sand*, 61.

126. Finnie, *Shifting Lines in the Sand*, 99–125.

127. Archibald H. T. Chisholm, *The First Kuwait Oil Concession Agreement: A Record of the Negotiations, 1911–1934*. For a discussion of the Kuwaiti-British relationship as an example of international cliency, see Tétreault, "Autonomy, Necessity, and the Small State."

128. Stephens, *The Arabs' New Frontier*, 31; Dickson, *Kuwait and Her Neighbours*, 281ff.

129. Tétreault, "Autonomy, Necessity, and the Small State," 582.

130. Al-Assiri, *Kuwait's Foreign Policy*, 100–10.

131. Theodore Draper, "American Hubris: From Truman to the Persian Gulf," *New York Review of Books*, July 16, 1987, 40–48.

132. This is covered in some detail in Tétreault, *The Kuwait Petroleum Corporation*, 130–38.

133. Al-Assiri, *Kuwait's Foreign Policy*, 32–48.

134. Tétreault, *The Kuwait Petroleum Corporation*.

4. Democratic Structures and Practices, 1921–1990

1. Crystal, *Oil and Politics in the Gulf*, chs. 3–4; Tétreault, "Autonomy, Necessity, and the Small State," 575ff.

2. Modern writers using these concepts include Hannah Arendt, *The Human Condi-*

tion; Eli Zaretsky, *Capitalism, the Family, and Personal Life*; and Robert N. Bellah et al., *Habits of the Heart: Individualism and Commitment in American Life.*

3. Here the use of "man" is not a synonym for "human being" but a gender-specific reference to male human beings.

4. Nazih Ayubi argues that the ancient distinction is still dominant in the Arab world, where privacy as it is known in the West is at a rudimentary stage of development (see *Over-stating the Arab State*, 439).

5. The term *mosque* is used here not simply to refer to a physical place of worship but also metaphorically to embrace the individuals, institutions, and organizations—including those whose purposes go beyond conventional definitions of "religious" but which still identify themselves as "Islamic." The term is analogous to the use of "the church" in the context of politics in Christian countries—see, for example, Claudia Koonz, *Mothers in the Fatherland: Women, the Family, and Nazi Politics*, who uses the term in this way to discuss the very different theological, institutional, and structural contexts of Protestantism and Catholicism in Germany.

6. Interviews with Kuwaitis, March, September-October 1992, in Kuwait. See also Jehan S. Rajab, *Invasion Kuwait: An English Woman's Tale*, 21–22; Shamlan Y. al-Essa, "The Political Consequences of the Crisis for Kuwait," in Ibrahim Ibrahim, ed., *The Gulf Crisis: Background and Consequences*, 169–85.

7. See, for example, Charles E. Lindblom, *Politics and Markets: The World's Political-Economic Systems*; Mary Ann Tétreault, "Regimes and Liberal World Orders," *Alternatives* 13 (January 1988): 13–16. The shift in the nature of the dominant interdependent institutions and their relationships in Europe is traced in Polanyi, *The Great Transformation*, chs. 4–5. The divergence between Islamist ideology regarding the integration of religion with every other aspect of life, and the practices of Muslim societies throughout history is discussed in the context of mosque-state relations in James P. Piscatori, *Islam in a World of Nation-States*. The relevance of such practice to democratization is discussed in Mernissi, *Islam and Democracy*.

8. The measure of Ahmad al-Jabir's acute self-regard can be assessed from a report on Kuwait compiled by the British Political Agent c. 1937–38, reprinted in Alan de Lacy Rush, ed., *Records of Kuwait, 1899–1961* 2:27–45. The author reports on cronyism (27–28), the country's and the amir's budgets—which include only Rs 2000 in unambiguously public expenditures out of a total of Rs 121,000 in "Shaikh's expenses private and public" (30), and the arrangements by which the amir and his family got free medical care while "charges are made for medicine and for all attentions, including those to out-patients, and even the poor—and they are very poor in Kuwait—have to bring something in kind, if not in cash" (42). After oil was discovered in Kuwait, Ahmad al-Jabir insisted that all revenues from it belonged to him by right, even though there was no support for such a position in tribal tradition and, as David Finnie notes, such an assertion was politically untenable as well. In the concession agreement outlining the relationship between the Kuwait Oil Company and the amir, Ahmad al-Jabir had "[taken] care to stipulate . . . that revenues . . . were to be paid to his personal account" (Finnie, *Shifting Lines in the Sand*, 88).

9. Rush, ed., *Records of Kuwait* 2:46; also Crystal, *Oil and Politics in the Gulf*, 52.

10. Phebe Marr, *Modern History of Iraq*, 78. Marr notes that this was the first time that an Iraqi ruler claimed sovereign rights to Kuwait. Crystal places the beginning of Iraqi efforts to tie Kuwait to Iraq in the early 1930s, with a campaign to woo the ruler to agree to voluntary merger in the face of the Saudi threat (see *Oil and Politics in the Gulf*, 52–53).

11. Rush, ed., *Records of Kuwait* 2:117.

12. Crystal, *Oil and Politics in the Gulf*, 52.

13. Rush, ed., *Records of Kuwait* 2:118–19.

14. Ibid., 140–43.

15. Ibid., 27–46, 134, 138–40.

16. Ibid., 136.

17. Ibid., 182.

18. Ibid., 208–209.

19. Ibid., 153–54.

20. Crystal, *Oil and Politics in the Gulf*, 49.

21. Tétreault, "Autonomy, Necessity, and the Small State," 576.

22. Rush, ed., *Records of Kuwait* 2:225. According to British records, the first council consisted of fourteen persons plus a president, the amir's cousin 'Abdullah al-Salim. The members in order of their vote totals were: *Muhammad bin Shahin al-Ghanim (103), *Shaikh Yusuf bin Issa (100), *Abdulla bin Hamad Al-Sagar (100), *Mash'an Al-Khudair (82), *Sulaiman Al-Adsani (77), *Sayid Ali Sayid Sulaiman (76), *Mishari Al-Hasan Al-Badur (62), *Sultan Al-Kulaib (62), *Abdul Latif Al-Thunayyan (61), *Yusuf Saleh Al-Humaidhi (59), *Saleh Al-Othman Al-Rashid (50), Yusuf Al-Marzook (45), *Hamad Al-Marzook (39), and *Khalid Al-Abdul Latif Al-Hamad (37)—see Rush, ed., *Records of Kuwait* 2:149. The twelve marked (*) were also elected to the second council, along with Ahmad bin Khamis, Ali al-Banwan, Ali al Abdul Wahhab, Mishairi al Hilal, Muhammad al Ahmad al Ghanim, Husf bin Yusuf, and Yusuf al Adsani. 'Abdullah al-Salim was again appointed president of the council. (Spellings of names are taken from the source.)

23. Rush, ed., *Records of Kuwait* 2:240–47.

24. The events of March 9–10, 1939, are drawn from the following sources: Rush, ed., *Records of Kuwait* 2:258–65; interviews with Jasim al-Qatami, veteran member of the political opposition and brother of a policeman slain in an altercation with anticouncil forces (see main text, later this chapter), March 17 and 21, 1990, in Kuwait; Alan Rush, *Al-Sabah*, 52–53; Crystal, *Oil and Politics in the Gulf*, 49–50.

25. Rush, ed., *Records of Kuwait* 2:260, 265.

26. Ibid., 2:228.

27. Crystal, *Oil and Politics in the Gulf*, 58.

28. Mernissi, *Islam and Democracy*, esp. ch. 3; Jamal al-Suwaidi, "Arab and Western Conceptions of Democracy: Evidence from a UAE Opinion Survey," in David Garnham and Mark Tessler, eds., *Democracy, War, and Peace in the Middle East*, 86–89; Shukri B. Abed, "Islam and Democracy," in ibid., 120–26.

29. Tétreault, "Autonomy, Necessity, and the Small State," 577.

30. Crystal, *Oil and Politics in the Gulf*, 51–53.

31. Gavrielides, "Tribal Democracy."

32. Rush, ed., *Records of Kuwait* 2:54.

33. Rush, *Al-Sabah*, 28–31; Gavrielides, "Tribal Democracy," 165; and chapter 7, this volume.

34. Tétreault, "Kuwait's Democratic Reform Movement," 17.

35. The Kuwaiti constitution provides for a National Assembly to resume meeting two months after a dissolution, "restored to its full constitutional authority . . . as if the dissolution had not taken place," and authorized to continue until the election of a new assembly (article 107). However, the 1975 assembly did not resume after the two-month period had ended. See Abdo Baaklini, "Legislatures in the Gulf Area: The Experience of Kuwait, 1961–1976," *International Journal of Middle East Studies* 14 (August 1982): 372–76.

36. The Group of Twenty-six refers to the parliamentarians who began meeting after the dissolution of the National Assembly. Its members are the core of the parliamentary opposition. They were joined gradually by six additional parliamentarians, and together composed the Group of Thirty-two. In 1989 the Thirty-two decided to enlarge its direct representation of groups in the Kuwaiti population by inviting selected members of these groups to join the leadership core. This body, augmented by nonparliamentarians, became the Group of Forty-five. (Interview with Ahmad al-Sa'doun, March 17, 1990, in Kuwait.)

37. During the spring of 1990, in scores of interviews with politically active Kuwaitis, people referred over and over again to the events in Eastern Europe as harbingers of democratization in Kuwait and elsewhere in the Middle East.

38. Kuwaiti parliaments are identified by the year of their election.

39. Information about the opposition movement and conditions in Kuwait prior to the invasion was gathered in interviews conducted in Kuwait in the spring of 1990. Among those I interviewed were leaders of the opposition, including five members of the Group of Twenty-six, government officials, professors and students at Kuwait University, Kuwaiti businessmen, and members of expatriate communities in Kuwait.

40. *Kuwait Times*, April 23, 1990, 1. The newspaper notes that these were almost the same reasons cited for the 1975 suspensions by the amir at that time, Sabah al-Salim. See also Baaklini, "Legislatures in the Gulf Area," 373–74.

41. Other causes possibly contributing to the amir's actions included a series of terrorist attacks by Kuwaiti Shi'i supporters of the Iranian regime, and the nervous debility of the amir, whose mental state following an assassination attempt the year before was said to have remained fragile. However, the suspensions are "overdetermined," and reasons coming from other perspectives will be noted in subsequent chapters.

42. John Whelan, "Kuwait '88: A Model for Development," G2. The mechanics of the illegal Manakh market relied on dealings in postdated checks. In Kuwait a postdated check can be presented for payment even before the date indicated. The presentation of a large postdated check in September 1982 set off the crash. See John Train, *Famous Financial Fiascos*, 20.

43. When I interviewed him in Kuwait in May 1990, then Finance Minister Jasim al-Khorafy denied that debtors' assets had been transferred out of the country, but bank economists in Kuwait contradicted his statement.

44. Economist Intelligence Unit, *Kuwait Country Profile, 1986–87* (London: Business International, 1986), 21–23.

45. Tétreault, *The Kuwait Petroleum Corporation*, 34–39. The opposition also criticized the price KPC paid, which was appreciably in excess of the market value of the company's shares.

46. The economic situation in Kuwait, as in the Gulf as a whole, also was affected by external factors such as the long recession in the West which vastly reduced employment and the consumption of oil, the region's major export.

47. Shireen T. Hunter, "The Gulf Economic Crisis and Its Social and Political Consequences," *Middle East Journal* 40 (Autumn 1986): 593–613.

48. National Bank of Kuwait, *Kuwait & Gulf Cooperation Council Economic & Financial Bulletin* 11 (Fall 1987): 9–11.

49. Al-Assiri, *Kuwait's Foreign Policy*, 129. In 1990 this insecurity was fanned by pressures from Iraq and Saudi Arabia. According to a military officer whom I interviewed in late February, these included separate incursions into Kuwait by armed forces from each country.

50. Information about the pro-democracy movement and the activities of 1989–90 were obtained from interviews with speaker Ahmad al-Sa'doun, March 17, 1990, in Kuwait, and four other members of the 1985 parliament in March and May 1990; interviews with other participants, including members of previous parliaments and members of the press, in spring 1990 and fall 1992. Quotes in the text other than those attributed to someone else are from the interview with Ahmad al-Sa'doun. Some of these events also were discussed by Shafeeq Ghabra in a talk entitled, "The Democratic Movement in Historical Perspective," given at the Conference on Political Participation and Constitutional Democracy in Kuwait, sponsored by the National Republican Institute for International Affairs, Washington, D.C., April 29, 1991.

51. Interviews with 'Abdullah Nibari, former member of parliament, April and May 1990.

52. *Arab Times*, April 28, 1990 (quote from 1); April 23, 1990, 1; *Kuwait Times*, April 23, 1990, 1.

53. When each prisoner was released from jail, his friends sent piles of cards and letters congratulating him and wishing him well. One of 'Abdullah Nibari's messages of congratulation was posted on his office wall, a four-foot-long computer printout spelling out "mabrouk"—congratulations—in Arabic.

54. *International Herald Tribune*, June 18, 1990, 19.

55. Testimony by the company's managing director in the London suit for recovery of funds embezzled from the Kuwait Oil Tanker Company indicated that Kuwaiti production in this period went as high as three million barrels per day (bpd), but I have no supporting information from another source for this figure. The quarter-million bpd estimate comes from the trade press.

56. Tétreault, "Independence, Sovereignty, and Vested Glory," 96.

57. Samir al-Khalil, *Republic of Fear: The Inside Story of Saddam's Iraq*.

5. Iraqi Occupation and Kuwaiti Democracy

1. Good summaries of the diplomatic events leading up to the invasion can be found in Elaine Sciolino, *The Outlaw State: Saddam Hussein's Quest for Power and the Gulf Crisis*, 177–208; and Jean Edward Smith, *George Bush's War*, 46–62. Sciolino notes that the Israelis were virtually alone in expecting some kind of military action by Iraq in the late spring of 1990, though even they were not convinced this would be directed against Kuwait. Both authors blame the United States for "allowing" Saddam to think that he could take over Kuwait and get away with it although, if it is true that no one actually believed that Saddam would do this, their condemnation of the United States seems, at best, overdrawn.

2. Information about Kuwaiti opinions during this period comes from extensive interviews of Kuwaitis conducted January-May 1990 in Kuwait and in London. "Overproduction" refers to production in excess of Kuwait's OPEC-set quota—at that time, 1.5 million barrels per day (MBD).

3. I first encountered this vast disjunction between the evaluations of insiders and outsiders of Kuwait's economic policies during my 1990 fieldwork in Kuwait and in Europe for a study of the Kuwait Petroleum Corporation.

4. This increasing control included the absorption of private-sector oil industry investments—see Tétreault, *The Kuwait Petroleum Corporation*, ch. 5.

5. Interview with 'Abdullah Nibari, March 25, 1990, in Kuwait. 'Abdullah Nibari was a leader of the opposition in the 1971 parliament, where he spearheaded the challenges to government oil policy. In this interview he also discussed the Kuwaiti parliament's role in changing OPEC's oil-expensing agreement in the mid-1960s, which he nominated as the first instance of public discussion of oil policy in Kuwait, and ongoing parliamentary criticisms of natural gas exploitation.

6. Ibid.

7. Interviews in Kuwait, spring 1990. These issues are discussed more fully in subsequent chapters.

8. 'Ali al-Khalifa started out in what was then the Ministry of Finance and Oil shortly after receiving a master's degree in economics from London University. He rose to the rank of assistant undersecretary of petroleum affairs before becoming undersecretary of the newly separated Ministry of Finance in 1975. He served as minister of finance and chair of the National Investment Authority after 'Abd al-Latif al-Hamad resigned in 1983 due to a conflict over how to deal with the crash of the Suq al-Manakh. 'Ali al-Khalifa held on to both positions until a new cabinet was formed following the 1985 election. His decisions during that period led to many of the charges by his political opponents of cronyism and corruption that continue to haunt him today. 'Ali al-Khalifa headed the oil ministry in its various incarnations from 1978 to 1990, and was the chair of the Kuwait Petroleum Corporation from its founding in 1980 until mid-1990, when he was

moved from Oil to Finance in June, after the Majlis al-Watani election. He remained in that position until the first postliberation government was formed in 1991. See Alan Rush, *Al-Sabah*, 134; Economist Intelligence Unit, "Kuwait: Country Report" (various issues); Tétreault, *The Kuwait Petroleum Corporation*.

9. In 1990 interviews, Jasim al-Sa'doun, members of the Group of Thirty-two, and 'Abdullah Nibari were highly critical, along with most academic economists at Kuwait University. Representatives of the press, former minister of oil and finance 'Abd al-Rahman al-Atiqi, and private-sector investor Fawzi Mossad al-Saleh, among others, were highly laudatory.

10. Jasim al-Sa'doun interview, March 11, 1990, in Kuwait. 'Ali al-Khalifa *is* a Sabah, but not one able to aspire to the leadership of Kuwait because he is not a direct descendent of the amir Mubarak.

11. This attitude persisted well into 1992 when I interviewed him in Kuwait the day before the October election.

12. *MEES* is the *Middle East Economic Survey*, an influential oil industry weekly published in Nicosia, Cyprus.

13. Interviews with Kuwaitis working at Kuwait's embassy in Washington, D.C., conducted in August 1990, and with non-Kuwaiti employees of the Kuwait Petroleum Corporation, conducted in California in September 1990, elicited variations of the Iraqi version from all but one interviewee—a former Kuwaiti diplomat.

14. Mohammed al-Mashat, Iraqi ambassador to the United States, quoted in Smith, *George Bush's War*, 22.

15. Ibid., also 60–61.

16. Smith is convinced that this is because the Kuwaitis had assurances of U.S. military assistance should Saddam actually invade (see ibid., 51ff.).

17. For example, see the *Washington Post*, March 8, 1991, 1. But Elaine Sciolino reports that the Kuwaiti government was suspicious that the "United States was exaggerating the threat as a pretext for increasing its military presence in the Gulf" (*The Outlaw State*, 208).

18. Milton Viorst, "After the Liberation," *The New Yorker*, September 30, 1991, 40.

19. Smith, *George Bush's War*, 51.

20. Personal communication from Ghanim al-Najjar. Mubarak's attempts to defuse the crisis are noted in Sciolino, *The Outlaw State*, 207, and Smith, *George Bush's War*, 22–23.

21. Interview with Khaled Buhamrah, then deputy managing director (M) of KNPC, March 2, 1992, at Mina' al-Ahmadi.

22. Smith, *George Bush's War*, 51.

23. Interview with 'Eisa bu Yabis, then-superintendent of the Kuwait Oil Company's well-capping and fire-fighting unit, October 3, 1992, in Ahmadi.

24. Robin Allen, "Armed Forces: Trip-wire Role," *Financial Times*, May 23, 1995, "Survey of Kuwait," 7.

25. Interview with 'Eisa bu Yabis, October 3, 1992.

26. Interview in September 1990, in Alhambra, California.

27. Personal communication from Ghanim al-Najjar.

28. Ibid.

29. This trickle moved in both directions across the border (see later this chapter).

30. Milton Viorst, *Sandcastles: The Arabs in Search of the Modern World*, 257.

31. The stories of some of these men are recounted in Tétreault, *The Kuwait Petroleum Corporation*, ch. 6.

32. For the officially fostered family romance in preinvasion Kuwait (i.e., the concept of *al-'usra al-waheda*), see chapter 3, this volume. For the views of an insider who held onto the idealistic story of the killing of Shaikh Fahad, see Rajab, *Invasion Kuwait*, 5–6.

33. This is because bedrock constituencies of the regime, the Shi'a and tribal bedouins, were underrepresented among exiled activists. The Shi'a, including opponents as well as supporters of the regime, remained in Kuwait in large numbers, many for personal reasons but some as the result of having been denied entry into Saudi Arabia as refugees because of their religion. Bedouin refugees living in hotels and apartment blocks in neighboring countries had little political influence during this period because they lacked the tribal organization that coordinates them into a formidable force in domestic politics during normal times.

34. These included Arab intellectuals and mass publics—"the street" in the vernacular of Middle East politics—and influential intellectuals as well as mass publics in the coalition countries.

35. 'Ali al-Khalifa spent much of this time in London, rallying employees of KPC who streamed into the corporate headquarters of Kuwait Petroleum International (KPI), a KPC holding company. He arranged almost immediately for written delegations of authority from the amir to a handful of Kuwaitis, including KPI president Nader Sultan, empowering them to operate the oil company and manage Kuwait's investments during the occupation. See later this chapter and also Tétreault, *The Kuwait Petroleum Corporation*, 133–34.

36. Viorst, *Sandcastles*, 262; Tétreault, *The Kuwait Petroleum Corporation*, 138.

37. Sciolino, *The Outlaw State*, 217; Tétreault, *The Kuwait Petroleum Corporation*, 137–38.

38. Sciolino, *The Outlaw State*, 217; interviews with Lubna Saif 'Abbas 'Abdulla, daughter of political scientist Saif 'Abbas 'Abdulla and herself a leader of the ad hoc student group working with Citizens for a Free Kuwait, September-October 1992, in Kuwait.

39. Tétreault, *The Kuwait Petroleum Corporation*, 139.

40. Ibid., 136.

41. Ibid., 139.

42. Viorst, *Sandcastles*, 261. Information about the Jidda meeting comes from this source, from Tétreault, *The Kuwait Petroleum Corporation*, from the Economist Intelligence Unit, "Kuwait Country Report no. 4, 1990" (London: Business International, 1990), and from interviews with Kuwaitis.

43. EIU, "Kuwait Country Report no. 4, 1990," 7.

44. Viorst, *Sandcastles*, 262.

45. The chief elements in this discrediting included Ibrahim Shahin's decision to eliminate all but one primary contractor, Bechtel, from postwar oil industry reconstruction, touching off a barrage of rumors about favoritism and payoffs; and the results of his insistence on personally authorizing every purchase—he too had been informed about the "corruption" of the volunteer planners—which created unnecessary shortages, including food, water, and equipment needed for the fire-fighting.

46. I have discussed the deleterious effects of Ibrahim Shahin's operations on the oil well fire-fighting and other immediate problems of the postliberation period in *The Kuwait Petroleum Corporation*, 140–42. I discovered evidence of the campaign to discredit the committees in 1994, after that book went to press.

47. Economic Intelligence Unit (EIU), "Kuwait Country Report no. 1, 1991" (London: EIU, 1991), 7–8.

48. Ibid., 7.

49. Ibid., 8. However, this is not to say that the crown prince was held in high esteem or that there were not significant pockets of support favoring the amir.

50. No mention is made of Hamad al-Jou'an, his wife, or her speech in the official published account of this meeting, which was taped in its entirety. See National Republican Institute for International Affairs, "Political Participation and Constitutional Democracy in Kuwait," Washington, D.C., April 29, 1991. The proceedings are marked "edited transcript of a conference."

51. Viorst, "After the Liberation," 43–44, 55; memoirs of and interviews with persons remaining in Kuwait during the occupation. The interviews were conducted in the United States, Europe, and Kuwait. Evidence of the attention paid by the Iraqis to the work of the Resistance is shown by a collection of captured Iraqi military documents compiled by Ali Abdul-Lateef Khalifiouh, PSC. See Youssef Abdul-Mo'ati, ed, *Kuwaiti Resistance as Revealed by Iraqi Documents*. Such documents littered the Kuwaiti landscape following the rout of Iraqi troops by the coalition forces. On a drive through the Mutla Ridge area with Saif 'Abbas 'Abdulla in February 1992, we found a large cache of papers that included a ledger left behind by the occupiers.

52. See accounts of some of the activities of KPC employees in Tétreault, *The Kuwait Petroleum Corporation*, 126–30.

53. These were Athbi al-Fahad, who served in the military, and Sabah al-Nasir and 'Ali al-Salim, who were active in the civilian Resistance. (Personal communication from Ghanim al-Najjar.)

54. Information about the operation of this system comes mainly from interviews with Kuwaiti businessmen 'Abd al-Wahhab al-Wazzan and 'Abd al-'Aziz Sultan, both of whom remained in Kuwait during the occupation. These interviews were conducted in September 1992 and March 1994, in Kuwait.

55. Cooperative societies, which continue to be important Kuwaiti economic institutions, also are incubators of democracy. They are based in neighborhoods, and all Kuwaitis who are at least eighteen years old are eligible to subscribe. Members receive a share of their cooperative's annual profits and may both vote and run for election to the

cooperative's board. See Neil Hicks and Ghanim al-Najjar, "The Utility of Tradition: Civil Society in Kuwait," in Augustus Richard Norton, ed., *Civil Society in the Middle East*, 199–200 (New York: E. J. Brill, 1995).

56. Hicks and al-Najjar, "The Utility of Tradition," 201.

57. Interview with 'Abd al-Wahhab al-Wazzan, October 19, 1992, in Kuwait.

58. Interview with 'Eisa bu Yabis.

59. Personal communication from Ghanim al-Najjar.

60. Ibid.

61. Interview with 'Abd al-Wahhab al-Wazzan, September 21, 1992, in Kuwait.

62. Interview with Ghanim al-Najjar, May 23, 1999, in Cambridge, Mass.

63. Interview with 'Eisa bu Yabis, October 6, 1992, in Kuwait.

64. Interview with 'Eisa bu Yabis.

65. Interview with Kuwaiti attorney Saleh al-Hashem, candidate for parliament in 1992, September 29, 1992, in Kuwait.

66. Interview with Dr. Mohammad al-Muhanna, director of animal health, Kuwait Agricultural Authority, October 2, 1992, in Kuwait.

67. Interview with Ghanim al-Najjar, May 23, 1999.

68. Personal communication.

69. Interview with 'Eisa bu Yabis.

70. This is a constant refrain in occupation "diaries" such as Jadranka Porter's *Under Siege in Kuwait: A Survivor's Story*, Don Latham's *Occupation Diary*, and Julie D. Sharples's "Diary" (unpublished manuscript, 1992).

71. Interview with Eqbal al-Rahmani, September 23, 1992, in Kuwait. Even though the numbers were exaggerated, however, rapes did occur. Following liberation, careful estimates of the number of Kuwaiti women raped by Iraqis were compiled from a wide variety of data sources. On that basis, researchers concluded that about two thousand Kuwaitis had been raped. See Haya al-Mughni and Fawzia al-Turkait, "Dealing with Trauma: Cultural Barriers to Self-Recovery—The Case of Kuwaiti Women," paper presented at the Seminar on Effective Methods for Encountering the Psychological and Social Effects of the Iraqi Aggression, sponsored by the Social Development Office of the Amiri Diwan, Kuwait, March 1994; also, Mary Ann Tétreault, "Justice for All: Wartime Rape and Women's Human Rights," *Global Governance* 3 (1997): 197–212. The inhibitions on raping Arab women, which helped to keep the number of rapes of Kuwaiti women relatively low, did not hold for non-Arab women, who were reported to have been raped in much larger numbers, absolutely and relative to their proportion among the Kuwaiti population.

72. When stories about atrocities are told by insiders, their quality is different. Artist Lidia Qattan told me several stories about executions in her neighborhood, Qadisiya, where Iraqi military officers were concentrated. Lidia's status as an insider infuses her stories with a knowledge that goes beyond the fact of the executions to the persistence and strategies of survivors. Even without being put into words, the survival of Lidia, her artist husband Khalifa, and their house filled with years' worth of paintings, mosaics, and sculptures is a story of persistence and inner strength.

73. Interviews in Kuwait, October 1992.

74. Interview in Kuwait, September 1992.

75. See Mary Ann Tétreault, "Whose Honor? Whose Liberation? Women and the Reconstruction of Politics in Kuwait," in Tétreault, ed., *Women and Revolution in Africa, Asia, and the New World*, 300–301.

76. According to insiders, most of the money was exchanged through regular channels and at prevailing rates—nothing "favorable." 'Ali al-Salim al-Sabah, acting for the ruling family, would give merchants receipts for goods taken by Iraqis and distributed through cooperatives. The merchants also received receipts for the cash they distributed among the population. "The merchants gave goods to the cooperatives and the cooperatives gave the merchants money. The merchants gave the money to the people and the people [spent] the money at the cooperatives. It was a circle." Receipts for these various transfers could be "cashed" outside Kuwait. (Interview with 'Abd al-Wahhab al-Wazzan, September 21, 1992, in Kuwait, and personal communication from Ghanim al-Najjar. The quote is from the interview.)

77. For example, Jadranka Porter, in *Under Siege in Kuwait*, tells of the heroism of 'Abd al-'Aziz Sultan, a favored subject of "businessman as occupation entrepreneur" stories.

78. Hicks and al-Najjar, "The Utility of Tradition," 200.

79. Shamlan Y. al-Essa, "The Political Consequences of the Crisis for Kuwait," 169–85.

80. Interviews in Kuwait, September-October 1992.

81. Hicks and al-Najjar, "The Utility of Tradition," 200.

82. Interview with 'Abd al-Wahhab al-Wazzan.

83. Interview with a Kuwait University professor, September 19, 1992, in Kuwait.

84. Interview in Kuwait, October 11, 1992. This man remained concealed in Kuwait with his family until December 1990.

85. Interview with Lubna Saif 'Abbas 'Abdulla, September 17, 1992, in Kuwait. Lubna, a graduate of American University in Washington, was one of nine Kuwaiti women trained at Fort Dix to participate in the military phase of the liberation.

86. Interview with 'Eisa bu Yabis.

87. Interview with Muna al-Mousa, member of the staff of KPI's public relations department and a volunteer with the Free Kuwait Campaign, March 8, 1991, in London.

88. Interview with Khaled Buhamrah, then deputy managing director of KNPC (Kuwait National Petroleum Company), a subsidiary of KPC,, September 27, 1992, at Mina' al-Ahmadi.

89. Interview with 'Abd al-Wahhab al-Wazzan.

90. Interview with Khaled Sultan, businessman and candidate for parliament, September 30, 1992, in Kuwait.

91. Tétreault, *The Kuwait Petroleum Corporation*, 141–42.

92. PBS, "Frontline: The Gulf War," January 9, 1996.

6. The Election of 1992

1. Interviews in Kuwait, September-October 1992. According to Khaldoun al-Naqib and 'Abd al-Wahhab al-Zufayri, 60 percent of the candidates for parliament in 1992 had

not run for office before. Cited in Shafeeq Ghabra, "Kuwait: Elections and Issues of Democratization in a Middle Eastern State," *Digest of Middle Eastern Studies* 2 (Winter 1993): 7.

2. Interviews with Kuwaitis and political officers of Western embassies who attended some of these meetings, September-October 1992 in Kuwait.

3. Gavrielides, "Tribal Democracy," 166–70.

4. Shafeeq Ghabra, "Democratization in a Middle Eastern State: Kuwait, 1993," *Middle East Policy* 3 (1994): 105.

5. Ghabra, "Democratization in a Middle Eastern State," 109. The article implies that these laws were rescinded. However, in a postelection interview, Hamad al-Jou'an, the first winner in District 2, al-Murqab, emphasized that the laws permitting the government to ban public meetings and censor the press were not rescinded but merely not enforced. They remained on the books throughout the campaign, and their continuing status has been a subject of contestation in the 1992 parliament—in fact, arrests under the censorship law were resumed only a week after the election. See *Arab Times*, October 13, 1992, 3, and chapter 7, this volume.

6. Interview with Dr. Mohammad al-Muhanna, one of seven Khodary campaign managers, at campaign headquarters, October 2, 1992, and a volunteer working with the computerized files. The information tracked the number of times a voter had approached the candidate (and vice versa), and whether he had asked for and/or received any assistance through 'Abbas al-Khodary's good offices.

7. Ghabra, "Democratization in a Middle Eastern State," 108.

8. This meeting was held on September 28, 1992. It is discussed further in Tétreault, "Civil Society in Kuwait," 286.

9. *Arab Times*, February 7, 1994, 1. The amendment to the citizenship law reads, "Offspring of a naturalized Kuwaiti are treated as first-class citizens if their father was a Kuwaiti at the time of their birth." The issue of the numbers of persons involved was regarded as primary in the minds of the government by Kuwaiti political scientists. Speaking at a press conference held during the 1996 campaign, Ghanim al-Najjar used the enfranchisement of the sons of naturalized Kuwaitis to illustrate his point that enfranchisement of women might be implemented gradually, in steps, in order for the government to ensure that the results would not destabilize the regime—see chapter 9. (Press conference at Kuwait University, October 5, 1996.)

10. Shafeeq Ghabra notes that this suspension occurred shortly before the parliament took a vote on a measure the amir had refused to sign the previous year. Under the constitution, the parliament has two ways to pass a law over such an amiri "pocket veto." One is to pass it immediately with a two-thirds majority vote. The other is to pass it by a simple majority a year later. See "Democratization in a Middle Eastern State," 103.

11. Ibid., 104. See also Kamal Osman Salih, "Kuwait's Parliamentary Elections, 1963–1985" (unpublished paper).

12. Gavrielides, "Tribal Democracy," 160; Mary Ann Tétreault and Haya al-Mughni, "Modernization and Its Discontents," 412–13; Ghabra, "Kuwait and the Dynamics of Socio-Economic Change," 363–66; Salih, "Kuwait's Parliamentary Elections."

13. *Badu* are Sabah supporters because of their long collaboration during the heyday of the caravan trade, and because individual ruling family members, including many amirs, maintained personal relationships with tribal leaders, often through marriage with a woman from one of the major tribes. Shi'a supported the amir during the 1938–39 parliamentary crisis, both because of Sunni prejudice and because the self-anointed Sunni electorate and parliament had excluded them from participation in the two legislative councils elected during that era. *Badu* forces were used against parliamentarians and their supporters during the 1938–39 crisis.

14. Gavrielides, "Tribal Democracy," esp. appendix B. Kamal Osman Salih is most concerned by the absolute increase in the number of tribal representatives, whom he calls "traditional political forces"—see "Kuwait's Parliamentary Elections." Shafeeq Ghabra identifies the combination of bedouin enfranchisement and electoral redistricting as the beginning of the "desertization" of Kuwaiti politics (see "Kuwait and the Dynamics of Socio-Economic Change," 366–67).

15. Kamal Osman Salih, "Kuwait's Parliamentary Elections."

16. Gavrielides, "Tribal Democracy," 166–70.

17. Following the 1992 election, parliament's Legal and Legislative Affairs committee approved a bill to ban tribal primaries. The bill was then sent to the Interior and Defense Affairs committee, which refused even to discuss it—all five of its members had been elected after first having won tribal primaries. *Arab Times*, October 7, 1996, 1.

18. The term "new men" is one of several used for members of economic classes and social groups formed as a result of modernization that are not found in traditional social formations. For examples of this usage, see Huntington, *Political Order in Changing Societies*, and Lynn Hunt, *Politics, Culture, and Class in the French Revolution*.

19. Interview with Khaled Buhamrah, then deputy managing director of the Kuwait National Petroleum Company (KNPC), a subsidiary of KPC, at his office at Mina' al-Ahmadi, September 27, 1992.

20. Interview at the Shuwaikh campus of Kuwait University, October 10, 1992.

21. The Graduates Society's debate was held on September 26. The Kuwait University debate was held on September 27.

22. Interview, March 1994, in Kuwait.

23. Interview, September 29, 1992, in Kuwait.

24. Ibid.

25. Interview with Saif 'Abbas 'Abdulla, September 19, 1992, in Kuwait. A similar point about the widespread support among Kuwaitis of aid for Iraq during the first Gulf War can be found in Rajab, *Invasion Kuwait*, 12.

26. Interview with Saif 'Abbas 'Abdulla, September 19, 1992, in Kuwait.

27. Interview with Khaled Sultan, September 30, 1992, in Kuwait.

28. Information about the political groups comes from Ghabra, "Democratization in a Middle Eastern State," 9–10; the *Arab Times*, various issues, including the candidate listing by district and affiliation published on October 6, 1992, 3; and interviews with candidates and campaign staffs.

29. Political scientist and anthropologist James C. Scott sees the creation of sur-

names as a way for states to keep closer tabs on citizens. "In almost every case . . . the invention of permanent, inherited patronyms . . . . was a state project, designed to allow officials to identify, unambiguously, the majority of its citizens." Scott, *Seeing Like a State: How Certain Schemes to Improve the Human Condition Have Failed* (New Haven: Yale University Press, 1998), 64–73 (quote from 65). While I have no doubt that this is so, the inclusion of designated surnames in Kuwaiti electoral rolls strikes me as having a broader purpose.

30. Information about the candidate came from an interview with him on October 1, 1992, and interviews with other KDF members in September and October 1992. I was unable to get Ahmad al-Rubʻi to answer questions about his decision to run as an independent, but many other Kuwaitis in and out of the KDF were more than willing to speculate about his reasons as well as to offer comments on his character and prospects.

31. Interview with Ahmad Dayin at his campaign diwaniyya, October 1, 1992.

32. I infer the diversity of Ahmad al-Rubʻi's support from the ballots cast in the election. Ballots for Ahmad al-Rubʻi, who was a very strong first-place winner (see appendix 6.1), included votes for virtually every other candidate running in District 8, religious and secular, Sunni and Shiʻi.

33. Husain al-Qallaf also maintained a separate tent for women, but the women's tent was dark and deserted every time I passed his headquarters, even during events when the main tent was full of men. That, and the upheaval that resulted when, together with my Dutch colleague, Paul Aarts, and two young Kuwaitis, a man and a woman, I went there to interview him, convinced me that women rarely if ever attended events at Husain's headquarters. The small second tent was more symbolic than functional, a point to which I shall return later in the chapter.

34. Gavrielides sees tribal primaries and diwaniyya voting as similar and often jointly employed strategies for maximizing the chances that a group can elect one of themselves. He notes that single-vote ballots were employed by the supporters of the secularists (whom he refers to as the "Liberal/Left") in 1985, districts where secularists were too few to field two candidates and expect to win. See Gavrielides, "Tribal Democracy," 167.

35. Two of the people I discussed this with said that at least one diwaniyya had preferred Ahmad Dayin but were persuaded to choose Ismaʻil al-Shati for strategic reasons—so that the anti-Qallaf vote would not be scattered.

36. Interview with Mohammad al-Jasim, October 20, 1992. Two vote tally matrices from the 1996 election are reproduced in appendix 6.2.

37. The differences between various understandings of Islam and their impact on family and personal status laws, the issue area featuring the greatest religious influence, are explored in Mahnaz Afkhami, ed., *Faith and Freedom: Women's Human Rights in the Muslim World*, and in John L. Esposito, *Women in Muslim Family Law*.

38. Interview with attorney Badria al-ʻAwadhi, October 1992, in Kuwait.

39. This debate was held on September 22 at the ʻAdeliya campus. Information on the university's qualms at continuing the debates came from the university debate organizer, ʻAbdullah al-Shayeji, then acting chair of the political science department.

40. Interview with Nasir Sarkhou, October 2, 1992. However, candidate Sarkhou did eschew shaking my hand, the mark of a very religious man who does not touch women who are not related to him.

41. Interviews, Khaled Sultan, September 30, 1992; Khaled al-'Adwa, October 18, 1992; attendance at a diwaniyya on September 29, 1992, where candidate Mohammad al-Basiri and two of his supporters spoke—but only after I, the only woman present in a gathering of more than one thousand persons, had left the diwaniyya space and took refuge behind a row of cars in the parking lot where I could listen to what was going on while the others could pretend I was not there.

42. In District 24, ICM endorsee Sa'd Mohammad al-'Ajmy, finished fifth, only thirty-six votes behind the fourth vote-getter.

43. Information on voting procedures, the irregularities that have been common in Kuwait in the past, along with the measures adopted in 1992 to keep them at a minimum, was obtained in interviews with 'Ali Murad from Kuwait's Ministry of the Interior on September 21 and October 10, 1992. 'Ali Murad heads a staff of twenty-one persons charged with administering election procedures.

44. Voting outside one's district of residence became a major issue in 1996, as I shall discuss in the last chapter.

45. Interview with 'Ali Murad. There were charges made after the election that severe irregularities had occurred in the polling in District 14, Abraq Khaittan, and District 16, al-'Umariya. These elections were rerun in February under closer scrutiny. The primary focal point of the charges was that disqualified persons had voted—specifically, police and military personnel. (Interview with Mohammad al-Jasim, attorney for the challenger in District 16, October 20, 1992; *Arab Times*, February 16, 1993, 1.)

46. Many of these issues are discussed in Walter Dean Burnham, "The Changing Shape of the American Political Universe," *American Political Science Review* 59 (March 1965): 7–28.

47. Observers I talked to at the vote-counting in District 7, Kaifan, said that many ballots cast in 1990 for the Majlis al-Watani were technically invalid because of write-ins. The government was not concerned about the number of invalid ballots but very concerned about turnout. It was supposed to have set a target of 50 percent and, had fewer voters shown up, the election would have been canceled. One reporter put it this way: "Coming at all, even to vote for Donald Duck, was enough."

48. Susan Slyomovics, *The Object of Memory: Arab and Jew Narrate the Palestinian Village*, 162.

49. Ghabra, "Kuwait: Elections and Issues," 15.

50. Tétreault, "Individualism, Secularism, and Fundamentalism"; also Lerner, *The Passing of Traditional Society*, esp. ch. 2.

51. See, for example, Ayubi, *Over-stating the Arab State*, ch. 5. Ayubi opts for the term "intermediate classes" to describe the heterogeneity of this segment and its economic location between social groups of premodern origin such as merchants and landlords on the one hand, and *badu* and peasants on the other.

52. Ayubi, *Over-stating the Arab State*, 170–82.

53. For example, ibid.; also Longva, *Walls Built on Sand.*

54. Interview with Khaldoun al-Naqeeb, October 14, 1992. See also F. Gregory Gause III, *Oil Monarchies: Domestic and Security Challenges in the Arab Gulf States,* 93–94.

55. See Tétreault, *The Kuwait Petroleum Corporation,* 140–41. Shortly before the 1992 parliamentary elections, a number of other ruling family–allied merchants had run against the traditionals for places on the Chamber of Commerce's governing board. Faisal al-Marzouk was the only challenger who won a seat in the chamber election—see Gause, *Oil Monarchies,* 93–94.

7. Back to the Future: The Return of Normal Politics

1. I am indebted to Jorgen Rasmusen for his comments on earlier drafts of this chapter, and his suggestions with regard to selecting criteria for evaluating governing institutions.

2. Abdul-Reda al-Assiri and Kamal al-Monoufi, "Kuwait's Political Elite: The Cabinet," 49–50.

3. Winners do not sit at home and read congratulatory telegrams. They hold court every night in their diwaniyyas. Hundreds of well-wishers stand in line for hours to embrace them, reminisce about everything from the childhood of their grandparents to the heat of the just-finished campaign, and confide their needs and expectations. No Kuwaiti politician can afford to sidestep these ceremonies and few would even want to.

4. *Arab Times,* October 11, 1992, 1; October 12, 1992, 1; October 13, 1992, 1 (the issue with a photo of the women); interview with a demonstration participant.

5. *Arab Times,* October 13, 1992, 1.

6. The outcry against the inner core of the preinvasion cabinet had been strong enough to force a reshuffling in April 1991 that saw Shaikh Sabah al-Ahmad, a brother of the amir, dumped in favor of a member of the al-Salim branch of the ruling family to which the crown prince belongs. The reinstatement of Shaikh Sabah al-Ahmad is more likely to have come at the behest of the amir and his branch of the family than from the crown prince. See Economist Intelligence Unit (EIU), "Kuwait Country Report no. 2, 1991" (London: EIU, 1991), 10–11.

7. The difficulty of choosing a member of the ruling family in such a situation can be inferred from the history of conflicts over selecting the heir apparent. It should be noted that article 4 of Kuwait's constitution allots a period of one year for this process, unlike the two weeks between the election and the convening of the parliament allotted by article 87. Ruling family members with political ambitions see the parliament as an avenue for achieving them. This is reflected in their attempts to run for seats—attempts that were squelched by the amir in 1992 and 1996 (see chapter 9).

8. *Arab Times,* October 12, 1992, 1.

9. Interview with Hamad al-Jou'an, October 21, 1992, in Kuwait.

10. *Arab Times,* October 14, 1992, 1.

11. Interview with Hamad al-Jou'an, October 21, 1992.

12. Because the cabinet—including the parliamentary members—votes as a bloc on important issues. See discussion later in chapter.

13. Mubarak's flagging campaign for the speakership was revealed in the results of an "unorthodox private ballot" taken among parliamentarians at the diwaniyya of Nasir al-Sana', an independent and the top winner in District 9. The straw poll gave a large majority to Ahmad al-Sa'doun. *Arab Times*, October 18, 1992, 1.

14. Interviews with Hasan 'Ali al-Ebraheem and others, spring 1990.

15. I discuss some of these difficulties in *The Kuwait Petroleum Corporation*. 'Ali al-Baghli's problems were aggravated by his lack of experience—unlike Ahmad al-Rub'i, he was a new parliamentarian as well as a new minister. Cherished for his integrity by his patrons and supporters in the Shi'i business community, 'Ali's initial lack of political skills interfered with his ability to accomplish what they—and he—hoped he could achieve as oil minister. He performed well in his second showcase position, as head of the parliament's human rights group (see chapter 8, this volume). During the 1996 campaign, the managing director of one of KPC's Kuwait-based affiliates told me that he thought that 'Ali al-Baghli had begun badly but had become a good oil minister as well.

16. Nathan Brown, *The Rule of Law in the Arab World: Courts in Egypt and the Gulf*, 158–59.

17. *Arab Times*, October 13, 1992, 3.

18. See, for example, the priorities listed by Jasim al-Saqr in an interview published in the *Arab Times*, September 19, 1992, 1, 2.

19. Interview with Jasim al-Saqr, May 1990, in Kuwait.

20. *Arab Times*, October 15–16, 1992, 1.

21. EIU, "Kuwait Country Report no. 4, 1992," 9.

22. Hamad al-Jou'an, interview, October 21, 1992. Secularists outside the parliament analyzed the situation similarly in interviews also conducted in late October.

23. EIU, "Kuwait Country Report no. 4, 1992," 10.

24. Ibid.; also interview with Hamad al-Jou'an, October 21, 1992.

25. Longva, *Walls Built on Sand*, 55 (table 3.1).

26. This includes requiring a worker to stay with his employer for a certain length of time and giving the employer custody of the employee's passport. See ibid.

27. For the growing importance of investment income over oil income, see Thomas Stauffer, "Oil Revenues: Income or Capital?" *Middle East Economic Survey* (hereafter, *MEES*) 27 (November 7, 1983): D1–D4.

28. The World Bank, "Kuwait: A Privatization Strategy," four parts, October 29, 1993.

29. Information on KIA privatization comes from "The Kuwait Investment Authority's Privatisation Sales: An Update," *Economic and Financial Quarterly* (a publication of the National Bank of Kuwait) 2 (1996): 34–39; and on an interview with KIA managing director 'Ali al-Badr, October 8, 1996, in Kuwait.

30. Interviews with bank managers in Kuwait, spring 1990.

31. The early histories of the KPC domestic subsidiaries are told in Tétreault, *The Kuwait Petroleum Corporation*, ch. 5.

32. "KIA Privatization: An Update," 35. This page includes a table reporting dates and amounts of sales through September 1994.

33. Ibid., 36.

34. Interview with KIA managing director 'Ali al-Badr, October 8, 1996, in Kuwait.

35. See, for examples, Goldberg, "Smashing Idols and the State," 195–236; Roy, *The Failure of Political Islam*; and Gabriel Warburg, "Mahdism and Islamism in Sudan," *International Journal of Middle East Studies* 27 (May 1995): 219–36.

36. For example, Aziz al-Azmeh, "Populism Contra Democracy," 112–29.

37. Mernissi, *Islam and Democracy*.

38. See, for example, the essays in John Stratton Hawley, ed., *Fundamentalism and Gender*, and in Martin E. Marty and R. Scott Appleby, eds., *Fundamentalisms and Society: Reclaiming the Sciences, the Family, and Education*, especially those in part 2, "Family and Interpersonal Relationships."

39. Leila Ahmed, *Women and Gender in Islam*, ch. 8; Deniz Kandiyoti, "Introduction," in Kandiyoti, ed., *Women, Islam, and the State*, 1–9 (Basingstoke: Macmillan, 1991).

40. Goldberg, "Smashing Idols and the State"; Roy, *The Failure of Political Islam*, 58–59.

41. Goldberg, "Smashing Idols and the State," 219; Tétreault, "Spheres of Liberty," 282–83.

42. Roy, *The Failure of Political Islam*, 59.

43. On this issue, see Haya al-Mughni, *Women in Kuwait*, and "Women's Movements and the Autonomy of Civil Society in Kuwait"; Tétreault, "Civil Society in Kuwait," 275–91, and "Whose Honor? Whose Liberation?" 297–315. See also four jointly authored essays: Mary Ann Tétreault and Haya al-Mughni, "Modernization and Its Discontents," 403–17; "Al-Mar'at wal Demuqratiyya fil Kuwait," *Abwab* (January 7, 1996): 9–23; "Gender, Citizenship, and Nationalism in Kuwait," 64–80; and "Citizenship, Gender, and the Politics of Quasi-states," in Suad Joseph, ed., *Gender and Citizenship in the Middle East*.

44. Al-Mughni, *Women in Kuwait*; also al-Mughni and Tétreault, "Citizenship, Gender, and the Politics of Quasi-States."

45. These patterns in child-rearing are similar throughout much of the Middle East. For another example, see Susan Schaefer Davis, "Growing Up in Morocco," in Donna Lee Bowen and Evelyn A. Early, eds., *Everyday Life in the Muslim Middle East*, 23–33.

46. Tétreault, "Kuwait's Democratic Reform Movement," 17–18. These patterns also are class-based. Upper-class families are far more likely than middle-class families to restrict their male children, and are more likely to send them abroad for university training. At the same time, fewer women than men study abroad regardless of social class. One result is that the population of Kuwait University has been well over 50 percent female for some years, and includes large numbers of young women who are highly able along with average and poor performers. The top performers among young Kuwaiti men of every social class tend to study abroad, leaving the less able in their age cohorts to compete against a pool of women whose overall intellectual ability and social skills are better than theirs.

47. The speaker is a manager at the Kuwait Oil Company who was interviewed in April 1990. This rationale came up repeatedly in interviews with students, professors, and parents, both before the invasion and after liberation.

48. It is important here to remember that most parliamentary Islamists are independents or tribally endorsed rather than members of organized Islamist political blocs.

49. EIU, "Kuwait Country Report no. 1, 1992," 7.

50. Ayubi, *Over-stating the Arab State*, 142.

51. Theoretically, women also are supposed to refrain from veiling when driving, another safety-oriented prohibition, but veiled women continue to drive. Police are loathe to ticket a veiled woman, and Islamist organizations offer to pay fines, making ticketing a losing proposition.

52. See *Arab Times*, various issues, particularly January 5, 1993, 3, and February 6, 1993, 3.

53. A compromise was reached with university officials, who agreed that girls could veil "in case of utmost necessity," sidestepping the demand for formal legislation. *Arab Times*, March 2, 1994, 2.

54. *Arab Times*, December 8–9, 1994, 1.

55. Ibid.

56. *Arab Times*, December 2, 1995, 1, 8, and December 12, 1995, 6.

57. Their most recent success as of this writing occurred in August 1998. *MEES* 41.31 (August 3, 1998), from the *MEES* Archive.

58. *Arab Times*, March 10–11, 1994, 1.

59. See various issues of the *Arab Times*, particularly March 1, 1994, 1, 8, and March 2, 1994, 1–2, which summarize these events. Quotes in the text are from the March 1 issue.

60. *Kuwait Times*, January 31, 1994, 1; *Arab Times*, March 7, 1994, 1, 6.

61. At the first session of the trial, Hasan pled his innocence and asked to be released on bail. His attorneys also requested the return of the money he had paid a year earlier—with accrued interest—on the grounds that they were family resources and not embezzled funds.

62. Information about this case came from various issues of the *Arab Times*; proceedings of the March 22, 1994, session of the trial held in Kuwait City; and interviews with defendant Hasan Qabazard on March 22, 1994, and Salman al-Du'aij al-Sabah, attorney for 'Ali al-Khalifa, March 24, 1994.

63. *Arab Times*, January 12, 1994, 1, and January 19, 1994, 1.

64. This would require approval by the government and therefore was unlikely to happen. The arguments on both sides of this issue are analyzed in Brown, *The Rule of Law in the Arab World*, 170–79.

65. Provisions of this law are reviewed in *Arab Times*, August 8, 1995, 1, 6. It includes significant protections for accused ministers.

66. *Arab Times*, October 10, 1995, 1, 6, and October 18, 1995, 1, 8.

67. *Arab Times*, April 23, 1997, 8.

68. *Issues* 4.5 (June 1995): 2; also, interviews in Kuwait, March 1994.

69. In the debate on the amir's action, members of parliament identified the KOTC trial as the root cause of the amir's decision to reopen the issue of article 71. See *Arab Times*, April 12, 1995, 1.

70. *Arab Times*, March 21, 1995, 8.

71. EIU, "Kuwait Country Report no. 2, 1995," 6.

72. Ibid., 8.

73. *Arab Times*, March 11, 1995, 1, 8.

74. EIU, "Kuwait Country Report no. 2, 1995," 7. A foreign diplomat told me how he had sat listening while the prime minister called various members on the telephone, promising whatever it would take to get them to refrain from voting to censure.

75. *Arab Times*, April 17, 1995, 1.

76. *Arab Times*, April 4, 1995, 1, and April 17, 1995, 1.

77. In the 1993 cabinet reshuffle, 'Ali al-Baghli (I) and 'Abdullah al-Hajri (T) had been removed.

78. *Arab Times*, April 17, 1995, 8. The fourth, 'Abd al-Mohsin al-Mud'ej, had run as an independent and was not associated with the Forty-five.

79. Ibid., 8.

80. EIU, "Kuwait Country Report no. 2, 1995," 8–9.

81. *Arab Times*, October 10, 1995, 1, 6.

82. *Arab Times*, October 18, 1995, 8.

83. Quoted in *Arab Times*, November 25, 1995, 8.

84. *MEES* 39.40 (July 1, 1996).

85. But not beyond the jurisdictions of other nations' courts. In late February 1998, a case for recovery of the embezzled funds, titled *KOTC and Another v. Al-Badr and Others* began seventy-four days of litigation in a London court in an attempt to recover embezzled funds for KOTC and the state of Kuwait. See chapter 8 for a discussion of this trial and its results.

86. *Arab Times*, December 24, 1996, 1.

87. Ibid.; also, *Arab Times*, April 29, 1997, 1, 8. The decision made reference to the fact that the new law bore the amir's signature.

88. The original bill, which had passed on the floor with a smaller majority, required the segregation of private schools (government schools are already segregated) as well as of the university and postsecondary technical schools. Cabinet approval is necessary for a bill to be sent to the amir for his signature. The cabinet did approve gender segregation for the university and the technical schools, but removed the provision requiring segregation in private schools before sending the measure back to the assembly for a final vote.

89. Gender segregation interested foreign journalists in part because it was one of the easiest issues to explain to readers and viewers unfamiliar with the Kuwaiti political scene. Also, as Leila Ahmed and Judy Mabro note, Westerners have been obsessed by gender relations in the Middle East for hundreds of years and are avid consumers of stories feeding their orientalist preconceptions. See Ahmed, *Women and Gender in Islam*, esp. ch. 8, and Judy Mabro, *Veiled Half-Truths: Western Travellers' Perceptions of Middle Eastern Women*.

90. For example, Roger Owen, "Socio-economic Change and Political Mobilization: The Case of Egypt," in Salamé, ed., *Democracy Without Democrats?*, 184.

8. Getting By with a Little Help from Our Friends

1. Among the most highly nuanced analyses of the political, economic, social, and spiritual difficulties of late development is Eric R. Wolf's excellent *Europe and the People Without History*. Alexander Gerschenkron is most often associated with the view that there can be economic advantages to late development—see *Economic Backwardness in Historical Perspective*. My favorite analyst of the opportunities available to the oil producers among late-developing countries is Edith Penrose, *The Large International Firm in Developing Countries: The International Petroleum Industry*.

2. See, for example, Gilbert Rist, *The History of Development from Western Origins to Global Faith*.

3. Raymond D. Duvall and John R. Freeman, "The State and Dependent Capitalism," *International Studies Quarterly* 25 (1981): 99–118; Timothy W. Luke, "Dependent Development and the Arab OPEC States," *Journal of Politics* 45.4 (1983): 979–1003, and "Dependent Development and the OPEC States: State Formation in Saudi Arabia and Iran Under the International Energy Regime," *Studies in Comparative International Development* 20 (1985): 31–54. A more recent study of dependent development comparing dependency on oil revenues to dependency on labor exports in the same region is Chaudhry's *The Price of Wealth*.

4. For examples, see Walter J. Levy, "The Years That the Locust Hath Eaten: Oil Policy and OPEC Development Prospects," *Foreign Affairs* 57 (Winter 1978–79): 999–1015; Jahangir Amuzegar, "Oil Wealth: A Very Mixed Blessing," *Foreign Affairs* 60 (Spring 1982): 814–35; Hunter, "The Gulf Economic Crisis," 593–613; Paul W. H. Aarts, Gep Eisenloeffel, and A. J. Termeulen, "Oil, Money, and Participation: Kuwait's *Sonderweg* as a Rentier State," *Orient* 32 (June 1991): 205–16.

5. For example, see Basil Davidson, *The Black Man's Burden: Africa and the Curse of the Nation-State*.

6. Here the literature on the American war in Vietnam is a particularly rich source of information and analysis—see, for example, Gabriel Kolko, *Anatomy of a War: Vietnam, the United States, and the Modern Historical Experience*, and Truong Nhu Tang (with David Chanoff and Doan Van Toai), *A Viet Cong Memoir: An Inside Account of the Vietnam War and Its Aftermath*.

7. For example, Mark J. Gasiorowski, *U. S. Foreign Policy and the Shah: Building a Client State in Iran*.

8. Tilly, "War Making and State Making as Organized Crime," 186.

9. Giddens, *A Contemporary Critique of Historical Materialism* 2:11.

10. See Roger Keil, "Globalization Makes States: Perspectives of Local Governance in the Age of the World City," *Review of International Political Economy* 5 (Winter 1998): 616–46.

11. This literature is analyzed in Tamar Hermann, "From Unidimensionality to Mul-

tidimensionality: Some Observations on the Dynamics of Social Movements," *Research in Social Movements, Conflicts, and Change* 15 (1993): 181–202.

12. See the chapters by Jirina Šiklová, "Women and the Charta 77 Movement in Czechoslovakia"; Cheryl Logan Sparks, "How Grandmother Won the War: Strategic and Organizational Lessons of the Struggle for Suffrage"; and Haya al-Mughni, "Women's Movements and the Autonomy of Civil Society in Kuwait"—all in Teske and Tétreault, eds., *Feminist Approaches to Social Movements, Community, and Power*, vol. 1. The heterogeneity of new social movements is well shown in such studies of peace and human rights movements as David S. Meyer, *A Winter of Discontent: The Nuclear Freeze and American Politics*, and Caroline Blackwood, *On the Perimeter* (New York: Penguin, 1985).

13. This quality is emphasized by Šiklová with regard to the protection offered by international human rights organizations to activists. See "Women and the Charta 77 Movement."

14. Robin L. Teske, personal communication. Teske is an attorney who teaches international law at James Madison University in Harrisonburg, Virginia.

15. Every suspension of the parliament (1976, 1985, 1999) occurred after the National Assembly had initiated investigations into government finances.

16. United Press International (UPI), December 27, 1994 (from the archives of Gulf2000).

17. Reuters, September 1, 1995 (from the archives of Gulf2000).

18. *Arab Times*, February 2, 1997, 6.

19. See, for example, the analysis of the British Petroleum Company stock purchase in "KIO, BP and the $5bn Shell Game," *Financial Times*, September 24, 1993, 9; also Paul W. H. Aarts, Gep Eisenloeffel, and A. J. Termeulen, "The KPC Connection of 'Kuwait Inc.' " (Amsterdam: CEPS, University of Amsterdam, 1989); and Middle East Consultants, "The Background to Recent Changes in the KIO," January 18, 1990 (typescript). Many Kuwaitis I have interviewed—most notably, 'Abdullah Nibari and Jasim al-Sa'doun—make similar charges.

20. In a May 4, 1998, report in *al-Watan* (newspaper), government reserves were given as KD 12,009 million (U.S.$39.8 billion) in the RFFG and KD 5,780 million (U.S.$18.9 billion) in the General Reserve Fund. This was the first time that figures on Kuwaiti government reserves had been released to the public. In the *Middle East Economic Survey* (hereafter, *MEES*) report of the release (*MEES* Archives for 41.19 [May 11, 1998]), it was noted that most estimates of Kuwaiti reserves are lower than the nearly $60 billion revealed by *al-Watan*. In my many interviews with bankers and others in Kuwait since 1990, all report that the only liquid reserves held by the state are in the RFFG. If this is so, the report and the estimate, though nominally divergent, are functionally nearly identical.

21. Tétreault, "Kuwait: The Morning After," 9.

22. *Arab Times*, February 1, 1997, 1, 8.

23. *Arab Times*, January 2–3, 1997, 1, 8, and January 22, 1997, 1, 6.

24. *Arab Times*, March 10, 1997, 1, and March 11, 1997, 1. The eleven board members as reported in the *Arab Times* are Imad al-Saif, Ahmad Lari, Ahmad al-Serraf, Kawthar

Jawwan, Imran Mohammad, Khalifa al-Khorafy, 'Ali al-Baghli, 'Abdullah al-Roumi, Fatima Abdali, 'Abdullah al-Dughayshim, and Mohsen al-Mutairy. Ghanim al-Najjar, who attended that meeting, reports that the group applied for a license as a public benefit society, but that the license was denied (personal communication).

25. *Arab Times*, April 28, 1997, 1.

26. The speakership of the 1996 parliament was decided by a one-vote margin due to a single abstention. The loser of what otherwise would have been a tied race, Jasim al-Khorafy, asked for a ruling on the grounds that Ahmad al-Sa'doun did not receive an absolute majority of the entire body. The Constitutional Court ruled that Ahmad al-Sa'doun's election was valid.

27. *Arab Times*, May 4, 1997, 1.

28. An independent investigation later determined that the charges had been false, and the four prosecutors were exonerated. *Arab Times*, June 21, 1997, 1, and June 24, 1997, 1.

29. *Arab Times*, June 7, 1997, 8.

30. "Attempted Murder Convictions Upheld for 4 Men Who Shot at Deputy," *Deutsche Presse-Agentur*, March 23, 1999, from the Gulf2000 Archives.

31. *Arab Times*, June 18, 1997, 1. The assassin also was connected to Shaikh 'Ali Khalifa, and it was reported in the press that he had taken an envelope to 'Ali Khalifa at *al-Watan* immediately after the assassination attempt. When questioned, 'Ali Khalifa was reported to have said that the envelope had contained stock certificates. (Personal communication from Ghanim al-Najjar.)

32. The day after the assassination attempt against 'Abdullah Nibari, Mohammad Jasim al-Saqr, editor of *al-Qabas*, the newspaper owned by merchant traditionals, reported receiving a telephone death threat saying that he would be the next target.

33. *Mideast Mirror*, June 10, 1997, 11.

34. Government action also dissipated the momentum favoring populist critics. The suspects were caught and arrested within forty-eight hours of the crime.

35. Quoted in *Arab Times*, June 29, 1997, 1.

36. *Arab Times*, July 2, 1997, 1.

37. It should be noted that Ahmad al-Mulaifi, though not a member of an Islamist political group, often supported Islamist positions on issues.

38. *Arab Times*, July 16, 1997, 1, 8.

39. "Kuwaiti Government Issues Transparency Law on Public Sector Contracts," *MEES* 39.51 (September 16, 1996), from the *MEES* Archives.

40. Details on the case come from the draft judgment handed down on November 16, 1998, in the High Court of Justice, Queen's Bench Division, Commercial Court, by the Honorable Mr. Justice Moore-Bick between Kuwait Oil Tanker Company S. A. K. and Sitka Shipping Incorporated, Plaintiffs; Abdul Fattah Sulaiman Khaled Al Bader, Hassan Ali Hassan Qabazard, and Timothy St. John Stafford, Defendants; and H. Clarkson & Company Limited, Hugh O'Neill McCoy, Kuwait Petroleum Corporation, and Sheikh Ali Khalifa Al Sabah, Third Parties.

41. Brown, *The Rule of Law in the Arab World*, 158–59.

42. *Arab Times*, November 23, 1998, 1.

43. *Arab Times*, December 3–4, 1998, 4. The article notes that the court "froze world-wide assets held by the trio up to [$130 million, the] value [of the judgment]."

44. *Arab Times*, December 3, 1998, 2, and December 7, 1988, 3.

45. Both quotes in this paragraph are taken from a personal communication from Ghanim al-Najjar.

46. The list of committee members, including those who lost bids for committee slots, can be found in *Arab Times*, October 28, 1998, 4. Ahmad Baqr's health insurance proposal is outlined in ibid., June 30, 1998, 1.

47. See, for example, *Arab Times*, November 1, 1998, 1.

48. *Arab Times*, November 23, 1998, 1.

49. *Upstream* and *downstream* are terms that envision the oil industry as a continuous process with production as its pivot. "Upstream" includes production, along with exploration and development—installation of production capacity. "Downstream" from production are transportation, processing, and marketing. A vertically integrated firm owns interests in all phases of the industry. A multinational firm's holdings are located in more than one country.

50. Tétreault, *The Kuwait Petroleum Corporation*, 90.

51. Ragaei El Mallakh and Jacob K. Atta, *The Absorptive Capacity of Kuwait: Domestic and International Prospects*, 14, 20–22. The role of parliament in this policy is emphasized in J. E. Peterson, *The Arab Gulf States: Steps Toward Political Participation* (New York: Praeger, 1988), 40.

52. Tétreault, *The Kuwait Petroleum Corporation*, 90. 'Abdulla Nibari, then a member of parliament, was the leader of the pro-nationalization forces.

53. Tétreault, *The Kuwait Petroleum Corporation*, and "Political Consequences of Restructuring Economic Regimes."

54. World Bank, "Kuwait: A Privatization Strategy," Part 2 (Washington, D.C.: World Bank, October 1993), 31–38. The World Bank did not recommend strategies for upstream privatization, although it offered suggestions for improving efficiency at KOC, KPC's production subsidiary. The report concentrated on downstream privatization, reflecting the Bank's disapproval of Kuwait's multinational vertical integration strategy.

55. *Arab Times*, August 25, 1997, 4.

56. *MEES* 42.16, April 19, 1999, A1–A3; D1–D4.

57. Ibid., A2.

58. Ibid.

59. *MEES* 42.4, January 25, 1999, from the MEES Archives.

60. Ibid.

61. Ibid.

62. Ashraf Fouad, "Kuwait Goverment Backs Minister Before House Grilling," May 2, 1999, Gulf2000 Archives; "Kuwait MPs Set to Seek Minister's Resignation," Reuters, May 4, 1999, Gulf2000 Archives.

63. Ashraf Fouad, "Kuwait Election Could Bring Back Key Government Critics," Reuters, May 5, 1999, Gulf2000 Archives.

64. I have not focused on the 1976 dissolution in this volume. Discussions of the fi-

nancial and oil policy conflicts of that era, along with the regime's discomfort at parliamentary criticisms of ruling family business interests and the family's objection to the public airing of these issues, can be found in Crystal, *Oil and Politics in the Gulf*, 91–92, and Peterson, *The Arab Gulf States*, 39–41.

65. *MEES* 42.19, May 10, 1999, A3, B1; also "Kuwaiti MPs Accuse Cabinet of Orchestrating New Polls to Save Minister," AFP, May 5, 1999, Gulf2000 Archive. The sale of KIC shares had been annulled two months earlier on the grounds that the initial public offering (IPO) price was too low. Allegations that IPO prices were unnecessarily discounted were made in parliament regarding previous KIA privatizations, and underlay criticisms on this issue from the speaker that were noted in the text of this chapter. Setting IPO prices at very low levels is a common technique for directing quick capital gains to insiders—see John Kenneth Galbraith, *The Great Crash, 1929* (Boston: Houghton Mifflin, 1954); also Leon Levy and Jeff Madrick, "Hedge Fund Mysteries," *New York Review of Books* 45.20 (December 17, 1998): 73–77.

66. *MEES* 42.19, May 10, 1999, A2.

67. Ashraf Fouad, "Kuwait Politicians Mull Stance for July Elections," Reuters, May 6, 1999, Gulf2000 Archives.

68. *MEES*, May 31, 1999, B1.

69. Crystal, *Oil and Politics in the Gulf*, 90.

70. Ibid., 75–79, 89–92.

71. See the comments by political scientists Shafeeq Ghabra and Ghanim al-Najjar on Gulf2000.

72. See, for example, comments by political scientist 'Abdullah Alshayeji on Gulf2000; and an interview with Shamlan al-'Eisa reported in "Most Kuwaiti MPs to Retain Seats, Crisis to Continue, Analysts Say," AFP, May 6, 1999, Gulf2000 Archives.

73. Levy, "The Years That the Locust Hath Eaten," 287–305.

74. See, for example, Stauffer, "Oil Revenues: Income or Capital?"

75. For example, see Gould, *Rethinking Democracy*, and Shue, *Basic Rights*.

76. See, for examples, Raymond Bonner, "A Woman's Place," *The New Yorker*, 16 November 1992; "Alarming Death Sentences in Kuwait Spark World-wide Repercussions," *Arabia Monitor* 2.7 (July 1993): 1. I also discussed these issues in a number of interviews in 1992 and 1996 with Kuwaiti human rights activists, among them Shamlan al-'Eisa, Kholoud al-Feeli, Ghanim al-Najjar, and Jasim al-Qatami.

77. Ghanim al-Najjar, personal communication.

78. Ibid.

79. Neil Hicks and Ghanim al-Najjar, "The Utility of Tradition," 205.

80. "Kuwait Closes All Human Rights Organizations," *Middle East Watch* 5.6 (September 1993), 1–2.

81. Ibid.

82. A similar symbiosis between human rights groups and the parliament characterizes the link between Kuwaiti NGOs dealing with prisoner-of-war issues and their parliamentary counterpart, the Committee of the Detained and Welfare for Martyr's Families. See Hicks and al-Najjar, "The Utility of Tradition," 205.

83. Kuwait University political scientist Shamlan al-'Eisa notes that the effectiveness of the human rights organization lies in its ability to work discreetly, through informal networks, and thereby to capitalize on the desire of the government to improve Kuwait's reputation on human rights without embarrassing the country or the regime.

84. *Arab Times*, April 27, 1997, 2.

85. All the quotes in this paragraph are taken from the *Arab Times*, December 31, 1995, 1.

86. Ann Elizabeth Mayer, "Rhetorical Strategies and Official Policies on Women's Rights: The Merits and Drawbacks of the New World Hypocrisy," in Mahnaz Afkhami, ed., *Faith and Freedom: Women's Human Rights in the Muslim World*, 115. The Kuwaiti reservations were noteworthy among reservations made by other Muslim states for their political rather than religious rationales.

87. *Arab Times*, December 31, 1995, 1; also, interviews with Shamlan al-'Eisa, fall 1996.

88. Quoted in *Arab Times*, January 25, 1998, 3.

89. U.S. Department of State, "Kuwait Report on Human Rights Practices for 1997," report released by the Bureau of Democracy, Human Rights, and Labor, January 30, 1998 (from Gulf2000). The report included the phrase, "women do not have the right to vote or seek election to the National Assembly," a situation the government indicated it wished to see altered with the amir's May 1999 decree conferring full political rights on female Kuwaiti citizens.

90. Reuters, March 16 and March 23, 1998 (from Gulf2000).

91. *Mideast Mirror*, May 27, 1998, 16–17, and June 10, 1998, 15–20.

92. For example, Mubarak al-Duwailah led the National Assembly in referring an attempt, in his words, to "buy scrap" from the United States to supply the Kuwaiti armed forces (regarding a proposal to buy howitzers and military vehicles) to the Protection Public Funds Committee. See *Arab Times*, June 3, 1998, 1, 4.

93. *Mideast Mirror*, June 10, 1998, 19.

94. Quoted in *Mideast Mirror*, May 27, 1998, 17 (preceding quote also taken from this source).

95. *Arab Times*, June 2, 1998, 1, 4.

96. Ibid.; also, *Mideast Mirror*, June 15, 1998, 18.

97. *Arab Times*, June 3, 1998, 1.

98. *Arab Times*, June 8, 1998, 1, 4.

99. On June 13 he praised the impending dissolution as "the right step" for bringing Kuwait "back to balance." *Arab Times*, June 13, 1998, 1.

100. *Arab Times*, June 10, 1998, 1, 4.

101. *Mideast Mirror*, June 16, 1998, 16–17.

102. See, for example, *Arab Times*, June 8, 1998, 1, 4.

103. *Arab Times*, June 17, 1998, 1. Husain told a press conference that he had been forced to choose between two unattractive options, "either to kill one of the most important tools in the National Assembly or to kill the grilling itself. I choose the latter because I don't want to establish a bad precedent that the government may use in the future."

104. *Mideast Mirror*, June 16, 1998, 14–15 (quotes from 15).

105. *Mideast Mirror*, June 18, 1998, 15.

106. Mary Ann Tétreault, "Out of Body Experiences: Migrating Firms and Altered States," *Review of International Political Economy* 6.1 (Spring 1999): 55–78.

107. Ghabra, "Kuwait and the Dynamics of Socio-economic Change," 358–72.

9. Stories of Democracy

1. Interviews on October 23, 1992.

2. See, for example, Macpherson, *The Political Theory of Possessive Individualism*, and Jeffrey C. Isaac, "Oases in the Desert: Hannah Arendt on Democratic Politics," *American Political Science Review* 88 (1994): 156–68.

3. Among the recent calls to "abandon Western-style democracy" is one by a new Kuwaiti Islamist organization calling itself the Shura Advocates Group. See *Arab Times*, May 15–16, 1997, 5.

4. Haya al-Mughni, "Women's Movements and the Autonomy of Civil Society in Kuwait," in Robin L. Teske and Mary Ann Tétreault, eds., *Feminist Approaches to Social Movements, Community, and Power*.

5. Interview with Khaled Buhamrah, October 3, 1996, in Kuwait.

6. According to the announcement made at the rally held in conjunction with the strike, 570 Kuwaiti women signed pledges to stay home from work on the strike day.

7. *Mideast Mirror*, June 4, 1997, 12–13.

8. *Arab Times*, April 3–4, 1997, 1.

9. Shamlan al-'Eisa, quoted in *Mideast Mirror*, May 8, 1997, 13–14.

10. The National Democratic Rally included six women among its seventy-two founding members. They are Adela al-Sayer, Shaikha al-Nusif, Ma'suma al-Mubarak, Kawshar al-Jou'an, Nabila al-Mulla, and Moudhi al-Hmoud. All six of these women are members of the Women's Cultural and Social Society, Kuwait's oldest continuing feminist organization.

11. *Mideast Mirror*, June 4, 1997, 15.

12. *Mideast Mirror*, June 6, 1997, 14.

13. *Mideast Mirror*, June 4, 1997, 15.

14. Gulf2000, "Kuwait's FM Hands in Resignation," May 18, 1998.

15. *Arab Times*, January 30–31, 1997, 3.

16. Tétreault, *The Kuwait Petroleum Corporation*, 54.

17. *Mideast Mirror*, June 17, 1998, 15. This source reports that all the Kuwaiti newspapers declined to publish Shaikh Nasir's statement.

18. Giddens, *Modernity and Self-Identity*; see also Peter Gay, *The Bourgeois Experience: Victoria to Freud*, vol. 1, *Education of the Senses*. For a negative interpretation of these phenomena and their influence on public life, see Eli Zaretsky, *Capitalism, the Family, and Personal Life*.

19. Habermas, *Structural Transformation of the Public Sphere*.

20. Not only Habermas in ibid., but others, most notably Benedict Anderson, iden-

tify commercial publishing as a powerful engine spreading modern ideas and behaviors rapidly through society. See Anderson, *Imagined Communities*.

21. *Mideast Mirror*, June 6, 1997, 14.

22. Quoted in ibid.

23. *Mideast Mirror*, June 17, 1998, 15.

24. Interview with Sa'oud al-'Enezi, October 9, 1996, in Kuwait City.

25. Because the law specified that the *sons* of naturalized Kuwaitis would be given the right to vote and run for office, expectations were that the newly enfranchised would be relatively young and well educated. Even so, the concentration of these new voters in the Jahra' area also promised that some would be influenced by the leaders of tribes who saw themselves as having been denied fair representation—a fair share of services and other benefits—for more than thirty years. *Arab Times*, January 25, 1994, 1, 6.

26. Interview with Fadel al-'Abbas al-Khodary, campaign worker for and son of 'Abbas al-Khodary, October 4, 1996, in Rumaithiya. The "bad paper" he refers to is the blank sheet that is the first "ballot" cast in the ballot-switching scam described in chapter 6. If ten persons (cars) are buying votes, there will be ten blank ballots.

27. Ibid.

28. Ghanim al-Najjar, October 5, 1996, at Kuwait University.

29. In March 1998 the parliament showed its intransigence in this regard once again when a bill to allow women to vote and run for office was struck down—unanimously—in committee. "Kuwaiti Women Demand Right to Vote," *Khaleej Times*, March 8, 1998, Gulf2000 Archive.

30. An earlier example was the naturalization and enfranchisement of large numbers of *badu*, and the redistricting of electoral constituencies that preceded the 1981 elections.

31. Giddens, *The Consequences of Modernity*, 50.

32. Ibid., 33–34.

33. Jill Crystal notes that a corruptly organized and badly run system of public financing forced the amir 'Abdullah al-Salim to go to the merchants for money in the mid-1950s. The merchants lent him the money but demanded that he in turn "guarantee their wealth and see that they received a sizable portion of the new oil revenues." The social contract they arrived at left as much of the private sector to Kuwaitis as the merchants wanted, and required the Sabah to stay out of Kuwaiti business, or at least engage in business locally with great discretion. See Crystal, *Oil and Politics in the Gulf*, 73–78 (quote on 75).

34. Most Kuwaitis I have talked to over the years believe that the rulers have interfered directly in elections since 1967, though not all agree with respect to the details of the alleged interference.

35. See, for example, statements by parliamentarian Talal al-Ayyar and Professor Shafeeq Ghabra in *Arab Times*, January 25, 1994, 1, 6.

36. A committee statement quoted in *Arab Times*, June 5–6, 1997, 6.

37. *Arab Times*, May 22–23, 1997, 1. The total elected in the two polls would be fifty persons, the same number as are elected under the current system.

38. Interviews with 'Eisa bu Yabis, head of joint operations, Kuwait Oil Company, October 1, 1996, in Wafra; and with Ahmad al-Baghdadi, chair of the political science department at Kuwait University, October 2, 1996, in Kuwait.

39. Interviews with 'Ali Murad, September 21 and October 10, 1992, in Kuwait.

40. *Arab Times*, June 17, 1997.

41. *Arab Times*, June 16, 1999, 6.

42. "Kuwait Tribesmen Set to Consolidate Power," AFP, June 30, 1999, Gulf2000 Archive.

43. Ibid.

44. Ibid. Interviewed after his release, Khaled said, "There is no evidence that we held any primary, and our tribe has unanimously decided to support us." He also called the detention of tribesmen "shameful and defying democracy." The penalties for violating the law against primaries include a jail term of not more than three years and/or a KD 2000 fine. *Arab Times*, June 16, 1999, 6.

45. Lani Guinier, *The Tyranny of the Majority: Fundamental Fairness in Representative Democracy*.

46. Guinier, *The Tyranny of the Majority*, 74–91.

47. This is a point made by Barbara Geddes throughout her book—see *Politician's Dilemma*.

48. For an analysis of the ram sacrifice and its political significance in Morocco, see M. E. Combs-Schilling, *Sacred Performances: Islam, Sexuality, and Sacrifice*. Michael Sells examines the use of religious and quasi-religious rituals to mobilize Serb nationalists to attack Bosnian Muslims in *The Bridge Betrayed: Religion and Genocide in Bosnia*. Both Combs-Schilling and Sells emphasize the sexualization of religious symbols in these contexts, an indication of their deep embeddedness in the unconscious mind. The incommensurability of mythic and philosophic knowledge systems is discussed in Hatab, *Myth and Philosophy*.

49. The contribution of religious myths to centuries of European anti-Semitism, and the use of religious symbols and stories to mobilize nationalist movements today, for example, in the former Yugoslavia, are subjects of intensive study. For the former, examples include the writings of Gavin I. Langmuir, such as his exemplary *History, Religion, and Antisemitism* (Berkeley: University of California Press, 1990). A more recent examination of the latter phenomenon can be found in Sells, *The Bridge Betrayed*. The civil war in Algeria as it is described by novelists such as Aïcha Lemsine echoes the patterns of interwoven politics, sexuality, and religion documented by Langmuir and Sells in these other cases. Studies of religious justifications of violence in the modern Middle East (though not including Algeria) can be found among the articles in Mark Juergensmeyer, ed., *Violence and the Sacred in the Modern World*.

50. Connections between "real violence" and "symbolic violence" are explored in Mark Juergensmeyer, "Is Symbolic Violence Related to Real Violence?" in *Violence and the Sacred*, 1–8.

51. Olivier Roy shows this in great detail in *The Failure of Political Islam*. Others support his contention that political Islam is without an adequate theory or practical plan

for governance—see, for example, John Waterbury, "Democracy Without Democrats? The Potential for Political Liberalization in the Middle East," in Salamé, ed., *Democracy Without Democrats?*, 39–44; also, Aziz al-Azmeh, *Islams and Modernities*, esp. ch. 2.

52. This is depicted very well for Iran in Haideh Moghissi's *Populism and Feminism in Iran*. Deniz Kandiyoti has written for many years about the use of female subjection as attesting a group's traditional values and goals. See, for example, "Women and the Turkish State: Political Actors or Symbolic Pawns?" in Nira Yuval-Davis and Floya Anthias, eds., *Woman–Nation–State*, 126–49.

53. Mernissi, *Islam and Democracy*.

54. The complexity of Islamic tradition in this sense is discussed in ibid.; see also James P. Piscatori, *Islam in a World of Nation-States*, and the articles in Mahnaz Afkhami, ed., *Faith and Freedom*.

55. For example, *MEES*, July 12, 1999, C2; Mark Huband, "Kuwait: Islamists and Liberals in Poll Victory," *Financial Times*, July 6, 1999, FT Archives; "A Bolder Kuwait," *The Economist*, July 9, 1999, Gulf2000 Archive.

56. Reuters reported that ten "newly elected MPs" were approached to take cabinet portfolios. Among those named in news reports were 'Abdullah Nibari, Ahmad Baqr, Mishairy al-'Anjari, 'Abd al-Mohsen Jamal, Muhammad al-Saqr, 'Abd al-Mohsen al-Mud'ej, Walid al-Jari. See "Opposition Figures Turn Down Kuwait Cabinet Invite," Reuters, July 12, 1999, Gulf2000 Archive; "Kuwaiti Oppostion MPs Not Impressed by Offers of Cabinet Posts," *Mideast Mirror*, July 17, 1999, Gulf2000 Archive.

57. Tétreault, "Out of Body Experiences," 69–70, 73–74.

58. "Ouster of al-Sa'doun 'an ICM-Govt. Plot,'" *Kuwait Times*, July 22, 1999 (issue no. 11121) from <http://www.paaet.edu.kw/ktimes>.

59. AFP, "Islamists Seek to Strengthen Grip on Kuwait's Parliament," June 29, 1999, Gulf2000 Archive.

60. The *Kuwait Times* notes that the ICM's role in this alleged deal was not welcomed by younger members of the association, another example of the progression of issue-based internal differences within the Islamist movement. "Ouster of al-Sa'doun 'an ICM-Govt. Plot,'" *Kuwait Times*, July 22, 1999.

61. Ghanim al-Najjar, "Kuwait Election Results," July 12, 1999, Gulf2000.

62. Quoted in *MEES*, July 19, 1999, B4.

63. Mary Ann Tétreault, "Gulf Winds," 23–24.

64. Jane Mansbridge, *Beyond Adversary Democracy*.

65. This issue is discussed in Augustus Richard Norton, "The Future of Civil Society in the Middle East," *Middle East Journal* 47 (1993): 215.

Bibliography

Aarts, Paul. 1992. "Democracy, Oil, and the Gulf War." *Third World Quarterly* 13.3: 525–38.

———. 1993. "Les Limites du 'Tribalisme Politique': Le Koweit d'après-guerre et le Processus de Démocratisation." *Monde Arab Maghreb-Machrek* 142: 61–79.

Aarts, Paul W. H. and Gep Eisenloeffel. 1990. "Kuwait Petroleum Corporation and the Process of Vertical Integration." *OPEC Review* 14: 203–22.

Aarts, Paul W. H., Gep Eisenloeffel, and A. J. Termeulen. 1989. "The KPC Connection of 'Kuwait Inc.' " Working Paper no. 10. Amsterdam: Stichting Center for Economic and Political Studies (CEPS), University of Amsterdam.

———. 1991. "Oil, Money, and Participation: Kuwait's *Sonderweg* as a Rentier State." *Orient* 32.2: 205–16.

Abdul-Moa'ti, Youssef, ed. 1994. *Kuwaiti Resistance as Revealed by Iraqi Documents*. Kuwait: Center for Research and Studies on Kuwait.

Abed, Shukri B. 1995. "Islam and Democracy." In David Garnham and Mark Tessler, eds., *Democracy, War, and Peace in the Middle East*, 120–26. Bloomington: Indiana University Press.

Abu-Hakima, Ahmad Mustafa. 1983. *The Modern History of Kuwait, 1750–1965*. London: Luzac.

———. 1972. "The Development of the Gulf States." In Hopwood, ed., *The Arabian Peninsula*, 31–53.

Afkhami, Mahnaz, ed. 1995. *Faith and Freedom: Women's Human Rights in the Muslim World*. Syracuse, N.Y.: Syracuse University Press.

Ahmed, Leila. 1992. *Women and Gender in Islam*. New Haven: Yale University Press.

Ajtony, M. A. No date (c. 1967). *The Expanding Role of KNPC in the Oil Business*. Printed in Munich by DANUBIA-Druckerei.

Allison, Mary Bruins, M.D. 1994. *Doctor Mary in Arabia*. Austin: University of Texas Press.

Alshayeji, 'Abdullah K. 1992. "Kuwait at the Crossroads: The Quest for Democratization." *Middle East Insight* 8.5: 41–46.

Amos, Deborah. 1992. *Lines in the Sand: Desert Storm and the Remaking of the Arab
World*. New York: Simon and Schuster.

Amuzegar, Jahangir. 1982. "Oil Wealth: A Very Mixed Blessing." *Foreign Affairs* 60.4:
814–35.

Anani, Ahmad and Ken Whittingham. 1986. *The Early History of the Gulf Arabs*. London:
Longman.

Anderson, Benedict. 1991 (rev. ed.). *Imagined Communities: Reflections on the Origin and
Spread of Nationalism*. London: Verso.

Angell, Roger. 1996. "True Tales—Well, Maybe." *The New Yorker* (January 22): 37–43.

Anscombe, Frederick F. 1997. *The Ottoman Gulf: The Creation of Kuwait, Saudi Arabia,
and Qatar*. New York: Columbia University Press.

Apter, David D. 1963. "Political Religion in the New Nations." In Edward Shils, ed., *Old
Societies and New States*, 57–104. New York: Free Press.

Arendt, Hannah. 1959. *The Human Condition: A Study of the Central Dilemmas Facing
Modern Man*. Garden City, N.Y.: Doubleday Anchor.

———. 1965. *On Revolution*. New York: Compass Books.

al-Assiri, Abdul-Reda. 1987. "Teaching Political Science in the Gulf States: The Case of
Kuwait." *International Studies Notes* 13.3: 78–81.

———. 1990. *Kuwait's Foreign Policy: City-State in World Politics*. Boulder, Colo.: Westview.

al-Assiri, Abdul-Reda and Kamal al-Monoufi. 1988. "Kuwait's Political Elite: The Cabinet." *Middle East Journal* 42.1: 48–58.

Ayubi, Nazih N. 1995. *Over-stating the Arab State: Politics and Society in the Middle East*.
London: I. B. Tauris.

al-Azmeh, Aziz. 1994. "Populism Contra Democracy: Recent Democratist Discourse in
the Arab World." In Salamé, ed., *Democracy Without Democrats?*, 112–29.

———. 1996 (2d ed). *Islams and Modernities*. London: Verso.

Baaklini, Abdo. 1982. "Legislatures in the Gulf Area: The Experience of Kuwait, 1961–
1976." *International Journal of Middle East Studies* 14.3 (August): 372–76.

Barber, Noel. 1973. *The Sultans*. New York: Simon and Schuster.

Baz, Ahmed A. S. 1981. "Political Elite and Political Development in Kuwait." Ph.D. diss.,
George Washington University.

Beblawi, Hazem. 1990. "The Rentier State in the Arab World." In Luciani, ed., *The Arab
State*, 85–98.

Beetham, David. 1992. "Liberal Democracy and the Limits of Democratization." *Political Studies* 40 (Special Issue): 40–53.

Bellah, Robert N., Richard Madsen, William M. Sullivan, Ann Swidler, and Steven M.
Tipton. 1986. *Habits of the Heart: Individualism and Commitment in American Life*.
New York: Harper Perennial.

Benjamin, Roger and Stephen L. Elkin, eds. 1985. *The Democatic State*. Lawrence: University of Kansas Press.

Berlin, Isaiah. 1969. "Two Concepts of Liberty." In Berlin, *Four Essays on Liberty*, 118–72. Oxford: Oxford University Press.

———. 1998. "The First and the Last." *New York Review of Books* 45.8 (May 14): 52–60.

Bloom, Harold and David Rosenberg. 1990. *The Book of J.* New York: Grove/Weidenfeld.

Bond, George C. and Angela Gilliam, eds. 1994. *Social Construction of the Past: Representation as Power*. London: Routledge.

Bonine, Michael E. 1980. "The Urbanization of the Persian Gulf Nations." In Alvin J. Cottrell, ed., *The Persian Gulf States: A General Survey*, 225–78. Baltimore: Johns Hopkins University Press.

Bonner, Raymond. 1992. "A Woman's Place." *The New Yorker* (November 16): 56–66.

Bowen-Jones, Howard. 1984. "The Philosophy of Infrastructural Development." In M. S. El Azhary, ed., *The Impact of Oil Revenues on Arab Gulf Development*, 81–90. London: Croom Helm.

Brandell, Inga. 1996. "North Africa: From Social to Political Citizenship?" Paper presented at the Conference on Citizenship and the State in the Middle East, University of Oslo, November 22–24.

Brockopp, Jonathan E. 1998. "Early Islamic Jurisprudence in Egypt: Two Scholars and Their *Mukhtasars*." *International Journal of Middle East Studies* 30.2 (May): 167–82.

Bromley, Simon. 1994. *Rethinking Middle East Politics*. Austin: University of Texas Press.

Brown, Nathan J. 1997. *The Rule of Law in the Arab World: Courts in Egypt and the Gulf*. Cambridge: Cambridge University Press.

Burnham, Walter Dean. 1965. "The Changing Shape of the American Political Universe." *American Political Science Review* 59.1 (March): 7–28.

———. 1970. *Critical Elections and the Mainsprings of American Politics*. New York: Norton.

Chaudhry, Kirin Aziz. 1997. *The Price of Wealth: Economies and Institutions in the Middle East*. Ithaca, N.Y.: Cornell University Press.

Chisholm, Archibald H. T. 1975. *The First Kuwait Oil Concession Agreement: A Record of the Negotiations, 1911–1934*. London: Frank Cass.

Cnudde, Charles F. and Deane E. Neubauer, eds. 1969. *Empirical Democratic Theory*. Chicago: Markham Publishing.

Cole, Juan R. I., ed. 1992. *Comparing Muslim Societies: Knowledge and the State in a World Civilization*. Ann Arbor: University of Michigan Press.

Combs-Schilling, M. E. 1989. *Sacred Performances: Islam, Sexuality, and Sacrifice*. New York: Columbia University Press.

Cox, Robert W. 1981. "Social Forces, States, and World Orders: Beyond International Relations Theory." *Millennium* 10.2 (Summer): 126–55.

Crystal, Jill. 1989. "Coalitions in Oil Monarchies: Kuwait and Qatar." *Comparative Politics* 21: 427–43.

———. 1990. *Oil and Politics in the Gulf: Rulers and Merchants in Kuwait and Qatar*. Cambridge: Cambridge University Press.

———. 1992. *Kuwait: The Transformation of an Oil State*. Boulder, Colo.: Westview.

Dahl, Robert A. 1990 (rev. ed.). *After the Revolution? Authority in a Good Society*. New Haven: Yale University Press.

Daniels, John. 1971. *Kuwait Journey*. Luton, UK: White Crescent Press.

Davidson, Basil. 1992. *The Black Man's Burden: Africa and the Curse of the Nation-State*. New York: Random House.

Davis, Susan Schaefer. 1993. "Growing Up in Morocco." In Donna Lee Bowen and Evelyn A. Early, eds., *Everyday Life in the Muslim Middle East*, 23–33. Bloomington: Indiana University Press.

Devine, Pat. 1988. *Democracy and Economic Planning: The Political Economy of a Self-governing Society*. Boulder, Colo.: Westview.

Diamond, Larry and Marc F. Plattner. 1993. *The Global Resurgence of Democracy*. Baltimore: Johns Hopkins University Press.

Dickson, H. R. P. 1956. *Kuwait and Her Neighbours*. London: Allen and Unwin.

Dickson, Violet. 1971. *Forty Years in Kuwait*. London: Allen and Unwin.

Dommen, Edward and Philippe Hein, eds. 1985. *States, Microstates, and Islands*. London: Croom Helm.

Doran, Charles F. 1977. *Myth, Oil and Politics: Introduction to the Political Economy of Petroleum*. New York: Free Press.

Draper, Theodore. 1987. "American Hubris: From Truman to the Persian Gulf." *New York Review of Books* 34 (July 16): 40–48.

——. 1992a. "The Gulf War Reconsidered." *New York Review of Books* 39 (March 26): 46–53.

——. 1992b. "The True History of the Gulf War." *New York Review of Books* 39 (January 30): 38–45

Duvall, Raymond D. and John R. Freeman. 1981. "The State and Dependent Capitalism." *International Studies Quarterly* 25.1: 99–118.

al-Ebraheem, Hasan 'Ali. 1975. *Kuwait: A Political Study*. Kuwait: Kuwait University.

——. 1984. *Kuwait and the Gulf: Small States and the International System*. Breckenham, Eng.: Croom Helm.

Eickelman, Dale F. and James P. Piscatori. 1996. *Muslim Politics*. Princeton: Princeton University Press.

El Mallakh, Ragaei and Jacob K. Atta. 1981. *The Absorptive Capacity of Kuwait: Domestic and International Perspectives*. Lexington, Mass.: D. C. Heath.

Esposito, John L. 1982. *Women in Muslim Family Law*. Syracuse, N.Y.: Syracuse University Press.

al-Essa, Shamlan Y. 1992. "The Political Consequences of the Crisis for Kuwait." In Ibrahim Ibrahim, ed., *The Gulf Crisis: Background and Consequences*, 169–85. Washington, D.C.: Center for Contemporary Arab Studies.

Evans, Peter B., Dietrich Rueschemeyer, and Theda Skoçpol, eds. *Bringing the State Back In*. New York: Cambridge University Press, 1985.

Fallers, Lloyd. 1963. "Equality, Modernity, and Democracy in the New States." In Edward Shils, ed., *Old Societies and New States*, 158–219. New York: Free Press.

Farrar, Cynthia. 1988. *The Origins of Democratic Thinking: The Invention of Politics in Classical Athens.* New York: Cambridge University Press.

Fergany, Nader. 1984. "Manpower Problems and Projections in the Gulf." In M. S. El Azhary, ed., *The Impact of Oil Revenues on Arab Gulf Development,* 155–69. London: Croom Helm.

Fieldhouse, D. K. 1967. *The Colonial Empires: A Comparative Survey from the Eighteenth Century.* New York: Delacorte.

Finnie, David H. 1992. *Shifting Lines in the Sand: Kuwait's Elusive Frontier with Iraq.* Cambridge: Harvard University Press.

Freeth, Zahra. 1972. *A New Look at Kuwait.* London: Allen and Unwin.

Fromkin, David. 1989. *A Peace to End All Peace: The Fall of the Ottoman Empire and the Creation of the Modern Middle East.* New York: Avon.

Gasiorowski, Mark J. 1991. *U.S. Foreign Policy and the Shah: Building a Client State in Iran.* Ithaca, N.Y.: Cornell University Press.

Gause, Gregory, III. 1994. *Oil Monarchies: Domestic and Security Challenges in the Arab Gulf States.* New York: Council on Foreign Relations.

Gavrielides, Nicolas. 1987. "Tribal Democracy: The Anatomy of Parliamentary Elections in Kuwait." In Linda L. Layne, ed., *Elections in the Middle East: Implications of Recent Trends,* 187–213. Boulder, Colo.: Westview.

Gay, Peter. 1984. *The Bourgeois Experience: Victoria to Freud,* vol. 1, *Education of the Senses.* New York: Oxford University Press.

Geertz, Clifford. 1980. *Negara: The Theatre State in Nineteenth-Century Bali.* Princeton: Princeton University Press.

Geddes, Barbara. 1994. *Politician's Dilemma: Building State Capacity in Latin America.* Berkeley: University of California Press.

Gellner, Ernest. 1983. *Nations and Nationalism.* Ithaca, N.Y.: Cornell University Press.

Gerschenkron, Alexander. 1962. *Economic Backwardness in Historical Perspective.* New York: Praeger.

Ghabra, Shafeeq. 1991a. "The Democratic Movement in Historical Perspective." Presented at the Conference on Political Participation and Constitutional Democracy in Kuwait, sponsored by the National Republican Institute for International Affairs (NRIIA), Washington, D.C., April 29, 1991.

——. 1991b. "The Iraqi Invasion of Kuwait: An Eyewitness Account." *Journal of Palestine Studies* 20.2: 112–25.

——. 1993. "Kuwait: Elections and Issues of Democratization in a Middle Eastern State." *Digest of Middle East Studies* 2.1 (Winter): 1–27.

——. 1994. "Democratization in a Middle Eastern State: Kuwait, 1993." *Middle East Policy* 3: 102–19.

——. 1997. "Kuwait and the Dynamics of Socio-economic Change." *Middle East Journal* 15.3 (Summer): 358–72.

Giddens, Anthony. 1987. *A Contemporary Critique of Historical Materialism,* vol. 1, *The Nation-State and Violence.* Berkeley: University of California Press.

———. 1990. *The Consequences of Modernity.* Stanford, Calif.: Stanford University Press.

———. 1991. *Modernity and Self-Identity: Self and Society in the Late Modern Age.* Stanford, Calif.: Stanford University Press.

———. 1992. *The Transformation of Intimacy: Sexuality, Love, and Eroticism in Modern Societies.* Stanford, Calif.: Stanford University Press.

Goldberg, Ellis. 1992. "Smashing Idols and the State: The Protestant Ethic and Egyptian Sunni Radicalism." In Cole, ed., *Comparing Muslim Societies,* 195–236.

Gould, Carol C. 1988. *Rethinking Democracy: Freedom and Social Cooperation in Politics, Economy, and Society.* Cambridge: Cambridge University Press.

Graz, Liesl. 1990. *The Turbulent Gulf.* London: I. B. Tauris.

Greenfeld, Liah. 1992. *Nationalism: Five Roads to Modernity.* Cambridge: Harvard University Press.

Guinier, Lani. 1994. *The Tyranny of the Majority: Fundamental Fairness in Representative Democracy.* New York: Free Press.

Habermas, Jürgen. 1991. *The Structural Transformation of the Public Sphere: An Inquiry into a Category of Bourgeois Society.* Translated by Thomas Burger and Frederick Lawrence. Cambridge: MIT Press.

Halliday, Fred. 1974. *Arabia Without Sultans.* London: Penguin.

Hallwood, Paul and Stuart Sinclair. 1981. *Oil, Debt, and Development: OPEC in the Third World.* London: Allen and Unwin.

Hartz, Louis. 1955. *The Liberal Tradition in America: An Interpretation of American Political Thought Since the Revolution.* New York: Harvest Books.

Hatab, Lawrence J. 1990. *Myth and Philosophy: A Contest of Truths.* La Salle, Ill.: Open Court.

Hawley, John Stratton, ed. 1994. *Fundamentalism and Gender.* New York: Oxford University Press.

Held, David. 1992 "Democracy: From City-states to a Cosmopolitan Order?" *Political Studies* 40 (Special Issue): 10–39.

Hermann, Tamar. 1993. "From Unidimensionality to Multidimensionality: Some Observations on the Dynamics of Social Movements," *Research in Social Movements, Conflicts, and Change* 15: 181–202.

Hewins, Ralph. 1963. *A Golden Dream: The Miracle of Kuwait.* London: W. H. Allen.

Hicks, Neil and Ghanim al-Najjar. 1995. "The Utility of Tradition: Civil Society in Kuwait." In Augustus Richard Norton, ed., *Civil Society in the Middle East* 1: 188–213. New York: E. J. Brill.

Hindess, Barry. 1993. "Citizenship in the Modern West." In Bryan S. Turner, ed., *Citizenship and Social Theory,* 18–35.

Hintze, Otto. 1975 (1902). "The Formation of States and Constitutional Development: A Study in History and Politics." In *The Historical Essays of Otto Hintze,* 159–77. Edited and translated by Felix Gilbert with the assistance of Robert M. Berdahl. New York: Oxford University Press.

Hirschman, Albert O. 1986. "Exit and Voice: An Expanding Sphere of Influence." In *Rival Views of Market Society, and Other Recent Essays,* 77–101. New York: Viking.

Holl, Otmar, ed. 1983. *Small States in Europe and Dependence.* The Laxenburg Papers. Boulder, Colo.: Westview.

Hollander, Anne. 1994. *Sex and Suits: The Evolution of Modern Dress.* New York: Kodansha International.

Hommersannd, Atle. 1996. "Citizenship and Levels of Political Organization in the Middle East: A Normative Approach." Paper presented at the Conference on Citizenship and the State in the Middle East, University of Oslo, November 22–24.

Hopwood, Derek, ed. 1972. *The Arabian Peninsula: Society and Politics.* London: Allen and Unwin.

Horowitz, Irving Louis. 1980. *Taking Lives: Genocide and State Power.* New Brunswick, N.J.: Transaction Books.

Howell, W. Nathaniel. 1995. "In the Wake of the Storm: Kuwaiti Society After Liberation." *Middle East Insight* 9.3: 6–8.

Hudson, Michael C. 1977. *Arab Politics: The Search for Legitimacy.* New Haven: Yale University Press.

——. 1991. "After the Gulf War: Prospects for Democratization in the Arab World." *Middle East Journal* 45.3: 407–26.

Human Rights Watch/Middle East. 1995. *The Bedoons of Kuwait: "Citizens Without Citizenship."* New York: Human Rights Watch.

Hunt, Lynn. 1984. *Politics, Culture, and Class in the French Revolution.* Berkeley: University of California Press.

——. 1992. *The Family Romance of the French Revolution.* Berkeley: University of California Press.

Hunter, Shireen T. 1986. "The Gulf Economic Crisis and Its Social and Political Consequences." *Middle East Journal* 40.4 (Autumn): 593–613.

Huntington, Samuel P. 1968. *Political Order in Changing Societies.* New Haven: Yale University Press.

——. 1994. "The Clash of Civilizations?" *Foreign Affairs* 72 (Summer 1993): 22–49, reprinted in *Foreign Affairs Agenda 1994: Critical Issues in Foreign Policy,* 120–47. New York: Council on Foreign Relations.

Isaac, Jeffrey C. 1994. "Oases in the Desert: Hannah Arendt on Democratic Politics." *American Political Science Review* 88.1: 156–68.

Ismael, Jacqueline S. 1982. *Kuwait: Social Change in Historical Perspective.* Syracuse, N.Y.: Syracuse University Press.

Jacobs, Jane. 1984. *Cities and the Wealth of Nations: Principles of Economic Life.* New York: Random House.

Jentleson, Bruce W. 1983. "Kruschev's Oil and Brezhnev's Natural Gas Pipelines." In Robert J. Lieber, ed., *Will Europe Fight for Oil?,* 33–69. New York: Praeger.

Jorgensen, Connie. 1994. "Women, Revolution, and Israel." In Mary Ann Tétreault, ed., *Women and Revolution in Africa, Asia, and the New World,* 272–96. Columbia: University of South Carolina Press.

Jurgensmeyer, Mark, ed. 1992. *Violence and the Sacred in the Modern World.* London: Frank Cass.

Kandiyoti, Deniz. 1989. "Women and the Turkish State: Political Actors or Symbolic Pawns?" In Nira Yuval-Davis and Floya Anthias, eds., *Women–Nation–State*, 126–49. London: Macmillan.

Kandiyoti, Deniz, ed. 1991. *Women, Islam, and the State*. Basingstoke, Eng.: Macmillan.

Katzenstein, Peter J. 1977a. "Conclusion: Domestic Structure and Strategies of Foreign Economic Policy." *International Organization* 31.4 (Autumn): 879–920.

———. 1977b. "Introduction: Democracy and International Forces and Strategies for Economic Policy." *International Organization* 31.4 (Autumn): 587–606.

Katzenstein, Peter J., ed. 1977. *Between Power and Plenty: Foreign Economic Policies of Advanced Industrial States*. A Special Issue of *International Organization* 31.4 (Autumn).

Keane, John. 1988. "Despotism and Democracy: The Origins and Development of the Distinction Between Civil Society and the State, 1750–1850." In Keane, ed., *Civil Society and the State*, 35–77. London: Verso.

Keil, Roger. 1998. "Globalization Makes States: Perspectives of Local Governance in the Age of the World City." *Review of International Political Economy* 5.4 (Winter): 616–46.

Khalaf, Jassim Muhammad. 1984. "The Kuwait National Assembly: A Study of Its Structure and Functions." Ph.D. diss., State University of New York, Albany.

al-Khalil, Samir. 1989. *Republic of Fear: The Inside Story of Saddam's Iraq*. New York: Pantheon.

Khouja, M. W. and P. G. Sadler. 1979. *The Economy of Kuwait: Development and Role in International Finance*. London: Macmillan.

Klapp, Merrie G. 1982. "The State—Landlord or Entrepreneur?" *International Organization* 36.3 (Summer): 575–607.

Kolko, Gabriel. 1985. *Anatomy of a War: Vietnam, the United States, and the Modern Historical Experience*. New York: Pantheon.

Kook, Rebecca. 1996. "Citizenship and Its Discontents: Palestinians in Israel." Presented at the Conference on Citizenship and the State in the Middle East, University of Oslo, November 22–24.

Koonz, Claudia. 1987. *Mothers in the Fatherland: Women, the Family, and Nazi Politics*. New York: St. Martin's.

Krasner, Stephen D. 1985. *Structural Conflict: The Third World Against Global Liberalism*. Berkeley: University of California Press.

Kuwait Petroleum Corporation (KPC). N.d. *Annual Report* (nos. 1–8). Kuwait: KPC.

———. N.d. *Kuwait Petroleum Corporation Information Booklet*. Printed in Kuwait by Alkhat.

Langmuir, Gavin I. 1990. *History, Religion, and Antisemitism*. Berkeley: University of California Press.

Latham, Don. 1991. *Occupation Diary*. Kuwait: Noureya al-Saddani.

Lauterpacht, E. (CBE, QC), C. J. Greenwood, Marc Weller, and Daniel Bethlehem, eds. 1991. *The Kuwait Crisis: Basic Documents*, vol. 1. Cambridge International Documents Series. Cambridge: Grotius.

Leca, Jean. 1994. "Democratization in the Arab World: Uncertainty, Vulnerability, and Legitimacy. A Tentative Conceptualization and Some Hypotheses." In Salamé, ed., *Democracy Without Democrats?*, 48–83.

Lerner, Daniel. 1958. *The Passing of Traditional Society: Modernizing the Middle East.* New York: Free Press.

Levy, Walter J. 1978–79. "The Years That the Locust Hath Eaten: Oil Policy and OPEC Development Prospects." *Foreign Affairs* 57 (Winter): 287–305.

Lewis, Bernard. 1993. "Islam and Liberal Democracy." *Atlantic Monthly* 271 (February): 89–94.

Lienhardt, P. A. 1972. "Some Social Aspects of the Trucial States." In Hopwood, ed., *The Arabian Peninsula*, 219–30.

Lindblom, Charles. 1977. *Politics and Markets: The World's Political-Economic Systems.* New York: Basic Books.

Lindholm, Charles. 1992. "Quandaries of Command in Egalitarian Societies: Examples from Swat and Morocco." In Cole, ed., *Comparing Muslim Societies*, 63–94.

Longva, Anh Nga. 1992. "When State Patriarchy Rests on Female Consensus: Kuwait Women as Nation Builders." *Proceedings of the 1992 Annual Conference of the British Society for Middle Eastern Studies*, 95–105. Scotland: University of St. Andrews (July 8–10).

——. 1993. "Kuwaiti Women at a Crossroads: Privileged Development and the Constraints of Ethnic Stratification." *International Journal of Middle East Studies* 25.3 (August): 448.

——. 1996. "Citizenship in the Gulf States: Conceptualisation and Practice." Paper presented at the Conference on Citizenship and the State in the Middle East, University of Oslo, November 22–24.

——. 1997. *Walls Built on Sand: Migration, Exclusion, and Society in Kuwait.* Boulder, Colo.: Westview.

Lowi, Theodore J. 1969. *The End of Liberalism: Ideology, Policy, and the Crisis of Public Authority.* New York: Norton.

——. 1995. *The End of the Republican Era.* Norman: University of Oklahoma Press.

Luciani, Giacomo, ed. 1990. *The Arab State.* Berkeley: University of California Press.

Luke, Timothy W. 1985. "Dependent Development and the OPEC States: State Formation in Saudi Arabia and Iran Under the International Energy Regime." *Studies in Comparative International Development* 20.1: 31–54.

——. 1991. "The Discipline of Security Studies and the Codes of Containment: Learning from Kuwait." *Alternatives* 16.3 (July): 315–44.

Mabro, Judy. 1991. *Veiled Half-Truths: Western Travellers' Perceptions of Middle Eastern Women.* London: I. B. Tauris.

Mackey, Sandra. 1998. *The Iranians: Persia, Islam, and the Soul of a Nation.* New York: Penguin/Plume.

MacPherson, C. B. 1962. *The Political Theory of Possessive Individualism: Hobbes to Locke.* Oxford: Oxford University Press.

Magnus, Ralph H. 1980. "Societies and Social Change in the Persian Gulf." In Alvin J.

Cottrell, ed., *The Persian Gulf States: A General Survey*, 369–413. Baltimore: Johns Hopkins University Press.

Mansbridge, Jane. 1983. *Beyond Adversary Democracy*. Chicago: University of Chicago Press.

Mansfield, Peter. 1990. *Kuwait: Vanguard of the Gulf*. London: Hutchinson.

Marr, David G. 1981. *Vietnamese Tradition on Trial, 1920–1945*. Berkeley: University of California Press.

Marr, Phebe. 1985. *The Modern History of Iraq*. Boulder, Colo.: Westview.

Marshall, T. H. 1950. "Citizenship and Social Class." In *Citizenship and Social Class and Other Essays*, 1–85. Cambridge: Cambridge University Press.

Marty, Martin E. and R. Scott Appleby, eds. 1993. *Fundamentalisms and Society: Reclaiming the Sciences, the Family, and Education*. Chicago: University of Chicago Press.

Mayer, Ann Elizabeth. 1995. "Rhetorical Strategies and Official Policies on Women's Rights: The Merits and Drawbacks of the New World Hypocrisy." In Mahnaz Afkhami, ed., *Faith and Freedom: Women's Human Rights in the Muslim World*, 104–32. Syracuse, N.Y.: Syracuse University Press:

——. 1995. "Reform of Personal Status Laws in North Africa: A Problem of Islamic or Mediterranean Laws?" *Middle East Journal* 49.3 (Summer 1995): 432–46.

Mernissi, Fatima. 1992. *Islam and Democracy: Fear of the Modern World*. Translated by Mary Jo Lakeland. Reading, Mass.: Addison-Wesley.

Meyer, David S. 1990. *A Winter of Discontent: The Nuclear Freeze and American Politics*. New York: Praeger.

Migdal, Joel S. 1988. *Strong Societies and Weak States: State-Society Relations and State Capabilities in the Third World*. Princeton: Princeton University Press.

Mikdashi, Zuhayr. 1972. *The Community of Oil-Exporting Countries*. Ithaca, N.Y.: Cornell University Press.

——. 1986. *Transnational Oil: Issues, Policies, and Perspectives*. London: Frances Pinter.

Mill, John Stuart. 1975 (1859). *On Liberty*. Edited by David Spitz. New York: Norton.

Miller, Aaron David. 1980. *Search for Security: Saudi Arabian Oil and American Foreign Policy, 1939–1949*. Chapel Hill: University of North Carolina Press.

Moghissi, Haideh. 1994. *Populism and Feminism in Iran*. New York: St. Martin's.

Morgan, Edmund S. 1997. "America's First Great Man." *New York Review of Books* 44 (June 12): 42–44.

Morse, Edward L. 1986. "After the Fall: The Politics of Oil." *Foreign Affairs* 64: 792–811.

al-Mughni, Haya. 1993. *Women in Kuwait: The Politics of Gender*. London: Saqi Books.

——. 2000. "Women's Movements and the Autonomy of Civil Society in Kuwait." In Robin L. Teske and Mary Ann Tétreault, eds., *Feminist Approaches to Social Movements, Community, and Power*, vol. 1, *Conscious Acts and the Politics of Social Change*. Columbia: University of South Carolina Press.

al-Mughni, Haya and Fawzia al-Turkait. 1994. "Dealing with Trauma: Cultural Barriers to Self-Recovery—The Case of Kuwaiti Women." Paper presented at the Seminar on Effective Methods for Encountering the Pyschological and Social Effects of the Iraqi

Aggression, sponsored by the Social Development Office of the Amiri Diwan, Kuwait, March.

al-Mughni, Haya and Mary Ann Tétreault. 2000. "Citizenship, Gender, and the Politics of Quasi-states." In Suad Joseph, ed., *Citizenship and Gender in the Middle East*. Syracuse, N.Y.: Syracuse University Press.

Munson, Henry, Jr. 1988. *Islam and Revolution in the Middle East*. New Haven: Yale University Press.

Munif, Abdelrahman. 1987. *Cities of Salt*. Translated by Peter Theroux. New York: Vintage.

al-Najjar, Ghanim Hamad. 1984. "Decision-Making Process in Kuwait: The Land Acquisition Policy as a Case Study." Ph.D. diss., University of Exeter.

al-Naqeeb, Khaldoun Hasan. 1990. *Society and State in the Gulf and Arab Peninsula: A Different Perspective*. Translated by L. M. Kenny. London: Routledge.

National Bank of Kuwait. 1987. *Kuwait & Gulf Cooperation Council Economic & Financial Bulletin* 11 (Fall). Kuwait: NBK.

National Republican Institute for International Affairs. 1991. *Political Participation and Constitutional Democracy in Kuwait*. Edited transcript of a conference. Washington, D.C.: NRIIA.

Niblock, Tim. 1982. "Iraqi Policies Towards the Arab States of the Gulf, 1958–1981." In Niblock, ed., *Iraq: The Contemporary State*, 125–49. New York: St. Martin's.

Nitzan, Jonathan. 1997. "Differential Accumulation: Toward a New Political Economy of Capital." Paper presented at the annual meeting of the International Studies Association, Toronto, March. Another version of this paper can be found in the *Review of International Political Economy* 5.2 (Summer 1998): 169–216.

Nitzan, Jonathan and Shimshon Bichler. 1995. "Bringing Capital Accumulation Back In: The Weapondollar-Petrodollar Coalition—Military Contractors, Oil Companies, and Middle-East 'Energy Conflicts.' " *Review of International Political Economy* 2.3 (Summer): 446–515.

Norton, Augustus Richard. 1993. "The Future of Civil Society in the Middle East." *Middle East Journal* 47.2: 205–16.

Nussbaum, Martha C. 1995. *Poetic Justice: The Literary Imagination and Public Life*. Boston: Beacon Press.

Olson, Mancur. 1965. *The Logic of Collective Action: Public Goods and the Theory of Groups*. Cambridge: Harvard University Press.

Organization of Petroleum Exporting Countries (OPEC). 1977. *Papers from the OPEC Seminar on the Present and Future Role of the National Oil Companies*. Vienna: OPEC.

Owen, Roger. 1994. "Socio-economic Change and Political Mobilization: The Case of Egypt." In Salamé, ed., *Democracy Without Democrats?*, 183–99.

Pagels, Elaine. 1988. *Adam, Eve, and the Serpent*. New York: Random House.

——. 1995. *The Origin of Satan*. New York: Random House.

Pateman, Carole. 1988. "The Fraternal Social Contract." In John Keane, ed., *Civil Society and the State*, 101–27. London: Verso.

PBS. 1996. "Frontline: The Gulf War." January 9.

Peled, Yoav and G. Shafir. 1996. "The Roots of Peacemaking: The Dynamics of Citizenship in Israel, 1948–93." *International Journal of Middle East Studies* 28.3 (August): 391–413.

Penrose, Edith. 1968. *The Large International Firm in Developing Countries: The International Petroleum Industry*. Cambridge: MIT Press.

———. 1972. "Oil and State in Arabia." In Hopwood, ed., *The Arabian Peninsula*, 271–85.

Penrose, Edith and E. F. Penrose. 1978. *Iraq: International Relations and National Development*. London: Ernest Benn.

Peterson, J. E. 1988. *The Arab Gulf States: Steps Toward Political Participation*. New York: Praeger.

Petroleum Intelligence Weekly. 1990. "What's Next for OPEC's Downstream Club?" *PIW—Special Supplement Issue* (January 15).

Phillips, Anne. 1992. "Must Feminists Give Up on Liberal Democracy?" *Political Studies* 40 (Special Issue): 68–82.

Pierson, Christopher. 1992. "Democracy, Markets, and Capital: Are There Necessary Economic Limits to Democracy?" *Political Studies* 40 (Special Issue): 83–98.

Piscatori, James P. 1986. *Islam in a World of Nation-States*. New York: Cambridge University Press.

———. 1996. *Muslim Politics*. Princeton: Princeton University Press.

Polanyi, Karl. 1944. *The Great Transformation*. New York: Farrar and Rinehart.

Porter, Jadranka. 1991. *Under Seige in Kuwait: A Survivor's Story*. Boston: Houghton Mifflin.

Quality Publications. N.d. *Kuwait Today: A Welfare State*. Nairobi: Quality Publications.

Raban, Jonathan. 1987. *Arabia Through the Looking Glass*. London: Pan Books.

al-Rahmani, Eqbal. 1996. "The Impact of Traditional Domestic Sexual Division of Labor on Women's Status: The Case of Kuwait." *Research in Human Capital and Development* 9: 79–101.

Rajab, Jehan S. 1996. *Invasion Kuwait: An English Woman's Tale*. London: Radcliffe Press.

Richards, Alan and John Waterbury. 1990. *A Political Economy of the Middle East*. Boulder, Colo.: Westview.

Rist, Gilbert. 1997. *The History of Development from Western Origins to Global Faith*. Translated by Patrick Camiller. London: Zed Books.

Roy, Olivier. 1994. *The Failure of Political Islam*. London: Verso.

Rush, Alan De Lacy. 1987. *Al-Sabah: History and Genealogy of Kuwait's Ruling Family, 1752–1987*. London: Ithaca Press.

Rush, Alan De Lacy, ed. 1989. *Records of Kuwait, 1899–1961*, vol. 1, *Internal Affairs, 1899–1921*; vol. 2, *Internal Affairs, 1921–1950*; vol. 5, *Petroleum Affairs*. London: Archive International Group.

al-Sabah, M. S. 1983. *Development Planning in an Oil Economy and the Role of the Woman: The Case of Kuwait*. London: Eastlords.

al-Sabah, Mohammad. 1988. "The 'Dutch Disease' in an Oil-Exporting Country: Kuwait." *OPEC Review* 12: 129–44.

Sadri, Ahmad. 1992. *Max Weber's Sociology of Intellectuals*. New York: Oxford University Press.

Said, Edward. 1979. *Orientalism*. New York: Vintage Books.

Sakr, Naomi. 1983. "Economic Relations Between Iraq and Other Arab Gulf States." In Tim Niblock, ed., *Iraq: The Contemporary State*, 150–67. New York: St. Martin's:

Salamé, Ghassan. 1990. " 'Strong' and 'Weak' States: A Qualified Return to the *Muqaddimah*." In Luciani, ed., *The Arab State*, 29–64.

——. 1994. "Small Is Pluralistic: Democracy as an Instrument of Civil Peace." In Salamé, ed., *Democracy Without Democrats?*, 84–111.

Salamé, Ghassan, ed. 1994. *Democracy Without Democrats? The Renewal of Politics in the Muslim World*. London: I. B. Tauris.

Salih, Kamal Osman. 1990. "Kuwait's Parliamentary Elections, 1963–1985: An Appraisal." Unpublished paper (Kuwait University).

Sampson, Anthony. 1975. *The Seven Sisters: The Great Oil Companies and the World They Shaped*. New York: Viking.

Sayigh, Yusif A. 1972. "Problems and Prospects of Development in the Arabian Peninsula." In Hopwood, ed., *The Arabian Peninsula*, 287–309.

Sciolino, Elaine. 1991. *The Outlaw State: Saddam Hussein's Quest for Power and the Gulf Crisis*. New York: John Wiley.

Sells, Michael A. 1996. *The Bridge Betrayed: Religion and Genocide in Bosnia*. Berkeley: University of California Press.

Sharabi, Hisham. 1988. *Neopatriarchy: A Theory of Distorted Change in Arab Society*. New York: Oxford University Press.

Sharoni, Simona. 1995. *Gender and the Israeli-Palestinian Conflict: The Politics of Women's Resistance*. Syracuse, N.Y.: Syracuse University Press.

Sharples, Julie D. 1992. "Diary." Unpublished manuscript.

Shue, Henry. 1980. *Basic Rights: Subsistence, Affluence, and U.S. Foreign Policy*. Princeton: Princeton University Press.

Šiklová, Jiřina. 2000. "Women and the Charta 77 Movement in Czechoslovakia." In Robin L. Teske and Mary Ann Tétreault, eds., *Feminist Approaches to Social Movements, Community, and Power*, vol. 1, *Conscious Acts and the Politics of Social Change*. Columbia: University of South Carolina Press.

Skoçpol, Theda. 1979. *States and Social Revolutions*. New York: Cambridge University Press.

Slot, B. J. 1998 (2d ed.). *The Origins of Kuwait*. Kuwait: Center for Research and Studies on Kuwait.

Slyomovics, Susan. 1995. "The Rebuilt Palestinian *Madaafeh* (Guest House) of Ein Houd in Jordan." Presented at the annual meeting of the Middle Eastern Studies Association, Washington, D.C., December.

——. 1998. *The Object of Memory: Arab and Jew Narrate the Palestinian Village*. Philadelphia: University of Pennsylvania Press.

Smith, Anthony. 1983 (2d ed.). *Theories of Nationalism*. London: Duckworth.

——. 1991. *National Identity*. Reno: University of Nevada Press.

Smith, Jean Edward. 1992. *George Bush's War*. New York: Henry Holt.

Sparks, Cheryl Logan. 2000. "How Grandmother Won the War: Strategic and Organizational Lessons of the Struggle for Suffrage." Robin L. Teske and Mary Ann Tétreault, eds., *Feminist Approaches to Social Movements, Community, and Power*, vol. 1, *Conscious Acts and the Politics of Social Change*. Columbia: University of South Carolina Press.

Spectorsky, Susan A., ed. 1993. *Chapters on Marriage and Divorce: Responses of Ibn Hanbal and Ibn Rahwayh*. Austin: University of Texas Press.

Springborg, Patricia. 1986. "Politics, Primordialism, and Orientalism: Marx, Aristotle, and the Myth of the Gemeinschaft." *American Political Science Review* 80.1 (March): 185–211.

——. 1994. *Western Republicanism and the Oriental Prince*. Austin: University of Texas Press.

State of Kuwait, Ministry of Guidance and Information, Department of Culture and Publicity. N.d. (c. 1964). *Kuwait Tourist Guide*. Kuwait: Kuwait Government Printing Press.

Stauffer, Thomas. 1983. "Oil Revenues: Income or Capital?" *Middle East Economic Survey* 27.4 (November 7): D1–D4.

Stephens, Robert. 1973. *The Arabs' New Frontier*. London: Temple Smith.

Stoakes, Frank. 1972. "Social and Political Change in the Third World: Some Peculiarities of Oil-Producing Principalities of the Persian Gulf." In Hopwood, ed., *The Arabian Peninsula*, 189–215.

Stone, Lawrence. 1979 (abridged ed.). *The Family, Sex, and Marriage in England, 1500–1800*. New York: Harper Torchbooks.

al-Suwaidi, Jamal. 1995. "Arab and Western Conceptions of Democracy: Evidence from a UAE Opinion Survey." In David Garnham and Mark Tessler, eds., *Democracy, War, and Peace in the Middle East*, 82–115. Bloomington: Indiana University Press.

Tekiner, Roselle. 1994. "The Nonexistence of Israeli Nationality." *Contention* 4.1: 29–46.

Tétreault, Mary Ann. 1985. *Revolution in the World Petroleum Market*. Westport, Conn.: Quorum Books.

——. 1988. "Regimes and Liberal World Orders." *Alternatives* 13.1 (January): 5–26.

——. 1990. "Kuwait's Democratic Reform Movement." *Middle East Executive Reports* (October): 9, 16–19.

——. 1991. "Autonomy, Necessity, and the Small State: Ruling Kuwait in the Twentieth Century." *International Organization* 45.4 (Autumn): 564–91.

——. 1992. "Kuwait: The Morning After." *Current History* 91 (January): 6–10.

——. 1993a. "Civil Society in Kuwait: Protected Spaces and Women's Rights." *Middle East Journal* 47.2 (Spring): 275–91.

——. 1993b. "Independence, Sovereignty, and Vested Glory: Oil and Politics in the Second Gulf War." *Orient* 34.1 (March): 87–103.

——. 1993c. "Kuwait's Economic Prospects." *Middle East Executive Reports* (January): 9–14.

——. 1994. "Whose Honor? Whose Liberation? Women and the Reconstruction of Politics in Kuwait." In Tétreault, ed., *Women and Revolution in Africa, Asia, and the New World*, 297–315. Columbia: University of South Carolina Press.

———. 1995. *The Kuwait Petroleum Corporation and the Economics of the New World Order*. Westport, Conn.: Quorum Books.

———. 1996. "Gulf Winds: Inclement Political Weather in the Arabian Peninsula." *Current History* 95 (January): 23–27.

———. 1997a. "Political Consequences of Restructuring Economic Regimes: The Kuwait Petroleum Corporation." *Millennium* 26.2: 379–401.

———. 1997b. "Justice for All: Wartime Rape and Women's Human Rights." *Global Governance* 3.2: 197–212.

———. 1998a. "Formal Politics, Meta-Space, and the Construction of Civil Life." In Andrew Light and Jonathan M. Smith, ed., *Philosophy and Geography*, vol. 2, *The Production of Public Space*, 81–97. Lanham, Md.: Rowman and Littlefield.

———. 1998b. "Individualism, Secularism, and Fundamentalism." Paper presented at the annual meeting of the British Society for Middle Eastern Studies, Birmingham, July.

———. 1998c. "Spheres of Liberty, Conflict, and Power: The Public Lives of Private Persons." *Citizenship Studies* 2.2 (July): 273–89.

———. 1999. "Out of Body Experiences: Migrating Firms and Altered States." *Review of International Political Economy* 6.1 (Spring): 55–78.

Tétreault, Mary Ann and Haya al-Mughni. 1995a. "Gender, Citizenship, and Nationalism in Kuwait." *British Journal of Middle Eastern Studies* 22.1&2: 64–80.

———. 1995b. "Modernization and Its Discontents: State and Gender in Kuwait." *Middle East Journal* 49.3: 403–17.

———. 1996. "Al-Mar'at wal Demuqratiyya fil Kuwait." *Abwab* (January 7): 9–23.

Tillion, Germaine. 1983. *The Republic of Cousins: Women's Oppression in Mediterranean Society*. Translated by Quinton Hoare. London: Al Saqi Books.

Tilly, Charles. 1985. "War Making and State Making as Organized Crime." In Peter B. Evans, Dietrich Rueschemeyer, and Theda Skoçpol, eds., *Bringing the State Back In*, 169–91. New York: Cambridge University Press.

Tilly, Charles, ed. 1975. *The Formation of National States in Western Europe*. Princeton: Princeton University Press.

Tocqueville, Alexis de. 1955 (1856). *The Old Regime and the French Revolution*. Translated by Stuart Gilbert. Garden City, N.Y.: Doubleday Anchor.

Tomeh, George. 1980. "Interdependence: A View from the Third World." In Peter Dorner and Mahmoud A. El-Shafie, eds., *Resources and Development: Natural Resource Policies and Economic Development in an Interdependent World*, 359–84. Madison: University of Wisconsin Press.

Tönnies, Ferdinand. 1955. *Communities and Association*. Translated by C. Loomis. London: Routledge and Kegan Paul.

Townsend, John. 1984. "Philosophy of State Development Planning." In M. S. El Azhary, ed., *The Impact of Oil Revenues on Arab Gulf Development*, 35–53. London: Croom Helm.

Train, John. 1985. *Famous Financial Fiascos*. New York: Clarkson N. Potter.

Truong Nhu Tang (with David Chanoff and Doan Van Toai). 1986. *A Viet Cong Memoir: An Inside Account of the Vietnam War and Its Aftermath*. New York: Vintage.

Truman, David B. 1952. *The Governmental Process*. New York: Knopf.

Turner, Bryan S., ed. 1993. *Citizenship and Social Theory*. London: Sage.

Turner, Patricia A. 1993. *I Heard It Through the Grapevine: Rumor in African-American Culture*. Berkeley: University of California Press.

Valensi, Lucette. 1993. *The Birth of the Despot: Venice and the Sublime Porte*. Translated by Arthur Denner. Ithaca, N.Y.: Cornell University Press.

Villiers, Alan. 1969. *Sons of Sinbad*. New York: Scribner's.

Viorst, Milton. 1991. "After the Liberation." *The New Yorker* (September 30): 37–40.

———. 1994. *Sandcastles: The Arabs in Search of the Modern World*. New York: Knopf.

Vital, David. 1971. *The Survival of Small States: Studies in Small Power/Great Power Conflict*. London: Oxford University Press.

Walzer, Michael. 1965. *The Revolution of the Saints: A Study in the Origins of Radical Politics*. Cambridge: Harvard University Press.

Warburg, Gabriel. 1995. "Mahdism and Islamism in Sudan." *International Journal of Middle East Studies* 27.2 (May): 219–36.

Ware, Alan. 1992. "Liberal Democracy: One Form or Many?" *Political Studies* 40 (Special Issue): 130–45.

Waterbury, John. 1994. "Democracy Without Democrats? The Potential for Political Liberalization in the Middle East." In Salamé, ed., *Democracy Without Democrats?*, 39–44.

Weber, Max. 1958. *The Protestant Ethic and the Spirit of Capitalism*. Translated by Talcott Parsons. New York: Scribner's.

Whelan, John. 1988. "Kuwait '88: A Model for Development." London: The MEED Group.

Wills, Garry. 1992. *Lincoln at Gettysburg: The Words That Remade America*. New York: Touchstone.

Wilson, Rodney. 1984. "The Future of Banking as a Gulf Industry." In M. S. El Azhary, ed., *The Impact of Oil Revenues on Arab Gulf Development*, 138–54. London: Croom Helm.

Winstone, H. V. F. and Zahra Freeth. 1972. *Kuwait: Prospect and Reality*. London: Allen and Unwin.

Wolf, Eric R. 1982. *Europe and the People Without History*. Berkeley: University of California Press.

Wood, Ellen Meiksins. 1995. *Democracy Against Capitalism: Renewing Historical Materialism* Cambridge: Cambridge University Press.

Zaretsky, Eli. 1986 (rev. and expanded ed.). *Capitalism, the Family, and Personal Life*. New York: Harper Perennial.

Internet Sources

Financial Times archive.

Gulf2000, a newsgroup and listserve sponsored by Columbia University.

Kuwait Times.

MEES Archives, through the courtesy of the publisher of the *Middle East Economic Survey*.

Index